KARL MARX'S ECOSOCIALISM

KARL MARX'S ECOSOCIALISM

Capitalism, Nature, and the Unfinished Critique of Political Economy

Kohei Saito

MONTHLY REVIEW PRESS

New York

Library of Congress Cataloging-in-Publication Data
available from the publisher.

ISBN (paper) 978-1-58367-640-0
ISBN (cloth) 978-1-58367-641-7

MONTHLY REVIEW PRESS
NEW YORK, NEW YORK

monthlyreview.org

Typeset in Minion Pro

5 4 3

Contents

Acknowledgments

This book is an English version of *Natur gegen Kapital: Marx' Ökologie in seiner unvollendeten Kritik des Kapitalismus* (Frankfurt am Main: Campus, 2016), which was based on my dissertation. In that German edition, I thanked Andreas Arndt, who, as my supervisor, always motivated and inspired me in Berlin, and my Japanese colleagues Shigeru Iwasa, Teinosuke Otani, Tomonaga Tairako, Ryuji Sasaki, Hideto Akashi, and Soichiro Sumida for their comments and constructive criticisms throughout the project. I was also grateful to the MEGA editors in the Berlin Brandenburg Academy of Sciences (BBAW), notably Gerald Hubmann, Claudia Reichel, and Timm Graßmann, who encouraged me to struggle with Marx's notebooks. Thanks also to Frieder Otto Wolf, Harald Bluhm, Michael Heinrich, Michael Perelman, Ingo Stützle, Kolja Lindner, and Elena Louisa Lange for their helpful comments in various conferences.

Preparing the English manuscript, I was lucky to receive additional help. First of all, I want to thank Kevin Anderson who kindly hosted me as a visiting scholar in the department of sociology at the University of California, Santa Barbara. He provided me with opportunities to share my research with the members of the department as well as the International Humanist Marxist Organization in Los Angeles. I cannot thank John Bellamy Foster enough. He has been very supportive, publishing my articles in *Monthly Review* and publishing this book with Monthly Review Press. At each stage of the project, his comments and editing always improved the clarity and preciseness of the writing. I also cannot give adequate thanks to Brett Clark, who read my first English draft and significantly improved it with his careful and accurate reading. Thanks to his help, it became possible to convey my interpretation in a

foreign language, although any remaining errors must of course be attributed to me. I am also grateful to Michael Yates from Monthly Review
Press, who together with its editorial committee offered an unknown
Japanese scholar this wonderful opportunity to publish my first English
book. Finally, I would like to thank Martin Paddio at Monthly Review
Press, and copy editor Erin Clermont, for their hard work during the
publication process.

The Japan Society for the Promotion of Science financed my research
at the University of California, Santa Barbara, enabling me to complete
this book.

Introduction

For quite a long time, the expression "Marx's ecology" was regarded as oxymoronic. Not just critics of Marx but even many self-proclaimed Marxists believed that Marx presupposed unlimited economic and technological developments as a natural law of history and propagated the absolute mastery of nature, both of which run counter to any serious theoretical and practical consideration of ecological issues such as the scarcity of natural resources and the overloading of ecospheres. Since the 1970s, when grave environmental threats to human civilization gradually but undoubtedly became more discernible in Western societies, Marx was repeatedly criticized by new environmental studies and an emerging environmental movement for his naïve acceptance of the common nineteenth-century idea advocating the complete human domination of nature. According to critics, such a belief inevitably led him to neglect the destructive character that is immanent in the modern industry and technology that accompanies mass production and consumption. In this vein, John Passmore went so far as to write that "nothing could be more ecologically damaging than the Hegelian-Marxist doctrine."[1]

In subsequent years, the critique against Marx's "Prometheanism," or hyperindustrialism, according to which unlimited technological development under capitalism allows humans to arbitrarily manipulate external nature, became a popular stereotype.[2] Consequently, it was not rare to hear the same type of critique, that Marx's theory, especially with regard to ecology, was fatally flawed from today's perspective. His historical materialism, it was said, uncritically praised the progress of technology and productive forces under capitalism and anticipated, based on this premise, that socialism would solve every negative aspect of modern industry simply because it would realize the full potential of productive forces through the radical social appropriation of the means of production that were monopolized by the capitalist class. Marx was depicted as a technological utopian who failed to grasp the "dialectics of Enlightenment," which would ultimately bring about the vengeance of nature when the ultimate productivism was realized.[3]

This particular critique, which was common in the Anglo-Saxon world, remains widely accepted in Germany, Marx's homeland. Even in recent years, Thomas Petersen and Malte Faber repeated the widespread critique against Marx's productivism, albeit without much textual analysis. According to these German scholars, Marx was "too optimistic in terms of his supposition that any production process can be arranged in such a manner that it does not incur any environmentally harmful materials.... This optimism of progress is certainly due to his great respect for the capitalist bourgeoisie, which is already documented in the *Manifesto of the Communist Party*."[4] Rolf P. Sieferle, another German scholar, also rejected the possibility of Marx's ecology because Marx wrongly believed, based on his historical understanding of capitalism, that the "limits of growth of natural factors would be uncoupled" in the future. Sharing the dominant modernist tendency of the time and the idea of mastery of nature, Marx's alleged Prometheanism succumbs to anthropocentrism.[5] Hans Immler, best known as the author of *Nature in Economic Theories* (*Natur in der ökonomischen Theorie*), which is regarded as one of the earliest works of political ecology in Germany, also recently reinforced his rebuttal of Marx's unacceptable productivism. According to Immler, Marx's unecologocial standpoint is grounded in his anthropocentric value theory, which absolutizes human labor as the sole source of value and dismisses nature's contribution in value production. He argues that "due to its one-sided concentration on value and value analysis and due to its fundamental neglect of the physical and natural sphere (use values, nature, sensuousness)," Marx's critique "remains unable to address and analyze . . . those developments of social practice that result not only in the most fundamental threats to life, but also represent decisive impulses toward a transformation of socio-economic reality, such as ecological politics."[6] Both Sieferle and Immler agree with other critics of Marx in asserting that the founder of historical materialism was decisively unecological in his faith in the positive effects of unlimited technological and economic growth, a view that can no longer be accepted in the twenty-first century. Immler thus concludes: "So forget about Marx."[7]

The current state of German debates over Marx's ecology surely gives an impression of outdatedness to English readers, who are more familiar with the development of Marxist ecology in the last fifteen years, initiated by two important works: Paul Burkett's *Marx and Nature* and John Bellamy Foster's *Marx's Ecology*.[8] Their careful reexaminations of Marx's texts convincingly showed various unnoticed or suppressed ecological dimensions of his critique of political economy and opened up a way to emancipate Marx's theory from the Promethean stereotype dominant in the 1980s and '90s. Today many Marxist scholars and activists do not regard it as an exaggeration when Burkett claims that Marx's critique of capitalism and his vision of socialism can be "most helpful" for the critical reflection upon ongoing global eco-crises.[9]

As Foster recounts recent developments with respect to socialist environmental thought in his introduction to the new edition of Burkett's *Marx and Nature*, the discursive constellation around Marx's ecology has significantly changed with a series of publications by Marxists inspired by Foster and Burkett. These analyze environmental crises as a contradiction of capitalism based upon the "metabolic rift" approach: "A decade and a half ago the contribution of Marx and Marxism to the understanding of ecology was seen in almost entirely negative terms, even by many self-styled ecosocialists. Today Marx's understanding of the ecological problem is being studied in universities worldwide and is inspiring ecological actions around the globe."[10] Various studies examine current ecological issues such as ecofeminism (Ariel Salleh), climate change (Del Weston, Brett Clark, and Richard York), ecological imperialism (Brett Clark), and marine ecology (Rebecca Clausen and Stefano Longo).[11] The concept of metabolic rift has subsequently become influential beyond a small circle of the radical left. Notably, Naomi Klein's critique of capitalist global warming in *This Changes Everything* draws upon Foster's approach in an affirmative manner, though she is not a Marxist.[12] The significance of "Marx's ecology" is now positively recognized on both theoretical and practical levels, to the point that allegations of Marx's Prometheanism are now generally regarded as having been proven false.

However, despite or precisely because of the increasing hegemonic influence of the "classical" Marxist tradition represented by "second-stage ecosocialists" such as Foster and Burkett in the environmental movement, there remains the persistent reservation toward accepting Marx's ecology among the so-called first-stage ecosocialists, such as Ted Benton, André Gorz, Michael Löwy, James O'Connor, and Alain Lipietz.[13] Recently, first-stage ecosocialists have found new adherents, who in various ways seek to downgrade Marx's ecological contributions. Recognizing the validity of Marx's ecological analysis only to a limited extent, these thinkers always end up claiming that his analysis was fatally flawed in its failure to be fully ecological and that his nineteenth-century discussions of the ecological problem are of little importance today.[14] For example, they argue that Marx was "no god of any kind" since he did not adequately anticipate today's climate change due to the massive usage of fossil energy. Daniel Tanuro maintains that Marx's time is now so distant in terms of technology and natural sciences that his theory is not appropriate for a systematic analysis of today's environmental issues, especially because Marx did not pay enough attention to the specificity of fossil energy in contrast to other renewable forms of energy.[15] Furthermore, Jason W. Moore, changing his earlier valuation of the metabolic-rift approach, now directs his critique against Foster, claiming that a theory of value is missing in Foster's metabolic-rift approach. Foster, Moore claims, fails to comprehend the dynamic historical transformation of the whole ecosystem—Moore calls it "oikeios"—through the process of capitalist accumulation. According to Moore, Foster's analysis describes no more than "a statistic and ahistorical theory of natural limits," and so it is inevitable for the metabolic-rift approach to have "apocalyptic" implications.[16] Critics of the theory of metabolic rift complain that "Marx's ecology" as such can at best point out the banal fact that capitalism is bad for the environment.

In order to refute such persistent misunderstandings of Marx's ecology and to demonstrate its larger theoretical significance, this book aims at a more *systematic* and *complete* reconstruction of Marx's ecological critique of capitalism. Although Foster and Burkett have carefully examined various texts by Marx for the purpose of demonstrating the power of his ecological theory, their analyses sometimes give a false impression that Marx did not deal with the topic in a systematic but only in a sporadic and marginal way. On the one hand, it is thus necessary to reveal the immanent systematic character of Marx's ecology, that there is a clear continuity with his critique of political economy. This constitutes the main task of Part I of this book. On the other hand, in Part II I offer a more complete examination of Marx's ecology than the earlier literature, scrutinizing his natural science notebooks that will be published for the first time in the new *Marx-Engels-Gesamtausgabe*, known as MEGA[2]. These notebooks will allow scholars to trace the emergence and development of Marx's ecological critique of capitalism in a more vivid and lively manner, unraveling various unknown aspects of his astonishingly encompassing project of *Capital*. The notebooks display just how seriously and laboriously Marx studied the rich field of nineteenth-century ecological theory and integrated new insights into his own dissection of capitalist society. In this process, Marx consciously parted from any forms of naïve Prometheanism and came to regard ecological crises as the fundamental contradiction of the capitalist mode of production. The key concept in this context is "metabolism" (*Stoffwechsel*), which leads us to a systematic interpretation of Marx's ecology.

The significance of a systematic reading becomes clearer if we take a look at a typical interpretation by first-stage ecosocialists. For example, believing that Marx's work can be used at best as a source of citations that might resonate with today's environmental concern, Hubert Laitko, a German Marxist, argues that Marx's ecology "lacks a systematic character and rigor, and it can possibly give some stimulation for theoretical works, but not more than that."[17] Obviously, it is true that Marx was by no means a "prophet," and thus his texts cannot be literally and directly applied to and identified with today's situation. Nonetheless, this rather trivial fact does not justify Laitko's judgment. If Marx's *Capital* could only be used for the purpose of mere citations, then why refer to Marx at all for conducting an ecological investigation of contemporary capitalism? Indeed, this is the hidden implication when the first-stage ecosocialists point to a fatal flaw of Marx's ecology, and this is precisely why one must be cautious when many ecosocialists seem to place value on this "precious heritage for political ecology" without actually providing any positive reason for returning to Marx. Alain Lipietz bluntly contends that "the general structure, the intellectual scaffolding of the Marxist paradigm, along with the key solutions it suggests, must be jettisoned; virtually every area of Marxist thought must be thoroughly reexamined in order to really be of use."[18] Similarly, André Gorz, another important figure among first-stage ecosocialists, goes further and explicitly admits that "socialism is dead."[19] If the general structure of Marx's thought, such as his theory of class, value, and socialism, must be abandoned because "socialism is dead," it becomes extremely hard to imagine why those who are seriously concerned with the current ecological crises should waste their time reading Marx's "obsolete" texts, when urgent actions are required on a global scale. By dismissing the pillars of Marx's critique of political economy, first-stage ecosocialists negate the entire significance of Marx's theorization of the capitalist mode of production.

In order to avoid this negative evaluation of Marx's intellectual legacy, in this book I will demonstrate that Marx's ecological critique possesses a *systematic character* and constitutes an *essential moment* within the totality of his project of *Capital.* Ecology does not simply exist in Marx's thought—my thesis is a stronger one. I maintain that *it not possible to comprehend the full scope of his critique of political economy if one ignores its ecological dimension.* In order to ground this statement, I will explore Marx's theory of "value" and "reification" (*Versachlichung*), because these key categories reveal that Marx actually deals with the whole of nature, the "material" world, as a place of resistance against capital, where the contradictions of capitalism are manifested most clearly. In this sense, Marx's ecology not only constitutes an immanent element for his economic system and for his emancipatory vision of socialism, it also provides us with one of the most helpful methodological scaffolds for investigating the ecological crises as the central contradiction of the current historical system of social production and reproduction. The "precious heritage" of Marx's theory can only be appreciated completely with his ecology.

To be sure, it is important to admit that Marx was in the beginning not necessarily "ecological" but sometimes appeared to be "productivist." Only after a long, arduous process of developing the sophistication of his own political economy, during which time he earnestly studied various fields of the natural sciences, did Marx become fully conscious of the need to deal with the problem of environmental disaster as a limitation imposed upon the valorization process of capital.

Yet it is vital to recognize that a key ecological motive is already present in Marx's notebooks of 1844 (known as *Economic and Philosophic Manuscripts of 1844*). In chapter 1, I show that Marx in 1844 is already dealing with the relationship between humanity and nature as the central theme of his famous theory of alienation. Marx sees the reason for the emergence of modern alienated life in a radical dissolution of the original unity between humans and nature. In other words, capitalism is fundamentally characterized by alienation of nature and a distorted relationship between humans and nature. Accordingly, he envisions the emancipatory idea of "humanism = naturalism" as a project of reestablishing the unity between humanity and nature against capitalist alienation.

However, Marx in *The German Ideology* discerns the inadequacy of his earlier project, which simply opposes a philosophical "idea" against the alienated reality. As a result of distancing himself from Ludwig Feuerbach's philosophical schema, Marx comes to examine the relationship between humans and nature using the physiological concept of "metabolism" to criticize the degradation of the natural environment as a manifestation of the contradictions of capitalism. In chapter 2, I trace the formation of the concept of metabolism in Marx's theory. Marx used it for the first time in his neglected *London Notebooks* and elaborated on it even more in the *Grundrisse* and *Capital*. The concept of metabolism allowed him not only to comprehend the transhistorical universal natural conditions of human production but also to investigate their radical historical transformations under the development of the modern system of production and the growth of forces of production. In other words, Marx examined how the historically specific dynamics of capitalist production, mediated by reified economic categories, constitute particular ways of human social praxis toward nature—namely the harnessing of nature to the needs of maximum capital accumulation—and how various disharmonies and discrepancies in nature must emerge out of this capitalist deformation of the universal metabolism of nature. Marx's seminal contribution in the field of ecology lies in his detailed examination of the relationship between humans and nature in capitalism.

To describe the unecological character of the specific modern relationship of humans to their environment, I provide in chapter 3 a systematic reconstruction of Marx's ecology through his theory of "reification" as developed in *Capital*. I focus on the "material" (*stofflich*) dimensions of the world as essential components of his critique of political economy, which is often underestimated in earlier discussions on *Capital*. Marx's *Capital* systematically develops the pure formal categories of the capitalist mode of production, such as "commodity," "value," and "capital," revealing the specific character of capitalistically constituted social relations of production, which operate as economic forces independent of human control. In this sense, in Germany, the "new reading of Marx" (*neue Marx-Lektüre*), first initiated by Helmut Reichelt and Hans-Georg Backhaus—and now put forward with more depth and rigor by Michael Heinrich, Ingo Elbe, and Werner Bonefeld—has convincingly reinterpreted Marx's critique of classical political economy as a critique of the fetishistic (that is, ahistorical) understanding of economic categories, which identifies the appearance of capitalist society with the universal and transhistorical economic laws of nature.[20] Marx, in contrast, comprehends those economic categories as "specific social forms" and reveals the underlying social relations that bestow an objective validity of this inverted world where economic things dominate human beings.[21] Marx's critique cannot be reduced to a simple categorical reconstruction of the historically constituted totality of capitalist society, however, because such an approach cannot adequately explain why he so intensively studied natural sciences. In fact, the "new reading of Marx" remains silent on this issue.

In contrast, I stress in this book that Marx's practical and critical method of materialism actually goes beyond this type of "form" analysis and deals with *the interrelation between economic forms and the concrete material world*, which is closely related to the ecological dimensions. Insofar as Marx's analysis regards the destruction of nature under capitalism as a manifestation of the discrepancy arising from the capitalist formal transformation of nature, it becomes possible, after examining formal economic categories in close relation to the physical and material dimensions of nature, to systematically reveal Marx's critique of capitalism. Thus I argue that "material" (*Stoff*) is a central category in Marx's critical project. This is not a minor point. If the systematic character of Marx's ecology in *Capital* is not correctly understood, his remarks about nature and its destruction under capitalism only appears sporadic and deviating, without offering a comprehensive critique of today's environmental destruction under capitalism. However, if it is possible to correctly conceive the role of "material" in its relation to economic "forms," Marx's ecology turns out not only to be an immanent component of his system but also a useful methodological foundation for analyzing the current global ecological crisis.

In this context, it is important to add that, even if I intend to present a systematic interpretation of Marx's ecology against the first-stage ecosocialists, Marx was not able to complete his own system of political economy during his lifetime. Volumes two and three of *Capital* were edited by Frederick Engels after Marx's death and published in 1885 and 1894, respectively. As Marx's system remained unfinished, its full reconstruction is an important task, which might be an impossible endeavor. Nonetheless, this implies that every attempt at a reconstruction might inevitably be in vain and unproductive. In recent years the historical and critically complete edition of Marx and Engels's works continues to publish a large number of new materials that remain unknown even more than one hundred years after Marx's death. They contain highly informative passages that document his long efforts to complete his own project of *Capital*. Notably, all of eight original manuscripts for volume 2 of *Capital* are published in the second section of the MEGA[2] in 2012, so that now instead of reading a mixture of manuscripts put together by Engels we can more clearly see how Marx's theory of capital circulation developed until the last moment of his life. The original manuscript for volume 3 is also available, and a careful comparison reveals important differences between Marx and Engels.[22]

Moreover, the significance of the MEGA project goes beyond such clarification of Marx's ideas in relation to those of Engels. The fourth section of the new complete works will publish Marx's excerpts, memos, and comments in his personal notebooks. These materials are of great importance for the current project. Insofar as Marx was unable to elaborate on what he published during his life, and his major work *Capital* remains unfinished, his notebook excerpts become all the more important. These excerpts are often the only source that allows us to trace Marx's theoretical development after 1868, as he did not publish much after the publication of volume 1 of *Capital*. Interestingly, during the last fifteen years of his life Marx produced one-third of his notebooks. Moreover, half of these deal with natural sciences, such as biology, chemistry, botany, geology, and mineralogy, whose scope is astonishingly wide.[23] Yet despite exhaustive efforts, Marx was not able to integrate most of his last research on natural science into his critique of political economy, so the importance of this work remained neglected for more than a century. However, carefully looking at these notebooks in relation to *Capital*, they turn out to be a valuable original source that allows scholars to see Marx's ecology as a fundamental part of his critique of political economy. I argue that Marx would have more strongly emphasized the problem of ecological crisis as the central contradiction of the capitalist mode of production had he been able to complete volumes 2 and 3 of *Capital*.[24]

It is regrettable that Marxist scholars have neglected and marginalized Marx's notebooks for such a long time. This was the case from the beginning when David Riazanov (1870–1938), the prominent Marxist philologist and the director of the Marx-Engels Institute in Moscow, made decisions about the publication plan for the older *Marx-Engels-Gesamtausgabe* (MEGA[1]). He certainly recognized that "roughly 250 excerpt notebooks that have been preserved . . . certainly constitute a very important source for the study of Marxism in general and for the critical account of Marx's individual works in particular."[25] Despite this statement, his plan was only a partial publication of Marx's notebooks without an independent section for excerpts. In other words, Riazanov did not see much value in the notebooks; he actually believed that most of them were "mere" copies taken out of books and articles and thus could only be useful for "Marx biographers."[26]

Riazanov's decision on the partial publication of the notebooks was criticized in 1930 by Benedikt Kautsky, who maintained that "excerpts

from excerpts would serve no purpose."[27] Furthermore, Paul Weller, a col-
league of Riazanov in the Marx-Engels Institute and another extremely
talented MEGA editor, later suggested creating an additional independent section of the MEGA[1], in fifteen volumes, for Marx and Engels's
study notebooks. This suggestion was unfortunately not realized due
to the terror of Stalinism and the disruption of the first MEGA project.
Riazanov was arrested in 1937 and executed the next year, and Paul Weller,
who survived the great terror and even finished editing the *Grundrisse*,
died in war soon after the opening up of the battles of the Eastern Front.
Much later, Weller's insight that Marx's notebooks precisely document his
research process proved right, so the editorial board of the second MEGA
project decided to follow his suggestion for the complete publication of
the excerpts of Marx and Engels, now in 32 volumes.

Thus, Hans-Peter Harstick, who edited Marx's ethnological notebooks in the 1970s, was correct when he emphasized the importance of
the fourth section of the MEGA during a conference in March 1992 in
Aix-en-Provence: "The group of sources consisting of excerpts, biblio-
graphical notes, and marginal comments constitutes a *material basis* of
the intellectual world and works of Marx and Engels, and for the research
and editiorial work of Marx and Engels it is *the key* that opens the door
to the intellectual workshop of both authors and thus *offers access* to the
historical context of Marx and Engels's time during the editors' conge-
nial reconstruction."[28] Every researcher who previously dealt with the
MEGA would agree with Harstick's statement. Martin Hundt, another
MEGA editor, noted that the fourth section is "most interesting" because
notebooks with changes in original sentence order, abbreviations, and
marginal lines offer a number of hints as to what Marx was interested
in, and what he was trying to criticize or to learn.[29] However, if there is a
weakness in current Marxian study twenty years after Harstick's remarks,
it is the continuing marginalization of Marx's notebooks.[30] It is a matter
of urgency to change this situation, in order to demonstrate to the public
the priceless importance of continuing the MEGA project.[31]

Through the reconstruction of Marx's working process documented
in his natural science notebooks, it will now be possible to see how ecology constantly gained a greater significance in his project. Along the way,
he quite consciously abandoned his earlier optimistic evaluation of the
emancipatory potential of capitalism. As already noted, Marx's historical materialism has been repeatedly criticized for its naïve technocratic
assumptions. A careful reading of his notebooks, however, reveals that
Marx actually did not dream up a utopian vision of the socialist future

based on the infinite increase of productive forces and the free manipulation of nature. On the contrary, he seriously recognized natural limits, treating the complex, intense relationship between capital and nature as a central contradiction of capitalism. In fact, he eagerly read various natural scientific books during the preparation of ground rent theory in *Capital*, most notably Justus von Liebig's *Agricultural Chemistry*, which provided him with a new scientific foundation for his critique of Ricardo's "law of diminishing returns." In *Capital* Marx thus came to demand the conscious and sustainable regulation of the metabolism between humans and nature as the essential task of socialism, which I discuss in chapter 4.

In this context, it is essential to emphasize that Marx's notebooks need to be analyzed in close connection with the formation of his critique of political economy rather than as a grandiose materialist project of explaining the universe. In other words, the notebooks' meaning cannot be reduced to his search for a scientific worldview. Earlier literature often claims that through new discoveries in natural sciences Marx followed the classical tradition of the philosophy of nature by Hegel and Schelling, trying to figure out the universal laws that materialistically explain all phenomena within the totality of the world.[32] In contrast, I inspect Marx's research on natural science independent of any totalizing worldview but examine it in close relation to his unfinished project of political economy.[33] For the sake of fulfilling this task, Marx's ecology is even more important because it is in his ecological critique of capitalism that he employed new discoveries of natural sciences to analyze the destructive modifications of the material world by the reified logic of capital.

As I discuss in chapter 5, Marx's reception of Liebig's theory in 1865–66 led him consciously to abandon any reductionistic Promethean model of social development and to establish a critical theory that converges with his vision of sustainable human development. In comparison with the *London Notebooks* in the 1850s, in which Marx's optimism rather neglected the problem of soil exhaustion under modern agriculture, his notebooks of 1865–66 vividly demonstrate that various scientists and economists such as Justus von Liebig, James F. W. Johnston, and Léonce de Lavergne helped him develop a more sophisticated critique of modern agriculture. As a result, Marx started to analyze the contradictions of capitalist production as a global disturbance of natural and social metabolism. Marx's critique of Ricardo, especially as seen in the "Ireland question," most plainly shows that his usage of natural sciences was not

simply restricted to the theory of ground rent but was also meant to prepare a foundation for his analysis of ecological imperialism.

Yet Marx did not absolutize Liebig's *Agricultural Chemistry* for his
critique of capitalism, despite the obvious importance of Liebig's theory
of metabolism. In chapter 6, I give an account of why Marx in 1868—that
is, right after the publication of the first volume of *Capital* in 1867—chose
to study further natural science books, doing so even more intensively.
Notably, he read a number of books at this time that were highly critical of Liebig's theory of soil exhaustion. After a while, Marx relativized
his evaluation of Liebig's theory and even more passionately argued for
the necessity for a post-capitalist society to realize a rational intercourse
with nature. The important figure in this context is a German agronomist, Carl Fraas, who was critical of Leibig. In Fraas's historical research,
Marx even found an "unconscious socialist tendency." Even if Marx was
not able to integrate his new evaluation for Fraas fully into *Capital*, his
excerpts from Fraas document why the natural sciences acquired increasing meaning for his economic project. In this sense, the year 1868 marks
the beginning of a new period for his critique of political economy, with
much wider scope than before. Unfortunately, this made the completion
of his critique extremely difficult.

In spite of its unfinished state, Marx's political economy allows us to
understand the ecological crisis as a contradiction of capitalism, because
it describes the immanent dynamics of the capitalist system, according
to which the unbounded drive of capital for valorization erodes its own
material conditions and eventually confronts it with the limits of nature.
Here it is important to understand that to refer to the limits of nature does
not mean that nature would automatically exert its "revenge" on capitalism and put an end to the regime of capital. On the contrary, it is actually
possible for capitalism to profit from the ruthless extraction of natural
wealth indefinitely, destroying the natural environment to the point that
a large part of the earth becomes unsuitable for human occupation.[34] In
Marx's theory of metabolism, nature nonetheless possesses an important
position for resistance against capital, because capital cannot arbitrarily
subsume nature for the sake of its maximum valorization. Indeed, by
attempting to subsume nature, capital cannot help but destroy, on an
expanding scale, the fundamental material conditions for free human
development. Marx found in this irrational destruction of the environment and the relevant experience of alienation created by capital a chance
for building a new revolutionary subjectivity that consciously demands
a radical transformation of the mode of production so as to realize free

and sustainable human development. In this sense, Marx's ecology is neither deterministic nor apocalyptic. Rather, his theory of metabolism emphasizes the strategic importance of restraining the reified power of capital and transforming the relationship between humans and nature so as to ensure a more sustainable social metabolism. Here exists the nodal point between the "red" and "green" project in the twenty-first century, about which Marx's theory still has a lot to offer.

Part I

Ecology and Economy

1

Alienation of Nature as the Emergence of the Modern

After marrying Jenny von Westphalen and moving to Paris in the autumn of 1843, Marx started to intensively study political economy for the first time. During this research process, he made a series of notebooks that contain excerpts and notes, which today are usually referred to as the *Paris Notebooks*. Marx was at that time not able to read in English and had to use French translations of major works of political economy by Adam Smith and David Ricardo. He was aware that he still had much to study in the discipline of political economy, so he did not publish any part of these notebooks during his lifetime and kept them for personal reference.[1] Famously, one part of these notebooks, written between May and August 1844, was published in the twentieth century as *The Economic and Philosophic Manuscripts*, a misnomer as they were not manuscripts. This text became controversial after some Marxists became enamored with it. These self-styled Marxist humanists found an entirely different philosophy in the young Marx than that found in his economic analysis in *Capital* and used it against the party dogma of Soviet dialectical materialism.[2] Their attempt to rescue the young Marx from the terror of Stalinism was to some extent successful and humanism became a trend within Marxist discourse, but without doubt the humanist interpretation was closely tied to a particular historical-political situation, and it subordinated Marx's intention to their own interests. Today after the collapse of "really existing socialism," it is necessary to analyze the *Paris Notebooks* from a more neutral perspective, with recent philological evidence, so that one can contextualize Marx's notebooks in the development of his theory instead of imposing arbitrary political interests upon them.

Surely it would be futile and a contradiction of Marx's intention if one were to try to discover a fully developed version of his ecology in his notebooks of 1844. However, these notebooks undeniably contain Marx's early recognition of the strategic importance of reestablishing a conscious "unity" between humans and nature as a central task of communist society. If Marx was later able to conceptualize environmental destruction as an immanent contradiction of capitalism, his ecological critique in *Capital* partially originates from his earlier insight into the modern disunion of the human-nature relationship. This is the case even if his later theorization required many years during which he went through an enormous amount of economic, historical, and natural science books and developed his own system of political economy, one much more sophisticated than that of 1844. The young Marx formulated the unity between humanity and nature in the future society as the idea of fully developed "humanism = naturalism," a conception that Marx retained even after various later modifications of his own theory.

Focusing upon the theme "humanism = naturalism" in this chapter, I will reconstruct the importance of the *Paris Notebooks* from the standpoint of Marx's *economic* critique, in contrast to the earlier debates between "humanist" and "scientific" Marxists about the philosophical concept of "alienation." According to Marx, the fundamental cause of alienation under capitalist production lies in the specific modern relation of the producers to their objective conditions of production. After the historical dissolution of the original unity between humans and the earth, the producers can only relate to the conditions of production as an alien property. Marx's claim that the dissolution of the original unity constitutes the paradigm of modern society marks a decisive difference from the standpoint of most economists, who take the existing social relation for granted, as a given.

However, Marx was then still very much influenced by Ludwig Feuerbach's philosophy. As a result, he tended to connect his historical analysis with an abstract and ahistorical "human essence," and further, his critical understanding of the capitalist mode of production was not very profound. Nevertheless, Marx soon came to notice the theoretical limitations of Feuerbach's philosophy of essence and succeeded in fully rejecting its abstract critique of alienation in his *Theses on Feuerbach* and

The German Ideology and thereby establishing in 1845 a theoretical basis for his later research in natural science.

"ALIENATION" AS PHILOSOPHICAL CATEGORY?

The popular Marxist concept of "alienation" and "estrangement" found in *The Economic and Philosophic Manuscripts* certainly documents the young Marx's brilliant insight into the negative characteristics of modern capitalist production. However, this concept was also an object of never-ending heated debates in the twentieth century. On the one hand, Marxist humanists argued that Marx always held on to the theory of alienated labor to criticize the central contradiction of capitalism and to envision human emancipation in post-capitalism.[3] On the other hand, Louis Althusser famously pointed to a radical "epistemological break" in Marx's theory, maintaining that Marx after *The German Ideology* completely abandoned his earlier anthropological and Hegelian scheme of 1844 and moved to a totally different "scientific" problematic.[4] Althusser notably criticized the delusions of humanists who fetishized *The Economic and Philosophic Manuscripts* and embraced Marx's Young Hegelian conception of alienation as an adequate foundation for historical materialism. The "epistemological break" was observed in the fact that alienation no longer played any important theoretical role after 1845. The endless debates between two entirely different interpretations served to deepen various dimensions of the concept of alienation, but at the same time a certain theoretical one-sidedness existed due to the heavily philosophic discussions of Marx's texts.[5]

A presupposition was taken for granted in this philosophic debate. Whether one advocated the continuity of or a break in Marx's theory, both interpretations regarded the text as a completed "work." However, this position is no longer acceptable after Jürgen Rojahn's careful philological examination showed in a convincing manner that the bundle of texts called *The Economic and Philosophic Manuscripts* do not constitute an independent work; that is, they are not a coherent and systematic treatise. Instead, they are a part of his study notes, similar to those in the *Paris Notebooks*. These texts were spontaneously written down as part of a process that included making excerpts (*Exzerpte*), without any intent of publishing them. As Rojahn argues:

> To summarize: Marx's *Manuscripts* of 1844 must not be seen as a distinct entity, isolated from his notebooks of that period. Their various

parts do not form a properly thought out "work," based on preceding studies, but rather, reflect different stages of the *development* of his ideas, which proceeding at a rapid pace at that time, was fueled by continued reading. Marx made his *exzerpte* but at the same time, also wrote down his thoughts. He did that alternately in his notebooks and his manuscripts. Only the *ensemble* of these notes, seen as a sequence of *exzerpte*, comments, summaries, reflections, and further *exzerpte*, gives an adequate idea of *how* his views developed.[6]

Thus, since the text today known as *The Economic and Philosophic Manuscripts* was written spontaneously in the very process of copying down excerpts from his readings, it does not include any final formulation of Marx's thought, and Marx would never have imagined that his notes would cause such heated debates after his death because he wrote his notebooks only for private use. In this sense, humanists exaggerate the theoretical significance of these "study notes." Humanists are not able to admit this philological fact, clinging to the idea that these notes are "manuscripts" for an independent work. The priority they give to *The Economic and Philosophic Manuscripts* tends to neglect Marx's later economic texts, in which the theory of alienation loses its central role. And even if they refer to them, they often do so in a superficial manner, merely looking at terms such as "alien" and "alienation" as claims for the continuity of Marx's thought.[7] If the concept of "alienated labor" is overestimated as a normative theory, such an approach contradicts Marx's non-philosophic position after *The German Ideology*, which rejects any opposition of a philosophic idea against the alienated reality.[8]

In contrast, the "scientific" interpretation represented by Althusser also neglects the unique critical aspect of Marx's theory in the notebooks of 1844 by overemphasizing the break without recognizing any value in them. It is true that Marx's Young Hegelian approach is problematic, and he later abandoned it. Still, it does not automatically follow that there is no continuity at all in Marx's theory before and after 1845 and that one can simply ignore the *Paris Notebooks*. Such an interpretation too hastily reduces the richness of Marx's critique to the Young Hegelian philosophy and cannot trace the formation of Marx's thought because it misses the true beginning point of his critique of political economy. In his analysis of alienation of 1844, there already exists a central theme of his critique of capitalism, that is, *the separation and unity between humanity and nature.* This is why, in contrast to the earlier philosophic discussions, it is necessary to conduct a systematic examination of the development of

Marx's concept of nature in relation to his political economy. Instead of treating only *The Economic Philosophic Manuscripts*, we need to take the *Paris Notebooks* as a whole into account in order to know what kind of theory emerged in 1844. *can a theory "emerge" from such disparate notes?*

First of all, it is helpful to have a general understanding of Marx's theory of alienation or estrangement in his *Paris Notebooks*. According to the standard interpretation, there are four types of alienation, starting with Marx pointing out the reality under the system of private property, where "labor's realization" appears as a "loss of realization" and the "objectification" of labor appears as "loss of the object."[9] The product of labor, in which workers objectify their own activity, appears not as their own product. It neither satisfies their needs nor confirms their creative abilities. On the contrary, it appears as an alien object to workers, as a power independent of the producers: "The more the worker spends himself, the more powerful the alien world of objects which he creates over and against himself, the poorer he himself—his inner world—becomes, the less belongs to him as his own. It is the same in religion. The more man puts into God, the less he retains in himself. The worker puts his life into the object; but now his life no longer belongs to him but to the object. Hence, the greater this activity, the more the worker lacks objects."[10] Apparently, Marx applies Feuerbach's critique of alienation in religion to the sphere of political economy to problematize the paradoxical situation in capitalism that an act of appropriation appears as a loss of the object. One cannot appropriate the sensuous world through a teleological act of laboring, but rather the external world of things dominates and impoverishes producers. It gets lost precisely through the act of production.

From this first type of estrangement of the sensuous external world, Marx deduces the second alienation of labor. If the product of laborers appears as alienated, it is, says Marx, because the activities of producers do not belong to themselves, but to someone else, resulting in the loss of self. In other words, the act of production is not a voluntary activity of objectification of one's own free subjectivity, but "forced labor":

> In his work, therefore, he does not affirm himself but denies himself, does not feel content but unhappy, does not develop freely his physical and mental energy but mortifies his body and ruins his mind. . . . His labor is therefore not voluntary, but coerced; it is *forced labor*. It is therefore not the satisfaction of a need; it is merely a *means* to satisfy needs external to it.[11]

As a result of reducing labor to a mere "means" of their own subsistence, there is no room for producers to realize their own free
self-affirmation through labor. The content of free human activity is now
limited to animal functions such as eating, drinking, and procreating,
and therefore the main objective of workers becomes the maintenance
of physical subsistence. Yet even the realization of this hope is not
guaranteed for them under alienated labor, when they are constantly
exposed to poverty and sickness. Marx problematizes the modern inversion of the free and conscious human activity of labor into the act of
dehumanization.

From these first two types of alienation Marx then infers the third
form of alienation: "In estranging from man (1) nature, and (2) himself,
his own active functions, his life activity, estranged labor estranges the
species from man."[12] Here Marx takes Feuerbach's concept and argues that
even if individuals are finite beings, humanity as such is universal and
infinite as a "species-being."[13] Marx sees the essential manifestation of
the universality of human species-being in its unique free and conscious
act of production. In laboring, the producers can reflect upon a given
situation and actively realize their own subjective ideas in the objective
world by freely modifying the latter. In this sense, humans are a "universal" being and differentiate themselves from other animals. According to
Marx, while animals remain trapped in a given particular situation and
can only work and consume in a certain manner—though we know now
that this is not quite true—humans can teleologically relate to nature
as their "inorganic" body and modify its current forms in accordance
with their own needs, inventing new technologies and creating a wholly
new environment.[14] Furthermore, Marx argues that human labor is also
a "free" activity because it is not always directed to the satisfaction of
immediate physical needs for the sake of a bare subsistence. Humans can
also produce something fully independent from their physical needs. For
example, one can produce an artistic object "in accordance with the laws
of beauty" and attain self-confirmation and pleasure in this act.[15] Marx
bemoans the fact that alienation negates this creative activity, which is
nothing but a manifestation of human species-being, since labor is now
subordinated to mere individual purposes as a means to sustaining one's
existence: "Estranged labor reverses this relationship, so that it is just
because man is a conscious being that he makes his life activity, his *essential being*, a mere means to his *existence*."[16] The universal dimension of
human labor gets lost as its functions are instrumentalized to increase
the wealth of others.

Finally, Marx adds the fourth form of alienation: "An immediate consequence of the fact that man is estranged from the product of his labor,
from his life activity, from his species-being is the *estrangement of man
from man.*"[17] If individuals have to strive desperately for their physical
existence, their intersubjective social cooperation and communication
becomes extremely problematic. Consequently, it is no longer possible to
enrich the physical and mental dimensions of the human species-being
together. Instead of free mutual intercourse and collaboration, there
emerges antagonistic and atomistic competition for survival.

To sum up, Marx's analysis of estranged labor delineates the modern
unfree reality where one cannot execute labor as an end in itself but rather
labor functions as a process of loss of reality, impoverishment, dehumanization, and atomization. Marx argues that the only way to overcome this
alienated reality is to transcend the system of private property so that
humans can relate to nature through labor in a thoroughly conscious,
free, universal cooperative manner and acquire self-affirmation with the
totality of the external world with their own objectified products. This
will lead to the absolute realization of human essence as species-being.
Marx envisions communism as a goal of the historical process, in which
humans overcome the estranged dichotomy of the subject and object
through a revolution to realize the absolute unity between humanity and
nature under the name of human species-being.

It is obvious that Marx's project of 1844 is heavily influenced by
Feuerbach, who is supposed to have achieved "the establishment of *true
materialism* and of *real science.*"[18] Feuerbach in his *Essence of Christianity*
put forward a theory of alienation as a critique of religion. Individuals
suffer from alienation in religion because they are finite beings and
project an infinite being (that is, God) in opposition to which they find
themselves powerless. Feuerbach argues that this religious estrangement can be overcome if they are able to recognize the hidden truth that
humans are actually projecting their own essence as a species-being onto
God. God is nothing but the product of human imagination that later
became more and more powerful and independent, dominating humans
as an alien existence. Against this inverted reality, Feuerbach opposes the
importance of "sensibility," and particularly "love," as the unique materialist foundation of truth:

Love is the middle term, the substantial bond, the principle of reconciliation between the perfect and the imperfect, the sinless and sinful
being the universal and the individual, the divine and the human.

Love is God himself, and apart from it there is no God. Love makes
man God and God man. Love strengthens the weak and weakens
the strong, abases the high and raises the lowly, idealizes matter and
materializes spirit. Love it the true unity of God and man, of spirit
and nature. In love common nature is spirit, and the preeminent
spirit is nature.[19]

Feuerbach claims that with the power of love humans will be able to
transcend religious estrangement, because through love they can coop-
erate with one another to overcome their isolated state of being and this
intersubjective unity allows them to see through their own essence as
species-being.

Feuerbach's explanation of alienation together with its transcendence
had a tremendous impact upon the Young Hegelians. Marx at the time
firmly believed that Feuerbach had carried out a thorough critique of
religion and revealed the true principle of a coming revolutionary "philosophy of the future." He felt it necessary only to extend its scope to
include other spheres of the modern bourgeois society: "For Germany
the *criticism of religion* is in the main complete, and criticism of religion
is the premise of all criticism."[20] Marx's *Paris Notebooks* document his
attempt to carry out this type of criticism of alienation, combining it with
his recent discoveries in the field of political economy. However, he neither published these notebooks nor discussed the concept of alienation
in an extensive manner again.

It has been heatedly disputed whether Marx stuck to his original
plan to extend the concept of alienation to political economy in later
works. Marx's theory of alienation was interpreted from a *philosophic*
perspective ever since the publication of the text as *The Economic and
Philosophic Manuscripts* in 1932. What is more, the participants in this
debate never questioned this tendency, something that must now change
based on recent philological findings. At the time, Marx was reading
various works of political economy, and if he started his discussion on
alienation rather spontaneously while he was making other excerpts of
political economy in his *Paris Notebooks*, political economy must have
affected his theoretical interest even with regard to alienation.

In terms of philosophizing the text and ignoring political economy,
Herbert Marcuse played a particularly important role. He published
an article on the newly discovered manuscripts in 1932 titled "The
Foundation of Historical Materialism" and shed light on the novel
dimension of Marx's "philosophical critique" of alienation. Marcuse

argued that there is an important "breakthrough" within the first manuscript, and that Marx's analysis "seems initially to proceed completely
on the ground of traditional political economy and its theorems. Marx
significantly starts by dividing his investigation into the three traditional concepts of political economy: 'The Wages of Labor,' 'The Profit
of Capital' and 'The Rent of Land.'" However, according to Marcuse,
Marx's radical critique of alienation and estrangement "point[ed] in
a completely new direction," and his critique emerged only after "this
division into three [was] exploded and abandoned." Marcuse went further, claiming that the "development of the concept of labor thus breaks
through the traditional framework for dealing with problems."[21] Thus,
Marx's philosophical critique of modern bourgeois society and political economy as its ideologue only begins when he supersedes the "three
traditional concepts of political economy." A radical break exists between
the economic and philosophic parts.

As Marcuse emphasized, Marx first excerpted relevant sentences
by Jean-Baptiste Say and Adam Smith from his notebooks into the
Manuscripts and then added detailed comments on them.[22] Subsequently,
he began his discussion of estranged labor only after page XXII of the
first "Manuscript." Yet, this fact does not mean that Marx's comments on
these economists within their framework are insignificant for his concept of alienation as Marcuse's interpretation implies. Marcuse's analysis
almost completely neglects Marx's economic critique in the first half
of the first manuscript.[23] This tendency of Marcuse to underestimate
the economic part of the first manuscript was widely shared by later
Marxists, showing that Marcuse's interpretation was quite influential.
For example, Erich Fromm shared the same view, and his popular edition of *The Economic and Philosophic Manuscripts* omitted the economic
part of the first manuscript, which reinforced the philosophic interpretation of alienation.[24] Marcuse and Fromm only recognized the original
theoretical contribution by the young Marx in his *philosophical* criticism
of "alienated labor," without going into the very beginning, which deals
with his critique of political economy.

The impression of Marx's "breakthrough" was reinforced by an editorial title, "Estranged Labor," at the beginning of the second half of the
first *Manuscript*, which *does not exist* in Marx's own notebooks. In contrast to the dominant tendency, I argue that the "emergence of a theory"
in Marx's notebook must be understood in a close relation to his analysis
of political economy because his original theory of alienation is formulated in the process of a critique of it. If one misses the importance of

the first part of the first *Manuscript*, one cannot avoid being confronted with a theoretical difficulty, as was the case in the earlier literature. In other words, the young Marx has been unjustly criticized being unable to explain *the cause of modern alienated labor.*

In 1844, Marx was trying to analyze the "facts" of private property, the existence of which bourgeois economists simply took for granted. He aimed at revealing the historical conditions of the system of private property, and he argued that its "essence" lies in a certain form of labor in capitalist society. In this sense, Marx stated that private property is the "product" and "necessary result" of estranged labor:

> *Private property* is thus the product, the result, the necessary conse-
> quence, of *alienated labor,* of the external relation of the worker to
> nature and to himself. *Private property* thus results by analysis from
> the concept of *alienated labor,* i.e., of *alienated man,* of estranged
> labor, of estranged life, of *estranged* man. True, it is as a result of the
> *movement of private property* that we have obtained the concept of
> *alienated labor (of alienated life)* in political economy. But analysis
> of this concept shows that though private property appears to be the
> reason, the cause of alienated labor, it is rather its consequence, just
> as the gods are *originally* not the cause but the effect of man's intel-
> lectual confusion. Later this relationship becomes reciprocal.[25]

Marx pointed to the "reciprocal" relationship, according to which both private property and alienated labor function as "cause" and "effect" and reinforce each other. However, this situation only emerged later. In this way, he intended to make it clear that at the beginning private prop-erty must not be treated as a given "fact" precisely because it is a specific historical and logical "result" that arose from alienated labor.

Then Marx continued to ask: "We have accepted the *estrangement of labor*, its *alienation*, as a fact, and we have analyzed this fact. How, we now ask, does *man* come to *alienate*, to estrange, his *labor*? How is this estrangement rooted in the nature of human development?"[26] Here his question seems to indicate that Marx felt the necessity to explain the ultimate cause of the estrangement of labor in capitalist society, but in the following sentences he did not explain it, and the notebook is disrupted without going into this question. The text gives an impres-sion that Marx had difficulty in revealing the cause of alienation, that is, when he tried to grasp the notion that private property arose from alienated labor, he seemed to fall into a circular explanation that labor is alienated because of the system of private property. Lars Tummers thus asked: "How can private property be both an effect of and a factor that influences alienation?" This question is a common one, and Tummers follows Ignace Feuerlicht, who also pointed to the young Marx's theoretical limitation in a similar manner: "One of the most conspicuous contradictions lies in the fact that young Marx considers private property sometimes as the cause and sometimes as the effect or symptom of alienation."[27] Feuerlicht moans that one can only try in vain to find the answer to the obvious question about the exact historical and logical genesis of alienated labor.

On the contrary, Michael Quante attempts to solve Marx's circular explanation, though he shares the same presupposition with Marcuse that Marx's "own philosophically founded analysis of national economic phenomena" is "expounded in the second part of the first manuscript with the concept of alienated labor." Since Quante neglects the economic critique by Marx in the first part of the first notebook, he naturally reaches another "philosophic answer" to the problem concerning the cause of alienation, which is the Hegelian logical and historical movement of "negation of negation." He explains that the emergence of alienation is an "inevitable intermediary step" on the way to the "conscious appropriation of species-being."[28] Without doubt, this type of schematic account does not provide any attractive and convincing solution to the problem because its reductionistic understanding of Hegel's logical and historical dialectics cannot avoid the criticism of determinism, although Quante is not interested in defending Marx from such consequences.

As will be shown in the next section, both Feuerlicht and Quante miss Marx's original intent and end up directing an "imagined" critique. It is "imagined" because the aporia of alienation does not exist at all. It appears to exist only because earlier studies arbitrarily divided the notebook's text into two parts and focused exclusively on the second "philosophic" part. A Japanese Marxist scholar, Masami Fukutomi, pointed out the importance of the first economic part, especially Marx's discussion of the "intimate ties of man with the earth."[29] It will provide us with a solid basis for consistently comprehending Marx's entire project.

THE DISSOLUTION OF THE ORIGINAL UNITY BETWEEN HUMANITY AND NATURE

In one paragraph in the first notebook that hardly gained attention in the philosophic literature, Marx compares the capitalist form of property with the feudalist form of possession. The neglect is surprising, because it is in this paragraph in the *Paris Notebooks* that Marx for the first time discusses the relationship between the pathological reality of modern production and the concept of estranged labor. After he describes the total commodification of landed property as the completion of capitalist relations, Marx provides a reason why this transformation of landed property exerts such a decisive impact on the emergence of alienated labor.

Marx first makes it clear that his historical comparison must not be confused with a romantic idealization of past feudal society, as if there had been no alienated labor in precapitalist societies. He argues that such an idealization occurs only through a lack of scientific investigation:

> We will not join in the sentimental tears wept over this by romanticism. Romanticism always confuses the shamefulness of *huckstering the land* with the perfectly rational consequence, inevitable and desirable within the realm of private property, of the *huckstering of private property* in land. In the first place, feudal landed property is already by its very nature huckstered land—*the earth which is estranged from man* and hence confronts him in the shape of a few great lords.[30]

The romantic bemoans the collapse of feudal domination and the resultant commodification of the land and the loss of the lords' noble values to the avarice of merchants. Rejecting such a view, Marx argues that "the huckstering" of the land also existed in feudal landed property, so that labor and land were estranged from humans *to some extent* under the dominion of "a few great lords."

Furthermore, "shamefulness," Marx says, is not the fundamental characteristic of the modern money aristocracy, because the boundless desire for money that the defenders of romantic ideals find unacceptable is actually an "inevitable" and even "desirable" result, viewed from a wider historical perspective, because it is nothing but an embodiment of the rationality of modern bourgeois society. In other words, the "shameful" behavior of the modern landowners is not a moral defect but makes concrete the new social rationality after a radical transformation of social structure. Romantics like Pierre le Pesant de Boisguilbert cannot recognize this; they can only moralistically reproach the shameful behavior of individuals in capitalism.[31] In clear opposition to the idealization of the past, Marx points to the fact that there were relations of domination grounded in feudal landed property, under the system of which people were also "estranged" from the land and "confronted" by it.[32]

Marx continues his analysis on feudal possession of land, illustrating the situation of serfs in opposition to the landlord:

> The domination of the land as an alien power over men is already inherent in feudal landed property. The serf is the adjunct of the land. Likewise, the lord of an entailed estate, the first-born son, belongs to the land. It inherits him. Indeed, the dominion of private property begins with property in land—that is its basis. But in feudal landed property the lord at least *appears* as the king of the estate. Similarly, there still exists the semblance of a more intimate connection between the proprietor and the land than that of mere *material* wealth. The estate is individualized with its lord: it has his rank, is baronial or ducal with him, has his privileges, his jurisdiction, his political position, etc. It appears as the inorganic body of its lord.[33]

Serfs, on the other hand, have lost their ability to conduct independent and free activity insofar as they cannot relate to the land as their own property but only as the lord's. Their existence is reduced to a mere "adjunct" of the earth, which is the foundation of material wealth. Marx recognizes that due to this subjugation there exists a certain level of alienation from nature and their own activity even under feudal social relations. Nature functions only as an "inorganic body" of the lord who can appropriate the product of the land and the labor of serfs. In this way, serfs become a part of the inorganic body in the production process. Land is as such "privatized" and "individualized" by the lord, which Marx considers the beginning of the "domination of private property."

However, without directly deducing the cause of modern alienated labor from this class antagonism in the feudal social system, Marx points to its important qualitative difference from landed property in capitalist society. According to Marx, feudal social relations are grounded on "personal" and "political" domination; that is, the appropriation of products of the land takes place through the lord's direct dominance over serfs with his personal and political power thanks to innate privileges and a monopoly of violence. Thus serfs are totally conscious of this personal domination by the lord, and this is why the lord's "family history, the history of his house etc." become so important to legitimate the relations of domination, as "all this individualizes the estate for him and make it literally his house, personifies it." The land and family history individualizes the landed property and legitimizes its monopoly, which transforms a piece of land into the "inorganic body" of the lord.[34]

The direct personal and political domination and exploitation in this precapitalist society is dependent on tradition and custom, which results in a unique relation of the laborer to the earth. Marx emphasizes the notable difference between serfs and day-laborers:

> Similarly those working on the estate have not the position of *day-laborers*; but they are in part themselves his property, as are serfs; and in part they are bound to him by ties of respect, allegiance, and duty. His relation to them is therefore directly political, and has likewise a human, *intimate [gemüthliche]* side. Customs, character, etc., vary from one estate to another and seem to be one with the land to which they belong; whereas later, it is only his purse and not his character, his individuality, which connects a man with an estate.[35]

Those working the land under feudal domination are negated in such a way that their personal independence is not recognized by their lord. Serfs are regarded as a part of the lord's landed property. This relation of domination and dependence essentially differs from the situation of day-laborers in modern bourgeois society because the latter are free from any direct political domination and recognized as "free" and "equal" legal subjects.

This does not mean, however, that day-laborers can enjoy a freer and better life than serfs. Marx argues that the opposite is the case. Precisely because serfs are negated and deprived of their rights, there remains their unity with the objective conditions of production and reproduction, so that the physical existence of serfs is guaranteed. As Masami Fukutomi pointed out, the unique relation of serfs to the land is decisive for Marx's analysis of alienation in the *Paris Notebooks*.[36] Notably, Marx emphasizes in the cited passage that personal domination in feudal society possesses "a human, *intimate* side" despite the antagonistic opposition of the land to those working on it. Though the concrete situation varies according to the different customs and characters of lords, the fundamental characteristic common to feudal production is the unity of producers with the land. In spite of the negation of their independence as legal subjects, they can attain a guarantee for their own physical existence as well as freedom and independence in the production process. There is no room for the reified domination by capital because direct personal domination prevents capital from penetrating its autonomous power. Under this situation, the producers provide surplus labor and surplus products only through the threat and often the reality of physical coercion, which inevitably impedes the increase of productivity. The feudal lord also does not strive to attain maximal advantage from his land, but rather "consumes what is there and calmly leaves the worry of producing to the serfs and the tenants."[37]

The lord's seemingly moderate behavior is praised by Romantics as a manifestation of his noble character, but it is clearly conditioned by the underlying objective relations of production. In this vein, the entire production in feudal society acquires a stable character because its aim is fundamentally directed to the satisfaction of concrete social needs. In contrast to the Romantics, Marx concludes that it is not the moral character of the lord but the relationship between humans and the earth that realizes the "nobility's relationship" to landed property and casts "romantic glory on its lord."[38]

Then Marx investigates modern bourgeois society, where, together with the dissolution of feudal personal domination, landed property has been fully transformed into an object of "huckstering." This change creates a wholly different type of domination, one that is the non-personal and reified domination of capital, accompanied by a specific form of alienated labor:

> It is necessary that this appearance be abolished—that landed property, the root of private property, be dragged completely into the movement of private property and that it become a commodity; that the rule of the proprietor appear as the undisguised rule of private property, of capital, freed of all political tincture; that the relationship between proprietor and worker be reduced to the economic relationship of exploiter and exploited; that all personal relationship between the proprietor and his property cease, property becoming merely *objective*, material wealth; that the marriage of convenience should take the place of the marriage of honor with the land; and that the land should likewise sink to the status of a commercial value, like man.[39]

As the landed property becomes a commodity and thus comes to be integrated into the huckstering system of private property after the dissolution of the earlier personal relationship of domination and dependence, individuals, on the one hand, can face each other as formally free and equal subjects. They are all uniformly recognized as legal subjects in the civil society. On the other hand, they also lose the direct connection with the earth, so that they now have to appear in the market to sell their labor power. In illustrations by political economists, this new modern relationship provides a foundation of an ideal and harmonious realm of freedom and equality in which the relationship of domination seemingly ceases to exist. Marx rejects this view and argues that the bourgeois ideal of "freedom" and "equality" is not the end of domination at all. This ideal turns out to be an appearance, for instead of the relationship of personal domination between the exploiting and the exploited, there comes an impersonal and reified relationship of domination. Day-laborers must be subordinated to a qualitatively different, modern form of alienation, and their working conditions prove much worse and more alienated in various aspects than in feudal society.

Domination in capitalist society must be strictly differentiated from that of the feudal world. Due to the commodification of land, the producers in modern society lose any direct connection with the earth and come to be separated from their original means of production, whereas serfs were still tightly connected to the land.[40] Consequently, modern individuals are all constantly obligated to sell their own labor power, the only commodity they have, to another person and thus become day-laborers suffering from estrangement from their own activity. According to Marx, this transformation of the relationship between humans and the earth is decisive in order to understand the specificity of the capitalist mode of production.[41]

Modern workers lose any guarantee of physical existence, and their activity becomes estranged, controlled and dominated by alien forces. Propertylessness, precariousness, alienation, and exploitation are tightly connected. It is true that exploitation existed for the serfs, and they had to provide the lord with surplus labor and surplus products. However, contrasting this with the situation of modern workers, Marx argues that the labor of serfs still possessed an "intimate side," because, thanks to the connection with the earth serfs maintained autonomy in the production process and their material life was secured. Ironically, this is a particular result of the negation of their personality in feudal society, which transforms them into a mere part of the objective means of production. In this regard, Marx without doubt recognizes a positive side of the feudal mode of production.

The regulation of the autonomous power of capital can take various forms, such as "craft, guild, corporation, etc., within which labor still has a *seemingly social* significance, still the significance of the *real* community, and has not yet reached the stage of *indifference* to its content, of complete being-for-itself, i.e., of abstraction from all other being, and hence has not yet become *liberated* capital."[42] Within a craft, guild, and corporation there no longer exists the direct unity between humans and land, but there is still a stable connection of the producers with their means of production thanks to the intersubjective coordination of the entire production, which hinders the full penetration of the power of capital. The complete dissolution of the tie between the workers and their objective means of production for the first time prepares "free" labor, in a "double sense," and thus the impersonal, reified dominance by "liberated capital."

Modern laborers, on the contrary, lose any direct connection to the land. On the one hand, they are free from personal dominance. On the other hand, they are also free from the means of production and thus can no longer relate to nature as their own "inorganic body." The original unity with the land disappeared with the collapse of precapitalist personal domination. Its result is alienation from nature, activity, species-being, and other people—or simply said, modern alienation arising from the total annihilation of the "intimate side" of production. When the land becomes a commodity, the relationship between humans and land is radically modified and reorganized for the sake of producing capitalist wealth. After the universalization of commodity production over the entire society, the whole of production is not primarily directed to the satisfaction of concrete personal needs, but to the valorization of capital alone. Following the new rationality of production, the capitalist does not simply let the workers conduct their job as they please; rather, in accordance with his "filthy self-interest," he actively transforms the entire production process in such a way that human activity is fully subjected to a reified dominance, without consideration of autonomy of work and material security.[43]

In societies where the logic of commodity production becomes dominant, the modern form of alienation takes up a fully different shape in comparison with precapitalist estrangement. Since the reified dominance of capital is not dependent upon legitimatization through personal history and honor, "liberated capital" ignores all kinds of "ties of respect, allegiance, and duty" and even the concrete material life of individual workers. Capital is simply indifferent even if those workers are dying as long as "the *race of laborers*" does not die out.[44] The concrete content of labor is fully abstracted for capital. Capital only counts the wages of labor as mere "costs" in addition to costs for maintaining other instruments. In other words, there is no significant difference between wages for workers and oil for wheels. According to the new social relations, capitalists act with self-interest and avarice. However, this is not a mere moral corruption, but a result of following the new rationality under competition for more profit. This is because "it is essential that in this competition landed property, in the form of capital, manifests its dominion over both the working class and the proprietors themselves who are either being ruined or raised by the laws governing the movement of capital."[45]

Marx thus points to a great historical transformation of the human-nature relationship underlying the estrangement of modern labor, as a result of which the activity of workers can no longer function as the subjective realization of the free and conscious capability of human beings in and with nature. Human beings are reduced to "wage laborers" who are dependent on capital for the sake of their own physical lives; and accordingly, their entire activity is minimized into "wage labor." Though humans as wage laborers can only survive in relation to alien capital, this relationship between capital and labor is "an indifferent, external and accidental relationship to each other" because liberated capital is not interested in workers and their concrete lives.[46]

Therefore, the circular argument that Tummers and Feuerlicht find in the first manuscript in terms of the specific historical condition of modern alienated labor does not exist. This is because in the section on "ground rent" in the same notebook Marx discusses the specificity of the capitalist mode of production and alienation in comparison to the feudal mode. For Marx, the cause of modern estrangement is quite clear, and his argument is consistent.[47] Though Marx in his private notebook, never intended for publication, did not repeat every single point in a reader-friendly manner, a careful analysis of the notebook, with attention paid to his excerpts from Engels's *Outline*, demonstrates that private property as the dominion of reified relations of commodity and money emerges out of a loss of the original unity between producers and their objective conditions of production.

If one does not take the section on ground rent into account, one faces a risk of an even greater misunderstanding. Without correctly understanding the fundamental cause of alienation, it is not possible to recognize Marx's vision of transcending it. Only if one comprehends the estrangement in capitalist society as a dissolution of humans' original unity with the earth does it becomes evident that Marx's communist project consistently aims at a conscious rehabilitation of the unity between humans and nature.

This idea builds the core of "humanism = naturalism," as Marx was already aware of the task of realizing free individuality in the future society, using the concept of "association":

Association, applied to land, shares the economic advantage of large-scale landed property, and first brings to realization the original tendency inherent in [land] division, namely, equality. In the same way association also reestablishes, now on a rational basis, no longer mediated by serfdom, overlordship and the silly mysticism of property, *the intimate [gemüthliche] ties of man with the earth, since the earth ceases to be an object of huckstering,* and through free labor and free enjoyment becomes, once more, a true personal property of man.[48]

Speaking of the practical task of association, Marx comes back to the earlier discussion and emphatically demands the reconstruction of "the intimate ties of man with the earth," now on a higher level after its destruction in capitalism. In contrast to the feudal society and its monopoly of lands, the conscious construction of the unity between humans and nature must be free of any personal and political subjugation and dominion, and association must realize free intersubjective relationships through the social appropriation of the means of production and products by the direct producers. Consequently, this totally new mode of production makes a "rational" relationship to the land possible on a social scale, which is radically different from its ruthless "huckstering" in capitalism. The entire social activity of production and its products thus does not confront the producers as alien objects, but thanks to the higher unity with the earth as "a true personal property of man," serves to make possible the "free labor and free enjoyment" of *all* producers. Marx's vision of the future society is without doubt fully consistent with his critique of modern alienated labor.

It is in this *economic* sense that Marx in 1844 insists that establishment of the absolute unity of humanity and nature is the central task of communism:

Communism as the *positive* transcendence of *private property as human self-estrangement,* and therefore as the real *appropriation* of the *human* essence by and for man; communism therefore as the complete return of man to himself as a *social* (i.e., human) being— a return accomplished consciously and embracing the entire wealth of previous development. This communism, as fully developed naturalism equals humanism, and as fully developed humanism equals naturalism; it is the *genuine* resolution of the conflict between man and nature and between man and man—the true resolution of the

strife between existence and essence, between objectification and
self-confirmation, between freedom and necessity, between the individual and the species.[49]

Marx depicts the historical movement toward the transcendence of
self-alienation and the loss of object under the system of private property as a process of the true reconciliation of humanity and nature. As a
condition for its realization, he points to the necessity of a radical transformation of the existing mode of production and the abolition of private
property. The "society" to come is nothing but a collective and conscious
organization and regulation of the relationship between humans and
nature: "Thus *society* is the complete unity of man with nature—the true
resurrection of nature—the accomplished naturalism of man and the
accomplished humanism of nature."[50] The unity between the organic and
inorganic body of humans can only be realized through a fully conscious
and rational regulation of their interaction with nature. Marx's critique
of alienation of 1844 regards the "rational" reorganization of the relationship between humans and nature as essential, and thus he envisions
the idea of communism as the accomplished "humanism = naturalism."
This is a beginning, even if it is only a beginning, of Marx's economic and
ecological critique of capitalism.

THE CONTINUITY OF A THEORY

Marx did not significantly alter his original, fundamental insight of 1844,
in terms of the unity of humans and nature, until *Capital*. In a consistent
manner, he criticized in his *Poverty of Philosophy* of 1847 the modern
commodification and huckstering of the land as separation of humans
from nature: "Rent, instead of *binding man to nature*, has merely bound
the exploitation of the land to competition."[51]

Another more notable paragraph is in *The Original Text* [*Urtext*] *of
a Contribution to the Critique of Political Economy* of 1858, where Marx,
employing the same terminology, refers to the dissolution of the unity
between humans and nature as the essential condition of modern society:

> The peasant no longer confronts the landowner as a peasant with his
> rural product and his rural labor, but as the money owner. . . . On the
> other hand, the landowner no longer regards him as an uncouth indi-
> vidual producing means of subsistence in peculiar living conditions,
> but as one whose product—exchange value become independent,

the universal equivalent, money—is no different from anyone else's product. Thus, the *intimate appearance* [*der gemühtliche Schein*] that covered up the transaction in its previous form is dispelled.[52]

In this passage, the theoretical continuity since 1844 is obvious, since Marx again deals with the dissolution of feudal personal dominion into the relationship among proprietors of commodity and money in the market and thematizes this change as the disappearance of the "intimate appearance that covered up" the production process. With similar words, he describes the transformation of the relation of domination into a pure economic form as a result of "the shedding of relationships of personal dependence, as a victory of bourgeois society."[53] The social relationships become reified as they are mediated through money and commodity, though unlike precapitalist society, individuals appear capable of behaving equally and independently of one another. The market transactions seem to take place between "free" and "equal" commodity owners, but it turns out in reality to be the expanding process of appropriating other people's wealth and concentrating social wealth to few people's hands. Thus, even the "intimate appearance" disappears in capitalist society.

Furthermore, in the 1860s, Marx repeatedly points to the separation of the producers from the land as a historical and logical presupposition for the emergence of the capitalist mode of production:

The formation of a class of wage laborers, whether in manufacture or in agriculture itself—at first all manufacturers appear only as *stipendiés*, wage laborers of the cultivating proprietor—requires the separation of the conditions of labor from labor capacity, and the basis for this separation is that the land itself becomes the private property of one part of society, so that the other part is cut off from this objective condition for valorization of its labor.[54]

In a similar manner, Marx argues in *Capital*:

In the section on primitive accumulation we saw how this mode of production presupposes on the one hand that the direct producers are freed from the position of mere appendages of the soil (in the form of bondsmen, serfs, slaves, etc.) and on the other hand the expropriation of the mass of the people from the land. To that extent, the monopoly of landed property is a *historical precondition* for the capitalist mode of production and remains its permanent *foundation*, as with all previous modes of production based on the exploitation of the masses in one form or the other. But the form of *landed property* which greets the capitalist mode of production at the start does not correspond to this mode. The form that does correspond to it is only created by the capitalist mode of production itself, through the subjection of agriculture to capital; and in this way feudal landed property, clan property, or small peasant property is transformed into the *economic* form corresponding to this mode of production, however diverse the legal forms of this may be. It is one of the great results of the capitalist mode of production that it transforms agriculture from a merely empirical set of procedures, mechanically handed down and practiced by the most undeveloped part of society, into a conscious scientific application of agronomy, insofar as this is at all possible within the conditions of private property; that on the one hand it completely detaches landed property from relations of lordship and servitude, while on the other hand it completely separates the land as a *condition of labor* from landed property and the landowners, for whom, moreover, this land represents nothing but a certain money tax that his monopoly permits him to extract from the industrial capitalist, the farmer. . . . Landed property thus receives its *purely economic form* by the stripping away of all its former political and social embellishments and admixtures.[55]

As clearly indicated in this paragraph, Marx repeatedly explains the specificity of the capitalist mode of production, with the monopoly of landed property as its "historical condition." Even if the monopoly of landed property is also a permanent condition in "all previous modes of production based on the exploitation of the masses in one form or the other," its capitalist form is distinct because it takes a "purely economic form," while the precapitalist exploitation is carried out through the political "relations of lordship and servitude." According to Marx, this qualitative transformation of the relationship between humans and the earth results from "the subjection of agriculture to capital." In this sense, Marx still holds his insight of 1844 that the absolute separation of humans from their objective conditions of production is the essential presupposition for the emergence of the relation of capital and wage labor, whereas in precapitalist societies, despite the monopoly of landed property as a condition of exploitation of bondsmen, serfs, and slaves, the access to the means of production remained guaranteed to these direct producers. Through the transformation of the form of landed property in the process of "original accumulation," a mass of peasants was driven out and lost their independent relationship to the land as the means of production and subsistence, so that they were forced to sell their own labor force as a commodity on the market. The emergence of the "purely economic form" of landed property—"huckstering of the land," which caused the modern alienation from nature—is the fundament of the capitalist mode of appropriation.

It is particularly in this sense that Marx's *Grundrisse* discusses the problem of "alienation" in terms of the dissociation of producers from the objective condition of production. In the precapitalist relations of the "working subject" to nature, the "first objective condition of his labor appear[s] as nature, earth, as his inorganic body; he himself is not only the organic body, but also the subject of this inorganic nature."[56] Marx calls this unity within the production process where both the subjective and objective sides of production are tightly combined "the natural unity of labor with its material presuppositions."[57] Alienation and impoverishment in the bourgeois society are, on the contrary, the products of this "absolute *divorce, separation* of property, i.e. of the objective conditions of labor from living labor capacity." Marx continues to argue that it is

> absolute separation between property and labor, between living labor capacity and the conditions of its realization, between objectified and living labor, between value and value-creating activity—hence also the alien quality of the content of labor for the worker himself—this divorce now likewise appears as a product of labor itself, as objectification of its own moments. . . . The worker emerges not only not richer, but emerges rather poorer from the process than he entered. For not only has he produced the conditions of necessary labor as conditions belonging to capital; but also the value-creating possibility, the valorization which lies as a possibility within him, now likewise exists as surplus value, surplus product, in a word as capital, as master over living labor capacity, as value endowed with its own might and will, confronting him in his abstract, objectless, purely subjective poverty.[58]

Even though Marx does not use the term "alienation" in this passage, the theoretical continuity since 1844 is quite obvious. The "objectless" and "purely subjective" condition of modern workers cannot allow them to realize their own labor capacity because they do not possess the necessary objective conditions for it. The realization of labor capacity is only

possible when they as voluntary and independent owners of a commodity—that is, labor power—sell it on the market only to be subjugated to
the alien dominance of capital. Without control over the material foundation of his or her own life, the "free" worker always remains a "virtual
pauper."[59] From the alien character of labor activity, which is inevitably
caused by the estrangement of the worker's subjective capacity in the
production process organized by capital, the alien character of the objective world is also produced because labor can only produce products of
its own realization as an alien reality. The producers cannot appropriate
the product of labor; under a reified dominion, their own activity only
realizes itself as a subjugating alien power. This process of de-realization
and impoverishment, together with accumulation of capital, produces a
constantly growing alien world beyond human control.

In the *Grundrisse*, Marx again contrasts this modern situation with
pre-bourgeois society: "In the relations of slavery and serfdom this separation does not take place," because labor in the form of the slave or that
of the serf "is classified as *an inorganic condition* of production along
with other natural beings such as cattle, as an accessory of the earth."[60]
Furthermore, Marx argues that in the "pre-bourgeois relation of the individual to the objective conditions of labor" an individual can appear as
a "working subject."[61] It is precisely in this form of the subjectivity of
the pre-bourgeois working subject that Fukutomi found the potentiality
for the free development of individuality of laboring serfs as direct producers.[62] Even if the serfs remained subjugated to personal dominance
and their existence was reduced to the objective condition of production
itself, they nonetheless maintained a certain independence and freedom
of activity in the production process, thanks to the unity with the earth,
and accordingly, they could appropriate the fruits of labor for themselves in the form of small-scale operations. Here existed the material
basis for the "free development of individuality" as it flourished during
the transition to capitalist landed property when producers actually got
emancipated from personal dominion in the aftermath of the collapse of
feudalism.

Marx calls this period after the downfall of the feudal system "a golden
age for labor in the process of becoming emancipated," as exemplified by
the yeomanry in England in the fourteenth and first half of the fifteenth
century.[63] Marx also writes about it in *Capital*:

> The private property of the worker in his means of production is
> the foundation of small-scale industry, and small-scale industry is a

necessary condition for the development of social production and of the free individuality of the worker himself. . . . But it [this mode of production] flourishes, unleashes the whole of its energy, attains its adequate classical form, only where the worker is the free proprietor of the conditions of his labor, and sets them in motion himself: where the peasant owns the land he cultivates, or the artisan owns the tool with which he is an accomplished performer.[64]

The development of "the free individuality of the worker" is an expression that Marx usually uses in the context of a future society established among the associated producers, but as an exception he uses it to characterize precapitalist small-scale family agriculture, where the worker can behave as "the free proprietor of the conditions of his labor," even if it is still a limited premodern form. This freedom of labor became possible because, after the dissolution of the relationship of personal dependence, the workers can freely relate to the earth as their own means of production. Consequently, the relation of humans to nature flourished as a free one in which the direct producer could now enjoy the "intimate" aspect of the earlier production, but without a landlord. Thus, in opposition to a popular critique that Marx's optimistic vision of technological development undervalues small-scale family agriculture, Marx explains why this type of production could more than adequately sustain farm families, even if after the introduction of the capitalist mode of production into English agriculture it had to decline because it is "unfitted to develop labor as *social* labor and the productive power of social labor. Hence the necessity for the separation, for the rupture, for the antithesis of labor and property."[65]

Insofar as the objective condition of one's physical existence is still present in feudal society—thanks to the intimate connection with the land—the universal commodification of laboring capacity cannot penetrate the entire society. Therefore, the reified dominion of capital first needs to secure the dissociation of the original unity between humans and the earth and replace it with a relationship of capital and wage labor. As a result of the separation of land, means of production, and subsistence manifested in the history of enclosure, the producers of small-scale operations in the countryside are now sent to the large cities as "doubly free" proletariats, not just freed from personal dominance but also freed from the conditions of production and reproduction. Without objective capacity for production, modern "free and rightless (*vögelfrei*)" workers are compelled to estrange their own living labor capacity and to work under the alien commands of capital for the sake of attaining a minimal amount of means of subsistence.[66] Marx calls this deprivation of all objective possibility of production the "absolute poverty" of modern workers:

> Labor separated from all means and objects of labor, from its entire objectivity. This living labor, existing as an *abstraction* from these moments of its actual reality (also, not-value); this complete denudation, purely subjective existence of labor, stripped of all objectivity. Labor as *absolute poverty*: poverty not as shortage, but as total exclusion of objective wealth.[67]

No matter how much salary workers attain, it does not allow them to escape this absolute poverty. The total exclusion of objective wealth remains the essential characterization of the worker's situation under the capitalist mode of production, and alienation of nature is the fundamental cause.

Throughout the process of the development of his critique of political economy, Marx never gave up his 1844 insight in terms of the original unity of humans and nature. From the beginning, Marx comprehended the historical negation of a certain relationship between humans and nature as a central characteristic of the capitalist mode of production, and its negation as a positive rehabilitation of the original unity on a higher level—"the negation of the negation"—is, as before, the essential task of the future society.[68] Thus Marx wrote: "The original unity can be reestablished only on the material foundation which capital creates and by means of the revolutions which, in the process of this creation, the working class and the whole society undergo."[69] In accordance with the cause of estrangement, Marx proposed the same necessity for the conscious rehabilitation of the original unity between humans and nature through "association": "The *alien property* of the capitalist in this labor can only be abolished by converting his property into the property of the non-individual in its independent singularity, hence of the *associated, social individual*."[70]

In contrast to Althusser's interpretation that simply dismisses Marx's texts before 1845, one finds important insights in his *Paris Notebooks* of 1844 that fundamentally characterize Marx's lifelong project of critique of political economy. His formulation is, however, not at all the final one, but a personal sketch without an intent to publish it. Thus the humanist interpretation of *The Economic and Philosophic Manuscripts* turns out to be one-sided, because though Marx preserved a certain *economic* insight attained in 1844, he also quickly gave up his *philosophical* conception of alienation, which he borrowed from Feuerbach and Moses Hess. The fact that Marx abandoned Feuerbach's anthropological philosophy was of significance with regard to his ecology as well because his new critique of philosophy in *Theses on Feuerbach* and *The German Ideology* prepared the theoretical basis for a more adequate understanding of the historical modifications of the relationship between humanity and nature. Why did Marx have to abandon his earlier Feuerbachian schema, while he kept his economic insight? How did Marx reconceptualize the relationship between humans and nature?

LEAVING PHILOSOPHY

The German Ideology, together with *Theses on Feuerbach,* documents the moment when Marx decisively distanced himself from philosophy and began to move forward to the non-philosophic conception of the unity between humanity and nature. His evaluation of Feuerbach rapidly changed during this time, and he came to realize that Feuerbach's avoidance of any practical engagement with the socialist movement was an inevitable consequence of his abstract philosophy, which aimed at educating the masses with the truth about species-being. As a result, Marx rejected not only Hegel's idealism but also Feuerbach's materialism, which claimed to have revealed the truth hidden under the estranged mystification by means of "sensibility." In this divergence from Feuerbach's philosophy, one can find a crucial development for Marx's entire theory. Although his critique of bourgeois society in 1844 still opposed Feuerbachian concepts such as "love," "sensibility," "species-being," etc., to an estranged reality, in order to describe historical progress as a process of reappropriating the human essence, the primacy of praxis in *The German Ideology* aims at the analysis of concrete social relations themselves, relations that structure the inverted consciousness and behaviors of individuals trapped within them.

One should be careful, however, not to confuse Marx's rejection of philosophical questioning with an "epistemological break" from an old paradigm. As shown above, the central economic insight of 1844 remains without doubt in the late Marx as well. It is necessary to ask different questions: Why did Marx, *in spite of this theoretical continuity*, change his evaluation of Feuerbach's materialism? How did he reconceptualize his earlier vision of "humanism = naturalism" as a truly materialist analysis of the relationship between humans and nature in accordance with this distancing from Feuerbach? In this context, the formation of Marx's "materialist method" is of importance.[71]

The main point of Marx's critique of Feuerbach and other Young Hegelians in *The German Ideology* is that they simply opposed a hidden "essence" to the estranged "appearance," without examining the specific social relations that bestow an objective reality to this appearance. For example, Feuerbach argues that religious alienation in front of God is an "illusion" that humans themselves produce in their heads due to the misrecognition of their own species-being, thereby allowing an inverted essence to dominate their consciousness and activity. Marx in the *Paris Notebooks* was highly supportive of this Young Hegelian discourse because he believed that through the application of Feuerbach's schema to labor alienation in bourgeois society it would be possible to envision the social abolition of private property as a way to reappropriate and realize human species-being.[72] However, Marx now argues that Feuerbach's critique is "purely *scholastic*" and incapable of leading to radical social change.[73] This is because Feuerbach's method only allows for the necessity of an epistemological change concerning the religious inversion "through the 'spectacles' of the *philosopher*" without an actual practical engagement.[74] In other words, Marx criticizes Feuerbach for naïvely (and wrongly) believing that he could simply educate the masses with his philosophy that the essence of God is really that of humans themselves without touching upon the alienated social relations at the root of the problem.

The difference between the standpoints of Marx and Feuerbach after 1845 becomes clearer if one follows Marx's various usages of "praxis" during this period. It is true that Marx from the very beginning consistently demanded the necessity of transcending philosophical dualism in actuality, in contrast to Hegel's idealist philosophy, which tries to overcome the contradiction only on a theoretical level.

In September 1843, Marx had already formulated, in a letter to Arnold Ruge, his demand for "ruthless criticism of all that exists" with the following words:

> The reform of consciousness consists *only* in making the world aware of its own consciousness, in awakening it out of its dream about itself, in *explaining* to it the meaning of its own actions. Our whole object can only be—as is also the case in Feuerbach's criticism of religion— to give religious and philosophical questions the form corresponding to man who has become conscious of himself.[75]

Here it is obvious that Marx, following Feuerbach's critique of religion, primarily aimed at the "reform of consciousness." The epistemological emancipation from illusion through ruthless criticism is, according to Marx, the most important task, from which radical praxis should emerge. This philosophical approach is also reflected in his political solution. In his *Contribution to the Critique of Hegel's Philosophy of Right*, written between March and August 1843, Marx dealt with the contradiction of the modern world as a dualistic opposition between the state and civil society. In order to overcome this "alienation," Marx opposed to alienated reality the philosophical idea of "democracy," in which every private individual should be able to participate in the public sphere, overcoming the dualist separation between the two spheres.[76]

In *On the Jewish Question*, Marx rapidly came to criticize this type of democratic idea after he recognized the limitation of "political emancipation." He realized that political emancipation through democracy simply contributes to the completion of the modern world, and not its transcendence. Marx argued that democracy alone cannot bring about a radical political action as long as the existence of bourgeois society is taken for granted. The political sphere remains *depoliticized* in order to protect the interests of "an *egoistic, independent individual*."[77] In this vein, Marx admitted that the abstract idea of "democracy" only reflects the abstract idea of the political state in modern society. Abandoning his naïve view of democracy, he began to problematize bourgeois society itself as the actual contradiction of the modern world. Here Marx was already carrying out a partial overcoming of Feuerbach's schema, recognizing that the actual antagonistic dualism between the state and bourgeois society cannot be brought into a unity solely through a philosophic idea of democracy.

Despite this theoretical development, Marx at the same time still cherished another aspect of Feuerbach's philosophy. Against the egoism of bourgeois society, with its endless desire to attain money, Marx opposed the concrete "sensibility" of human beings as the true principle for human emancipation. Thus, Marx argued in *Contribution to the Critique of Hegel's Philosophy of Right*, the Introduction of which was published in the journal *Deutsch-Französische Jahrbücher*, that a radical transformation of bourgeois society is not possible through a political ideal but only through a "passive element" (sensibility), that is, as a result of alienated workers grasping their "universal suffering," which can then become the basis for acting upon it.[78] This is why Marx emphasized the power of praxis, based on the workers' concrete sensible desires, as the sole means of solution for the modern contradiction: "As the resolute opponent of the previous form of *German* political consciousness, the criticism of speculative philosophy of law turns, not towards itself, but towards *problems* which can only be solved by one means—*practice*."[79] One finds a certain ambivalence in Marx's argument. On the one hand he recognized the limitation of a simple opposition of an abstract philosophical idea against the alienated objective reality and emphasizes the primacy of practice more strongly than Feuerbach. On the other hand Marx still followed him, appreciating his concept of "sensibility" precisely as the concrete materialist foundation of revolutionary practice.

The following sentence from the *Paris Notebooks* represents the same ambiguity. At first glance, Marx's claim may give an impression that he had already established the primacy of practice against Feuerbach's philosophical position:

> We see how the resolution of the *theoretical* antitheses is *only* possible in a *practical* way, by virtue of the practical energy of man. Their resolution is therefore by no means merely a problem of understanding, but a *real* problem of life, which *philosophy* could not solve precisely because it conceived this problem as *merely* a theoretical one.[80]

It is true that Marx without doubt acknowledged the necessity of practice for the transcendence of "theoretical antitheses" that reflect the contradictory reality, criticizing that idealist philosophy for failing to make any practical engagement with the concrete objective contradiction. However, his claim still accepted Feuerbach's schema when he also demanded overcoming the antitheses, such as those between "subjectivity and objectivity, spirituality and materiality, activity and suffering," through Feuerbachian "sensuous perception."[81] Since Marx's critique was directed only against the abstract nature of idealist philosophy from his own standpoint of sensuous perception, he, together with Feuerbach, recommended overcoming these philosophical antitheses with concrete sensuous praxis and, more precisely, "labor" that can actualize the free and universal subjectivity of human beings in the concrete objective world. Thus what Marx problematized in the notebooks of 1844 is essentially dependent upon the return to concrete "sensuous perception" in labor being the *true* principle of radical materialism, and in this vein Marx demanded that human beings should first correctly *recognize* their own species-being *and then* get engaged in revolutionary praxis against alienated reality under capitalism.

It is not hard to understand why Marx highly valued Feuerbach's concept of species-being. He was convinced that in contrast to Hegel's "spirit" and Bruno Bauer's "self-consciousness," the human subject conceptualized by Feuerbach could function as a real and true basis for the progress of historical movement and show the way to transcend alienation. His critique of philosophy in 1844 principally aims at correcting earlier *misrecognitions* of the true philosophical principle in a similar way that Feuerbach opposed his species-being to Hegel's spirit as the true subject of history. In this sense, Marx's demand for praxis in 1844 still clearly moved within the paradigm of the Young Hegelian philosophy.

On the contrary, in *The German Ideology* Marx rejects any antitheses that take place *within* philosophy:

> Since, according to their fantasy, the relations of men, all their doings, their fetters and their limitations are products of their consciousness, the Young Hegelians logically put to men the moral postulate of exchanging their present consciousness for human, critical or egoistic consciousness, and thus of removing their limitations. This demand to change consciousness amounts to a demand to interpret the existing world in a different way, i.e., to recognize it by means of a different interpretation. . . . The only results which this philosophic criticism was able to achieve were a few (and at that one-sided) elucidations of Christianity from the point of view of religious history.[82]

As before, Marx certainly emphasizes the importance of praxis in order to radically transform existing social contradictions. However, it is evident that Marx also points out that "a demand to change consciousness" through elucidations and education only ends up producing the "moral postulates" of what ought to be, without actually changing the real problems. He claims that the earlier debates among the Young Hegelians are barren because they are simply trying to discover a "true" philosophical principle for imagining the historical subject, whether "self-consciousness," "species-being," or "the ego."[83] Marx thus problematizes and rejects the entire debate within the Young Hegelians after realizing that the demand for another interpretation of the world alone is not at all capable of a radical social transformation.

According to Marx, Feuerbach's critique of religion may be able to educate the masses about God being a mere illusion whose predicates should be actually prescribed to humans as species-beings. The problem is that Feuerbach's critique ends there without posing a more substantial question: "How did it come about that people 'got' these illusions 'into their heads'?"[84] In other words, God is not a mere illusion that would disappear after its falseness was recognized. Rather, the illusion is an objective appearance produced by social relations. Thus Marx argues against Feuerbach's optimism that it is most essential to comprehend "the actual material premises as such." Without a radical transformation of social relations, the religious "illusion" will be repeatedly reproduced as an objective force through social practice. It is not possible to transcend the alienated reality by simply pointing out the alienated inversion of the objective world from a standpoint of philosophy. The real problem is not an epistemic misrecognition of a truth of the world but rather its inversion, which is based on objective social relations and social practice.[85] Since individuals are always already conditioned by social relations independently of their will, Feuerbach's demand to "change consciousness" alone cannot bring about any radical praxis, no matter how correct his critique of religion may be. In this sense, Feuerbach's concept of "sensuous perception" still remains for Marx within an abstract philosophical discussion, because the way Feuerbach poses questions is a mere epistemic one, trying to discover another "true" foundation that discloses the human "essence" hidden under the alienated reality.

Despite Feuerbach's assumption, however, there is no privileged standpoint for the philosopher from which the direct access to the "essence" can be guaranteed, as Marx writes in the third thesis:

> The materialist doctrine concerning the changing of circumstances and upbringing forgets that circumstances are changed by men and that the educator must himself be educated. This doctrine must, therefore, divide society into two parts, one of which is superior to society.[86]

Marx problematizes the presupposition of "the educator"—obviously he means Feuerbach—because there is no such thing as pure sensuous perception that guarantees access to essence independently of the existing objective social relations. The intuition of philosophy is not outside the world but always already within the inverted world and thus conditioned by it. Therefore Feuerbach's philosophic idea of "sensuous perception" and "love" remains inevitably abstract, insofar as he does not seriously take social conditions within the inverted world into account. If the philosopher is satisfied with a discovery of "essence," philosophy only hinders radical praxis by giving another expression to the alienated reality and leaving it unchanged. What it really needs, so says Marx, is a critical investigation of the objective social relations in order to comprehend the possibility of resistance from the really existing contradictions of society itself.

On the contrary, Feuerbach's idea amounts to a set of abstract theses without any specific social analysis. He does not take the objective force of the inverted world seriously enough, as if the alienated reality could be simply transformed through an alternative philosophical intuition. As a consequence, Feuerbach's philosophy ironically preserves the current estranged situation of the world, avoiding a serious theoretical confrontation with reality. For Marx, it is much more important to practically confront the existing order of things and radically change it. He emphasizes the significance of a social and historical investigation with regard to *how* and *why* the objectively inverted world beyond human control emerges out of social practice, so that the material conditions for its transcendence can be understood.

Because Marx distanced himself from philosophy, he came to acknowledge the limitations of his own earlier schema of 1844. Even though Marx was aware that humans always relate to nature through the mediation of labor and that modern alienation deforms this relationship, his entire project of communism in 1844 was dependent upon a philosophically conceptualized idea of "humanism = naturalism." Since his critique of alienation still roughly identified "capitalism" with "the system of private property," Marx inevitably fell into a deterministic understanding of history, one that failed to carefully analyze the historical specificity of the capitalist mode of production.

This is a reason why Marx's project of 1844 still inevitably possessed a "Romantic" tone; it could only oppose to the alienated reality the philosophical idea of species-being that is supposed to realize the unmediated absolute unity of humans and nature.[87] The more Marx depended on Feuerbach's concept of "species-being" to ground his claim for the realization of "humanism = naturalism," the more abstract his analysis of modern capitalism became. It is because of this that Marx initially envisioned the content of species-being ontologically, with abstract and ahistorical predicates such as "passion," "sensuality," and "universality."[88] Consequently, Marx's own critique of political economy, which was supposed to reveal the specificity of modern society, became invisible, buried under the transhistorical discourse of the Young Hegelian philosophy.

Meanwhile, Marx intensively studied the problem of commodity and money in his *Notes on James Mill* in his *Paris Notebooks*, so that instead of falling into a rough schema of human history he actually continued his investigation into the specificity of the capitalist system. In *The German Ideology*, Marx finally came to be fully conscious of the danger immanent in Feuerbach's abstractness: "Feuerbach's whole deduction with regard to the relation of men to one another is only aimed at proving that men need and *always have needed* each other."[89] An actual examination of the specific historicity of society is missing in Feuerbach's philosophy. According to Marx, who had now distanced himself from his earlier project, there is no "essence" in Feuerbach's sense such as "actual" nature and "actual" human beings, because both nature and humans are already thoroughly conditioned and constituted by social relations. The critical comprehension of the historically specific process of mediation now became the kernel of his scientific analysis:

> Because he still remains in the realm of theory and conceives of men not in their given social connection, not under their existing conditions of life, which have made them *what* they are, he never arrives at the actually existing, active men, but stops at the abstraction "man," and gets no further than recognizing "the actual, individual, corporeal man" emotionally, i.e., he knows no other "human relations" "of man to man" than love and friendship, and even then idealized. He gives no criticism of the present conditions of life. Thus he never manages to conceive the sensuous world as the total living sensuous *activity* of the individuals composing it; therefore ... he is compelled to take refuge in the "higher perception" and in the ideal "compensation in the species," and thus to relapse into idealism at the very point where the communist materialist sees the necessity, and at the same time the condition, of a transformation both of industry and of the social structure.[90]

Instead of praising the primacy of practice in Feuerbach's philosophy, Marx harshly criticizes it due to the separation between theory and practice. For Feuerbach, "man" as such is nothing but an abstract entity to which only ahistorical universal properties such as "human relations," "love," and "friendship" can be attributed. Feuerbach neglects real social relations as presupposition for actual individual activity and consciousness, so that he cannot explain *why* and *how* the inversion of the objective world in the modern society was produced and is constantly reproduced. "Man" as such, says Marx, exists only in "thinking which is isolated from practice."[91]

The same theoretical limitation of Feuerbach's philosophy manifests itself in his treatment of "nature." Marx criticizes "nature as such," which Feuerbach is seeking, because this does not exist anywhere. Nature as such, fully separated from humans, is a pure fantastic construction in thinking, which "today no longer exists anywhere (except perhaps on a few Australian coral islands of recent origin) and which, therefore, does not exist for Feuerbach either."[92] When he talks about nature, Feuerbach is always compelled to abstract it from existing social relations, fleeing into the world of "eternity" with his philosophical intuition. As a consequence, he overlooks the historical process of the formation of nature through the human activity of production.

It is true that Marx in 1844 recognized the necessity to treat nature and humans in their interrelationship: "But *nature* too, taken abstractly, for itself—nature fixed in isolation from man—is *nothing* for man."[93] However, his remark was only an abstract ontological statement according to which history needs to be understood as a labor-mediated process of the humanization of nature and the naturalization of human beings. In contrast to this early formulation, Marx in *The German Ideology* emphasizes the historical formation of what counts as "nature." Nature is not just there, but is constantly transformed through social production, in which both humans and nature work upon and constitute each other. Of course, the statement that humans and nature do not exist in reality without this reciprocal relation still sounds abstract and banal. To avoid this abstractness, it is essential for Marx's "materialist method" to analyze the process of social and natural formation in capitalism, paying particular attention to its specific historical interaction between humans and nature, mediated by labor. Marx clearly recognized this point in *The German Ideology* and later analyzed this historical reciprocal process much more carefully with the concept of "metabolism" (*Stoffwechsel*), as will be shown in the following chapters.

In *The German Ideology*, Marx does not yet discuss the reciprocal constitution of humans and nature in detail. But in contrast to Feuerbach, he comprehends the antagonistic relationship between humans and nature as a specific modern product that resulted from capitalist industrialization. Furthermore, Marx intentionally formulates this historical development as a critique against Feuerbach:

> The "essence" of the fish is its "being," water—to go no further than this one proposition. The "essence" of the freshwater fish is the water of a river. But the latter ceases to be the "essence" of the fish and is no

longer a suitable medium of existence as soon as the river is made to serve industry, as soon as it is polluted by dyes and other waste products and navigated by steamboats, or as soon as its water is diverted into canals where simple drainage can deprive the fish of its medium of existence.[94]

Marx criticizes Feuerbach's remarks in the *Principles of the Philosophy of the Future*: "That which is my essence is my being." The being of the fish is its being in water, and from this being you cannot separate its essence. Language already identifies being and essence. Only in human life does it happen, but even here, only in abnormal and unfortunate cases, that being is separated from essence."[95] Marx rejects Feuerbach's Romantic tone, which only asks for the return to the essence as a countermeasure against the loss of that very essence. If the "water" is always the "essence of the freshwater fish," there would be no room for a critique of water pollution. By opposing the polluted water to the "natural" fresh water as the essence of the fish, Feuerbach can at best show that the current water condition is "abnormal." But simply pointing to the abnormality, Feuerbach cannot sufficiently analyze and identify the social cause of water pollution and comprehend the conditions for the cleaning of water. What he shows is that when the "essence" (water) is lost, the "being" (fish) must disappear. This statement is correct but obviously banal. In other words, Feuerbach's analysis says nothing about the distorted relationship between humans and nature in modern society and laments the situation as an "unavoidable misfortune, which must be borne quietly."[96] Marx argues that this ironic affirmation of alienation is a necessary consequence of Feuerbach's philosophy, which despite its self-claimed radicality avoids any practical engagement with the negative cosnequences of the modern system of production.

Against Feuerbach's presupposition of an ahistorical nature, Marx argues that it is always necessary to deal with humans and nature in their concrete reciprocity. So he asks what kinds of social relations make nature undergo various modifications in an antagonistic and alienated manner, and he attempts to reconstruct the specific historical process of social production and reproduction. It is the task of his scientific investigation of history to reveal this point:

The first premise of all human history is, of course, the existence of living human individuals. Thus the first fact to be established is the physical organization of these individuals and their consequent relation to the rest of nature. Of course, we cannot here go either into the actual physical nature of man or into the natural conditions in which man finds himself—geological, oro-hydrographical, climatic and so on. All historical writing must set out from these natural bases and their modification in the course of history through the action of men.[97]

Humans must produce in order to live. Labor as an act of this pro-duction is inevitably conditioned by various natural and material factors. Under these conditions, humans also change their environment. According to Marx, any scientific investigation must pay attention to this historical transformation mediated by labor. In other words, Marx's approach to the problem of the alienation of humans and nature after leaving the Young Hegelian philosophy changed fundamentally. He no longer opposes the alien dominion of capital to the philosophical idea of "humanism = naturalism" but asks *why* and *how* an antagonistic sep-aration between humans and nature emerges and deepens under the capitalist mode of production.

This materialist orientation formulated in *The German Ideology* was only the beginning of a new period of research that lasted for the rest of Marx's life. Marx's intensive research in both political economy and the natural sciences in the following years represents nothing but the further development of his project to examine the historically specific mediation under capitalism of the transhistorically necessary act of production. In Marx's examination of the relationship between humans and nature, the physiological concept of "metabolism" acquires a central role.

---- 2 ----

Metabolism of Political Economy

A
ll living creatures must go through constant interaction with
their environment if they are to live upon this planet. The
totality of these incessant processes creates not a static but an
open-ended dynamic process of nature. Before Ernst Haeckel called this
economy of nature "oecology," this organic whole that consists of plants,
animals, and humans was often analyzed with a concept of "metabolism" (*Stoffwechsel*).[1] This physiological concept became popular and
in the nineteenth century was applied beyond its original meaning to
philosophy and political economy to describe the transformations and
interchanges among organic and inorganic substances through the process of production, consumption, and digestion on the level of both
individuals and species.

This new concept in chemistry and physiology also stimulated Marx
in the 1850s, and he was even prompted to give it a central role in his
political economy, using it to comprehend the dynamic and interactive relationship between humans and nature mediated by labor. Like
all other living creatures, humans are essentially conditioned by natural
laws and subject to physiological cycles of production, consumption, and
excretion as they breathe, eat, and excrete. However, Marx argues that
human beings are decisively different from other animals due to their
unique productive activity, that is, *labor*. Labor enables a "conscious" and
"purposive" interaction with the external sensuous world, one that allows
humans to transform nature "freely," even if the dependence on nature
and its laws remains insofar as humans cannot produce their means of
production and subsistence *ex nihilo*.

Though incessant metabolism between humans and nature penetrates the entirety of human history, an eternal necessity that cannot
be abolished, Marx emphasizes that the concrete performance of human
labor takes up various economic "forms" in every stage of social development, and, accordingly, the content of the transhistorical metabolism
between humans and nature varies significantly. The way alienated labor
in the modern industrial society mediates this metabolic interaction of
humans with their environment is not the same as how this occurred in
precapitalist societies. What is the difference? Why does the capitalist
revolution of production, with its rapid development of machines and
technology, distort the metabolic interaction more than ever before, so
that it now threatens the existence of human civilization and the entire
ecosystem with desertification, global warming, species extinction,
destruction of ozone layers, and nuclear disasters? As Marx argues, the
problem cannot be simply reduced to the inevitable consequences of
the rapid *quantitative* development of productive forces in the twentieth
century. His critique provides an insight into the *qualitative* differences
between the capitalist mode of production and that of all other preceding
societies. Marx shows that the modern crisis of the ecosystem is a manifestation of the immanent contradiction of capitalism, which necessarily
results from the specifically capitalist way of organizing social and natural
metabolisms. In this sense, Marx's ecological critique of capitalism still
possesses contemporary theoretical relevance, because—in spite of copi-
ous stereotypical critiques of Marx's Prometheanism—his analysis of the
emancipation of productive forces in capitalism comprehends the basic
structure and dynamics of modern bourgeois society as an unsustainable
system of production. What is more, he does not idealize modern efforts
to absolutely master nature. It thus offers a methodological foundation
for a critique of today's ecological problems as specifically capitalist ones.

Thus the concept of metabolic interaction between humans and
nature is the vital link to understanding Marx's ecological exploration
of capitalism. Nevertheless, the concept was often totally neglected or
subordinated to his analysis of specifically capitalist social relations, and
even if it was discussed, its meaning was not correctly understood. In
this situation, it is helpful to contextualize the concept of metabolism
within the natural scientific discourse in the nineteenth century to avoid
confusion in terms of its multiple meanings in Marx's critique of political
economy. In opposition to a dominant misinterpretation represented by
Alfred Schmidt and Amy Wendling in particular, the following discussion shows not only that Marx's concept of metabolism has nothing to do

with "natural scientific materialists" such as Jacob Moleschott, Karl Vogt, and Ludwig Büchner, but also that it possesses a theoretical independence from the works of Justus von Liebig, who significantly contributed to the development of this physiological concept. I also show that it is possible to comprehend Marx's unique methodological approach, which is characterized by the concepts of "form" and "material."

NATURE AS THE MATERIAL OF ALL WEALTH

A common criticism of Marx is that he "absolutizes human labor in his analysis of capitalism" and thus has "systematically excluded the value-creating nature" from it.[2] As explained in chapter 1, and as other Marxists also point out, Marx in 1844 clearly treated nature as an essential element in the realization of labor.[3] Even at the time, when he argued that external nature functions in every process of production as the "inorganic body" of human, Marx did not mean the arbitrary robbery or manipulation of nature by human with an aid of technology, but instead emphasized the role of nature as the essential component of every production: "Man *lives* on nature" because "the worker can create nothing without *nature*, without the *sensuous external world*." Nature is, said Marx, "the material on which his labor is realized, in which it is active, from which and by means of which it produces."[4] Thus the whole of nature must not be treated as an object isolated from human production, and humans are also "a part of nature." Marx used the physiological analogy and argued that the relationship between humans and nature as mediated by labor comprises a unity, in which humans can only produce something by combining the organic and inorganic body: "Nature is man's *inorganic body*—nature, that is, insofar as it is not itself human body. . . . Nature is his *body*, with which he must remain in continuous interchange if he is not to die. That man's physical and spiritual life is linked to nature means simply that nature is linked to itself, for man is a part of nature."[5] Thus humans cannot transcend nature; they realize a unity with it, mediated by labor.

This mediating activity of labor is a unique human activity, and it is through this labor that humans differentiate themselves from other animals, in that humans through labor can "purposefully" and "freely" produce in and with nature and transform their environment in accordance with their will. In contrast to the instinctive activity of animals, which is limited by a given environment and by their unreflected physical needs, humans are able to go beyond this and teleologically modify the sensuous world. The young Marx argued that the act of objectification through human labor cannot be reduced to a mere process of satisfying unmediated physical needs, which is only the case with modern alienated labor. He claimed that the universal freedom particular to humans becomes manifest as a historical process of the humanization of nature and the naturalization of humanity.

However, the interactive relationship between humans and nature undergoes a significant transformation due to the dissolution of their original unity. As a result, unity transforms itself into the opposite of what it should be, that is, a loss of freedom, dehumanization, and enslavement to the product of one's own labor. "In estranging nature from man," it is no longer possible to produce anything without the inorganic body. Thus the first and fundamental alienation in modern society is not arbitrarily defined by Marx as alienation from nature. It is the separation from the objective conditions of production that brings about the decisive change in the way humans relate to the earth. Marx dealt with various negative effects on workers as a consequence of their alienation from nature, such as serious impoverishment and the loss of meaning in life. Despite this original insight, his early analysis in the *Paris Notebooks* did not contain any noteworthy ecological critique of capitalism. Marx in the following years began to gradually close this theoretical blind spot.

Marx in his later economic works still maintained this insight of 1844, even as his research on political economy and other disciplines greatly deepened and developed it. In the *Grundrisse* Marx points to the same "separation" of the producers from nature as a decisive step toward the emergence of modern bourgeois society, but in the paragraph below, Marx illustrates the same phenomena with a physiological concept and no longer with Feuerbach's terminology. Marx now defines the "separation" as cutting off the natural objective conditions for humans' "metabolic interaction with nature":

It is not the *unity* of living and active humanity with the natural, inorganic conditions of their metabolic interaction with nature, and hence their appropriation of nature, which requires explanation or is the result of a historic process, but rather the *separation* between these inorganic conditions of human existence and this active existence, a separation which is completely posited only in the relation of wage labor and capital.[6]

It is true that Marx continues to regard the central characteristics of capitalist production as the disruption of the incessant interaction between humans and nature after the labor process is subsumed under capital. Yet it is noteworthy that Marx now characterizes the "separation between these inorganic conditions of human existence and this active existence" as the obstruction of humans' access to their "natural, inorganic conditions of their *metabolic interaction with nature.*" Of course, the "metabolic interaction" does not get completely interrupted insofar as humans still need to interact with nature in order to live. The interactive process of material exchange between humans and nature in the labor process nonetheless takes a fully different shape from that of pre-capitalist society in that it can take place only on the basis of the radical separation posited "in the relation of labor and capital." This specifically modern "separation"—which completely destroys the "original unity"—and its historical consequences in capitalist society are exactly what Marx regards as necessary for a scientific discipline of political economy to explain.

During the preparation of *Capital*, Marx intensively investigated this problem. He no longer propagated the realization of the philosophical idea of "humanism = naturalism" and instead tended more and more to describe the central task of the future society as the conscious regulation of this *physiological* metabolic exchange between humans and nature by the associated producers. This conceptual change is remarkable.

In this context, Michael Quante argues for the continuity of Marx's *philosophical* conception of the relationship between humans and nature "even if Marx no longer describes it with anthropological and philosophical categories but with the natural scientific category of 'metabolism.'"[7] But then he criticizes both Marx's "ambivalences" between philosophy and natural science and an "anti-philosophical trait" in *Capital* that is the result of this conceptual shift.[8] However, Quante refrains from going into the new dimensions of Marx's natural sciences in detail. Evidently his critique of Marx is grounded in his own interpretation, in which he hopes to rediscover the basic philosophical motives in the later economic works. The transition from a "philosophical" terminology to a "natural scientific" one is not a simple change of Marx's personal preference, but reflects the development of his "materialist method" in *The German Ideology* as a guideline for understanding the historical transformations of the metabolism between humans and nature. In this sense, even if there is an "anti-philosophical trait" there are no "ambivalences" in his later works.

In contrast to the earlier philosophical scheme that simply imposes a utopian ideal on the estranged reality, Marx learned to analyze the concrete process between humans and nature, which is, on the one hand, transhistorical as an "eternal necessity," but is, on the other hand, thoroughly socially mediated, given that the economic function of labor differs considerably in each mode of production. In *The German Ideology*, Marx became fully aware that the metabolic interaction takes place within a tight entanglement of both historical and transhistorical aspects. Marx carefully analyzed this dynamic social process in nature in order to comprehend the material conditions for transcending the "separation" in the metabolic interaction between humans and nature.

Marx's research in the following years became more and more characterized by this unique duality. He studied political economy as an analysis of the *social* forms of economic categories, and simultaneously studied the natural sciences to achieve a scientific basis with regard to *material* qualities in the physical sphere. As emphasized in the following section, Marx's ecology deals with the synthesis of the historical and transhistorical aspects of social metabolism in explaining how the physical and material dimensions of the "universal metabolism of nature" and the "metabolism between humans and nature" are modified and eventually disrupted by the valorization of capital. Marx's analysis aims at revealing the limits of the appropriation of nature through its subsumption by capital.

This enormous project nonetheless cost Marx time and energy, so much so that he was not able to finish his magnum opus. Nonetheless, this does not mean that the project was a failure because Marx succeeded in elucidating his theory of metabolism in *Capital* and various economic manuscripts. Furthermore, there are a number of hints for his further theoretical development in his excerpt notebooks that are of great importance. Before analyzing these notebooks, it is helpful first to trace his own description of "metabolism" in the context of its usage in natural scientific and political economy.

ON THE GENEALOGY OF METABOLISM

The concept of "metabolism" was first employed in physiology at the beginning of the nineteenth century, even though it is often claimed that Liebig's "book on *Organic Chemistry in Its Application to Physiology and Pathology* (1842) was the first formal treatise on the subject, introducing the concept of 'metabolism' (*Stoffwechsel*)."[9] The famous German chemist is today known as the "father of organic chemistry"; along with Friedrich Wöhler he conducted a series of experiments to analyze chemical elements to find out not only that two molecules with the same molecular formula can have different properties (an isomer) but also that millions of different kinds of organic compositions can be formed out of various combinations of the simple and presumed unchangeable structures of organic compounds, even though their assumption of unchangeability later proved false.[10] After 1837, Liebig conducted research in physiological chemistry and published the epoch-making *Organic Chemistry in Its Application to Agriculture and Physiology*, usually simply called *Agricultural Chemistry*, as the aforementioned *Organic Chemistry in Its Application to Physiology and Pathology* is usually called *Animal Chemistry*. In these books Liebig applied his newest discoveries in chemistry to an analysis of the organic process of plants and animals. He investigated the reciprocal relationship of plants, animals, and humans as chemical interactions of organic and inorganic substances, even claiming that "the animal organism is a higher kind of vegetable."[11] Liebig opened up the new field of chemical analysis of metabolism, which synchronized nicely with the newly discovered law of conservation of energy.[12] He was highly critical of the dominant vitalist dualism of Jean-Baptiste André Dumas and Jean Baptiste Boussignault, who postulated the clear difference between "two kingdoms of plants and animals."[13]

In one of the earliest usages of the term *metabolism* Liebig depicted the constant interactive process of formation, transformation, and excretion of various compounds within an organic body:

> It cannot be supposed that metabolism in blood, the changes in the substance of the existing organs, by which their constituents are converted into fat, muscular fiber, substance of the brain and nerves, bones, hair &c., and the transformation of food into blood, can take place without the simultaneous formation of new compounds which require removal from the body by the organs of excretion. . . . every motion, every manifestation of organic properties, and every organic action being attended by metabolism, and by the assumption of a new form by its constituents.[14]

Metabolism is an incessant process of organic exchange of old and new compounds through combinations, assimilations, and excretions so that every organic action can continue. Liebig also maintained that the chemical reaction in combination and excretion is the ultimate source of electric current as well as that of warmth and force. Liebig's theory of metabolism prepared a scientific basis for further analyses of a living organism as pure chemical process.[15]

The concept of metabolism, under the influence of Liebig, soon went beyond the nourishment of individual plants, animals, and humans. That is, it could be used to analyze their interaction within a certain environment. Today's concept of metabolism can be applied not just to organic bodies but also to various interactions in one or multiple ecosystems, even on a global scale, whether "industrial metabolism" or "social metabolism."[16] This physiological and chemical concept about an extensive organic whole in nature found a wide reception and was employed beyond natural science, in philosophy and political economy, where it has been used to describe a social metabolism by way of analogy. This was the case in Marx's writings. However, out of this extension there emerged a certain ambiguity due to the term's multiple meanings, and it is necessary to distinguish them with commentary.

A careful conceptual differentiation of metabolism in Marx's writings is of importance, for there are a number of debates in the earlier literature in terms of how he integrated this concept into his political economy.[17] Even if it is difficult to determine every single source of his inspiration, given that he actively modified the concept for the purpose of his own analysis, this does not mean that one can use text in an arbitrary manner as a source for the sake of justifying a certain interpretation of Marx. Liebig is without doubt one of the most important intellectual sources, as has been convincingly demonstrated by John Bellamy Foster.[18] The intellectual heritage of Liebig first became manifest in *Capital*. Yet Marx did not simply take the concept from Liebig's *Agricultural Chemistry*, in which the term metabolism appears only twice, but developed and modified the concept through his study of various texts in chemistry and physiology.

It is worth discussing Marx's first usage of the concept of metabolism, which was not at all referred to in the earlier debates about his ecological perspective. The relevant text is in one of his *London Notebooks* of March 1851, titled *Reflection*, which was later published in the MEGA².[19] The date clearly indicates that Marx knew the concept of metabolism *before* his reading of Liebig's book in July 1851.

Because of the scant attention the fourth section of the MEGA² received, the key passages in *Reflection* about metabolism were not taken into account in the debates. However, the text provides a helpful hint for Marx's reception of the physiological concept, for he was not studying natural science so intensively then, so it is safe to assume that he took up the concept right before writing *Reflection*.

The term "metabolic interaction" (*Stoffwechsel*) appears three times in *Reflection*:

> Unlike ancient society where only the privileged could exchange this or that [item], everything can be possessed by everybody [in capitalist society]. Every *metabolic interaction* can be conducted by everyone, depending on the amount of money of one's income that can be transformed into anything: prostitute, science, protection, medals, servants, cringer—everything [becomes a] product for exchange, just like coffee, sugar, and herring. In the case of rank [society], the enjoyment of an individual, his or her *metabolic interaction* is dependent on a certain division of labor, under which he or she is subsumed. In the case of class [it is dependent] only on the universal means of exchange that he or she can appropriate. . . . Where the type of income is still determined by the type of occupation, and not simply by the quantity of the universal medium of exchange like today but by the quality of one's occupation, the relationships, under which the worker can enter into society and appropriate [objects], are severely restricted, and the social organ for the *metabolic interaction* with the material and mental productions of the society is limited to a certain way and to a particular content from the beginning.[20]

In *Reflection*, Marx again explicates his critique of the money system with a method of comparison between various forms of society, revealing the class antagonism hidden under the formally free and equal relationship of the bourgeois society. In order to illuminate the specificity of the mode of appropriation under the monetary system, Marx contrasts the appropriation of products in capitalist society with that in precapitalist societies, comprehending the problem as different ways of organizing the "metabolic interaction." In this sense, the concept of "metabolic interaction" is clearly used to deal with the transhistorical character of the necessity to organize social production.

Since in the precapitalist societies the appropriation of products took place based on the direct personal and political dominance legitimated by tradition, innate privileges, and violence, the variability of labor was limited to that within a certain "rank," and thus "the social organ for the metabolic interaction with material and mental productions of society" remained much narrower than in capitalist society. In capitalist society, the appropriation and transfer of products takes place on a much larger scale among the formally free and equal owners of commodities and

money. The commodity exchange appears totally free from class con-
flicts, and the "metabolic interaction" seems to enlarge with an increasing
amount of money. Equality and freedom "without class character," however, soon turns out to be an "illusion."[21] In reality, the quantitative
volume of money decides the "enjoyment of an individual, his metabolic
interaction," totally independent of actual concrete needs. Marx points
to the brutal fact that the abstract formal equality under the system of
money is inverted into the restriction of freedom and equality. To sum
up, Marx in *Reflection* argues that the individual and social "metabolic
interaction" in the capitalist mode of appropriation ends up heavily limited, particularly because of the hidden class character of money, so that
individuals are thoroughly impoverished and subjugated to the alien
power of money independently of their concrete needs.

Marx used the concept of metabolism in *Reflection*, and not in the earlier part of the *London Notebooks*. Despite this fact, it is possible to find
out the source. Gerd Pawelzig, in his analysis of Marx's concept of metabolism, offers the information that in February 1851 Marx received from
his friend Roland Daniels a manuscript for a book titled *Mikrokosmos:
Entwurf einer physiologischen Anthropologie*.[22] Daniels was an "excellent,
scientifically educated doctor" according to Marx and Engels, and he was
a member of the Communist League.[23] His intellectual relationship with
Marx was built on a close friendship, and Marx dedicated his book *The
Poverty of Philosophy* to Daniels.

Daniels wrote to Marx in a letter of February 8, 1851, asking for a
"sharp and candid" critique of his manuscript.[24] As he explained in his
next letter, the principal aim of his *Mikrokosmos* was to ground, in contrast to the spiritualist theory, "the *possibility*" to understand "human
society in a materialist manner," based on a "*physiological* description of
activity."[25] Daniels conveyed to Marx that he was attempting to apply the
newest physiological knowledge in order to treat the material and mental
activity of humans on both individual and social levels as an object of
(materialist) scientific investigation. In this context metabolism played
an important role. Notably, Daniels used the term in his very first letter
to Marx: "I would risk my organic metabolism against a mental metabolism, and I doubt if I would be able to digest and assimilate so many
things well to reproduce something ordinary."[26]

Marx carefully studied Daniels's manuscript in the next month and
commented on it critically, as Daniels had asked in his letter dated March
20.[27] The first usage of the concept of "metabolism" in *Reflection* is certainly closely connected with his critique of Daniels's *Mikrokosmos,* as

both texts were written in the same month. Pawelzig was nonetheless not conscious of the relevant paragraph in *Reflection* and simply concluded that Marx and Engels in 1851 did not use the term *metabolism* in their notes and letters.[28] But this statement is incorrect.

In Daniels's *Mikrokosmos*, the concept of "organic metabolism" appears many times. For instance, he defines it as *"simultaneous destruction and regeneration, through which these bodies maintain their individuality as they incessantly and newly produce this individuality— this is a uniqueness whose analogy cannot be found in inorganic bodies."*[29] Though there is some affinity between Daniels and Liebig in their treatment of metabolism, Daniels's discussion displays his originality when he divides "organic metabolism" into "animal and mental metabolism" and criticizes the ungrounded supposition of "vital force."[30] His materialist understanding of mental metabolism is directed both against the philosophical dualism of "body" and "spirit" and against the Hegelian speculative philosophy of "absolute spirit."[31] Nonetheless, Daniels's materialist orientation tends toward a naïve materialism because he interprets human thought, freedom, and history as pure "nerve physiological" phenomena.[32] Even if Daniels, in accordance with Marx's *German Ideology*, sometimes demands historical explanation through an analysis of "each type of production of material needs of life," he tends to reduce all dimensions of human activities to a compound of pure physiological—and thus totally ahistorical—"reflex movement" that functions independently of historical production. Consequently, his theory turns out to be mechanistic and deterministic. Marx was not really content with Daniels's *Mikrokosmos*, as he reported to Engels: "What little sense there is in his letter is a reflection of my own to him."[33]

Marx's critique of Daniels does not mean that he entirely dismissed the importance of the manuscript. Daniels's replies to Marx's criticisms indicate that he patiently provided him with critical comments and explanations to his questions. Even if Marx did not accept the general direction of Daniels's materialist project, intensive discussions between them prompted Marx to use the concept of metabolism in his private notes in *Reflection*, and he came to be more interested in physiology, as documented in the *London Notebooks* after July 1851, most notably in excerpts from Liebig's work. Marx shared an opinion with Daniels that the new physiological concept could be usefully applied to social analysis. In this vein, Marx used the concept not only in terms of "enjoyment of the individual," in the sense of consumption and digestion, but also in the context of "material and mental production" on a social scale.

Using the analogy to physiological metabolism, he endeavored to comprehend the modern social dynamics of production and consumption where, under a particular form of social division of labor, individuals as organs for "material" and "mental" production are ruinously alienated and impoverished. In *Reflection*, Marx applied the new concept to national economy, following in this sense the direction of Daniels's program: "The theory of human organism and its relationship to society and nature also builds the *sole stable foundation* for the reform of the communal institution, that is, for the reform of society."[34]

Unfortunately, further intellectual exchange between Marx and Daniels was interrupted when the latter was arrested in June 1851 in Cologne because of his political activity. He suffered terrible conditions in prison, and after his release died, on August 29, 1855. Marx wrote on September 6, 1855, to his widow, Amalie Daniels:

> It is impossible to describe the grief I felt on hearing that dear, unforgettable Roland had passed away.... Seen amongst the others in Cologne, Daniels always seemed to me like the statue of a Greek god deposited by some freak of fate in the midst of a crowd of Hottentots. His premature decease is an irreparable loss not only to his family and friends but also to science, in which he gave promise of the finest achievements, and to the great, suffering mass of humanity, who possessed in him a loyal champion.... It is to be hoped that circumstances will some day permit us to wreak upon those guilty of cutting short his career vengeance of a kind sterner than that of an obituary.[35]

Even if Marx did not discuss the concept in detail in *Reflection*, his reading of *Mikrokosmos* clearly prepared a foundation for the further integration of natural sciences into political economy before his excerpts from Liebig's *Agricultural Chemistry*.

Subsequently, Marx's usage of the term *metabolism* became more general and systematic during the process of witing the *Grundrisse*. In the passage from the *Grundrisse* quoted above, Marx deals with the incessant interaction between humans and nature with this physiological analogy, treating nature as the inorganic body of humanity. In this vein, Marx discusses the labor process as "metabolic interaction with nature," that is, as material interaction of three moments of production taking place within nature: raw materials, means of production, and human labor. According to Marx, this "production process in general" is "common to all social conditions" as long as humans produce within nature.[36]

Humans must work and produce, constantly taking out raw materials from nature, modifying nature to create various means of production and subsistence, and giving back waste materials. Labor is an essential moment in this process, and it is a transhistorical and material activity in nature, which Marx also calls "natural force."[37] After comprehending these three moments, Marx then analyzes how this incessant material exchange between humans and nature transforms itself when it receives a specific capitalist function as "valorization process of capital." This point is the most important aspect, and I will come back to this theme in the next chapter.

In the *Grundrisse*, there are other meanings of metabolism that Marx continued to use until *Capital*. "Changes of material (*Stoffwechsel* = metabolism)" is contrasted with "changes of form (*Formwechsel*)." "Change of form" signifies exchanges of economic forms between money and commodity during the circulation process—"C-M-C" and "M-C-M"—and "change of material" has to do with the constant changes among use values within capitalist society:

> Simple circulation consisted of a great number of simultaneous or successive exchanges. . . . A system of exchanges, changes of material [*Stoffwechsel*], from the standpoint of use value. Changes of form [*Formwechsel*], from the standpoint of value as such.[38]

Stoffwechsel in this sense takes place as changes of different commodities through their exchanges, and *Formwechsel* between money and commodity occurs at the same time. *Stoffwechsel* proceeds within the sphere of circulation, when necessary use values are distributed among private producers similar to the way blood provides each organ with necessary nutrients. In this usage Marx usually adds the adjective "social": "Insofar as the process of exchange transfers commodities from hands in which they are non-use-values to hands in which they are use-values, it is a process of social metabolism. . . . We therefore have to consider the whole process in its formal aspect, that is to say, the change in form or the metamorphosis of commodities through which the social metabolism is mediated."[39] This juxtaposition of *Formwechsel* and *Stoffwechsel* in *Capital* also indicates Marx's original methodological approach to treat the objects of his investigation from both "material" (*stofflich*) and "formal" (*formell*) aspects.

Marx's usage of *Stoffwechsel* and *Formwechsel* differentiates from that of Wilhelm Roscher, who employed the same set of categories before

Marx's *Grundrisse*. This comparison is particularly interesting because Marx read volume 1 of Roscher's *Principles of Political Economy*, published in 1854, before writing the *Grundrisse* and wrote down a number of vertical lines to highlight relevant paragraphs in his personal copy.[40] Roscher also integrated new discoveries of physiology and opposed his own "historical and physiological method" of national economy to the "idealist" one, so that Marx encountered various physiological analogies while he read the book.[41] Furthermore, Roscher openly refers to the physiological analogy of "metabolism" in a national economy:

> The greater portion of the national capital is in a state of constant transformation. It is being continually destroyed and reproduced. But from the standpoint of private economy, as well as from that of the whole nation, we say that capital is preserved, increased or diminished accordingly as its value is preserved, increased or diminished.

In a footnote to the last sentence, Roscher continues to argue: "J. B. Say, *Traité d'Economie Politique* I, ch. 10. Only think of the famous principle of metabolism (*Stoffwechsel*) in physiology!"[42] Unfortunately, the relevant pages in Marx's personal copy are missing, so we cannot tell how he reacted to this passage.

Referring to Say's *Traité*, Roscher also deals with the *Formwechsel* of capital in the production process, in which capital is consumed and transformed into another shape without interruption. With *Formwechsel*, Roscher means change of material shapes, rather than changes of economic forms between money and commodity, as Marx does. Say writes in one of the relevant passages in chapter 10 of the *Traité*: "In manufacture, as well as agriculture, there are some branches of capital that last for years; buildings and fixtures for instance, machinery and some kinds of tools; others, on the contrary, lose their form entirely; the oil and pot-ash used by soap-makers cease to be oil and pot-ash when they assume the form of soap."[43] Roscher calls these constant transformations of various materials in the everlasting process of production and consumption within a society *Stoffwechsel*, similar to Liebig's comprehension of the physiological process of an organ that sustains its equilibrium in spite of the constant changes of production, consumption, assimilation, and excretion. This analogy nonetheless marks Roscher's theoretical limitation, for, though he contrasts "form" and "material," he is not able to abstract the pure economic exchanges of form between commodity and money, but instead confuses the role of exchanges of form with the transformation of matter. Despite this decisive difference between Marx and Roscher, Roscher's argument clearly shows that Marx's contemporary economists were also willing to use the physiological concept for their own analysis of the modern economy.

The connection between the *Stoffwechsel* of physiology and political economy was often mentioned at the time. Even Liebig himself referred to an analogy between organisms and the state economy in his *Familiar Letters on Chemistry*:

> As in the body of an individual, so also in the sum of all individuals, which constitutes the state, there goes on a change of matter [Stoffwechsel], which is a consumption of all the conditions of individuals and social life. Silver and gold have to perform in the organism of the state the same function as the blood corpuscles in the human organism. As these round discs, without themselves taking an immediate share in the nutritive process, are the medium, the essential condition of the change of matter, of the production of the heat and of the force by which the temperature of the body is kept up, and the motions of the blood and all the juices are determined, so has gold become the medium of all activity in the life of the state.[44]

Liebig's analogy, based on an organic theory of the state, is crude, absent an analysis of money within the capitalist society. It is still interesting that the proponent of the concept of metabolism tried to connect physiology and political economy, a project soon taken up by Roscher and Marx.

Also, the agriculturalist in Munich, Carl Fraas, whom Marx intensively studied in 1868, emphasized the importance of "metabolism" for political economy: "Organism and metabolism—therefore, metabolism in the national economy, too! It builds the natural scientific foundation of national economy that was almost completely neglected until now in order to develop mere mathematical economics. However, such national economy only investigates and combines data without grasping their cause!"[45] Even if there is no direct proof that Marx read Liebig's *Familiar Letters on Chemistry* or Fraas's article, it is conceivable, given the scientific discourse then, that Marx was also led to adopt this new physiological concept in his system of political economy.[46]

In the *Grundrisse*, there is one more usage of metabolism, the "metabolism of nature," which proceeds independently of human intervention. Use values "are dissolved by the simple metabolism of nature if they are not actually used."[47] This "natural metabolism (*natürlicher Stoffwechsel*)," as chemical dissolution or modification of material substances, for example, occurs through oxidation and decomposition. Marx refers to this phenomenon again in *Capital*: "A machine which is not active in the labor process is useless. In addition, it falls prey to the destructive power of natural metabolism."[48] Labor alone cannot create natural substances; it can only modify their shapes according to various purposes. Labor provides the "natural substance" with "*external form.*"[49]

For example, the form of a desk that labor provides to the "natural substance" of wood is "external" to the original substance because it does not follow the "immanent law of reproduction." Although the immanent law maintains the wood in its specific form of a tree, the new form of a desk cannot reproduce its substances in the same way, so that it now starts to get exposed to the natural force of decomposition. In order to protect the product of labor from the power of natural metabolism, a purposeful regulation of metabolism through productive consumption is required, which nonetheless cannot overcome the force of nature. Marx on the one hand emphasizes the human ability of labor to consciously and purposefully modify nature, but on the other hand he recognizes the inevitable limitations and restrictions imposed by nature on the human ability to control the metabolism of nature. He is aware of a certain tension between the immanent law of nature and the external form of nature artificially created by labor. The negligence of this material necessity results in decay and destruction of products by natural laws and natural forces.

To sum up, Marx in the *Grundrisse* employed the concept of metabolism of political economy with three different meanings and continues to do so until *Capital*: "metabolic interaction between humans and nature," "metabolism of society," and "metabolism of nature." His sources of inspiration are not so apparent after his reading of Roland Daniels and Wilhelm Roscher because, following his own purpose of developing a system of political economy, Marx generalized and modified the concept as well. Precisely because of this generalization, Marx's concept of metabolism is exposed to the risk of arbitrary interpretations, discussed together with irrelevant theorists, whose ideas actually have nothing to do with Marx's theory of metabolism. In the earlier debates, one witnesses such cases that totally neglect Daniels and Liebig and focus only on the influence of "natural scientific materialists" (or "vulgar materialists" as Marxists often call them), such as Jacob Moleschott, Karl Vogt, and Ludwig Büchner. Such claims immediately sound very suspicious, considering that Marx referred to these authors only in private letters in a negative and pejorative tone.[50] This misinterpretation shows the importance of correctly grasping Marx's parting from Feuerbach's anthropological materialism and the originality of Marx's theory of metabolism, which must be understood not just philosophically but in a close relation to his system of political economy.

THE LIMITATION OF ANTHROPOLOGICAL MATERIALISM

Those who overvalue natural scientific materialism misinterpret not only Marx's metabolism theory but also his entire project, because the theoretical affinity between Feuerbach and these natural scientific materialists often hides Marx's non-philosophical, practical standpoint after *The German Ideology*. A typical misunderstanding of Marx's project through the lens of Feuerbachian materialism and natural scientific materialism is characteristic of Alfred Schmidt's famous book, *The Concept of Nature in Marx*: "It may be concluded with some certainty that Marx made use of Moleschott's theory of metabolism, not, of course, without altering it."[51] Although Schmidt's view is widely accepted, a careful examination of the texts makes his claim difficult to accept. There is no philological evidence for his claim; Schmidt and his admirers should have seen that Moleschott's view, as elaborated in *The Cycle of Life* (*Kreislauf des Lebens*, 1852), is hardly compatible with Marx's alliance with Liebig.[52]

Accordingly, Schmidt underestimates, perhaps intentionally, Liebig's influence on Marx, but provides no convincing reason for doing so. In only one footnote, he succinctly refers to Liebig: "The chemist J. von Liebig, whose views were not without influence on Marx (cf. *Capital*, Vol. I, p. 506, n. 1), compared the metabolism in nature with the same process in the body politic, in his book *Chemische Briefe*, Heidelberg, 1851, p. 622 et seq."[53] Schmidt's book does not go into Liebig's *Agricultural Chemistry* because he believes that Marx "made use of the term 'metabolism,' which, for all its scientific air, is nonetheless speculative in character."[54] He clings to the philosophical concept of nature in the young Marx, no matter what it costs in terms of the truth. For Schmidt, Liebig is too "natural science" compared to Moleschott. However, it is not necessary to interpret the concept of metabolism in such a "speculative" manner, and Schmidt's remark also contradicts the fact that Marx did not study various disciplines of natural science in accordance with a definite program of the philosophy of nature, as Hegel and Schelling did.

In order to ground his own claim, Schmidt quotes from Moleschott's theory of metabolism in *The Cycle of Life*:

What man excretes nourishes the plant. The plant changes the air
into solids and nourishes the animal. Carnivorous animals live on
herbivorous animals, to fall victim to death themselves and so spread
abroad newly germinating life in the plant world. The name "metabolism" has been given to this exchange of material.[55]

Moleschott's explanation of metabolism, which is also expressed
as "metempsychosis" among all material substances, is so general and
abstract that one cannot immediately infer his influence on Marx's
theory.[56] Thus it is necessary to look at Moleschott's theory of metabolism more closely to judge whether Marx would be willing to integrate it
"not, of course, without altering it."

Moleschott was a Dutch doctor and physiologist who participated with
Ludwig Büchner and Karl Vogt in a heated "materialism debate" in the
1850s. He advocated a radical materialist view that every mental activity is
"only a function of substances in the brain," and that "the thought stands
in the same relation to the brain as bile to the liver or urine to kidneys."[57]
Moleschott also reduced thought to a product of the movement of matter
in the brain: "Thought is a movement of matter [Stoff]."[58] While Liebig
in his *Agricultural Chemistry* emphasized the importance of phosphoric
acid for an ample growth of plants, Moleschott argued its importance for
humans in a provocative manner: "No thought without phosphorus."[59]
Admitting the necessity of further research on the functioning of the brain,
he put forward a view that with the development of materialist physiology, both physical and mental activities and talents can be determined by
measuring the assimilation and excretion of matter. In this vein, he argued
that nourishment plays an important role in determining these activities.
For example, he contrasted the English worker with the Italian lazzarone:
"Who doesn't know the superiority of the English worker fortified by roast
beef compared to the Italien lazzarone whose predominat vegetable diet
explains the large part of his disposition to laziness."[60]

Moleschott's mechanistic understanding of the relationship between
mental and physical characteristics and nourishment is also reflected in
his theory of metabolism, in terms of which he supported the "humus
theory" of Gerardus Mulder in Utrecht and criticized Liebig's "mineral
theory." Liebig maintained, as a result of various chemical experiments,
that the direct effect of humus—that is, the dark material of decayed
plants in the top layer of soil—upon plant growth occurs only as a result
of its decomposition into water and carbonic acid. In contrast, Moleschott
and Mulder insisted, in agreement with Albrecht Thaer, on the direct and

essential contribution of a soil nutrient called *Dammsäure* contained in humus for plant growth: "In contrast [to Liebig,] Wiegmann and Mulder, getting rid of any doubt, proved through experiments that neither carbonic acid nor ammonia can replace the effect of *Dammsäure*."[61]

As he counted ammonium compounds of *Dammsäure* as the "most important substance of nourishment," Moleschott undervalued Liebig's theory of inorganic substances for plant growth, a theory still valid today, and ignored the concrete chemical reactions of bonding and dissolving among various organic and inorganic substances in the atmosphere, soil, and plants.[62] While Liebig argued for the importance of a chemical analysis of soil composition, Moleschott reduced the chemical and physiological process of plant growth into an abstract and overgeneralized "metempsychosis," forgoing concrete investigations.

In this metempsychosis that subsumes everything under it humans also lose their own labor-mediated historicity and functions within the social and natural metabolism. Moleschott simply stated that humans as ephemeral beings are decomposed into "*Dammsäure* and ammonia" in the soil after death, so that plants can again grow on the soil without exhausting it:

> The same carbon and nitrogen that plants take from carbonic acid, *Dammsäure*, and ammonia become grass, clover and wheat, then animal and humans, one after the other, then finally crumble again into carbonic acid and water, *Dammsäure* and ammonia. Here is the natural miracle of cycle. . . . The miracle lies in the eternality of matter throughout the changes of form [*Wechsel der Form*], in the change of matter [*Wechsel des Stoffs*] from one form to another, and in metabolism [*Stoffwechsel*] as the ultimate ground of earthly life.[63]

According to Moleschott's monistic understanding, humans function only as an element in the eternal cycle of matter, so that the "metabolism between humans and nature" receives no particular theoretical and practical attention at all. Moleschott's explanation about the conditions for sustaining the material basis of interaction between various organisms on the earth is simply about the abstract and ahistorical cycle of indestructible matter in which every animal and human goes back to the soil after death, all for the sake of nourishing new plants.

So Liebig was fully right when in his lecture in 1856 he called Moleschott one of the "dilettantes who stroll at the edge of natural science," who act like "children in knowledge of natural laws."[64] One can expect the same reaction from Marx. Subsequent to his intensive discussion with Daniels in the beginning of the 1850s, when he became familiar with Liebig's *Agricultural Chemistry* and Johnston's *Lectures on Agricultural Chemistry*, he found both highly critical of humus theory. Given this, Schmidt's claim about Moleschott's influence upon Marx's metabolism theory is not plausible. Furthermore, Moleschott's materialist view of the world overlaps to some extent with that expressed in Daniels's *Mikrokosmos*,[65] and in this sense Marx's critical remark that Daniels's explanation is "on the one too mechanistic, on the other too anatomic" can be applied to Moleschott's materialism.[66] Moleschott neglected the mediating role of labor in the production process and explains the totality of the world only in terms of the transhistorical movement of matter and force. What is missing in his explanation is the specific historical "economic form determination" (*ökonomische Formbestimmung*), the analysis of which Marx regarded as the central task of his critique of political economy.

Like Vogt and Büchner, Moleschott stood close to Feuerbach's philosophy of essence. He often corresponded with him, and gave Feuerbach the impulse to study the new disciplines of physiology and medicine. Later, Moleschott reflected that Feuerbach's anthropology was the "task of my entire life."[67] He particularly saw the affinity with Feuerbach's project of anthropology, a materialist attempt to overcome all dualist oppositions between body and mind, matter and soul, God and world:

> Feuerbach made it clear to the consciousness that *humans* as the foundation for all intuition and all thoughts are the starting point. Feuerbach carried the banner for the science of human beings, i.e., anthropology. This flag becomes victorious through the research on matter and its movement. . . . The angel around which today's world wisdom rotates is the theory of metabolism.[68]

Moleschott envisioned his physiological theory of metabolism in continuity with Feuerbach's program, reducing all appearances of the world to the true materialist principle of essence, that is, of "matter."

Inspired by new discoveries in the natural sciences made by his followers, Feuerbach also praised Moleschott's work, claiming it possessed a "universal and revolutionary significance of natural science."[69] In his review of Moleschott's *Theory of Nutrition* (*Lehre der Nahrungsmittel*), titled "Natural Science and Religion," Feuerbach in a totally positive tone quoted Moleschott's remark that "life is metabolism." He even considered Moleschott's reduction of human functions to nourishment correct, arguing that the "doctrine of foods is of great ethical and political importance. Food becomes blood, blood becomes heart and brain, thoughts and mind-stuff. . . . Man is what he eats (*Der Mensch ist, was er isst*)."[70] Feuerbach believed that his philosophical program, the historical reform of consciousness, now acquired a new scientific foundation, although the failure of the revolution in 1848–49 clearly demonstrated the practical limitation of the Young Hegelian "radical" philosophy and significantly weakened its attractiveness.[71] It is not merely a purely epistemological issue, as he repeatedly pointed to the possible *political* consequences emerging out of Moleschott's radical metabolism theory because it could refute the Christian worldview. In his praise for Moleschott's new pantheism ("*Hen kai pan*" or "One-and-All"), which advocated "nourishment" as the foundation of all physical and mental activity and existence, without recourse to any God-like transcendence, one can confirm Feuerbach's theoretical continuity from *The Essence of Christianity* in the post-revolutionary period.[72]

One can also infer from the affinity between Feuerbach and Moleschott that Marx after 1845 neither accepted nor praised natural scientific materialism. Moleschott was, like Feuerbach, too easily satisfied with reducing all perceptions and appearances to their "essence," that is to say, "matter" and "force," in order to oppose his radical materialist worldview to philosophical dualism. As a result of his crude materialism, he fell into a naïve realism that identifies all of reality with matter and force, and into dogmatism due to the impossibility of proving the existence and exact functions of matter and force. Moleschott was not interested in the concrete historical transformation of the relationship between humans and nature, because it was presupposed from the beginning that essence must remain the same due to the eternity and indestructibility of matter, no matter how much its shapes get modified in history. Marx's *German Ideology*, by contrast, rejected any direct reduction of a phenomenon into its "essence" because it is not possible to overcome the objectively inverted world by simply pointing out its hidden truth and essence on an epistemic level. Thus Marx attempted to investigate the historical social relations that constantly produce and reproduce the inverted world of objective "appearance." While Feuerbach still clung to the same scheme of philosophy of essence as a basis for a radical social change even after the failure of revolution of 1848 and found himself in sympathy with Moleschott, Marx determinedly parted from philosophy, devoting himself to the study of political economy and natural science.

If Schmidt, in spite of the incompatibility between Marx and Feuerbach, argues for the importance of Moleschott's metabolism for Marx, the reason for it lies in his own ontological understanding of nature, which has nothing to do with Marx's theory. Schmidt claims to find the "negative ontology" of nature in Marx's thought, according to which nature exists as the totality that encompasses both nature and society, and penetrates even into society: "The whole of nature is socially mediated and, inversely, society is mediated through nature as a component of total reality."[73] Schmidt believes that nature in its entirety cannot be completely reduced to "second nature" because there is a "material side (*stoffliche Seite*)" that cannot be arbitrarily modified: "In the direct labor-process, i.e. the metabolism between man and nature, the *material side* triumphs over the historically determined form."[74]

Schmidt does not explain what exactly of this "material side" remains against the historically determined form, however, but mystifies it. This result is not accidental. Because Feuerbach and Moleschott reduced the relationship of humans and nature to a transhistorical ontology, Schmidt expresses sympathy to their conception of nature, due to his own philosophical interest. Schmidt consequently simplifies Marx's theory of metabolism, rather in a Moleschottian manner, in favor of "'ontological' dignity" associated with a mere recognition of an "eternal nature-imposed necessity."[75] Such an abstract irreducibility of nature is so obvious and banal, removed from all concrete context, as to scarcely require mysterious philosophic jargon, such as "negative ontology."

Theodor Adorno, Schmidt's supervisor, criticized Marx for his alleged optimistic belief in the possibility of abolishing natural laws: "That the assumption of natural laws is not to be taken à la lettre—that least of all is it to be ontologized in the sense of design, whatever its kind, of so-called man—this is confirmed by the strongest motive behind all Marxist theory: that those laws can be abolished."[76] It is plausible that Schmidt's "negative ontology" of nature is aimed at showing the non-transcendence of natural laws in Marx against Adorno's critique, but this defense has nothing to do with Marx's project. Adorno missed Marx's point from the start. Indeed, Marx deals with the relationship between the "formal" and "material" sides of the metabolism between humans and nature in its historical dynamics in a much more nuanced way than Schmidt does.

The fact that Schmidt's theory of metabolism deals only with the ontological dimension of nature without examining its concrete modifications under the historical dynamics of the capitalist mode of production is closely tied to his own philosophical standpoint, which praises Feuerbach's philosophy as "anthropological materialism."[77] Schmidt's theoretical limitation manifests itself in his new introduction to the German fourth edition of *The Concept of Nature in Marx,* in which Schmidt attempts to develop "ecological materialism." Admitting that his earlier work on Marx's concept of nature did not pay enough attention to its ecological aspects, Schmidt now rethinks the possibility of the ecological critique in Marx's theory, but in the end he only strengthens his earlier critique of Marx's "anthropocentrism" as being anti-ecological because Marx transforms nature into the object of technological exploitation and manipulation.[78] Schmidt writes: "It is evident that Marx's—mature—theory also illustrates nature under the historical a priori of administration, domination and oppression."[79] In order to avoid the instrumentalization of nature and to ground the truly materialist standpoint of "ecological materialism," Schmidt, in line with his philosophy of negative ontology, goes back to Feuerbach's *Essence of Christianity.* He is dependent on Feuerbach's explanation about the worldview of the Greeks who wanted to find the harmony of humans with their environment realized in a "beautiful object":

> It is clear that Feuerbach's recourse to the pretechnical and mythical worldview of the Greeks is not a mere reflex of his Romantic longings. Feuerbach reminds us of the possibility that was buried under many layers at his own time, the possibility to experience nature not only as an object of science or raw material, but "aesthetically" in a sensuous and receptive sense as in art.[80]

What is at stake in Schmidt's "materialist ecology" is a transformation of consciousness, so that one can reach a new image of nature as a unity of humans and nature beyond the dominant modern instrumentalization of nature. However, the main point of Marx's critique of Feuerbach in *The German Ideology* reminds us of the powerlessness of an attempt to change consciousness without changing social and material conditions. Abstract sensuous perception or intuition, he suggests, is not in itself capable of transforming real-world conditions—a view that is incompatible with Schmidt's "materialist ecology."

BEYOND "NATURAL SCIENTIFIC MATERIALISM"

Amy E. Wendling's 2009 book, *Karl Marx on Technology and Alienation,* put forward another interpretation of Marx's theory of metabolism, again in support of Marx's alleged "natural scientific materialism." Insisting upon the influence of Ludwig Büchner's *Matter and Force* (1855), her argument may look convincing at first glance, but it is necessary to examine her interpretation, especially with regard to the incompatibility between Marx and the natural scientific materialists.

Wendling points to a major transformation of Marx's concept of "labor" as a result of his exposure to the natural sciences and natural scientific materialism. While Marx's concept of labor in the 1840s was still "ontologically" understood, in that he comprehended the essence of human beings under the influence of Aristotle, John Locke, Adam Smith, and Hegel, Marx, after the *Grundrisse,* in agreement with Büchner and Moleschott, began to emphasize the "thermodynamic" theory of value in contrast to Liebig. Although there is no direct evidence that Marx seriously studied thermodynamics in the 1840s and 1850s, Wendling argues that it is possible to find its traces in his texts. She quotes one passage from the *Grundrisse*, where Marx discusses the metamorphosis of individual capitals with an analogy to the organic body:

> This change of form and matter [*Form und Stoffwechsel*] [of capital] is like that in the organic body. If one says, e.g., the body reproduces itself in 24 hours, this does not mean it does it all at once, but rather that the shedding in one form and renewal in the other is distributed, takes place simultaneously. Incidentally, in the body the skeleton is the fixed capital; it does not renew itself in the same period of time as flesh, blood.[81]

In this passage Marx argues that different organs of the body, which are produced and reproduced through the same process of metabolism, require different time periods for replacement and destruction depending on their material properties. According to Wendling, this is an adequate physiological analogy of political economy, for "fixed capital" also remains within the production process longer than "circulating capital." By this time, Marx was so familiar with the natural sciences in applying their concepts to political economy that he did not provide his source here.

Wendling claims to have found a relevant source for this passage and quotes a passage from Büchner's *Matter and Force,* published in 1855, to ground her thesis that Marx's *Grundrisse* documents his transition to a "thermodynamic" paradigm. She refers to the following passage in an English translation of the book:

> With each breath that passes from our lips we exhale part of the
> food we eat and of the water we drink. The[se] change so quickly
> that we may well say that in a space of from four to six weeks we are
> materially quite different and new beings—*with the exception of the
> skeletal organs of the body, which are firmer and therefore less liable
> to change.*[82]

This passage makes a clear distinction between bone and other
organs in the incessant metabolic process within the organic body. Bone
is harder than other parts, and thus is capable of lasting over a longer
time. Therefore it can function as an analogy of the fixed capital, which
lasts longer than circulating capital.[83]

If one casually reads Wendling's book, it seems plausible that Büchner
plays an important role because Marx, in the passage above, makes an
effort to establish the key categories of "fixed" and "floating" capital. At
the same time, Wendling's claim that Marx's concept of labor moves
toward a thermodynamic paradigm after reading Büchner's book will
also appear convincing.

However, Wendling's claim immediately becomes suspect once one
reads Büchner in the German original. It turns out that he is discussing
a completely different point in the relevant passage:

> With each breath that passes from our lips we exhale part of the
> food we eat and of the water we drink. We change so rapidly
> that we may well say that in a space of from four to six weeks
> we are materially quite different and new beings—*The atoms are
> exchanged, but the type of their combination remains the same.*[84]

As clearly indicated, Büchner does not actually talk about bones in
comparison with other organs. He deals with the "combination" of elements in each organic part; that is, he talks about a general physiological
characteristic of the organs, which, despite the constant changes of their
elements throughout the metabolic process, their "combination" in each
organ remains the same. Through breathing and eating, the organic body
is continuously replaced and renewed. Despite this, the chemical analysis
shows that the composition of organic compounds of each part of the
body, whether blood, muscle, or bone, remains the same. Thanks to the
equivalence between the constant assimilation and excretion, it is possible that the combination of each organ remains constant, and this is

why Büchner describes metabolism as the "eternal and continuous cycle of the minute particles of substance."[85]

The English translator of *Matter and Force* made a modification of the original text, which Wendling unfortunately focused on. This is not just a careless mistake; there is a reason for it. Wendling chose a passage in the *Grundrisse* where Marx employs the concept of metabolism, which is usually discussed in relation to Liebig, a harsh critic of natural scientific materialism, but her intent was to emphasize the importance of natural scientific materialism for Marx's political economy. This was necessary if she was to prove her thesis about Marx's "thermodynamic" transition in the 1850s.[86]

Wendling challenges the importance of Liebig's theory, repeatedly criticizing his theory as false "vitalism," as Büchner and Moleschott did. She even claims that distancing from the "Liebigian Enlightenment ideal" allowed Marx to move to the thermodynamic paradigm.[87] It is true that Liebig's physiology sometimes reverts to the supposition of "vital force." But this does not mean that his chemical analysis and method can be fully reduced to vitalism.[88] Wendling on the one hand neglects the theoretical development of Liebig's physiology, and on the other marginalizes Marx's strong interest in Liebig's theory of metabolism in favor of Büchner. This negligence leads her to a serious one-sidedness. Her interpretation of Marx's research on natural sciences does not reveal his ecological interests due to her rejection of Liebig's theory and her support for natural scientific materialism. A theory that argues for an ahistorical, eternal cycle of material cannot adequately trace the historical problem of exhaustion of natural resources, which, as Liebig posits, is the result of the disturbance of the metabolic interaction between humans and nature. His ecological critique of "robbery agriculture" has nothing to do with vitalism, and it is this aspect of Liebig's agricultural chemistry that contributes to the ecological development of Marx's critique of political economy.

In terms of a possible text source that really emphasizes the various reproduction periods of different organs, one can turn to the work of Carl Gustav Carus, a German physiologist and natural philosopher. Marx knew of his work, as his name appears not just in Daniels's letter to Marx but also in Daniels's *Mikrokosmos*.[89] In his *System of Physiology*, Carus explicated the same point as Marx in the *Grundrisse*:

> It might be now also necessary to refer to the *time ratio* in which the transformation of elementary parts of the organism takes place. . . . 1) In any case the components of parenchymatous fluid change fastest,

because it is this fluid that conditions the change of all solid elementary parts, and furthermore, it, like any living thing, must be engaged in a continuous process of perishing and generating. . . . 2) Among solid elementary parts, soft parts change their substance more rapidly than the totally rigid ones. This proposition necessarily follows from the earlier one; since the soft elementary parts are penetrated by the formative fluid even more than the rigid ones, a more rapid metabolism takes place in the former, even if this cannot be so easily proved by experiments compared to the latter.[90]

With the concept of metabolism, Carus explained how different organs are destroyed over different time periods and then newly replaced. The liquid, that is, blood, is fastest, and muscles and skins come to the next, and bones are slowest. It is possible that Marx knew Carus's discussion, and if he did not, other physiologists at the time also emphasized the same point. Carl Fraas described it in his *Nature of Agriculture*, from which Marx later made excerpts:

It is true that metabolism takes place everywhere, but it is much weaker in the firmly organized tissues without considerable contribution to excretions that indicate the total replacement than in fluids, first of all, in blood, its cells (granules), and plasma.[91]

Thus, despite Wendling's argument, there is no convincing reason to believe that Büchner's materialism was crucial for the *Grundrisse*. His philosophical and physiological views are less sophisticated than those of other contemporary natural scientists.

Marx's discussion on the different periods for reproducing different organs also documents his theoretical originality, which cannot be fully reduced to Liebig's theory of metabolism. Not only did Marx use in *Reflection* the concept of metabolism before reading Liebig's work, but he also integrated in the *Grundrisse* various aspects of physiological discourses. Certainly, Liebig emphasized the necessity of the equivalence between assimilation and excretion of each organ:

If we reflect, that the slightest motion of a finger consumes force; that in consequence of the force expended, a corresponding portion of muscle diminishes in volume; it is obvious, that an *equilibrium between supply and waste of matter* (in living tissues) can only occur when the portion separated or expelled in a lifeless form is, at the same instant in which it loses its vital condition, restored in another part.[92]

Liebig recognized that the "equilibrium between supply and waste of matter" must proceed during the constant metabolic process. Otherwise, each organ would continue increasing or decreasing, which is the case with children and old people. It would not have been difficult to add that each organ has a different time period for this replacement, given that other physiologists such as Carus and Fraas had pointed this out. Liebig, however, ended with simply pointing out the necessity of the equilibrium without going into the material difference among various organs.

Though Liebig's contribution to the development of Marx's theory of metabolism is undeniable, the *Grundrisse* also confirms that Marx was not simply following Liebig's concept of metabolism. He also took different aspects of metabolism from other authors. This relative independence of Marx's use of metabolism becomes important later, when Marx started reading various works against Liebig, although he continues to have the highest praise for Liebig's theory of soil exhaustion. This reading will lead him to the extension of his ecological theory of metabolism after 1868.

Marx clearly recognized that the natural scientific materialists were not dealing with the different reproduction periods among various organs, and that this was their theoretical defect. He explicitly conveyed his opinion to Engels in a letter dated March 5, 1858, while he was writing the *Grundrisse*: "In considering the reproduction of machinery, as distinct from *circulating capital*, one is irresistibly reminded of the Moleschotts who also pay insufficient attention to the period of reproduction of the bony skeleton, contenting themselves, like the economists, with the average time taken by the human body to replace itself completely."[93] Without doubt, "the Moleschotts" include not only Moleschott himself but also Büchner and Vogt. In this quote, Marx criticized Büchner's physiological analysis precisely in terms of what Wendling praises about him, because he did not take into account the relationship of concrete material properties to the whole process of metabolism. What is typical about the natural scientific materialists is a cognition of materialist "essence," such as the quantity of phosphorus in bones or the unchanging balance of atoms of organs. When Marx analyzed the relation of fixed and circulating capital, his physiological analogy showed, in contrast to Büchner, that he actually paid particular attention to material differences in relation to economic forms.

THE ROLE OF PHYSIOLOGY IN THE *GRUNDRISSE*

The discussion above helps in understanding why, in contrast to the analysis of Moleschott and Büchner, who stood closer to Feuerbach's philosophy of essence, Marx's theory of metabolism needs to be examined in relation to his own political economy. As shown earlier, Moleschott and Büchner reduced, like Feuerbach, historical and social relations into an ahistorical essence. They went so far as to dissolve the entire world into various combinations of eternal and unchangeable matter. Schmidt tried to go beyond Moleschott, comprehending the "material side" of nature in relation to its historical modifications in capitalist society. He was not able to fulfill this task because his "negative ontology" was still trapped in Feuerbach's philosophy of essence. Marx, after 1845, began to analyze this "material side" of political economy, such as use value, nature, human needs, in a very different way.

In the *Grundrisse*, Marx reflects on his own method of political economy, which deals with the relationship between "matter (*Stoff*)" and "economic form determinations." First he argues that economic forms are the object of his investigation, but he also recognizes the importance of matter:

> Above all it will and must become clear in the development of the individual sections to what extent use value exists not only as presupposed matter, outside economics and its forms, but to what extent it enters into it.[94]

Marx's analysis in the *Grundrisse* at first excludes use value from the object of political economy, treating it simply as something given, in order to systematically develop the pure economic categories, such as "commodity," "value," "money," and "capital." For example, various different things with a wide range of use values can all be "commodity," and different types of labor produce "value." Marx first aims at answering the general questions, such as "What is the commodity?" and "What is value?" and at clarifying under what social relations these categories attain objective validity. Here Marx does not talk about particular material properties or use values.

His project does not end there, however, and his analysis proceeds to ask to what extent "presupposed matter" is modified by economic forms, and to what extent it still retains its own independence in reality. Marx's systematic analysis of economic categories includes the process by which economic form determination by capital actively modifies the material dimension of the world, but at the same time repeatedly confronts various limitations.

In this context, natural science is useful for Marx's project because it helps him to comprehend the material aspects of economic analysis, as can be seen in his letter to Engels, where Marx distinguishes "fixed" and "floating" capital with the use of physiological concepts. His research in natural science was not complete when he was writing the *Grundrisse*, but he tried to integrate it into his critique of political economy. In the *Grundrisse* he again emphasized the same physiological analogy:

> In the human body, as with capital, the different elements are not exchanged at the same rate of reproduction, blood renews itself more rapidly than muscle, muscle than bone, which in this respect may be regarded as the fixed capital of the human body.[95]

The difference of the period of reproduction for the attrition and renewal of capital is conditioned by the natural properties of each material, like the reproduction of the human body. In the labor process, there are raw and auxiliary materials, such as oil, tallow, wood, and coal that cannot be used more than one time and thus must be replaced after every labor process, whereas other means of production, such as a building or a machine, last over many years and can go into the labor process many times. This difference in terms of the caducity of each element in the labor process is at first *purely material*, so it exists "outside economics."

Marx argues that the distinction between "fixed capital" and "circulating capital" is in the first instance to be regarded as a "merely formal distinction," because both forms of capital are distinguished by the different types of return of value.[96] Thus, says Marx, the same material can function as fixed as well as circulating capital. Raw materials for constructing a building or machine that the producers buy are circulating capital for them, but the same material can function as the fixed capital for those who use them over multiple production processes. The same material thus receives different economic form determinations depending on its purely economic function in the valorization process of capital. In this sense, Marx writes that capital, "as value, is indifferent to every specific form of use value."[97]

Marx quickly adds, however, that this indifference of economic form determination is not completely freed from the material characteristics of its bearers. They can have a "determinant" impact upon the economic form because their actual existence as fixed capital indeed requires less caducity, so that they can persist over multiple production processes. Different material durableness receives economic form determinations in the production process. Whereas the earlier distinction of "variable" and "invariable" capital was a "merely formal" distinction from the perspective of the valorization of capital, which makes the difference of use value fall "entirely outside the capital's specific character as form [*Formbestimmung*]," now, in the analysis of capitalist production, "with the distinction between circulating capital (raw material and product) and *fixed capital* (means of labor), the distinctness of the elements as use value is posited simultaneously as a distinction within capital as capital, on its formal side [*Formbestimmung*]."[98] Marx also says that the material difference in the production process that earlier fell outside the economic analysis "now appears as a qualitative division within capital itself, and as a determinant of its total movement (turnover)."[99] The material bearer of capital now plays an active and determinant role as a physical basis for the categorical differentiation of floating and fixed capital. Capital is inevitably conditioned by the material nature of use values: "The *particular nature of use value*, in which the value exists, or which now appears as capital's body, here appears as itself a *determinant* of the *form* and of the action of capital."[100]

This material nature of use value exerts a great influence on the accumulation of capital. Because of a bigger proportion of more durable fixed capital, the turnover of capital becomes slower because only a smaller aliquot of fixed capital goes into the valorization process each time. The slower turnover of capital results from the historical tendency of capitalism, the process of which is accompanied by the introduction and further development of the machinery system, impacting the rate of profit, and generating a tendency for this to fall. Marx analyzes how the pure economic form determinations must be incarnated by certain material bearers, and how they can condition capital's accumulation.

Marx later discusses this material limitation imposed on the valorization of capital on the level of reproduction in more detail with regard to the difference of fixed and circulating capital. As indicated by the physiological analogy, circulating capital must be provided and replaced faster than fixed capital in order to continue the production process without interruption. Capital can valorize itself only when all necessary raw and auxiliary materials are existent in addition to labor power and machines. Capital is inevitably interested in establishing access to abundant and cheap raw and auxiliary materials because this can increase the rate of profit. The equilibrium of consumption and renewal of circulating capital can suddenly become difficult or even get interrupted, for example, due to a lack of raw and auxiliary materials, whose production is often dependent on changing natural conditions. The bigger the forces of production become and the faster and bigger the required amount of raw materials (wood and iron) and auxiliary materials (oil and coal) for renewal, the more unstable the entire production becomes because it is more and more dependent on natural conditions. Crop failure or exhaustion of soil and mines can harm capital accumulation and totally interrupt the production process:

> Since the reproduction of raw material is not dependent solely on the labor employed on it, but on the productivity of this labor which is bound up with *natural conditions,* it is possible for the volume, the *amount* of the product of *the same* quantity of labor, to fall (as a result of *bad seasons*). *The value of the raw material therefore rises....* More must be expended on *raw material,* less remains for *labor,* and it is not possible to absorb the same quantity of labor as before. Firstly this is *physically impossible,* because of the deficiency in raw material. Secondly, it is impossible because a greater *portion of the value of the product* has to be converted into raw material, thus leaving less for conversion into *variable capital.* Reproduction cannot be *repeated* on the same scale. A part of *fixed capital* stands idle and a part of the workers is thrown out on the streets.[101]

Marx points to the possibility of an economic crisis partly due to the unfavorable factors imposed by the natural conditions of the production process and partly due to the unregulated desire of capital for accumulation. While the turnover of capital is a purely formal movement of value, in reality its actual valorization is necessarily conditioned by its material side, so that without adequate material equilibrium of fixed and circulating capital its valorization becomes "physically impossible." Writing in this way, Marx is without doubt conscious of the potential for crisis immanent to capital's inability of the absolute mastery over nature. The crisis is nothing but the disturbance of the equilibrium in the social and natural metabolism.[102]

Of course, capital does not passively accept this material obstacle imposed on its endless desire for accumulation. Whenever it encounters a limit, it immediately tries to overcome it. In this sense, Rosa Luxemburg is wrong in her analysis of Marx's "scheme of reproduction" when she argues that the disturbance of the equilibrium within the scheme would directly result in the fatal crisis of capitalism.[103] She underestimates the stubbornness of capitalism because, as Marx repeatedly emphasizes, there is an "elastic power of capital" with which it can react to the digression of the social and natural metabolism from its ideal equilibrium. Marx argues that

> capital is not a fixed magnitude, but a part of social wealth which is elastic, and constantly fluctuates with the division of surplus-value into revenue and additional capital. It has been seen further that, even with a given magnitude of functioning capital, the labor-power, science and land (which means, economically speaking, all the objects of labor furnished by nature without human intervention) incorporated in it form elastic powers of capital, allowing it, within certain limits, a field of action independent of its own magnitude.[104]

Capital develops the system of transportation and interchanges and furthermore always tries to exploit new free or cheap natural resources and labor power. In this sense, the "elastic power of capital" is actually based on various elastic characteristics of the material world that can be both intensively and extensively exploited according to capital's needs.

As can be observed in the history of capitalism, capital invents various counteractions in order to overcome every limit to capital accumulation, out of which there emerges a tendency of capital to construct "a system of general exploitation of the natural and human qualities" and "a system of general utility":

> Hence exploration of all of nature in order to discover new, useful qualities in things; universal exchange of the products of all alien climates and lands; new (artificial) preparation of natural objects, by which they are given new use values. The exploration of the earth in all directions, to discover new things of use as well as new useful qualities of the old, such as new qualities of them as raw materials etc.[105]

Capital exploits the whole world in search of new useful and cheap raw materials, new technologies, new use values, and new markets, and it develops new natural sciences so that neither bad seasons nor resource scarcity bring about difficulty for capital accumulation. What is essential for capital in this process is the transcendence of all material limits existing in nature through technological mastery of nature. The enormous elasticity of capital is based on this exploitation of all utilities in the world, and in the history of capitalism, capital always endured small and large disturbances in production and circulation but developed even more through them. This universal exploitation of the world transforms nature for the first time into "an object of humankind, purely a matter of utility," and Marx famously calls it the "great civilizing influence of capital," which proceeds with constant destruction of old ways of life, as well as nature itself.[106]

However, Marx also argues that this transcendence of all limits through the mastery of nature can be achieved only "ideally": "But from the fact that capital posits every such limit as a barrier and hence gets ideally beyond it, it does not by any means follow that it has really overcome it, and, since every such barrier contradicts its character, its production moves in contradictions which are constantly overcome but just as constantly posited."[107] Since the material elasticity is not infinite, there inescapably remains a certain material limitation that capital cannot overcome in reality. The limitation is not fixed a priori but can be altered as new technologies resist the exhaustion of natural resources by discovering new reserves or other replacements and expand the disposable natural forces with lower costs, or even manage to do so free of charge. Marx calls this the unity of the opposing tendencies that are part of capitalism's "living contradiction."[108] Its manifestations require a concrete historical analysis, which is beyond the scope of the current investigation of this book. Nonetheless, one can formulate the general historical tendency of capitalism: Capital always tries to overcome its limitations through the development of productive forces, new technologies, and international commerce, but, precisely as a result of such continuous attempts to expand its scale, it reinforces its tendency to exploit natural forces (including human labor power) in search of cheaper raw and auxiliary materials, foods, and energies on a global scale. This process deepens its own contradictions, such as with massive deforestation in the Amazon region; pollution of water, soil, and air by extractive industry in China; the oil spill in the Gulf of Mexico; and the nuclear catastrophe in Fukushima.

Despite various creative innovations and rapid technological progress, capital brings about more and more disturbances in the metabolic

interaction between humans and nature and inevitably impedes the free
and sustainable development of human individuality. However, the ecological crisis does not automatically lead to a collapse of capitalism, as
Paul Burkett rightly argues: "To put it bluntly, capital can in principle continue to accumulate under any natural conditions, however degraded, so
long as there is not a complete extinction of human life."[109] Long before
capital accumulation becomes impossible due to the ecological degradation of the world—as expressed in the famous "second contradiction
of capitalism"—human civilization will very likely no longer be able to
subsist.[110] This is why the capitalist system must be judged as irrational
from a perspective of sustainable human development.[111]

My illustration here is not a systematic analysis of Marx's ecology and
crisis theory, as his theory of value and reification is still missing. The
discussion above can nonetheless provide the basic idea that the natural
conditions of production can impede capital accumulation. There is a
tension between nature and capital, and Marx treats the irrationality of
purely formal economic categories from the perspective of the physical
and natural world in his economic analysis. In this vein, he avoids falling
into the abstract theory of "negative ontology" by seriously studying natural sciences to understand which properties of the "material sides" can
be used for the sake of an effective capital valorization and what works
against it. Marx attempts to comprehend the possible resistance against
capital from the perspective of the material world.

In the end, it is important to emphasize once again that Marx's concept of metabolism does not simply remain on the level of the abstract
dialectics of humans and nature in the *Paris Notebooks*. "Matter" (*Stoff*)
is for Marx not a mere Romantic idea, which, as Feuerbach assumes,
exists independently of every human intervention. Marx's critique after
The German Ideology refuses any type of transhistorical treatment of the
relationship between humans and nature; rather, he analyzes how the
concrete labor process, as an incessant metabolism between humans and
nature, is radically modified by the logic of capital. The unique art of
Marx's questioning is thus the following one: "To what extent [is] the
character of the labor process ... changed by its subsumption under capital?"[112] If the character of labor in the labor process is transformed due
to the reified dominion of capital, it follows that the entire metabolism
between humans and nature is radically disrupted. How this contradiction is made concrete needs to be analyzed with Marx's *Capital*.

—— 3 ——

Capital as a Theory of Metabolism

D
espite recent robust discussions of "Marx's ecology," one still repeatedly hears the critical view that a systematic illustration of Marx's ecology is not possible. Critics argue that there are only sporadic ecological references in his written works, demonstrating that Marx's ecological interest was unfortunately not a serious one and thus his overall theory is fatally flawed.[1] In this vein, Jason W. Moore argues that John Bellamy Foster's theory of "metabolic rift" inevitably "has reached an impasse."[2] Though the potentiality of a classical Marxist approach is widely undervalued by first-stage ecosocialists, their critique at least brings up an important challenge for a further development of an ecological critique of capitalism oriented to Marx's own method and system. However, they mistakenly believe that Marx's theory of metabolism does not have a systematic character related to his value theory in *Capital*. This is why critics argue that Foster and Burkett merely gather Marx's isolated and sporadic remarks about ecology, and their analysis is misunderstood as an "apocalyptic" warning about ecological catastrophes.[3]

Only a *systematic* analysis of Marx's theory of metabolism as an integral part of his critique of political economy can convincingly demonstrate, against the critics of his ecology, how the capitalist mode of production brings about various types of ecological problems due to its insatiable desire for capital accumulation. And why radical social change on a global scale, one that consciously constructs a cooperative, non-capitalist economic structure, is indispensable if humanity is to achieve a sustainable regulation of natural and social metabolism.

In this chapter, I provide a systematic interpretation of *Capital*, arguing that Marx's critique of metabolic rifts can be consistently developed from his value theory. His analysis of abstract labor reveals the fundamental tension between a reified commodity production and a sustainable intercourse with nature. Marx's *Capital* analyzes this tension to demonstrate that capital as the "subjectification" (*Versubjektivierung*) of value can interact with nature only in a one-sided manner, insofar as, according to the logic of capital, the squeezing of abstract labor consti- tutes the sole source of the capitalist form of wealth. With this insight, *Capital* prepares a theoretical foundation for further analyses of the historically specific dynamics of production in capitalism, in which the logic of capital radically modifies and reorganizes the incessant mate- rial interaction between humans and nature and finally even destroys it. In this context, Marx's "theory of reification" is of great importance, because it explains how capital, going beyond the production process, transforms human desires and even all of nature for the sake of its own maximal valorization.

By dealing with the relationship between "ecology" and "reifica- tion," it becomes necessary to displace the focus of the critique of political economy from social and economic "forms" to the "material" (*stofflich*) dimensions of the world. The material dimensions undergo various discrepancies and disharmonies precisely as a result of economic form determinations. Though Marx often points to the significance of "matter" (*Stoff*) in *Capital* and its preparatory manuscripts, the material dimension of his critique was largely underestimated in recent debates within Western Marxism. Good examples of this are "*Kapitallogik*" by Hans-Georg Backhaus and Helmut Reichelt, the "new reading of Marx" of Michael Heinrich and Ingo Elbe, and the "New Dialectics" of Chris Arthur and Tony Smith.[4]

Thus, after describing the labor process as a transhistorical metabo- lism, in this chapter I will make a "detour" to a Japanese interpretation of Marx that is seldom heard in the West, that which is based on the "Kuruma School." With this Japanese reading of *Capital*, it is possible to construct a stable theoretical foundation for further analysis in terms of how Marx thought of the exhaustion of the labor force and the soil not just as manifestation of the contradictions of capitalism but as a place of resistance against capital.

THE LABOR PROCESS AS TRANSHISTORICAL METABOLISM

To reveal the historical modifications of the metabolic interaction between humans and nature through the economic logic of capital- ism, we must first deal with the *transhistorical* and universal aspect of production abstracted from concrete social aspects. Indeed, it is this type of abstraction that Marx carries out in chapter 5, "Labor Process," in volume 1 of *Capital*, elaborating on the metabolic interaction between humans and nature as the production of use values "independent of any specific social form." In this chapter Marx defines labor as "a process between man and nature, a process by which man, through his own actions, mediates, regulates, and controls the metabolism between himself and nature."[5] Furthermore, labor is characterized as a specific *human* activity, in that in contrast to the instinctive operations of animals (such as spiders weaving webs or bees constructing honeycomb cells) humans are able to work upon nature *teleologically*, realizing an idea in their heads as an object in the external world. Labor is a purposeful and conscious act of production, a mediation or regulator of the metabolic interaction between humans and nature.

Labor as a metabolic mediation is essentially dependent on and conditioned by nature. Human production cannot ignore natural properties and forces; humans must acquire their assistance in the labor process. Thus labor cannot arbitrarily work upon nature; its modification faces certain material limitations:

> When man engages in production, he can only proceed as nature does herself, i.e. he can only change the form of the materials. Furthermore, even in this work of modification he is constantly helped by natural forces. Labor is therefore not the only source of material wealth, i.e. of the use-values it produces. As William Petty says, labor is the father of material wealth, the earth is its mother.[6]

Nature as the "mother" of material wealth provides not just objects of labor, but it also actively works together with producers during the labor process. Marx in *Capital* recognizes the essential function of nature for the production of any material wealth, and this aspect will without doubt remain essential for a post-capitalist society. Concrete labor as a regulator of this permanent metabolic interaction between humans and nature not only takes away from nature but also gives back the products of labor, including waste, to the sensuous world. In this way, a circular process proceeds as an untranscendable material condition of human life.

Marx summarizes the labor process as a material process:

> The labor process . . . is purposeful activity aimed at the production of use values. It is an appropriation of what exists in nature for the

requirements of man. It is the universal condition for the metabolic interaction [*Stoffwechsel*] between man and nature, *the everlasting nature-imposed condition of human existence*, and it is therefore independent of every form of that existence, or rather it is common to all forms of society in which human beings live.[7]

This definition of the labor process clearly indicates the fundamental physiological and transhistorical fact that the production and reproduction of humans must without exception occur through constant interaction with their environment. In other words, it is only through this incessant intercourse with nature that humans can produce, reproduce, and, in short, live on the earth.

This definition is only a beginning of Marx's theory of metabolism, and so the labor process is presented here only "in its simple and abstract elements."[8] Indeed, the statement that human production is inevitably dependent upon nature alone seems banal. Marx cautions elsewhere against its overvaluation because these types of transhistorical conditions are "nothing more than the essential moments of all production," and they are only "characteristics which all stages of production have in common, and which are established as general ones by the mind; but the so-called *general conditions* of all production are nothing more than these abstract moments with which no real historical stage of production can be grasped." Obviously, it is not possible to fully develop Marx's ecological critique of capitalism out of "a few very simple characteristics, which are hammered out into flat tautologies."[9] Any attempt to find an ecological aspect in Marx's discussion of the labor process alone will remain abstract and futile. Its further characterization is required to avoid a merely moralistic critique that we should respect nature because we owe our existence to it. If one is to develop Marx's ecology as a part of his economic system, it is necessary to comprehend the modern destruction of the environment in its relation to the capitalist mode of production as a historically specific stage of human production. It is exactly this task that Marx undertakes with his theory of value and reification in *Capital*. He demonstrates why the transhistorical process between humans and nature can only be mediated *in a one-sided manner* by a specific historical form of labor in capitalism.

REIFICATION AS THE KERNEL OF MARX'S THEORY

Marx's *Capital* begins with an analysis of "the commodity" as the "elementary form" of the capitalist mode of production. The commodity has two aspects, "use value" and "value," and the labor that produces commodities also possesses characteristics that include "concrete useful labor" and "abstract human labor." Concrete useful labor suggests a series of qualitatively different types of labor, such as weaving and tailoring, which, accordingly, produce qualitatively diverse use values such as linen and coats. This aspect of human labor as a concrete activity that pro- duces various use values through the modification of matter expresses a physiological, material, and transhistorical moment of the metabolic interaction of humans with their environment. Marx's characterization of concrete labor is not controversial. On the contrary, his claim that abstract labor is also *material* has been highly contentious.

Abstract human labor that creates the value of commodities within society with commodity production is, according to Marx's defini- tion, abstracted from all concrete characteristics, so it is invisible and untouchable. Moreover, he states quite explicitly that value as such is a pure social construction. But he also clearly maintains that abstract labor is physiological and transhistorical: "All labor is *an expenditure of human labor-power, in the physiological sense*, and it is in this quality of being equal, or abstract, human labor that it forms the value of commodities."[10] He also writes: "However varied the useful kinds of labor, or productive activities, it is a physiological fact that they are functions of the human organism, and that each such function, whatever may be its nature or its form, is essentially the expenditure of human brain, nerves, muscles and sense organs."[11] This "physiological fact" is true of any expenditure of labor power, and in this sense abstract labor is also as material and transhistorical as concrete labor.

Writing against this claim in *Capital*, Isaak Rubin's interpretation has found a wide audience, and a number of Marxists such as Michael Heinrich, Riccardo Bellofiore, and Werner Bonefeld today argue that abstract labor is neither material nor transhistorical, but a purely social form of labor characteristic only of the capitalist mode of production.[12] Against this dominant current, it is necessary to emphasize that Marx's theoretical aim in chapter 1 of volume 1 of *Capital* is often not correctly understood, and this leads to the claim that Marx's theory is funda- mentally "ambivalent."[13] Actually, a consistent interpretation of Marx's explanation of abstract labor is not only possible but also all the more important in the current context because it constitutes the theoretical basis for a systematic analysis of his ecology. As I will argue, ecology pro- vides an eminent example of how the focus on the materiality of abstract labor can open up an attractive and productive reading of Marx's value

theory. In this context, it is worth taking a look at an important Japanese
interpretation of Marx presented by Samezo Kuruma and Teinosuke
Otani.[14]

Heated debates on the first three chapters of volume 1 of *Capital*
occurred in Japan as well. The Kuruma school put forth one of the most
consistent interpretations, which will function here as a basis of the
current investigation. Kuruma's contribution to Marxist study is relatively unknown, with some exception in Germany, where his name has
attained distinction thanks to his fifteen volumes of *Marx-Lexikon zur
politischen Ökonomie*, which his student Teinosuke Otani and others co-
edited. Kuruma's main work, *Marx's Theory of the Genesis of Money: How,
Why and Through What Is a Commodity Money*, is largely neglected.[15] So
I hope this chapter will help introduce the unknown legacy of Samezo
Kuruma to readers outside of Japan.

Marx, in beginning his analysis in *Capital* with the category of the
commodity, first deals with the characteristics of simple commodity production.[16] Commodity production is a form of social production that
is founded on a historically specific division of labor. In his *History of
Political Economy*, Samezo Kuruma (along with his co-author Yoshiro
Tamanoi) explicates the specific characteristics of commodity production, pointing to "private labor" as the key to comprehend the modern
relations of production.[17] By doing so, Kuruma follows Marx's explanation in *Capital* about the social division of labor based on "private
labors." Marx writes:

> Objects of utility become commodities only because they are the
> products of the labor of private individuals who work indepen-
> dently of each other. The sum total of the labor of all these private
> individuals forms the aggregate labor of society. Since the producers
> do not come into social contact until they exchange the products of
> their labor, the specific social characteristics of their private labors
> appear only within this exchange. In other words, the labor of the
> private individuals manifests itself as an element of the total labor of
> society only through the relations which the act of exchange estab-
> lishes between the products, and, through their mediation, between
> producers.[18]

Marx clearly argues that *only* products of labor made by "private
labors" carried out by "private individuals" become commodities. The
concept of "private labor" should not be confused with labors that are

carried out by individuals in isolation from social production just for the sake of private enjoyment and hobby. Rather, the concept characterizes those labors that are a part of the social division of labor (in which people are dependent on others' products) but nonetheless carried out "independently of each other," without any social arrangement, so that producers must produce without knowing what other individuals actually want.

Kuruma explains how the "social division of labor" founded on private labor can be successfully arranged. The sum total of all available labors in one society is finite without exception because its members can only work for a certain amount of time in a year. This is simply a physiological fact. In any society where individuals cannot satisfy their own needs and are dependent on others, an adequate "allocation" of the entire supply of labor into each branch of production must be somehow arranged and realized so that the reproduction of a society can actually take place. If some of the necessary products are oversupplied and others are undersupplied, the needs of individuals will not be satisfied, and further production will not alter this fact. Moreover, the successful reproduction of society also requires an appropriate mode of "distribution" of products to the members of society. The allocation of the sum total of labor and the distribution of the sum total of products are two fundamental and transhistorical material conditions for the existence of society.[19]

To comprehend the specificity of the modern social division of labor, it is helpful to compare it with other, non-capitalist forms of social production. In forms of the social division of labor not based on private labor, allocation and distribution are regulated by a certain personal will, *before* labor activities are actually carried out, whether the method of this organization is despotic, traditional, or democratic. As a result, the sum total of society's labor can be allocated into each concrete labor and the products can also be distributed among members of society. This kind of social production is possible because social needs are always known before the act of production. If the entire production is arranged in accordance with this knowledge about society's needs, the labor of each individual *directly* possesses a social character, owing to its guaranteed contribution to the reproduction of the society.

Since a society with commodity production, like all other forms of society, is subjected to this transhistorical material condition, it is necessary for such a system to somehow organize the allocation of labor and the distribution of products. Commodity production differs significantly from other forms of the social division of labor in that the activity of labor carried out by individuals is organized *as a private* act, which does not become a part of the entire social labor at the moment of labor's execution. It is thus necessary to realize the adequate "allocation" and "distribution" not before but *after* labor is performed. Private labors as such thus do not possess any immediate social character and do not constitute a part of entire social labor. In the moment of production, the possibility always exists that labor is exercised in vain for some products that will not find any needs for them. In a society with commodity production, there is a *real contradiction* that in spite of the mutual material dependence of all producers—which forces everyone to step into a social contact with others for the sake of satisfying one's own needs—the labors of individuals must be carried out as a matter of fully private calculations and judgments. According to Kuruma, this real contradiction requires a "detour" in order to realize the continuation of social production and reproduction under private labor.[20]

Kuruma argues that this detour takes place when private producers relate to each other through the mediation of the products they produce. Since they cannot directly relate to each other, they must first come into contact with others through the reified relation of "the act of exchange between the products." When their products actually satisfy the needs of others through a commodity exchange and prove their social characteristics as use values, it is *retrospectively* possible to confirm the social character of expended private labor that is now considered socially useful labor. On the one hand, since the product actually met the needs of people, the successful commodity exchange means that the allocation of this labor took place fruitfully and was not wasted in the production of something that society does not need. On the other hand, the distribution of products among members of society occurs at the same time, through this exchange between commodities. This is the specific way of organization of the material conditions of production and reproduction under commodity production.

This social relation among private producers becomes possible thanks to certain material characteristics of labor's products. In other words, the social contact mediated by such products is possible because the material use value can be an object of others' desire. Since private producers mutually desire others' products, the sociality of a use value enables producers to have mutual contact. This sociality of a use value is dependent on whether it can satisfy a certain human need (which is, of course, socially conditioned), but it is fundamentally based on a material characteristic of each product.

There still remains a difficulty: it is still necessary to comprehend what functions as a *criterion* in the exchange of diverse products. The use value of each product is so different that there seems to exist no common measure for the exchange. However, as Marx argues, such a measure does exist, and it is this measure that characterizes the commodity exchange. In commodity exchange, in contrast to other forms of exchange, the *value relation* is characteristic. Marx writes that it "is only by being exchanged that the products of labor acquire a socially uniform objectivity as values, which is distinct from their sensuously varied objectivity as articles of utility."[21] Commodities with qualitatively different use values go into an equivalent relation of value in the process of commodity exchange. "Value" functions as a common criterion through which various products are made comparable. Mediated by the value relation between various commodities, private labors can relate to one another as social ones. Since value is required because of the specific characteristic of private labor, it is not a natural property of matter, and it does not exist in other forms of social production. Value is a "purely social" character of a thing that, independent of material characteristics, exists only under the historically specific social relations of commodity production.

Marx maintained that the "substance" of value is abstract labor. He said that, as a result of abstracting from concrete characteristics of labor, private labors are objectified in products as an expenditure of human labor power, in the physiological sense. In terms of the relationship between "value" and "abstract labor" it is clear first of all that the category of value has an essential connection with a specific modern social division of labor. The objectification of abstract labor as value necessarily occurs within societies with commodity production because the social allocation of the sum total of all available labor must take place. As objectification of abstract labor, value is a purely social property of matter with which private producers can enter into a social contract with others. As a pure social construction, value does not possess a sensuous form that we can touch or smell like a use value. Marx thus appropriately calls value a "phantom-like objectivity" because abstract labor cannot be materially objectified after abstraction of all concrete aspects. It appears only in a "phantom-like" manner.[22]

However, it does not follow that abstract labor is also "purely social." Rather, it is necessary strictly to distinguish "value" and "abstract labor." Many argue that when value is purely social, abstract labor is also purely social because it is value-creating labor. This explanation is simply not very convincing because it says no more than that "value-creating-labor creates value." This is merely a circular argument.

Thus it is necessary to differentiate value and abstract labor and make the content of the latter more fruitful. As said, value is purely social because in a specific society with commodity production, where social contact among private producers can only take place through the mediation of their products, one aspect of human labor must be objectified as value. In other words, the objectification of abstract labor occurs only through this specific social behavior of private producers that unconsciously but forcibly emerges under commodity production.

Abstract labor is, in contrast, physiological because it plays a social role in a transhistorical fashion in any society. Insofar as the total quantity of labor as expenditure of the human labor force is inevitably limited to a certain finite amount at any time, its adequate allocation for the sake of the reproduction of society is always of great significance for the reproduction of society. Labors as concrete labors are diverse and not compatible to each other, but they are *physiologically* the same and comparable in that, without exception, they consume a part of the finite sum of labor in the society. This aspect of abstract labor is essential in any social division of labor and thus plays a transhistorical role, as Marx argues: "In all situations, the labor-time it costs to produce the means of subsistence must necessarily concern mankind, although not to the same degree at different stages of development."[23] Any society must pay attention to the sum total of labor because it has to use it cautiously in order to attain necessary products every day of every year.

To sum up, in a society with commodity production, due to the private character of labor a social contract can only be realized through the social character of matter, that is, use values that become the object of other people's desires. In the exchange between different use values, value is required as their common criterion, in which abstract labor as one aspect of human labor is objectified through social praxis as a pure social character of matter. In this way, the allocation of social labor is unconsciously carried out through value, and the distribution of products takes place through commodity exchanges as well.

Now, it is understandable that abstract labor in societies with commodity production also functions as a specific social form of private labor. In other types of society, concrete labors are directly social labor despite the variety of their content because the allocation of the entire labor is arranged before performing concrete labors. As seen above, private labor, in contrast, does not possess such a social character in itself, so that the performance of concrete labor as such cannot arrange an adequate allocation of the sum total of labor. In a society with commodity production, abstract labor instead of concrete labor functions as a historically specific social form of labor in the moment of exchange, so that private labors can be socially comparable and related to one another. In other words, private labor can attain a socially meaningful form only with the aid of the "generality of labor," as abstract labor in which their diversity disappears. Marx's point is that a certain material aspect of human activity, in this case labor's pure physiological expenditure, receives a specific economic form and a new social function under capitalistically constituted social relations.

In this way, capitalist social relations bring new social characteristics into the transhistorical metabolic interaction between humans and nature. The allocation of the entire labor and the distribution of the entire product under commodity production are arranged through the mediation of "value," that is, objectified abstract labor. There is no conscious agreement on the general production among producers because they simply follow price changes in the market. Value is the fundamental sign for producers with regard to what they should produce. Since social production is nothing but the regulation of the metabolic interaction between humans and nature, value is now its mediator, which means that the *expenditure of abstract labor* is primarily taken into account in the metabolic process. Other elements of that metabolic interaction, such as concrete labor and nature, in contrast play only a secondary role and are taken into account only as long as they relate to value, even if they continue to function as essential material factors in the labor process. Insofar as abstract labor is also a material element of the labor process, its expenditure cannot completely ignore other material elements that work with it. However, thanks to the material elasticity of these elements, they can be subordinated to abstract labor. A germ of a contradictory relationship lies between nature and humans, and it grows to a great antagonism between nature and society with the development of capitalist production. This point is decisive for the systematic illustration of Marx's ecology. In order to follow its concretization in reality, we will now continue Marx's discussion about the *theory of reification* in *Capital*.

Since private producers can only relate to each other through the mediation of commodity exchange, it is necessary that they behave in such a way that the products of their labor attain a unique social property so that they can exchange diverse use values under a single common criterion, that is, "value." In other words, value is a social power that private producers unconsciously bestow on their products of private labor for the sake of constructing social ties. Marx emphasizes in a famous passage that this social practice is not a conscious but an unconscious act:

> Men do not therefore bring the products of their labor into relation with each other as values because they see these objects [*Sachen*] merely as the material [*sachliche*] integuments of homogeneous human labor. The reverse is true. By equating their different products to each other in exchange as values, they equate their different kinds of labor as human labor. They do this without being aware of it.[24]

Without equating products as values in the market, the social contacts necessary for social production and reproduction are not possible. This is an objective reality. This social practice of equating "different products to each other in exchange as values" is thus *forced* upon the members of the society as an unconscious act that is necessary for the material existence of society.

With a particular focus on Marx's theory of reification, Teinosuke Otani, a student of Samezo Kuruma, developed the theoretical structure of the first three chapters of the first volume of *Capital*, revealing the fundamental characteristics of societies with commodity production. According to Marx's own description, here is the basic characteristic of reification under commodity production:

> To the producers, therefore, the social relations between their private labors appear as what they are, i.e. they do not appear as direct social relations between persons in their work, but rather as material relations between persons and social relations between things.[25]

Otani characterizes this inversion within modern society as the "reification of a person," that is, as an alien domination of things that exerts its influence independent of human consciousness. This inversion of the world emerges out of the objective social structure in which the social relations of the producers do not directly appear as relations between persons but only as relations between things. Consequently, the "social character of labor" transforms into the "value character of labor product," the "continuity of labor in time" into the "value quantity of the labor product," and "social relation" into the "exchange relation of labor products."[26] This inversion is not a mere epistemic fallacy, in the sense of concealing and mystifying some kind of "essence" of fundamental human relations, but is a practical and objective phenomenon because private producers in reality cannot relate to one another without the value-mediated commodity exchange in the market. Human practice is inverted into the movement of labor products and dominated by it, not in a person's head, but in reality. As Marx writes: "Their own movement within society has for them the form of a movement made by things, and these things, far from being under their control, in fact control them."[27]

Producers are interested in the proportion of exchange with other commodities in order to effectively satisfy their own needs, but they cannot control this proportion—it constantly changes and does so suddenly against their calculations and expectations. Rather, producers are controlled by the movement of values, without guarantee that they can actually exchange their products with other use values they want. They do not even know whether they can exchange their products at all. The movements of commodities and money confront the producers as something alien because these determine the behavior of producers, and not the other way round. There exists an actual inversion of the relationship between the subject and the object, whose analogy Marx finds in religion: "This is exactly *the same* relation in the sphere of material production, in the real social life process . . . as is represented by *religion* in the ideological sphere: the inversion of the subject into the object and *vice versa*."[28] This objective inversion extends to the entire society with further self-developments of value as "money" and "capital."

Despite the reified movement that appears independent of the will of the producers, it is evidently not possible for a commodity to go into the market as an independent "subject." Commodities need humans as their "bearers (*Träger*)" who bring them to the market and exchange them for the sake of consumption. This commodity exchange is, of course, regulated by value. In this way, reification modifies human behavior and desires as the logic of value independently penetrates humans, turning them into the "bearers of commodities," wherein a further practical inversion of the world emerges. In order to realize the exchange of commodities, the possessors of a commodity must relate to each other in the market, recognizing each other as the "owner" of the commodity. In the exchange process, their functions are abstracted and reduced to a mere "bearer" of their products as commodities, which Otani, following Marx, calls the "personification of things."[29] The more the social power of commodity, money, and capital expands over the world, the more human functions are subordinated and integrated to these reified, economic relations in accordance with the logic of value. Out of these

modifications emerges a model of modern subjectivity, which internal-
izes the "rationality" of this inverted world, so that "Freedom, Equality,
Property, and Bentham," as Marx bitingly characterizes the capitalist
market, become absolutized as the universal norms, without taking into
account the fundamental inverted structure of this society, what Otani
calls "homo economicus illusion."[30]

As indicated, this "homo economicus illusion," the false view glori-
fied by capital's apologists, is the reflex of the actual inversion in the
objective structure construed in the society based on private labors.
The social inversion gets strengthened even further with this illusion
because individuals not only observe the surface of the world and
accept economic categories such as "value" and "commodity" while
unaware of the inverted social structure that produces them, but they
also, in conformity with this illusion, gradually internalize a new subjectivity with a set of behaviors and judgments, on the basis of which
they *consciously* come to obey the bourgeois utilitarian ideals of "freedom," "equality," and "property." These new desires and views of the
world in many cases determine the mode of behavior as an objective
force, because without conforming to a certain type of social rationality in the inverted world individuals cannot survive under these social
relations. They often do not have plausible alternatives other than
following the rules if they wish to live under the current social and
economic system. Through social practice, the social relations of this
inverted world are constantly reproduced and in the end naturalized.
Obeying the economic reduction of subjectivity, individuals volun-
tarily function as bearers of commodity and money. As a result, they
appropriate a series of norms, rules, and other value standards as sole
markers of human "rationality."

Due to the reified construction of the social structure, capitalists are,
on the one hand, forced by the logic of the system to reduce any "unnecessary" costs, including those of sanity, health, and safety for the workers,
to pressure the labor force as much as possible for the valorization of
capital, and constantly seek to increase productivity without thinking
about the sustainable reproduction of natural resources. Laborers are
compelled, on the other hand, to work harder than ever, are disciplined
under the directions of the capitalists, and are forced to withstand poor
working conditions if they wish to sell their labor forces successfully. No
matter what they wish, the threat of losing a job is enough to make workers endure a bad situation so that they can receive the wages necessary

for the purchase of their means of subsistence. All these behaviors reproduce the objective inversion of society and deepen workers' dependence on commodities and money.

The first three chapters in *Capital* volume 1 show that the modification of the material world begins with the category of "value." The inversion of relations between persons into relations between things causes not only alien, reified domination of the actions of individuals— "reification of persons"—but also causes the modification of human needs and rationality, that is, the "personification of things." Reification of the world deepens in the course of deducing further economic categories, to the extent that value first becomes independent as "money" and then becomes even stronger when value becomes a definite subject as "capital" and begins actively to transform the entire world.

"FORMS" AND "CONTENT"

Marx showed in his analysis of the commodity in *Capital* how the inverted, alienated economic form determinations not only transform ordinary judgments about the world, but also affect the material dimensions of humans in, for example, desires, will, and behaviors. However, such modifications are not limited to the human side, because Marx analyzed capitalist transformations of the material world in various spheres. As we will see, this methodological approach overcomes the confusion and dualism of "form" and "material" in classical political economy. Marx's critique of political economy can be understood, in this sense, as encompassing a dialectic of material spheres. Marxists generally conceive the historicity and sociality of economic forms as the kernel of Marx's project, but this discussion goes into the second, often neglected, aspect of "material" in his political economy.

Marx in the *Grundrisse* criticized a "fetishistic" misunderstanding that comes from the identification of social characteristics with natural properties of things:

> The crude materialism of the economists who regard as the *natural properties* of things what are social relations of production among people, and qualities which things obtain because they are subsumed under these relations, is at the same time just as crude an idealism, even fetishism, since it imputes social relations to things as inherent characteristics, and thus mystifies them.[31]

Ricardo, for example, defined capital as "accumulated (realized) labor (property, objectified labor), which serves as the means for new labor." He abstracted the economic "form" of capital, Marx argued, so that he ended up emphasizing only the "content" or the simple material of capital as "*a necessary condition for all human production*."[32] In Ricardo's analysis of economic forms, the form determination of capital is transformed into a material property of a thing and consequently naturalized as a transhistorical condition of production. Marx's first critique denounces this clumsy separation of "form" and "content" among classical political economists. Their fetishism is due to the unmediated identification of economic forms with a natural property of their material bearers.

Nonetheless, Marx also recognized a gradual progress among the classical political economists to build up economic categories precisely as a result of the separation of "form" and "content." The second aspect of his critique is directed at this point. He argued that this separation alone is not enough for the construction of a science. In contrast, Marx pointed to the necessity to analyze as economic categories not only the economic "form" but also "material" itself, because material properties play a specific economic role under certain social relations as a result of the development of capitalist categories, as seen in the example of "fixed" and "floating" capital.

Marx explicitly stated in the *Grundrisse* that material properties also require a theoretical analysis as economic categories in that their characteristics can reveal the specificity of capitalism. In the last part of the *Grundrisse* where Marx finally singled out the commodity as the first category of his critique of political economy, he wrote:

> The commodity itself appears as unity of two aspects. It is *use value*, i.e. object of the satisfaction of any system whatever of human needs. This is its material side, which the most disparate epochs of production may have in common, and whose examination therefore lies beyond political economy.[33]

This seems to confirm the traditional reading of Marx's critique of political economy as an analysis of economic forms, but then he continues to argue in the next sentence:

> Use value falls within the realm of political economy as soon as it becomes modified by the modern relations of production, or as it, in turn, intervenes to modify them. What it is customary to say about

it in general terms, for the sake of good form, is conditioned to commonplaces which had a historic value in the first beginnings of the
science, when the social forms of bourgeois production had still laboriously to be peeled out of the material, and, at great effort, to be
established as independent objects of study.[34]

Classical political economy was with "great effort" gradually able to
separate the economic "form" from the "material" and to treat the former
as "independent objects of study." The separation marks great progress
for political economy, but it is valuable only in "the first beginning of science," for the classical school could comprehend the categories only in
abstract forms, which it rapidly transformed into mere "commonplaces."
In order to save political economy from falling into this banality, Marx
proposed a more nuanced way of treating "form" and "material." It is in
this method where Marx's originality becomes apparent, in contrast to
his predecessors like Smith and Ricardo.

In his analysis, the material aspect of wealth that is common to all
the stages of production first lies outside the scope of an investigation of
political economy, because political economy analyzes the "social forms"
that reveal the particular characteristics of capitalist wealth and its production. Nonetheless, since capitalist commodity production like other
modes of production cannot exist without material elements such as labor
power, means of production, and raw materials, Marx treated the material side of the production process simply as "a given presupposition—the
material basis in which a specific economic relation presents itself."[35]

However, this presupposition does not mean that the material side
should never be taken into consideration in an analysis of economic
relations. Marx maintained the opposite in the quoted passage: where
use value is "modified" through the modern economic relations and
even "intervenes to modify them," it becomes the subject of scientific
observation. Marx emphasized in the *Grundrisse* that in addition to the
description of economic forms, the capitalist modification of use values
through economic-form determination is an important object of political economy.

This is not an isolated, minor remark in the *Grundrisse*. Marx emphasized at other places that use value functions as an economic category
under certain economic relations:

As we have already seen in several instances, nothing is therefore
more erroneous than to assert that the distinction between use value

and exchange value, which falls outside the characteristic economic form in simple circulation . . . falls outside it in general. We found, rather, that in the different stages of the development of economic relations, exchange value and use value were determined in different relations, and that this determination itself appeared as a different determination of value as such. Use value itself plays a role as an economic category. Where it plays this role is given by the development itself.[36]

Marx again criticized the absolute opposition of form and material because their various relations represent economic relations. In reality, the economic forms cannot exist without "the material basis." In many cases, Marx said, "use value itself plays a role as an economic category." It is a "bearer" *par excellence*, whose material properties are penetrated by economic relations. Like the "personification of things," the objective materialization of economic form determinations in the inverted world is not an epistemological inversion, but this "materialization" (*Verdinglichung*) of economic relations is to be understood as the deepest modification of a material property of a use value, as the "ossification" of social relations of production.[37]

Notably, Marx did not lose his interest in this topic even in the last stage of his life. He wrote in his *Notes on Adolph Wagner's Lehrbuch der politischen Ökonomie* in 1881: "Use value plays an important part quite different from its part in economics hitherto, but *nota bene* it still only comes under consideration when such a consideration stems from the analysis with regard to economic formations, not from arguing hither and thither about the concepts or words 'use value' and 'value.'"[38] Here again, Marx clearly emphasized the economic role of the material side of use value that contributes to comprehending the specificity of the capitalist system under certain conditions.

Marx's point is that the capitalist modifications of material characteristics are not limited to people's desires and behaviors but extend to properties of the things themselves. These modifications increase "in the different stages of the development of economic relations," and are more and more captured in his descriptions as the analysis moves from abstract categories to concrete ones. According to Marx, a thing under social relations does not simply exist with given natural properties but is historically modified by capitalistically constituted economic relations, so that the economic determination now comes to be ossified into a thing. It ultimately "appears as a *thing*, just as value appeared as the quality of a thing and the *economic determination* of the thing as a *commodity* appeared as its quality as a thing; and just as the social form assumed by labor in money expressed itself as the *qualities of a thing*."[39] With the development of capitalist production, various material dimensions are gradually modified by this process of "materialization" (*Verdinglichung*)—that is, modification of material properties according to the logic of capital—in such a way that the valorization of capital can proceed under more favorable conditions. Both the analysis of material in Marx's treatment and his form analysis point to the historical specificity characteristic to capitalist relations and even their contradictions. Moreover, this process of transformation must not be analyzed from the perspective of capital alone but also from the material side, especially in terms of the entire metabolic interaction between humans and nature. Marx's critique of political economy fulfills this double theoretical task in contrast to the classical political economists.[40]

Despite Marx's clear remarks about the economic role of the "material basis," its importance is often underestimated among Marxists compared to the form analysis. This tendency is not coincidental because many Marxists developed their interpretations based on the pure sociality of abstract labor.[41]

Alfred Sohn-Rethel's interpretation is a typical one in this context, as he argued: "In fact, 'not an atom of matter' enters into the objectivity of commodity as values, upon which the socializing effect of exchange is dependent. Here the socialization is a matter of pure human composition, uncoupled from humans' metabolism with nature."[42] Sohn-Rethel's form analysis surely recognizes the pure social character of the objectivity of value, but he reduces value to a mere social relation existing in the commodity exchange and the abstract labor to a pure social construct. Consequently, value is separated from the metabolism between humans and nature in his explanatory scheme.

Since Sohn-Rethel completely cut off the category of "value" from its material aspects, focusing only on its purely social character, he ended up falling into a dualism of "first nature" and "second nature":

I include the entire formal side of commodity exchange under the expression of *second nature*, which should be understood as a pure social, abstract and functional reality *in opposition to the first or primary nature*, in which we find ourselves on the same level with animals. In the expression of the second nature as the form of money, what is specifically human attains its first, objective, distinct and real manifestation in the history. It comes to exist due to the necessity of a socialization *dissociated from any modes of operation of material metabolism between humans and nature.*[43]

Sohn-Rethel opposed the first (animal-like, natural) nature to the second (specific human, social) nature. It is true that the social power of value does not include any "material content" of the commodity because it is a product of social praxis. However, one cannot infer that the objectivity of value has nothing to do with the transhistorical necessity of human metabolism with nature.

Marx's point is actually the opposite. As seen above, Marx in *Capital* consistently asked why the emergence of such a pure social category of value is at all necessary in capitalism. As an answer, Marx claimed that it is because the transhistorical metabolic interaction between humans and nature must be organized despite the private character of labor, and this metabolism can only be mediated by the pure social value. Thus the most fundamental reason for the existence of value indicates the material and transhistorical necessity to regulate the metabolism between humans and nature. This explanation must be contrasted to Sohn-Rethel's problematic understanding because he could not provide a convincing reason why abstract labor in society with commodity production must be objectified into commodities as value. Rather, he simply assumed that abstract labor is also purely a social construct. His dualism separates "value" from the "human metabolism from nature," because abstract labor as "second nature" has nothing to do with the transhistorical natural metabolism.

This opposition of the transhistorical and the historical in Sohn-Rethel's *Intellectual and Manual Labour* risks theoretical one-sidedness, as if value had nothing to do with the transhistorical sphere of production. If Marx's critique of political economy is primarily understood as "form analysis," this neglect of the material dimension does not seem so problematic because its examination *at first* "lies beyond political economy." However, as soon as one confronts Marx's detailed notebooks on natural sciences and asks how they can be integrated into the project of *Capital*, the absolute separation of "value" and "metabolism between humans and nature" becomes extremely problematic. Sohn-Rethel's explanation does not provide a key for understanding how a scientific investigation of the "first nature" can contribute to his critique of political economy whose primary field is supposedly the "second nature."

The debate on the material character of abstract labor is not an irrelevant deviation from the theme of Marx's ecology. The concept of abstract labor as a "pure social" category has serious consequences. It makes it much harder to explain why the capitalist dominance of abstract labor, to which no material property belongs, destroys various dimensions of the universal metabolism of nature more devastatingly than ever. In order to avoid a vague statement that the dominion of a social abstract destroys nature, it is necessary to explain the connection between abstract labor and social and natural metabolism by comprehending value in its relation to the latter's "eternal necessity." The strict opposition between "nature" and "society" excludes the influence of economic determinations over the material dimensions. In contrast, it is Marx's aim to reveal how the material natural properties receive social modifications and internalize them as their own thing-like properties, and how, particularly because of this entanglement of material and social properties, there emerge real contradictions. That is to say, the material natural properties cannot be completely subsumed under capital. Out of this limit to capital, various "living contradictions" come to exist even if the exact manifestations of these contradictions are not predetermined thanks to the "elasticity of capital," and are strongly dependent on the development of technologies and natural sciences. Marx's theory of reification comprehends the contradictory process of the capitalization of the material world and the conditions for its transcendence.

An analysis of Marx's project thus needs to go beyond the earlier interpretation and include the analysis of the material world as a central object of study. This analysis is primarily about how the capitalist mode of production tends to undermine the material conditions for the sustainable, that is, how production, by the logic of reification, organizes a social practice increasingly hostile to nature, resulting in a crisis of sustainable human development.

The material contradiction of capitalism is implicated at the abstract level of generalized commodity production in the first three chapters of *Capital*. But this is not sufficient. The tension between "form" and "material" crystallizes more clearly with the development of the category of "capital." Marx analyzes how capital, this "automatic subject," radically reorganizes the metabolic interaction between humans and nature and finally destroys it.

THE CAPITALIST TRANSFORMATION OF METABOLISM

Marx's explanation of the inverted world in *Capital* contributes to comprehending the necessity of disturbance in the material world under capitalism. Without explaining the dynamics immanent to the capitalist mode of production, Marx's ecology would be reduced to a simple proposition that capitalism destroys the ecological system because capitalists seek to attain profits with no care at all about environmental sustainability. This would be against Marx's "materialist method." Thus investigation of the objective social structure is also required because Marx's method is opposed to those approaches that simply aim at introducing new "moralistic" or "correct" values that claim to be environmentally friendly. In contrast, Marx examined in a detailed manner how the mediation of the social and natural interaction between humans and nature by the logic of capital's valorization organizes social production and circulation in such a way that their metabolic interchange necessarily gets disrupted. While the capitalist mode of production structures a particular human metabolism with nature on a national and global scale, the forces of nature are, though elastic, always limited in various ways, resulting in eco-crises in multiple spheres.

Since the allocation of the sum total of labor and the distribution of the sum total of products in capitalism are arranged through the mediation of value, the metabolic interaction between humans and nature is inevitably carried out under the primacy of abstract labor. As mentioned earlier, this mode of mediation contains within itself a certain tension, because the concrete material dimensions of humans-nature interaction can only be taken into account within the value expression in a very limited and deficient manner. This characterizes an important difference in relation to all other forms of social production, where the various material (and even ecological) aspects are normally incorporated at the moment of "allocation" of social labor and the "distribution" of products.[44]

The fact that humans work upon nature under the primacy of value might not seem so ecologically unfriendly. However, the problem of this reified mediation appears more distinctively with the emergence of fully developed "capital," because value then functions not just as a "mediation" of social production, but now becomes the "goal" of production. Capital threatens the continuation of humanity's metabolism with nature by radically reorganizing it from a perspective of maximally squeezing out abstract labor.

Once again, remember that according to Marx the category of "value" in a society of generalized commodity production is an economic category that shows an essential connection with material conditions for the reproduction of the metabolism between humans and nature. The particularity of capitalism is that, due to "private labors" and "reification," the production and reproduction of a society can proceed only with the mediation of value. Private producers socially relate to each other only with the aid of value, to secure the existence of society (more or less!).

With "money" the power of reification increases. As Marx explains, value incarnates itself as an independent object—money—that bestows a specific social use value to a commodity, gold. Gold functions as a "general equivalence" that is "directly exchangeable with other commodities." This social power of direct exchangeability means that its possession allows the acquisition of any desired object, and this generates a new desire for money hoarding, which is "boundless in its nature."[45]

Yet an even more radical change occurs when the sole objective of the production becomes the maximal objectification of abstract labor. With the subjectification of value as "capital," the transformation of the world proceeds even more drastically:

On the other hand, in the circulation M-C-M [money-commodity-money] both the money and the commodity function only as different modes of existence of value itself, the money as its general mode of existence, the commodity as its particular or, so to speak, disguised mode. It is constantly changing from one form into the other, without becoming lost in this movement; it thus becomes transformed into an automatic subject. If we pin down the specific forms of appearance assumed in turn by self-valorizing value in the course of its life, we reach the following elucidation: capital is money, capital is commodities. In truth, however, value is here the subject of a process in which, while constantly assuming the form in turn of money and commodities, it changes its own magnitude, throws off surplus-value from itself considered as original value, and thus valorizes itself independently.[46]

In the circulation of C-M-C [commodity-money-commodity], the process is directed at the final goal of a use value that one can only attain through commodity exchanges in the market. Here value mainly operates as a general measure for various products of private labors, and so at the end of the process value disappears together with the consumption of the desired use value. In other words, value simply functions as a mediator of social metabolism. With gold, value becomes an independent object as money, so that one can own value as a thing and hoard money. However, money must be exchanged with another use value sometime in the future if it is to function as money at all.

The economic determination of value as "capital" brings about a totally different situation. Value as capital is an "automatic subject" that repeatedly goes through the process of M-C-M' [M' includes surplus value] without losing its determination as capital and even grows bigger. The pure sociality of value turns into an infinite movement because the sole goal is pure quantitative increase. Value itself, or more precisely its valorization, has become the final goal of production. Surely enough, money as an independent value is always the beginning and the end of the process of M-C-M', but even this money is but a temporary figure for capital because its valorization can only take place through constant changes in forms (*Formwechsel*) between commodities and money. As Marx says, value is thus an "encompassing subject" of the process of M-C-M', in which "it alternately assumes and loses the form of money and the form of commodities, but preserves and expands itself through all these changes."[47] The entire process of production is still dependent on use values as the bearers of capital. However, this material component of production is now subordinated to the pure quantitative movement of capital. In accordance with this new economic characteristic of value as capital, the transhistorical "labor process" must be fundamentally reorganized as capital's "self-valorizing" process.

The statement that the metabolic interaction between humans and nature mediated by labor represents an "eternal natural necessity" in every society is abstract. The entire process of social production now takes a more concrete shape as Marx analyzes it in relation to transformations by capital according to the logic of its valorization. Through this new objective of the production process, abstract labor also receives an additional, specific economic function, namely, the sole source for increasing capitalist wealth.

Capital treats labor only as a means for its endless self-valorization, in which concrete labor yields to the primacy of abstract labor. What matters in capitalist production is no longer the satisfaction of social needs, as they are only casually satisfied under the anarchy of capitalist competition. The desire for capital accumulation can never be satisfied with a certain qualitative use value; it is an "endless" movement of an incessantly growing quantity.[48] As a consequence, all of capitalist production is directed at squeezing out abstract labor, and this one-sided expenditure of human labor power cannot help but distort humanity's relation to nature. Since both labor power and nature are important for capital *only* as a "bearer" of value, capital neglects the various aspects of these two fundamental factors of production, often leading to their exhaustion.

Indeed, Marx's *Capital* carefully describes how this neglect of material dimensions in the labor process leads to the erosion and destruction of human life and the environment.

As value becomes a subject in the form of "capital," this new subject, following its "blind and measureless drive, its insatiable appetite for surplus labor," aims at the objectification of abstract labor into commodities as encompassingly and effectively as possible.[49] This is now the main objective of social production. In contrast, this specific drive did not appear in precapitalist societies because surplus labor was generated only through the exercise of external compulsion. There was no motivation to work further once basic needs were satisfied, and the range of use values was, accordingly, relatively small. There existed the producer's "intimate tie" with the earth despite the relations of personal-political exploitation and dominion.

The situation is totally different in capitalist society. Marx carefully illustrates the destructive uniqueness of capitalist production in chapters on "The Working Day" and "Machinery and Large-Scale Industry" in volume 1 of *Capital*. Referring to parliamentary reports and investigations by factory inspectors and commissioners, Marx depicts the modern transformations of the labor process as a result of its "formal" and "real subsumption" under capital. These chapters, a couple hundred pages long, are often neglected by theoreticians as boring, inessential detours from the main dialectical development of economic categories under capitalism. The predominance of capital is a real process since the inversion manifested in the subjectification of capital is not taking place in our heads but exists objectively in social production. Marx's careful treatment of the concrete lives of workers indicates his strong interest in those transformations that cause workers to fall into a slave-like condition with regard to their moral, social, physical, and intellectual lives. One can say that Marx's project in *Capital* is not primarily motivated by the goal of overcoming Hegel's idealist philosophy but is fundamentally characterized by his sympathy for the actual situation of the working class.[50]

If *Capital* were reduced to a mere dialectical development of the economic categories of bourgeois society, Marx's project would be mainly about a *conceptual* reconstruction of the capitalist totality. On the contrary, it is important to emphasize that Marx seriously analyzed empirical materials in his investigation of capitalist society. In this context, these two chapters in *Capital* are exemplary because they deal not only with the process of the destruction of the material world by the logic of capital but also with the manifestation of capital's limits. That is to say, they reveal the way that the social formation of the inverted world causes a series of contradictions. Even if capital constantly tries to overcome contradictions with technological development and scientific discoveries, capital cannot fully establish its mastery over the material world and ends up devastating the social and natural metabolism, which ends up inducing resistance against the regime of capital.

Marx first illustrates the disharmony of the metabolic interaction between humans and nature, paying particular attention to the human side. Capital both extends and intensifies the working day for the sake of the effective valorization of capital, during which the performance of concrete labors is subordinated to the primacy of the expenditure of abstract labor. Without doubt, this production of "absolute" and "relative" surplus value" causes alienation and suffering in workers' lives. Even if there are certainly "physical limits to labor-power" and "moral obstacles" for capital, both of them possess a "very elastic nature."[51] Capital attempts with its "boundless thirst for surplus labor" to profit from this elastic characteristic of human labor power and to appropriate the labor beyond a given limit, even all twenty-four hours of the day.[52] Since the labor process is primarily the place for producing surplus value, capital, following its own formal logic, exploits labor power without caring about the lives of individual workers. Consequently, the tendency toward impoverishment strengthens itself, so that workers lose their free time due to the extension of the workday, even though disposable time is essential for physical recovery from work and for the cultivation of the mind.

The elastic nature of labor power, which enables the intensification and extension of the workday, has certain material limitations.[53] The boundless desire of capital inevitably confronts the "exhaustion" of labor-power:

> By extending the working day, therefore, capitalist production, which is essentially the production of surplus-value, the absorption of surplus labor, not only produces a deterioration of human labor-power by robbing it of its normal moral and physical conditions of development and activity, but also produces the premature exhaustion and death of this labor-power itself. It extends the worker's production-time within a given period by shortening his life.[54]

Capitalist production asks for a "cruel and incredible extension" of the workday not simply because it is the most direct way to an absolute increase of surplus labor and surplus value, but also because the constant operation of the factory avoids physical and moral depreciation and allows constant capital to be used more efficiently, saving time, for example, by not having to warm up the machines in the morning. Capital valorizes itself with a sacrifice of welfare and the security of workers: "What could be more characteristic of the capitalist mode of production than the fact that it is necessary, by Act of Parliament, to force upon the capitalists the simplest appliances for maintaining cleanliness and health?"[55] As Marx carefully depicted, the working class suffers from various physical deformities, moral degradation, and premature death due to a dangerous amount of work that is harmful for health. There is, in effect, torture through overwork, night work, and Sunday work. Child labor also becomes the norm unless regulated by law, as was clearly documented in a series of parliamentary reports that Marx was reading. If children of seven or eight years of age are forced to work from six in the morning until ten at night, mental and physical diseases prevail. Despite the gravity of the situation, individual capitalists would not take any countermeasures against this situation unless they were compelled to do so by the enforcement of a law. A beneficent capitalist who did otherwise would find that his or her profit diminished if other capitalists failed to do the same.

This "blind and measureless drive" or "boundless thirst for surplus labor" is therefore not a moral deficit of individual capitalists. They are obliged to follow such behavior due to competition with other capitalists if they want to survive as capitalists. The decision to act in accordance with that blind drive appears rational to them, out of which emerges again a social consciousness and practice seeking after a more and more efficient exploitation of labor power. To be concerned about the life of workers appears as something unnecessary. The first watchword of the capitalists is: "*Après moi le déluge!* . . . Capital therefore takes no account of the health and the length of life of the worker, unless society forces it to do so."[56]

When this type of decision making appears rational, individual capitalists are acting as the "personification of capital."[57] The social system that obliges them to adopt this mode of behavior is, however, totally irrational from another perspective because it makes sustainable reproduction of the laboring class impossible over the long term. The logic of capital does not know any limitation of surplus value because the pure quantitative movement of self-valorizing does not recognize the material aspect of labor-power: "We see then that, leaving aside certain extremely elastic restrictions, the nature of commodity exchange itself imposes no limit to the working day, no limit to surplus labor."[58] So the limit of the labor day cannot be derived from the formal logic of capital alone, and this is why the restriction of the power of reification must be imposed through an external compulsion. This is how workers' conscious resistance against the "measureless drive" appears, and Marx illustrates this process as "the struggle for a normal working day."

In the context of a brutal extension of the workday, workers demand the enforcement of a normal workday and the prohibition of child labor in order to protect their existence. Since individual capitalists are not ready to accept such a regulation if other capitalists still continue to profit from the same old method, the enforcement of a normal workday of eight or ten hours must be by law. Marx in *Capital* carefully reproduces actual struggles between capitalists and workers in the legislation process. Even if the length of a normal workday varies in each society, depending on the power balance between the two classes, factory legislation as such is "the necessary product of large-scale industry" because otherwise reproduction of the working class would be impossible. It is remarkable that Marx highly values factory legislation and even calls it the "first conscious and planned [*planmäßig*] reaction of society against the spontaneously developed form of its production process."[59] For Marx, the "struggle for a normal working day" is strategically of great importance precisely because it consciously transforms the social practice that unconsciously bestows the power of reification. It is true that production as a whole still remains oriented toward the valorization of capital and workers are exploited. However, the restriction of the workday and the corresponding improvement of working conditions, with legislative clauses on health, sanity, wages, and education, are significant achievements of the nascent labor movement.

If one assumes that Marx would have rejected the legislation of a normal working day as a social democratic or reformist policy, one misses his point. On the contrary, Marx passionately supported social attempts for the regulation of the reified power of capital. This is because the legislation *results* from a conscious transformation of a reified social practice. Thus Marx, who was actively engaged in the International Workingmen's Association, wrote a text for the Congress of the IWA held in Geneva, from which he directly quotes in *Capital*: "We declare that the limitation of the working day is *a preliminary condition without which all further attempts at improvement and emancipation must prove abortive. . . .* The Congress proposes eight hours as the legal limit of the working day."[60] The restriction of the working day creates free disposable time, which also prepares workers for further struggles against the alien power of capital. This legislation is a first conscious regulation of the reified power of capital from the standpoint of the material characteristics of labor power.

In terms of the real subsumption of labor under capital, Marx also describes in the chapter "Machinery and Large-Scale Industry" how the material conditions of the labor process are radically reorganized for the sake of the production of relative surplus value. The capitalist mode of production reduces individuals to workers with "ossified particularities" confined to a narrow activity. The development of machinery enables capital to replace skilled labor with unskilled labor, and workers are robbed of independence and autonomy in the production process. As Harry Braverman splendidly explicates in *Labor and Monopoly Capital*, the dominance of capital is not simply based on its monopoly of the means of production, but rather on its monopoly of technology and knowledge. As a result of the real subsumption, the labor process is organized independently of workers' skills, tradition, and knowledge, which Braverman argues is the "first principle" of the capitalist mode of production, namely the "dissociation of the labor process from the skills of the workers." Capitalist production is freed from the abilities of workers and instead it manages them. Workers are no longer able to conduct labor based on their own conception. What Braverman calls the "second principle" of modern-day Taylorism, the "separation of conception from execution," strengthens the dominion of capital.[61] Marx defines labor as a unique human activity, due to its purposeful and conscious character, objectifying humanity's ideal conception through the execution of labor. In its original shape, there is a unity of conception and execution. However, workers under the advanced capitalist division of labor are only accessories of machines. They are unable to impose their will upon the labor process; instead the latter is imposed upon them. Braverman shows that the dominance of capital is rooted in a much deeper dimension than is usually assumed. As a result of real subsumption, workers are not simply deprived of the objective means of production but also of their own subjective capacities, when neither technology nor knowledge as a material basis for autonomous production is accessible to them. These deficiencies are evident not just in the loss of object but also that of subject. This is why workers must be so thoroughly subjugated to the commands of capital in order to be able to produce something at all. Their degradation and domestication are as a result enormously facilitated.

The incessant revolution of the production process under this logic, however, dialectically creates *the conditions* for all-sided mobility, variety, and flexibility of these workers, who are therefore able to adapt to the different kinds of work required. Marx calls them "totally developed individuals." Since capital constantly revolutionizes the entire production process mechanically and chemically and creates new spheres of production, the quick accommodation of workers to changing conditions becomes a "question of life and death" to capitalism:

> But if, at present, variation of labor imposes itself after the manner of an overpowering natural law, and with the blindly destructive action of a natural law that meets with obstacles everywhere, large-scale industry, through its very catastrophes, makes the recognition of variation of labor and hence of the fitness of the worker for the maximum number of different kinds of labor into a question of life and death. This possibility of varying labor must become a general law of social production, and the existing relations must be adapted to permit its realization in practice. That monstrosity, the disposable working population held in reserve, in misery, for the changing requirements of capitalist exploitation, must be replaced by the individual man who is absolutely available for the different kinds of labor required of him; the partially developed individual, who is merely the bearer of one specialized social function, must be replaced by the totally developed individual, for whom the different social functions are different modes of activity he takes up in turn.[62]

Out of this development of the capitalist mode of production there emerges the social necessity for publicly financed institutions for training workers' skills and knowledge. As Ryuji Sasaki rightly emphasizes, Marx, in addition to the struggle for a normal workday, emphasizes the strategic importance of "the establishment of technical and agricultural schools" and of "écoles d'enseignement *professionnel,*" in which the children of the workers receive a certain amount of instruction in technology and in the practical handling of the various implements of labor.[63] It is clear why Marx so highly values the technological education offered in publicly financed schools. These schools provide, even if only to some extent, the basis for the conscious reappropriation of knowledge and skills required in a labor process but monopolized by the capitalist technology. Marx calls this possibility of reappropriation "revolutionary ferments."[64] Against the one-sided transformation of the labor process under its real subsumption under capital, Marx finds in the reappropriation of knowledge and skills the construction of essential material conditions for the rehabilitation of workers' freedom and autonomy in the production process.

To sum up, Marx, after analyzing the destructive consequences of the pure economic determination of the labor process, illustrates the possibility and necessity for regulating, as an emancipatory progress of the labor movement, the formal logic of capital's valorization *from a perspective of the material side of labor power*. This analysis takes place in two steps. Marx first elucidates the pure economic form determinations, and then he investigates how it subsumes and transforms the production process, causing various resistances to it. His discussion about formal and real subsumption in *Capital* indicates his clear support for concrete attempts that consciously struggle against the destruction of labor-power through the regulation of the reified power of capital. His standpoint is one of more sustainable and autonomous social production. Obviously, the shortening of the workday and technological education alone do not transcend the capitalist mode of production, yet they create the essential foundations for further struggles against capital by protecting workers' lives from capital's blind and measureless drive for surplus value.

The discussion about the working day might at first glance seem as if it had nothing to do with Marx's ecology. However, it provides us with insight into capital's influence over the physical and natural sphere, for according to Marx there is another place where the contradiction of reification crystallizes, that is, nature.

CONTRADICTION OF CAPITAL IN NATURE

Marx's illustration of the labor process does not neglect the fact that nature is working together with humans, as he clearly designated both labor and the earth as the two "original factors" of the metabolic interaction between humans and nature.[65] The powers of both labor and nature function as common transhistorical elements in all types of production. If the whole production is organized under the primacy of abstract labor in a one-sided manner, one can infer from the previous observation that capitalist production, in addition to its exhaustion of labor power, causes the exhaustion of natural power as well. Marx pointed to the close connection between the two original factors as he problematized the wasteful usage of natural resources as well as labor powers in various places, even if he did not elaborate on the squandering of natural resources in as much detail as the cruel exploitation of labor power. This is understandable in that Marx planned to deal with the problem of natural powers in the chapter on "ground rent" in volume 3 of *Capital*, but its manuscript remained unfinished. Nevertheless, there is no doubt that Marx intended to treat the problem of modifications of the metabolic interaction between humans and nature with a particular focus on the negative and destructive tendency of capitalist production.[66]

This interpretation is confirmed by how Marx paralleled the destruction of workers' lives and that of nature's fertility:

> Capital asks no questions about the length of life of labor-power. What interests it is purely and simply the maximum of labor-power that can be set in motion in a working day. It attains this objective by shortening the life of labor-power, in the same way as a greedy farmer snatches more produce from the soil by robbing it of its fertility.[67]

This juxtaposition of "labor-power" and "fertility" of the soil is not arbitrary because labor is nothing but the realization of humans' natural power. In both cases, Marx dealt with the exhaustion of natural power under the capitalist mode of production. Instead of simply focusing on the subjective factor of production, he analyzed the social transformation of the other objective side of it as well. As seen above, capital with its immanent logic of valorization is only interested in objectifying abstract labor into commodities as much as possible in the shortest period of time. The same indifferent attitude can be observed toward the soil, too, as a "greedy farmer" ends up "robbing it of its fertility." One must thus comprehend the robbery of soil fertility in conjunction with the theory of reification because it is nothing but another manifestation of the contradiction of the one-sided mediation of the metabolic interaction between humans and nature.[68]

If all of production is organized for this valorization, the destructive power over nature becomes stronger with the development of productive forces. In the *Manuscripts of 1861–63*, Marx explains why capitalist production inevitably and boundlessly exploits nature. It is in this context that the differentiation between the "formal" and "material" aspects of the production process becomes decisive. Marx argues that nature's powers do not go into the "process of valorization" but into the "labor process":

> But, apart from fixed capital, all those productive forces which cost *nothing*, i.e. those which derive from the division of labor, cooperation, machinery (insofar as this costs nothing, as is for example the

case with the motive forces of water, wind, etc., and also with the advantages which proceed from the social arrangement of the workshop) as well as forces of nature whose application does not give rise to any costs—or at least to the degree to which their application does not give rise to any costs—enter into the labor process without entering into the valorization process.[69]

An increase of productivity through "the division of labor, cooperation, machinery" brings about changes only on the material side of production (that is, the labor process) without, however, going into the formal side of production (that is, the valorization process), because the new increased social force of production does not require additional costs. The increased productivity appears under the monopoly of the means of production as a "productive force of capital," and this allows capitalists to acquire a greater amount of surplus products, so that the price reduction of products not only increases the "relative surplus-value" but also provides "extra surplus-value," if they can be produced with an amount of labor below the social average. This "extra surplus-value" offers the main motivation for capitalists to constantly revolutionize the production process.

With the application of natural forces to the production process, with the aid of natural science and technology, which is freely appropriated or has minimal costs that reduce the total production costs, it functions, Marx argues, in the same way as the social forces of capital attained through "the division of labor, cooperation, machinery." The forces of nature go into the labor process and work together with human labor power. Their appropriation appears as the productive force of capital because knowledge and the means of their application are monopolized by capital: "Science, generally speaking, costs the capitalist nothing, a fact that by no means prevents him from exploiting it. 'Alien' science is incorporated by capital just as 'alien' labor."[70] Even if they are not free, requiring some installation of machines or extra labor, new raw materials and auxiliary materials can reduce the constant part of the circulating capital and increase the productivity, so that the same amount of use value can be produced with lower costs. The "free natural power of capital" (land, wind, and water) and the availability of cheap raw materials and energy (wood, coal, and oil) exert a great influence upon the maximization of surplus-value.[71] Thus, this is yet another example of "how *use value*, which originally appears to us only as the material substratum of the economic relations, itself intervenes to determine the economic category."[72]

This situation has negative implications. The instrumental behavior toward nature becomes dominant, as sciences are developed from the standpoint of utility for capital. There also emerges a tendency of capital toward brutal exploitation of the free forces of nature and to a global competitive race after cheaper natural resources. Capital strives for secure and cheaper access to natural resources while problems such as the pollution of air and water, desertification, and exhaustion of natural resources are neglected or viewed merely as externalities. The main principle of technological development is more efficient exploitation of labor power and natural resources with minimal costs. The aim of the application of technology in modern large-scale industry and agriculture is not sustainable intercourse with nature but its profitable employment. As labor power is exhausted and destroyed due to the intensification and extension of production for the sake of greater surplus value, the forces of nature also suffer from the same destiny.

Without a doubt, capital is concerned about the material dimensions of the world. Natural resources are carefully and economically treated, insofar as they go into the valorization process, because their value must be transferred to new products without any loss.[73] "Economy" of constant capital is in this sense an immanent tendency of the capitalist mode of production, including today's popular idea of green capitalism, which is based on reduction of waste and recycling. Capitalist economies are "*economies in the creation of waste, i.e., reduction of refuse to a minimum*, and the maximum direct *exploitation of all the raw and ancillary materials that enter the production process*."[74] However, it is wrong to conclude from this description that according to Marx "this strong force will ultimately lead to a reduction of the production of waste by-products to zero."[75] Marx is neither so naïve nor does he believe that such a tendency is truly ecological. Recycling only occurs to the extent that it lowers production costs. Sustainable production is not an objective of these economies in the employment of capital. Insofar as massive commodity production and the squandering of free forces of nature continue under the capitalist system, there is no convincing reason to believe that capitalist production will become sustainable one day through economies of constant capital. Rather, with the development of productive forces under capitalism, the universal extravagant use of the forces of nature expands as capital pursues creating a "system of general utility" with lower costs.

Marx's ecological critique shows that a certain use value of nature is deeply modified under capitalism in favor of valorization, and that this elasticity of nature is the reason for capital's intensive and extensive exploitation of nature. A number of anti-Marxists contend that Marx believed that ecological crises arise out of a human inability to sufficiently master nature, which will be overcome with the future development of the forces of production. They thus reject what they suppose to be Marx's anthropocentric and Promethean demand for the absolute mastery over nature as fatally unecological.[76] However, this type of critique misses Marx's theory of reification. The cause of modern ecological crises is not the insufficient level of technological development but *economic form determinations of the transhistorical process of metabolic interchange between humans and nature.*

The problem of capitalism's disturbance of natural metabolism cannot thus be resolved through an augmentation of productive forces. To the contrary, the situation often gets even worse because the capitalist form of technological and scientific development for the sake of attaining more profit continues to neglect the universal metabolism of nature. Capital's drive to exploit natural forces is "boundless" because these forces function as free or cost-minimizing factors in production. However, natural forces and resources are "limited," so the disturbance of the ecosystem arises out of the contradiction between nature and capital. In this context, Marx does not simply claim that humanity destroys the environment. Rather, his "materialist method" investigates how the reified movement of capital reorganizes the transhistorical metabolism between humans and nature and negates the fundamental material condition for sustainable human development. Accordingly, Marx's socialist project demands the rehabilitation of the humans-nature relationship through the restriction and finally the transcendence of the alien force of reification.

The capitalist tendency to degrade nature is derived from the law of commodity exchange. Capital pays for value as the objectification of abstract labor and not for social and natural forces that do not enter into the valorization process—though it fully appropriates the surplus products that they produce. Moreover, capital ignores costs that are necessary for the recovery of natural power after every use. Those costs that natural power requires due to its material characteristics are not reflected in the value of a commodity because value only expresses the expenditure of abstract human labor. Capital follows the logic of equivalent commodity exchange and justifies its own behavior. This discrepancy between "commodity value" and "natural properties" clearly indicates the unecological character of social production mediated by value.[77] As capital without compulsion does not take any action against the destruction of workers' lives, it is also indifferent to various destructive consequences in nature because, according to its logic of equivalent commodity exchange, its procedure is fully justified in that it pays for every single value. This fact clearly shows that value cannot be an effective criterion for sustainable production.

Even if the recovery of the original condition after capital's extravagant use of natural resources costs a lot more in the future, capital cannot give up its freeloading, for the "elasticity of capital" is dependent on the elasticity of nature. Even if capital does not pay the costs for maintaining natural resources, these resources will not be exhausted immediately. Neither water contamination nor massive carbon dioxide emissions directly cause a crisis for capitalism. Rather, capital profits from this: through extensive and intensive appropriation of nature, capital not only increases productive forces but also counteracts any tendency for the rate of profit to fall. It attempts to compensate for this tendency with the mass production of cheaper commodities and with a usage of cheaper natural resources. However, these countermeasures only impose more burdens upon nature, and it is clear that these countermeasures cannot last forever. There is a material limitation for the capitalist squeezing the forces of nature, just as workers cannot avoid rapid physical and mental degradation under an excessive extension of the working day.

Remarkably, Marx in his later economic manuscripts pointed to cases where natural forces can no longer serve the valorization process "freely" because of their exhaustion:

> The quantity of productive force of labor can increase in order to obtain the same or even decreasing produce, so that this increase of labor's productive force serves only as compensation of decreasing natural conditions of productivity—and even this compensation may be insufficient—as seen in certain cases of agriculture, extractive industry etc.[78]

Marx was thus aware of those cases where the profit rate sinks as a result of the increasing costs of the floating part of constant capital. Consequently, capitalist production tries desperately to discover new sources and technological methods on a global scale in order to counter the falling rate of profit. Or it tries to produce a greater mass of commodities in order to compensate for a falling rate of profit with a larger *magnitude* of profit. As a result, capital undermines its own material foundation even more rapidly, because individual capitalists are forced to accumulate at an accelerating rate to secure such an increase in the magnitude of profit.[79]

Forced by economic competition, capital still does not hesitate to exploit nature ever more extensively and intensively without calculating the additional burdens of the ecosystem. Individual capitalists in this profit-driven society are not able to stop the destruction of nature; they must act with a popular motto of *Après moi le déluge*. Against this situation, Marx's socialism envisions an ecological struggle against capital. Ecosocialist strategy needs to aim at the construction of a sustainable humans-nature relationship through the restriction of reification. Otherwise, the capitalist development of productive forces only deepens the fundamental contradiction on an increasing scale:

> The more the productivity of labor increases, the more the working day can be shortened, and the more the working day is shortened, the more the intensity of labor can increase. From the point of view of society the productivity of labor also grows when economies are made in its use. This implies not only economizing on the means of production, but also avoiding all useless labor. The capitalist mode of production, while it enforces economy in each individual business, also begets, by its anarchic system of competition, the most outrageous squandering of labor-power and of the social means of production, not to mention the creation of a vast number of functions at present indispensable, but in themselves superfluous.[80]

In contrast to a popular claim that Marx was overly optimistic regarding the progressive character of capitalism, we find that he did not actually praise economizing on the means of production and labor under capitalist production. This is because such economizing only takes places for the sake of attaining greater profit. On the contrary, Marx emphasized that the capitalist development of production inevitably squanders the forces of labor and nature under its "anarchic system of competition."[81] Despite the reduction of necessary labor time as a result of increasing productivity, the entire labor time will not be reduced in capitalism, but on the contrary is intensified and even extended in order to produce more surplus value. In addition, the unorganized system of production requires various mediating "superfluous" expenditures such as those devoted to accountants and investors, who also demand extra consumption of labor power and natural resources. Capitalist production is driven toward the mass production of products that often do not find any effective demand, the inevitable result of anarchistic competition, so that a vast amount of commodities must be immediately discarded as garbage. On the social level, this anarchic development of productivity annuls the trivial economizing attempted by individual capitalists.

The capitalist mode of production must produce with its incessantly increasing productivity an enormous quantity of use values, which presupposes corresponding measureless desires for the realization of surplus values that squanders them. Under mass production the social use values multiply in various spheres, and the satisfaction of human needs becomes more and more dependent on commodity exchanges. Nonetheless, there emerges another material limitation to capital accumulation. No matter how much human desires proliferate, they are never infinite. In this material limitation there lies, in addition to the disturbance of "natural metabolism," another possibility of a disruption of "social metabolism": economic crisis due to overproduction. Economic crisis is nothing but the disturbance of material flux in the society by the economic form determination.

It has become clear that Marx, far from being optimistic about sustainable capitalist development in his theory of value, criticizes how the one-sided mediation of the metabolic interaction between humans and nature by abstract labor exhausts and desolates the forces of labor and nature. The main problem of capitalist eco-crises is not just that capitalism, as a result of wasteful mass production, will *sometime in the future* suffer from the increasing price and lack of raw materials (and a possible corresponding falling rate of profit) and will no longer efficiently satisfy human needs. Rather, the problem lies in the subjective experience of alienation, ensuring that the capitalist mode of production undermines the material foundation for sustainable human development due to the metabolic rift. Once the historical vocation of capitalism in increasing productive forces has been realized, the further development of human freedom and talents demands a transition to another stage of human history. However, as Marx argues, this transition is not an automatic one. It requires socialist theory and praxis.

At this point, it is possible to articulate a hypothesis addressing a remaining question of Marxism: Why did Marx so intensively study the natural sciences? Marx engaged in serious studies of a wide range of books in the fields of natural science, we can surmise, in order to analyze the contradictions of the material world as a result of its modifications by capital. To ground this hypothesis, the second part of this book investigates Marx's treatment of agriculture, focusing on agricultural chemistry, geology, and botany. In this context, the German agricultural chemist Justus von Liebig plays a central role.

PART II

MARX'S ECOLOGY AND THE *MARX-ENGELS-GESAMTAUSGABE*

4

Liebig and *Capital*

The productive power at mankind's disposal is immeasurable. The productivity of the soil can be increased *ad infinitum* by the application of capital, labor and science."[1] This statement, which is hardly valid today, is not from Marx's text but from the young Engels's *Outline of a Critique of Political Economy*. Yet it reflects to some extent the widespread nineteenth-century view regarding future technological and scientific development, which was supposed to dramatically increase productivity in industry and agriculture beyond given natural limits.[2]

This is why critics feel justified to attribute such a fatally flawed optimistic ideology to Marx as well. Ted Benton, one of the earliest ecosocialists, criticizes Marx's "flight from any recognition of 'natural limits'": "The blindness to natural limits already present in the industrial ideology is compounded and intensified by the overriding intentional structure, with its indifference to the concrete character of raw materials, labor *or* product."[3] This chapter puts Benton's claim into question. Analyzing Marx's theory of ground rent, which Benton surprisingly ignores despite its direct treatment of "nature" and the "soil," I will demonstrate that Marx clearly reconceptualized the problem of "natural limits" and the relevant contradictions of capitalism as his political economy deepened. Consequently, he came to envision the sustainable interaction of humans with their environment as a central practical task of a future socialist society. In the course of his theoretical development, Marx actually began to pay particular attention to "the concrete character of raw materials, labor *or* product."

Without doubt there are difficulties in reconstructing Marx's treatment of natural limits because he was not able to complete volume 3 of *Capital* during his lifetime, so it is not possible to find a final version of his analysis of agriculture in his manuscripts. In this context, it is necessary to study carefully those economic manuscripts that are now completely available in the second section of the MEGA². Marx's excerpt notebooks published in the fourth section, however, are as important as his economic manuscripts because they document a number of aspects that are not fully discussed in his economic manuscripts. In many paragraphs and footnotes to volume 3, Marx noted only a name or a comment without going into detail, and his intentions are not always clear. Though his notebooks have been marginalized in the earlier literature on *Capital*, they help in understanding what Marx would have said if he had been able to complete the final draft of *Capital*.[4] His theory of ground rent also attains a new context when taking his excerpt notebooks into account, especially in terms of a *genetic emergence* of an ecological critique of capitalism.

The central figure of our current investigation is Justus von Liebig, whose *Chemistry and Its Application to Agriculture and Physiology* (7th ed., 1862) had a great impact upon Marx's theory. While earlier research on the intellectual relationship between Marx and Liebig clearly demonstrated their ecological critique of modern agriculture, it is noteworthy that the original reason for Marx's reading of Liebig was an *economic* one.[5] It would be an exaggeration to say that Marx was ecological from the start, because there are sometimes naïve Promethean indications in his earlier texts, which are similar to the one found in Engels's quoted passage. Thus it is worth inquiring how Marx came to recognize the environmental unsustainability of the capitalist mode of production as *the* contradiction of capitalism, and to urge realizing sustainable production in the future society.

For this current investigation, Marx's analyses of the "law of diminishing returns" from different periods are useful to reconstruct the development of his view of nature. They document that Marx, as a result of deepening his natural science knowledge, consciously parted from the young Engels's myth about the infinite progress of agricultural productivity and recognized the insurmountable limitation of the natural conditions of agriculture, which must be respected in any post-capitalist society.[6] This recognition of natural limits did not, however, prompt Marx to fall into apocalyptic pessimism. Rather, he began to argue more passionately for a rational interaction with nature through the transcendence of the reified power of capital.

MARX'S THEORY OF GROUND RENT BEFORE 1865

Marx's theory of ground rent does not appear all of sudden in *Capital*; instead it has a long prehistory that begins with a reception of David Ricardo's rent theory in his polemic work against Pierre-Joseph Proudhon, *The Poverty of Philosophy*. I will first sketch out Ricardo's influential argument with a particular focus on the "law of diminishing returns," so that the significance of Marx's Ricardo reception becomes apparent.

Ricardo put forward his theory of rent in an epoch-making book, *On the Principles of Political Economy, and Taxation*, published in 1815. His analysis first abstracts from concrete reality and presupposes a linear process of land reclamation in the course of civilization, according to which, with an increase of population, the demands for food grow at the same time, so that farmers are continuously compelled to cultivate land with more and more infertile soil. Ricardo assumes that if plenty of land is available, the best land is cultivated first so as to spare extra labor and capital. With a continuous increase of the population under the development of civilization, the best lands are quickly cultivated since their availability is limited. Given the supposition that the value of all products is determined by the production under the most unfavorable conditions, Ricardo claimed that the prices of agricultural products necessarily go up in the course of the development of society, so that the owner of the better land who continues to produce with lower labor and capital can receive the deduction as differential rent.[7]

According to Ricardo, the additional investment of capital on the same lands cannot compensate the various different natural fertilities because the output does not increase proportionally to the investment but only at a decreasing rate, so that, for example, the price of corn inevitably rises in the long run:

> It often, and, indeed, commonly happens, that before No. 2, 3, 4, or 5, or the inferior lands are cultivated, capital can be employed more productively on those lands which are already in cultivation. It may perhaps be found, that by doubling the original capital employed on No. 1, though the produce will not be doubled, will not be increased by 100 quarters, it may be increased by eighty-five quarters, and that this quantity exceeds what could be obtained by employing the same capital, on land No. 3.[8]

Edward West, whom Marx also regards as one of the first economists to theorize on differential rent, argues in the same way in his *Essay on the Application of Capital to Land*, published in 1815:

> Thus, suppose any quantity of land such that 100*l.*[100 English pounds] capital laid out on it would reproduce 120*l.* that is 20 per cent profit, I say that a double capital, viz. 200*l.*, would not produce 240*l.* or 20 per cent profit, but probably 230*l.* or some less sum than 240*l.* The amount of the profit would no doubt be increased, but the ratio of it at the capital would be diminished.[9]

What both Ricardo and West understand as the law of diminishing returns is that the produce of the soil cannot proportionally increase through successive capital investments. Doubling the investments does not result in the doubling of the produce, but it always brings about a smaller portion of corn, meat, milk, etc.[10]

The law of diminishing returns purports to describe, on the one hand, the constant retreat toward less fertile soils, and on the other, the diminishing production from the soil as a result of successive capital investments on the same land. Both factors increase differential rent for the owner of better lands, who continues to attain the output at the same costs but sells it at a higher price. This view, advocated by Ricardo and West, found wide acceptance at the time, and this is the way "bourgeois economists" dealt with the idea of natural limits to capital, which industrial development cannot overcome.[11] It is still open whether and how far this presupposition of "natural limits" and "the law" on an abstract level is adequate for the explanation of ground rent in capitalist society. Marx struggled with this problem for quite a long time.

In *The Poverty of Philosophy*, published in 1847, Marx principally accepted the mechanism of Ricardo's differential rent theory, arguing similarly that the owners of produce of fruitful soils can attain a surplus due to the price difference compared with production under unfavorable conditions. At the same time, Marx attempted to diverge from Ricardo's law. He summarized Ricardo's argument:

> If one could always have at one's disposal plots of land of the same degree of fertility; if one could, as in manufacturing industry, have recourse continually to cheaper and more productive machines, or if the subsequent outlays of capital produced as much as the first, then the price of agricultural products would be determined by the cost price of commodities produced by the best instruments of

production, as we have seen with the price of manufactured products. But from this moment rent would have disappeared also.[12]

Marx correctly summarized Ricardo's presupposition that in reality
both the availability of good lands and the increase of agricultural productivity through successive capital investments are limited, so that the
insurmountable differences in soil fertility continue to offer the foundation for the category of "ground rent."

Marx agreed with Ricardo only in terms of the mechanism of ground
rent, but not his supposition of diminishing returns. Marx's critique of
"bourgeois economy" rejects its fetishistic, ahistorical treatment of economic categories, including ground rent. At the end of the section on
ground rent, Marx parted from Ricardo's presupposition, pointing to the
possibility of a great improvement in soil productivity:

> Wherein consists, in general, any improvement, whether in agricul-
> ture or in manufacture? In producing more with the same labor; in
> producing as much, or even more, with less labor. Thanks to these
> improvements, the farmer is spared from using a greater amount of
> labor for a relatively smaller product. He has no need, therefore, to
> resort to inferior soils, and installments of capital applied succes-
> sively to the same soil remain equally productive.[13]

Ground rent should *diminish* in the course of the development of
civilization in contrast to Ricardo's assumption, due to progress in agriculture. The material foundation of rent could even disappear in the future
if private property is abolished and if "improvements" brought about
by the free application of modern natural sciences, such as chemistry
and geology, and of technology that can increase agricultural productivity *proportionally*. Moreover, agricultural productivity can increase to
such an extent that the difference of fertility among various lands can be
equalized, so that ground rent tends continuously to diminish.

Marx's remark that "installments of capital applied successively to
the same soil remain equally productive" shares the optimistic opinion
about the possibility of infinite improvements of agricultural productivity with young Engels. Without the need "to resort to inferior soils," it is
possible to receive ground rent in relation to the *proportional* improvements of soil fertility.

Marx comes back to the same point in his letter to Engels of January
7, 1851, criticizing Ricardo's theory of ground rent once again. Marx

argues that Ricardo's understanding must not be completely rejected, but requires some modifications so that Ricardo's law of differential rent "*still holds good*" despite his critique. Marx's critique still supports the refutation of the law of diminishing returns, which contradicts "historical facts": "The main point of all this is to adjust the law of rent to progress in fertility in agriculture generally, this being the only way, firstly, to explain the historical facts."[14] In contrast to Ricardo's ahistorical abstraction, Marx's analysis tries to find empirical ground characterized by the "progress" of agriculture. He argues that Ricardo's scheme would explain increasing rent in the last fifty years with the cultivation of less fertile soils due to increasing demands of agricultural produce. However, according to Marx, Ricardo's assumption of diminishing fertility is not necessary. The increase of rent can take place even if agricultural produce becomes cheaper. This is because more products are produced thanks to the development of technology, and the sum total of rents becomes bigger than before.[15] With the general improvement of the land, it is possible, Marx argues, that more lands are cultivated for the purpose of attaining ground rent, so the sum total of rent increases, while, *contra* Ricardo, the price of corn continuously diminishes thanks to technological development.

At the end of the letter to Engels, Marx writes:

> As you know, the real joke where rent is concerned is that it is generated by evening out the price for the resultants of varying production costs, but that this law of market price is nothing other than the law of bourgeois competition. Even after the elimination of bourgeois production, however, there remains the snag that the soil would become relatively more infertile, that, with the same amount of labor, successively less would be achieved, although the best land would no longer, as under bourgeois rule, yield as dear a product as the poorest. The foregoing would do away with this objection.[16]

Marx tells Engels why Ricardo's law of diminishing returns needs to be rejected; that is, he is worried that if Ricardo's presupposition is correct, the future socialist society would be threatened by the problem of insufficient means of subsistence forever, and Malthus's theory of absolute overpopulation would prove correct. Marx believes that he succeeded in removing this concern after proving the increase of ground rent derived precisely out of a historical tendency of general improvement of the land through successive capital investment. While this demonstration does not directly refute the law of diminishing returns, in claiming to have refuted the objection that "the soil would become relatively more infertile, that, with the same amount of labor, successively less would be achieved," Marx still assumes that successive capital investment should be able to realize a *proportional* increase in agricultural productivity. Engels reacts positively to this letter, and his reaction relieves Marx.

As shown, some of the main aspects of Marx's theory of differential ground rent were already existent in the 1850s. Yet another theoretical development came at the beginning of the 1860s when Marx once again intensively engaged with Ricardo's ground rent theory, in the *Economic Manuscripts 1861–63*. First of all, in contrast to Ricardo's theory, Marx formulated the theory of rent in such a way that increasing as well as decreasing tendencies of agricultural development in the history can be analyzed with *one* law. He tried to provide a proof for "the incorrectness of the Ricardian concept that differential rent *depends* on the diminishing productivity of labor, on the movement from the more productive mine or land to the less productive. It is just as compatible with the *reverse* process and hence with the growing productivity of labor."[17] Thus, this time, Marx carefully went into concrete calculations of differential rent so that it can be flexibly extended and generalized to include those cases that start with less fertile soils and proceed to more fertile ones with increasing productivity of labor.

Furthermore, Marx formulated the possibility of "absolute land rent," which Ricardo did not deal with at all. Marx criticized Ricardo for only considering the difference of land fertility as the source of ground rent. However, there exists, argued Marx, another source. Because of its backwardness and the natural conditions that surround it, the "organic composition of capital," that is, the proportion of value between constant and variable capital (c/v) determined by the technological composition of capital, is lower in agriculture than in industrial branches. So, by selling agricultural products, it is possible to attain higher profit than the social average. Due to the natural limitations in the amount of disposable land, capital, seeking higher profit, cannot freely move from other production branches to agriculture. There is limited competition in agriculture, which allows the proprietor of the land to continue appropriating a part of surplus value as surplus profit without worrying about the typical adjustment to production price. Marx argued that surplus profit that arises from the difference of value and production prices constitutes the source of absolute rent.[18]

After discussing the two forms of ground rent, Marx outlined his plan for section 3, "Capital and Profit," which in terms of content largely corresponds to the order of volume 3 of *Capital*:

1) Conversion of surplus value into profit. Rate of profit as distinguished from rate of surplus value. 2) Conversion of profit into average profit. Formation of the general rate of profit. Transformation of values into prices of production. 3) Adam Smith's and Ricardo's theories on profit and prices of production. 4) *Rent.* (Illustration of the difference between value and price of production.) 5) History of the so-called Ricardian law of rent. 6) Law of the fall of the rate of profit. Adam Smith, Ricardo, Carey. . . .[19]

In this note, it is possible to see clearly the task of Marx's theory of ground rent: "Illustration of the difference between value and price of production." The theory of ground rent does not possess an independent character similar to that of the category "profit rate," but instead plays a secondary role because it only functions as an example for illustrating the difference between "value" and "price of production," which Ricardo failed to recognize. Accordingly, it is the category of "absolute rent" that Marx used as his primary category. In Marx's plan of 1861–63 for volume 3 of *Capital*, the theory of differential rent is theoretically subordinated to absolute rent, as he intended to describe it simply as the "history" of an economic category. The theoretical preeminence of the theory of absolute rent is understandable because it is this category that demonstrates Marx's original insight, contrasting with Ricardo, which is based on his distinction of "surplus value" from "profit" and "value" from "price of production."

But this plan is not identical with the one that Marx wrote down in his manuscript of 1864–65. Now the construction of the chapter on ground rent has a different outlook:

A1. The *concept of differential rent* as such. The example of waterpower. Then the transition to agricultural rent proper.
A2. *Differential rent I*, arising from the varying fertility of different tracts of land.
A3. *Differential rent II*, arising from successive capital investments on the same land. This should be *divided further* into:
    (a) differential rent with the *price of production stationary,*
    (b) differential rent with the *price of production falling,*
    (c) differential rent with the *price of production rising,* and

(d) *the transformation of surplus profit into rent.*
A4. The influence of this rent on the *rate of profit.*

B. *Absolute rent*
C. *The price of land.*
D. *Final considerations on ground-rent.*[20]

Notably, in the manuscript, rent theory becomes an independent chapter like the chapter on "profit." It no longer aims at an exemplary "illustration" of profit theory. In this manuscript, Marx first began to write the section on absolute rent. He then wrote the section on differential rent, but he ended up writing many more pages (80 printed pages in the MEGA[2] volume). After a new examination, the theory of differential rent appears to attain a more important position than absolute rent in the manuscript for volume 3 of *Capital.*

Since this later plan for the ground rent theory was not final, it is not certain whether Marx would have followed it in volume 3 of *Capital.* Yet, it is at least in the order that Engels followed more or less during his editorial work. This newer plan indicates that Marx was at the time prompted to develop the theory of differential rent in much more detail, so that absolute rent now seems to possess a secondary importance. The reason for this modification is to be found in the manuscript itself, and, in comparing it with that of 1861–63, it is noticeable that Marx now added a new subsection in the chapter on differential rent: "*Differential rent II*, arising from successive capital investments on the same land." Indeed, there is a new discussion on the "law of diminishing returns" and a new treatment of natural fertility in the manuscript. This is a result of Marx's reception of Liebig's theory.

As seen above, in terms of the "successive capital investments on the same land," Marx, like Engels in the 1840s and 1850s, and in his *Poverty of Philosophy* and letters, assumed the proportional increase of agricultural productivity. In the economic manuscripts of the 1860s, it is still possible to find this earlier assumption, as observed in the table dealing with two cases, A and B, where double capital investments accordingly produce the proportionally increased amount of crops. I have reproduced a shorter version of the table with relevant numbers (see Table 1, p.151).[21]

The land "II" produces proportionally to the successive capital investments. Furthermore Marx provided various calculations in his *Economic Manuscripts of 1861–63*, but he did not treat the cases with diminishing returns under successive capital investments. However,

Marx in his *Economic Manuscript of 1864–1865* reflected upon this theoretical blind spot.

Moreover, Marx anticipated in his *Economic Manuscripts of 1861–63*
that, due to the future capital intensification in agriculture associated
with the transition to socialism, agricultural production would increase
much faster, and that the disproportion of the development between
industry and agriculture would cease to exist:

> Furthermore, it [Marx's modification of the Ricardian rent theory]
> does away with the superstructure, which with Ricardo himself was
> anyhow only arbitrary and not necessary for his presentation, namely,
> that the agricultural industry becomes gradually less productive; it
> admits on the contrary that it becomes more productive. Only on the
> bourgeois basis is agriculture *relatively less productive*, or slower to
> develop the productive forces of labor, than industry.[22]

Marx then continues to argue:

> But when industry reaches a certain level the disproportion must
> diminish; in other words, productivity in agriculture must increase
> relatively more rapidly than in industry. This requires: 1) The
> replacement of the easygoing farmer by the businessman, the farm-
> ing capitalist; transformation of the husband-man into a pure wage
> laborer; large-scale agriculture, i.e., with concentrated capitals. 2) In
> particular, however: Mechanics, the really scientific basis of large-
> scale industry, had reached a certain degree of perfection during
> the eighteenth century. The development of chemistry, geology and
> physiology, the sciences that *directly* form the specific basis of agri-
> culture rather than of industry, does not take place till the nineteenth
> century and especially the later decades.[23]

The rapid increase of agricultural productivity through intensification by means of successive capital investment and the application
of natural sciences is the reason why absolute rent could disappear in
the future due to the increase of the organic composition of capital in
agriculture up to the level of industry.[24] Marx's argument sounds as if
agricultural production could increase its productivity with the application of modern natural sciences and technologies, as in industrial
production, without much difference. It is not clearly discernible how
much Marx still believed in the possibility of the proportional increase

Table 1.

A	Capital	No. of tons	Total value	Market value per ton
I	100	60	120	2
II	100	65	130	2
III	100	75	150	
Total	300	200	400	

B	Capital	No. of tons	Total value	Market value per ton
II	50	32½	60	$1=1l$ 16 $^{12}/_{13}$s.
III	100	75	$138^6/_{13}$	$1=1l$ 16 $^{12}/_{13}$s.
IV	100	95½	$170^{10}/_{13}$	$1=1l$ 16 $^{12}/_{13}$s.
Total	250	200	369	

of productivity with successive capital investments, but he nonetheless clearly propagated the possibility of a general rapid improvement of agricultural productivity in the future society in such a way that is incompatible with Ricardo's ahistorical abstract treatment of the law of diminishing returns. In this sense, Marx's critique does not yet take the problem of soil exhaustion and scarcity of natural resources in agriculture and in extractive industry seriously enough, because it supposes that such a problem only occurs in capitalism. Marx believed that this problem would be overcome in socialism *through the free development of productivity in the future.*[25]

In regard to the problem of natural limits in Marx's theory, Michael Perelman argues that Marx, as a result of the cotton crisis of 1863, became aware of the importance of natural resource scarcity under the increasing demands for circulating capital together with fixed capital, but Marx did not explicitly emphasize this point because he was afraid that he would be identified with Malthusianism, one of his main theoretical enemies.[26] This is an interesting hypothesis, but it is misleading to argue that Marx fled from this problem and suppressed this dimension of scarcity in his critique of political economy. In fact, Marx changed his understanding of the law of diminishing returns through his study of Liebig's agricultural chemistry in 1865–66. He remained convinced of the overall theoretical validity of his own theory of ground rent, but as a result of his reception of newer natural sciences Marx refuted the ungrounded assumption of classical political economy from a new perspective and began a more nuanced treatment of the problem of natural limits.

LIEBIG'S RECOGNITION OF NATURAL LIMITS

In 1865, Marx returned to studying natural sciences in order to bestow a more up-to-date scientific foundation for his own investigation of ground rent. After reading various books and writing his manuscript for volume 3 of *Capital*, Marx told Engels, in a letter of February 13, 1866, about his fascination with the rapid development of chemistry:

> As far as this "damned" book [*Capital*] is concerned, the position now is: it was *ready* at the end of December. The treatise on ground rent alone, the penultimate chapter, is in its present form almost long enough to be a book in itself. I have been going to the Museum in the daytime and writing at night. I had to plough through the new agricultural chemistry in Germany, in particular Liebig and Schönbein, which is more important for this matter than all the economists put together, as well as the enormous amount of material that the French have produced since I last dealt with this point. I concluded my theoretical investigation of ground rent two years ago. And a great deal had been achieved, especially in the period since then, fully confirming my theory.[27]

One immediately notices a surprisingly positive evaluation that Liebig, together with Schönbein, is "more important . . . than all the economists put together." Marx said that his theoretical investigation of ground rent was already "concluded" two years ahead in the *Economic Manuscripts of 1861–63*, but he also admitted that in the last two years "a great deal has been achieved." It was a positive progress, "confirming" Marx's theory. It is useful now to examine his notebooks because they will show how this new progress of agricultural chemistry confirmed and deepened his theory of ground rent.

In terms of Marx's reception of Liebig, it is important to note that, despite his remark about the "confirmation" of his own theory by recent developments in chemistry, he seems to correct his earlier thesis in the economic manuscript for volume 3 of *Capital* when he mentions the necessity to refer to Liebig in one paragraph and reminds himself of the importance of dealing with successive capital investment in a different manner than in the past: "*On the declining productivity of the soil when successive capital investments are made.* Liebig should be consulted on this question. We have seen that successive declines in surplus productivity always increase the rent per acre when the price of production is constant, and that the rent may increase even when the price is falling."[28] In this remark, Marx suddenly seems to accept the opposite idea that agricultural produce cannot continue to increase as industry does but *decreases* with successive capital investments. Does Marx accept the law of diminishing returns?

This remark is all the more interesting (though confusing as well) because Marx in another passage in volume 1 of *Capital* seems to criticize Liebig precisely in terms of the law of diminishing returns. Marx expresses his reservation toward Liebig after he praises his "immortal merits" in agricultural chemistry:

> It is, however, to be regretted that he ventures quite at random on such assertions as the following: "By greater pulverizing and more frequent ploughing, the circulation of air in the interior of porous soil is aided, and the surface exposed to the action of the atmosphere is increased and renewed; but it is easily seen that the increased yield of the land cannot be proportional to the labor spent on that land, but increases in a much smaller proportion. This law," adds Liebig, "was first enunciated by John Stuart Mill in his *Principles of Political Economy*, Vol. 1. p. 17, as follows: 'That the produce of land increases, *caeteris paribus*, in a diminishing ratio to the increase of the laborers employed' (Mill here reproduces the law formulated by the Ricardian school in an erroneous form, for since the advance of agriculture in England was accompanied by a 'decrease of the laborers employed,' this law, although discovered in, and applied to, England, could have no application in that country) 'is the universal law of agricultural industry.' This is very remarkable, since Mill was ignorant of the reason for this law" (Liebig, op. cit., Vol. 1, p. 143, and note).[29]

Liebig as a chemist is not so familiar with the history of political economy. As Marx comments, it is "really droll" that Liebig recognizes John Stuart Mill as the discoverer of the law of diminishing returns.[30] What is so regretful for Marx is the danger that Liebig's "random" remark raises a wrong impression, as if he confirmed the law of the Ricardian school about the non-proportional relationship between labor and the yield of the soil. In this passage, Marx still seems to reject the law of diminishing returns and to condemn Liebig's acceptance of the Ricardian view.

Confronted with those two seemingly contradictory passages from volume 1 and 3 of *Capital*, some earlier literature pointed out that Marx changed his opinion and finally and correctly accepted the law of diminishing returns in volume 3, as Joseph Esslen argued: "However, it looks as if Karl Marx had later changed his view."[31] If one looks at the history of *Capital* more carefully, this speculation is hardly plausible because Marx worked again on volume 1 of *Capital* for publication after writing the manuscript for volume 3, adding the section on "Large-Scale Industry and Modern Agriculture," in which he referred to Liebig to integrate his newest findings into the published work. So it is misleading to point to a theoretical modification within *Capital*. When Marx refers to Liebig twice on the same theme, it is to find his theoretical consistency.

In this context, Liebig's "law of replenishment" (*Gesetz des Ersatzes*) plays an important role. His main contribution in *Agricultural Chemistry* lies in the first systematic demonstration of the role of organic *and* inorganic soil constituent components for the healthy growth of plants. Liebig convincingly illustrates that a one-sided input of organic substances or nitrogen alone cannot guarantee a maximal amount of crop when other essential soil nutrients are missing. So Liebig claims that *all* essential nutrients, including inorganic substances, must be existent in the soil with more than a minimum amount—"law of the minimum." Liebig's "theory of mineral nutrition" here puts a particular importance on inorganic substances, for in contrast to organic materials, which plants can directly and continuously assimilate through atmosphere and rain, inorganic substances in the soil can be provided only to a limited extent, so that their loss in the soil must be heavily limited. To grow crops successfully and sustainably, it is absolutely necessary to constantly return to the soil those mineral substances that are taken away by plants in order to minimize their loss. As the "law of replenishment," Liebig formulates the necessity to give back nutrients and postulates a "full replenishment of all plant compounds taken from the soil by harvested crops" as the main proposition of his rational agriculture.[32] In this way, Liebig insists on the importance of the undisrupted cycle of organic and inorganic materials as the basic principle of sustainable production.

In terms of the law of diminishing returns, however, Liebig shows an ambivalence, which, interestingly, is *not* reflected in Marx's notebook, where Marx intentionally focuses on one aspect but neglects the other. Marx's excerpts from Liebig's *Agricultural Chemistry* reveal his theoretical interest.

Though Liebig's fame has been recently rehabilitated, primarily due to his critique of the "robbery system" of agriculture that neglects the law of replenishment, he shared, at least until the 1850s, a popular optimistic idea of the rapid and boundless progress of agriculture, which appeared plausible with the introduction of machinery and chemical fertilizer. Even before Liebig, James Anderson, who also influenced Marx as a defender of the ideal of agricultural development and as the founder of the theory of differential ground rent, wrote in an optimistic manner about the "proportional" increase of agricultural productivity:

> The melioration of the soil must ever be proportioned to the means that are used to augment its productiveness. . . . Under skillful management, the degree of melioration will be *proportioned to* the labor that is bestowed upon the soil. . . . In other words, the productiveness of the soil will be *proportioned to* the number of persons who are employed in active labor upon the soil, and the economy with which they conduct their operations.[33]

Contrary to Malthus's famous assumption about the "arithmetical" increase of agricultural productivity, Anderson proposed, so to speak, a "geometrical" model. When such an optimistic evaluation of the agricultural revolution was dominant, not only among practical farmers but also among scholars and appeared to reflect the actual development, it is fully understandable that the young Marx and Engels attempted to refute the law of diminishing returns by pointing to the possibility of a proportional increase in agricultural productivity.

Liebig underscored, with the same modernist spirit of Anderson, the potentiality of the soil proportionally to increase with the mineral substances contained in the soil. For example, he argued in the sixth edition of *Agricultural Chemistry* (1846):

> Hence it is quite certain, that in our fields, the amount of nitrogen in the crops is not at all in proportion to the quantity supplied in the manure. . . . The crops on a field diminish or increase in exact proportion to the diminution or increase of the mineral substances conveyed to it in manure.[34]

Also, John Bennet Lawes, whose "theory of nitrogen" in contrast to Liebig's "theory of mineral nutrition" stressed the primary importance of nitrogen for ample plant growth, did not doubt the increase of agricultural productivity in exact proportion to the quantity of nitrogen added to the soil:

The various contradictory results obtained by the application of mineral manures to wheat are completely accounted for, when it is known that they only increase the produce *in proportion to the available azotized matter* existing in the soil.[35]

In the famous debates between Liebig's mineral theory and Lawes's nitrogen theory, their main difference concerned which soil constituent components can bring about a "proportional" increase of crops, and not about whether such an increase would be possible.

However, in the seventh edition of *Agricultural Chemistry* published in 1862, Liebig put forward another view. He recognized that there are natural limits to agricultural improvements, particularly due to the finite amount of available mineral nutrients in the soil and the finite absorption ability of roots and leaves. The latter aspect is one of the most important themes that interested Marx, as observed in his excerpt notebooks. Liebig's book explicates the relationship between the intensification of agriculture and diminishing crops. In a paragraph to which Marx referred in a footnote in *Capital,* quoted above, Liebig wrote:

A *double amount of labor* cannot insure the *availability of twice the material nutrients* that ordinary tillage would have provided in a given amount of time. The *quantity of these material soil constituents is not equal in all fields,* and *even in those fields where there is sufficient supply* their transformation into an immediately effective form is *not directly dependent on labor* but on external agencies, which like *the air are limited in their oxygen and carbonic acid contents,* and which, in accordance with their quantity, must be increased in the same proportion as the increase of labor if the latter is to bring about a *proportionally* useful result.[36]

Marx documents Liebig's claim in his notebook, indicating that the intensification of agriculture through successive capital investments does not bring about a proportional increase of crops because the speed of chemical reaction and the sum total of available nutrients in the soil are always limited by nature. Liebig admitted that double labor cannot result in a double amount of crops. It is, however, not because of an abstract universal law of diminishing returns but because of a physiological limitation that cannot be overcome through chemical fertilizer or soil irrigation.

Despite various attempts for soil improvement, the limitation to increase agricultural productivity becomes tangible, for in agricultural production it is not only human labor but the "atmosphere," including air, light, and warmth, that affects the soil and plants. These effects of nature are as important as inorganic substances in the soil, as Liebig implicitly admitted in responding to critics. Irrigation, drainage, and other physical improvements increase crops by facilitating air circulation in layers of soil, so carbon dioxide and oxygen can more effectively react on soil components. If crops are proportionally increased with the amount of chemical mineral or azotized fertilizer, the physical aspects need to be proportionally increased as well because both chemical and physical elements constitute the essential conditions of plant growth. It is, however, obvious that these cannot always provide necessary nutrients in exact proportion to labor and capital because the weathering of the soil and the absorption ability of roots and leaves is physiologically restricted.

Marx documented the above passage from *Agricultural Chemistry* in his notebook and integrated it into *Capital*, not incidentally. In fact, it is this aspect on which Marx focused during his reading of Liebig in 1865–66. Here marginal additions, which highlight important passages in Marx's notebooks, turn out to be very useful. After he carefully made excerpts from Liebig's *Agricultural Chemistry*, which amounts to more than a thousand pages, he added a number of lines in margins of the notebook with pencil for the purpose of classifications and highlighting for future use. A thematic commonality of those lines indicate a striking fact: Marx was interested in the results of experiments that report a *nonproportional* increase of the soil productivity.

In a passage in volume 2 of *Agricultural Chemistry*, Liebig summarized an experiment conducted in a botanical garden in Munich by Nägeli and Zoeller to demonstrate the effects of absorption by plant roots of dissoluble material. They filled pots with various mixtures of peat powder, in which they had mixed different quantities of nutrient salts. The experiment showed that this artificial soil became fertile after the addition of the mineral salts, which made the nutrient absorbed in the peat powder dissoluble to water and thus assimilable to plants as their nutrients.[37] In regard to this experiment, Marx documented Liebig's concluding remarks and bestowed a vertical line to highlight its importance:

The larger amount of crops in the relatively poorer soil demonstrates that only the soil surface that contains nutrient matter is effective and that the productive power of a soil is not proportional to the quantity of nutrient matter detected by chemical analysis.[38]

It is true that the soil with rich nutrients provided more seeds, but Liebig admitted that the crops did not increase in exact proportion to the mineral substances in the soil, but the soil with less mineral nutrients provided more crops than its chemical analysis had expected.

Marx paid attention to another passage, adding another vertical line to emphasize it:

> The abundance or the lack of nutrient matter in the soil exerts influence upon the *amount* and *weight* of seeds produced, but it is not *proportional to elements existent in the soil.* . . . Deviations in the percentage of potash, lime and magnesia . . . are often discernible in all kinds of plants, and like tobacco, wine and clover, lime can be replaced by potash and vice versa. In this case, for example, a decrease of potash . . . corresponds to the increase in the amount of lime and vice versa etc.[39]

Here Marx again reveals that he is interested in learning about the *non-proportional* increase of soil productivity. And it is exactly this passage that he was thinking about when he later referred to the case of diminishing returns under successive capital investments in volume 3 of *Capital*, though he did not go into details there.

In the context of the law of diminishing returns, one sees the reason why Liebig's *Agricultural Chemistry* was of great importance for Marx's project. It is certainly possible that crops increase with both an artificial introduction of inorganic nutrients (such as bone, guano, and chemical fertilizer) and mechanical operations on the soil, which promote the process of weathering through air and warmth. However, as Liebig argued, it is not possible to aim at an infinite increase of crops on the same land. At one point, the soil will not produce more, even if on other lands there are still possibilities for proportional increases. This limit of nature varies according to the characteristics of the soil, and Liebig argued that this is why his theory of chemical analysis of the soil is highly important for agricultural practice.

Marx's focus on this point becomes more striking because Liebig's statements about the non-proportional increase of crops in this new edition of *Agricultural Chemistry* show a certain ambivalence or even "inconsistency" compared with earlier editions.[40] Liebig thus did not emphasize that he changed his earlier view. Marx, however, did not overlook this hidden modification and documented it, confirming his strong interest in this topic. Even if Liebig discussed the problem marginally,

Marx cautiously integrated the point into his political economy in order to oppose a scientific explanation to the ungrounded supposition of the Ricardian school.

What Marx problematized in volume 1 of *Capital* becomes clearer when he said it was to be "regretted" that Liebig believed he had found an affinity between his theory and Mill's though the chemist without a doubt knew that of which Mill was "ignorant." The difference between Liebig and Mill should be apparent; the latter's *Principles of Political Economy* simply repeated the famous "dogma" of the Ricardian school, after the law of diminishing returns was "vulgarized" by his father, John Stuart Mill:

> Apart from Liebig's incorrect interpretation of the word "labor," a word he used in quite a different sense from that adopted by political economy, it is, in any case, "very remarkable" that he should make John Stuart Mill the first proponent of a theory which James Anderson was the first to publish, in the days of Adam Smith, and which was repeated in various works down to the beginning of the nineteenth century; a theory which Malthus, that master in plagiarism (his whole population theory is a shameless plagiarism), appropriated in 1815 which West developed at the same time and independently of Anderson; which in the year 1817 was linked by Ricardo with the general theory of value, then made the rounds of the world as Ricardo's theory and in 1820 was vulgarized by James Mill, the father of John Stuart Mill; and which was finally reproduced by John Stuart Mill and others as a dogma already quite commonplace, and known to every schoolboy. It is undeniable that the second Mill owes his certainly "remarkable" authority almost entirely to such mistaken attributions.[41]

Marx argued that Mill's claim only distorted the old law into a wrong statement as if a population engaged with agriculture would increase under industrialization. Mill's fallacious thesis could not scientifically ground the phenomenon of diminishing returns, but he presupposed Ricardo's "dogma" as given. Liebig's incorrect understanding in the sphere of political economy is a matter of regret because his *scientific* analysis has a basis entirely independent from the Ricardian theory and shows the material mechanism of decreasing agricultural productivity. There lies Liebig's unique merit compared to other modern political economists.[42]

Thanks to Liebig's *Agricultural Chemistry*, the discursive constellation around the law of diminishing returns receives a new shape. Liebig
provided a scientific explanation of the "actual natural causes for the
exhaustion of the land, which incidentally were unknown to *any* of the
economists who wrote about differential rent, on account of the back-
ward state of agricultural chemistry in their time."[43] Thus, in the earlier
debates, not only the defenders of the law of diminishing returns but
also its critics tended to presuppose a historical tendency of agricultural development. Neither Ricardo nor West, nor Malthus, provided a
chemical and physiological proof in terms of why crops must gradually
sink with successive capital investments. Resorting to James Anderson
and Arthur Young, the critics of the law, including the young Marx and
Henry Charles Carey, also insisted without convincing reasons that a
further "proportional" development on the same land should be possible
when technological progress continues rapidly enough. Liebig proved
that both of the arguments are only *hypothetical*, and without scientific
basis.[44]

In 1865, Marx clearly recognized the shortcomings of the debate on
the limitations of agricultural productivity. After he found a convincing explanation by a scientist for diminishing crop returns to successive
increases in capital, it became possible for Marx to treat the problem of
diminishing productivity in detail in his theory of ground rent without
falling prey to what Perelman calls Marx's fear of Malthusianism. This
theoretical development, supported by new scientific discoveries, was
decisive for him, because he was now clearly conscious of the importance of investigating the different causes of diminishing productivity
in agriculture. And, from that, ascertaining the central problem of the
capitalist form of agriculture.

It is worth noting the general theoretical relevance of this issue to the
critique of political economy. Marx in 1865 deepened his own insight
that nature cannot be arbitrarily subordinated and manipulated through
technological development. There are insurmountable natural limits.
This fact must be contrasted with the popular critique that he totally
neglected such limits. For example, Leszek Kołakowski denounces
Marx's "utopian" idea:

> Marx can scarcely admit that man is limited either by his body or
> by geographical conditions. As his argument with Malthus showed,
> he refused to believe in the possibility of absolute overpopulation,
> as determined by the earth's area and natural resources. . . . Marx's

ignoring of the body and physical death, sex and aggression, geography and human fertility—all of which he turns into purely social realities—is one of the most characteristic yet most neglected features of his Utopia.[45]

Marx emphasized the possibility of technological improvement in agriculture and of modifications of natural fertility in the context of his critique of Ricardo and Malthus. However, he did not end up negating "geographical" and other natural conditions. Instead, he focused on such natural conditions of soil fertility during his reading of Liebig, as his notebook conveys. Material properties of the soil play a role as an economic category in Marx's political economy, for they provide a material basis for the category of ground rent. Thus, Marx had to carefully study agricultural chemistry, physiology, and geology. His investigation of the problem of diminishing returns in 1865 shows that he clearly recognized diverse, insurmountable limitations of the material world and that he decisively parted from the technocratic optimism suggested by Kołakowski. He understood that future production cannot transcend such limits, showing that Kołakowski's critique is both reductionist and false.

As discussed in chapter 3, Marx rejected the one-sided development of technology brought about by capitalism, which inevitably exhausts both workers and the earth. More important is that Marx did not naïvely believe that the socialist usage of technology would automatically result in positive effects and transcend all natural limits. Rather, he was more concerned about the negative consequences of the capitalist mode of production as a manifestation of the contradictions of capitalism, resulting from its neglect of natural limits.

Accordingly, Marx's demand for the conscious regulation of the metabolic interaction between humans and nature consists in the insight that precisely due to natural limits social production must be radically reorganized, with particular attention paid to the interaction of humans with their environment. Marx clearly recognized the merits of the development in modern natural sciences and technologies as fundamental material conditions for establishing the future society, but they must be applied to the production process in a fundamentally different way from that in capitalist society, not in order to overcome the limits of nature, but to conduct a sustainable metabolic interaction between humans and nature. This rational intercourse with nature is, however, not possible in capitalism because the whole of social production is organized by private labor, and, accordingly, the social-metabolic interaction is mediated by value. For a democratic and sustainable management of the metabolic interaction between humans and nature, Marx argued that it is necessary to transform the social practice that bestows capital with an independent force beyond human control. The uniqueness of Marx's approach becomes more apparent by contrasting it with Wilhelm Roscher's reception of Liebig.

ROSCHER'S RECEPTION OF LIEBIG

Despite his confusion, Liebig's theory contributes to the critique of the Ricardian school, scientifically explaining what the latter simply presupposed. Liebig's scientific treatment of the soil enables a rigorous analysis of various causes of diminishing land productivity. In this vein, a particular problem of diminishing returns comes to the foreground in Marx's theory, that is, *the problem of agricultural intensification characteristic of modern society.*

In this context an important contemporary political economist of Marx's time in Germany, who witnessed the intensification of agriculture, and who referred to Liebig's *Agricultural Chemistry* even before Marx, is Wilhelm Roscher. Carl-Erich Vollgraf has already pointed out the influence of this German theorist on Marx's research on agriculture in 1865–66.[46] Such a claim might at first seems dubious, for Marx in the *Economic Manuscripts of 1861–63* rejected Roscher without recognizing a single merit in his ideas. He even said in his discussion on ground rent theory that Roscher's "sentence contains as many falsehoods as words."[47] Notably, his negative comments on Roscher do not appear in his discussion of ground rent in the manuscript for volume 3 of *Capital*, even though he continues to mock Roscher in other contexts.

In the fourth, improved edition of *National Economy of Agriculture and Relevant Basic Productions (Nationalökonomie des Ackerbaues und der verwandten Urproductionen)*, which constitutes the second volume of his *System of National Economy*, Roscher states in the new preface that he "strove to integrate the results of Liebig's recent researches on agricultural chemistry . . . into national economy."[48] In newly added passages and footnotes, Roscher repeatedly emphasizes the significance of Liebig's new findings: "Even if many of Liebig's historical assertions are highly disputable . . . ; even if he misses some important facts of national economy, the name of this great natural scientist will always maintain a place of honor comparable to the name of Alexander Humboldt in the history of national economy as well."[49] Here one finds a clear similarity between

Roscher and Marx, as the latter also affirmatively refers to Liebig, in volume 1 of *Capital*: "To have developed from the point of view of natural science the negative, i.e., destructive side of modern agriculture, is one of Liebig's immortal merits. His historical overview of the history of agriculture, although not free from gross errors, contains more flashes of insight than all the works of modern political economists put together."[50] Furthermore, the list of books that Marx read and possessed includes a number of authors Roscher also discussed, such as Johann Heinrich von Thünen, Hermann Maron, Franz Xavier von Hlubek, and Carl Fraas. Carl-Erich Vollgraf even argues that Marx was prompted to read Liebig's *Agricultural Chemistry* in 1865 after reading Roscher's book. In fact, Roscher's book appeared in 1865, which corresponds to Marx's remark in his letter of February 11, 1866, cited above: "I concluded my theoretical investigation of ground rent two years ago. And a great deal had been achieved, especially in the period since then, fully confirming my theory."

Unfortunately, there are no excerpts from Roscher's book in Marx's notebooks. Marx's personal copy of the fourth edition of Roscher's *National Economy of Agriculture* was apparently lost.[51] Yet Marx's treatment of agricultural intensification as a "natural law of agriculture" seems to possess a commonality with Roscher. In the manuscript for volume 3 of *Capital*, Marx writes:

> It follows from *the natural laws of agriculture,* moreover, that given a certain level of agriculture and the corresponding exhaustion of the soil, capital, which in this sense is synonymous with means of production already produced, becomes the decisive element in the cultivation of the soil.[52]

The reference to the "natural laws of agriculture" in the historical development of agriculture as a process of transition from extensive to intensive agriculture is striking. Roscher also talks about the "transition from extensive to intensive agriculture" as one of its "three most important natural laws."[53] It is thus interesting to trace this transition following Roscher's argument.

Similar to Marx, Roscher claims that the transition occurs because extensive agriculture "exhausts" the soil. He writes: "Among barbarous peoples, and in their very extensive agriculture, what is primarily at stake is to gain access to plant nutrients naturally offered by the soil simply with little developed technique, unsophisticated machines, lean work animals, etc. Thus [they only cultivate] the large part of light soils, which of course get exhausted soon, and natural grasslands."[54] Due to soil exhaustion and increasing population, Roscher argues, people confront the necessity of a transition to a more intensive agriculture through the introduction of cultivation of clover, drainage, and fertilizer, as is shown in the three-field system and crop rotation. More capital and labor must be invested into the land. Roscher points out that, in order to cover the increasing demand for food from a growing population, the transformation of pasture lands into arable fields was necessary. Arable fields can produce more food within a limited availability of the soil; later Wilhelm Abel, following Roscher, calls this historical transition "destocking" (*Depekoration*).[55]

Roscher does not see any contradiction in the process of intensification. His tendency to naturalize historical development becomes more striking because of his high evaluation of Liebig's theory of soil exhaustion. In the paragraph of the fourth edition where Roscher introduces the difference between "extensive" and "intensive" agriculture, he adds new points taken from Liebig's *Agricultural Chemistry* and highlights the importance of "*statics of agriculture*." He demands the "equilibrium between the operations that consume soil power and the operations that replenish it" as the principal condition of sustainable agriculture.[56] Referring to Liebig's mineral theory, Roscher emphasizes that without replacement of mineral soil nutrients absorbed by plants the soil will sooner or later get exhausted.

Roscher then formulates the problem of increasing costs of agricultural products as a result of the intensification of agriculture: "The less plentiful the supply of natural fund becomes, the more urgent the necessity becomes to take some measure against it, and the costs that one can and must use for this purpose increase."[57] He points out that the costs for the replacement of soil nutrients go up as under intensification more labor and capital must be invested. In this context, Roscher says: "From a perspective of natural science Liebig is also totally right in proving that robbery agriculture can only be disguised by manuring the soil . . . and by plowing up the subsoil."[58] Intensification of capital (manuring) and labor (plowing up) can increase crops only for a short period of time. The intensive assimilation of the soil's constituent components is a necessary result of the development of civilization, but as "robbery" from the soil intensifies, soil exhaustion comes faster, and costs for countermeasures also increase. Liebig thematizes this difficulty of modern intensive agriculture in his analysis of "robbery agriculture."

Although he is aware of the danger of robbery agricultural practice, Roscher in the end decisively parts from Liebig's analysis. He even claims that the robbery system of agriculture can be justified: "From the point of view of mere natural science Liebig is totally right to call agriculture that does not fulfill the full replenishment *robbery agriculture*. However, from the point of view of economics, such robbery agriculture can be exactly the right choice for a long time."[59] Thus it is not necessary to keep up with Liebig's law of replenishment because expensive costs of replenishment often make production unprofitable. Roscher believes that the squeezing out of natural forces without full compensation in many cases makes perfect sense from an "economic" perspective, though not from a natural scientific one. Later on, the continuation of robbery of natural forces will be hindered by the logic of market price: when the produce decreases, the market price increases. Roscher predicts that with an increase in market price, more capital investment will be prompted, and then technical innovations will reduce production costs again.

In this sense, Roscher's argument shares the popular myth of the omnipotent regulating ability of market price. Ups and downs of production costs would automatically lead to a solution of the problem of soil exhaustion because otherwise agricultural production would no longer be profitable at all, or the profit rate in industry would decrease due to the increasing price of food. According to Roscher, the problem of soil exhaustion in a more extensive agriculture will be in accordance with natural laws, and will automatically be replaced by a more intensive and effective system, not only because of increasing demands from industry but because it is more profitable than the old system that exhausts the soil. In this vein, Roscher recognizes a "reformist spirit" in Liebig's theory, which is useful in the transition to intensive agriculture in that it propagates the importance of constant replenishment of soil nutrients to the public. A more practical solution to soil exhaustion would simply be left to future generations.[60] Consequently, there is no serious critique of modern agriculture in Roscher's discussion, despite his explicit reference to Liebig's warning about the irrationality of modern agriculture.

Marx's reception of Liebig fundamentally differs from Roscher's uncritical praise of the historical tendency to agricultural intensification. In a clear contrast to Roscher, Marx claims that the obstacle to the realization of sustainable agriculture is nothing but its dependence on market price, as he sees the central contradiction between the "permanent conditions" of nature and the law of capitalist mode of production:

But the way that the cultivation of particular crops depends on fluctuations in market prices and the constant changes in cultivation
associated with these prices fluctuations, as well as the entire spirit
of the capitalist mode of production, which is directed towards the
most immediate monetary profit, stands in contradiction to agriculture, which has to concern itself with the whole range of permanent
conditions of life required by interconnected human generations.[61]

Marx's text does not share Roscher's optimism; rather, he warns
that under the regulation by market price alone agriculture will remain
far from sustainable. His point is easily understandable because price
can take the metabolic interaction between humans and nature even
more one-sidedly than value does, while the sustainable maintenance,
preservation, and improvement of the soil requires conscious and careful treatment with the mechanisms of the material world. Capitalism's
improvement of the soil does not aim at sustainable production in the
long run but only the "*most immediate* monetary profit," investing capital
and labor only on profitable lands, so that their overloading leads them
to quick exhaustion, while other lands that can be improved and cultivated do not receive enough additional capital investment or are left to
lie fallow. Nor are long-term improvements through drainage and irrigation introduced when they are not profitable. In contrast to the capitalist
mode of production directed toward immediate profit, which "stands in
contradiction" to sustainable agriculture, Marx explicitly demands an
agriculture that is not mediated by value but instead is conducted from a
perspective of "interconnected human generations."

Marx's rejection of the unsustainable intensification of agriculture
is also documented in his critical comments in volume 3 of *Capital* on
Léonce de Lavergne, an enthusiastic supporter of English agriculture and
farming. Lavergne praises agricultural progress thanks to crop rotation,
which was first introduced in Norfolk in eastern England toward the end
of the seventeenth century. "Norfolk rotation" abolishes the fallow year
in the four-course rotation of wheat, turnip, barley, and clover together
with ryegrass. They take out different nutrients in the soil, allowing time
for replenishment. The fodder crops do not just better nourish cattle and
sheep, whose excrement can provide rich animal manure, but clover, for
example, also fixes nitrogen from the atmosphere to the soil. Lavergne
praises this efficient system in England, which Marx documents in his
notebooks with his own short comment in brackets:

At that time (around the time of the French Revolution) the *Norfolk rotation* emerged . . . *forage plants* [according to Mr. Lavergne, this is a theory recognized not only by him but also by "everyone"] derive from the atmosphere the principal elements of their growth, *while they give to the soil more than they take from it*; thus both directly, and by their conversion into animal manure, contributing in two ways to repair the mischief done by cereals and exhausting crops generally; one principle, therefore, is that they *should at least alternate with these crops*: in this consists the Norfolk rotation.[62]

Notably, Marx calls Lavergne's explanation a "fairy tale."[63] It is true that neither Liebig nor Marx knew the exact function of clover in fixing nitrogen at the time. Liebig's and Schönbein's hypothesis about the source of ammonia in the soil later turned out to be false; the exact mechanism of fixing nitrogen by rhizobia in legume was discovered in 1866 by Hermann Hellriegel and Hermann Wilfarth. This later discovery does not refute the validity of Liebig's "law of the minimum" and "law of replenishment," however, and it is overhasty to criticize Liebig and Marx on this point alone.[64] Crop rotation alone does not fulfill the law of minimum nor avoid soil exhaustion because more intensive production takes not only nitrogen but also other mineral substances from the soil. Rotation alone accelerates soil exhaustion when these substances are not replenished in an adequate manner. But Lavergne is only interested in the short-time increase of crops, which is nothing but a cause of the rapid exhaustion. This is exactly what Marx rejects as a "fairy tale."

Roscher, on the contrary, would agree with Lavergne because the abolition of fallow land through the constant input of nitrogen realizes the squeezing of natural forces for a greater profit. After reading Roscher's book Marx was prompted to study agricultural chemistry again, especially in terms of extensive and intensive agriculture. However, he soon developed his own critique of capitalist agriculture. He began to understand the historical specificity of diminishing crop returns in modern agriculture as a result of the introduction of machinery, the application of chemical fertilizer, and crop rotation. Because Marx recognized, through Liebig's *Agricultural Chemistry*, the causal relationship between capitalist intensification of agriculture and the successive decrease of its productivity, his theory of ground rent in *Capital* could for the first time clearly thematize, without fear of Malthusianism, the distortion of the material world that results from the logic of capital's valorization.

NEGATIVE INTENSIFICATION OF MODERN AGRICULTURE

Clearly, Marx in *Capital* analyzes the problem of declining agricultural productivity as a contradiction of the modern operational mode of agriculture, whose sole goal is the production of monetary profit. In the beginning of the 1860s, Marx already recognized the possibility of the exhaustion of the soil due to its maltreatment, but he attributed its cause to *extensive* agriculture, finding an example in the contradiction of southern slave states in the United States, where slave owners produced cotton for export only to exhaust the land. Marx wrote in an article on October 25, 1861, for the Vienna newspaper *Die Presse*:

> The cultivation of the southern export articles, cotton, tobacco, sugar, etc., carried on by slaves, is only remunerative as long as it is conducted with large gangs of slaves, on a mass scale and on wide expanses of a naturally fertile soil, which requires only simple labor. Intensive cultivation, which depends less on fertility of the soil than on investment of capital, intelligence, and energy of labor, is contrary to the nature of slavery. . . . Even in South Carolina, where the slaves form four-sevenths of the population, the cultivation of cotton has been almost completely stationary for years due to the exhaustion of the soil.[65]

For Marx the problem of soil exhaustion in the southern states was a result of extensive cotton production based on slave labor. He argued that it is precisely this exhaustion that made the "acquisition of new Territories ... necessary." Notably, he did not problematize the corn production in the Union and its export to Europe, which also caused soil exhaustion, even if his analysis should be read in a political context of support for the Union during the Civil War. The necessity of constant expansion toward the West existed in New England as well due to the rapid exhaustion of the soil, against which James F. W. Johnston warned in his book *Notes on North America*.

In the *Economic Manuscripts of 1861–63*, Marx still argued in the same direction when he wrote:

> The development of productive power is not even. It is in the nature of capitalist production that it develops industry more rapidly than agriculture. This is not due to the nature of the land, but to the fact that, in order to be exploited really in accordance with its nature, land requires different social relations. Capitalist production turns

towards the land only after its influence has exhausted it and after it has devastated its natural qualities.[66]

Marx certainly recognized the reality of soil exhaustion, but what is striking is its cause. Capitalist production itself "turns towards the land" only *after* the exhaustion of the soil, so that machinery is introduced and natural sciences are applied. Here Marx possibly thought about the United States again. The problem of soil exhaustion as a result of intensive cultivation is, by contrast, not discernible in his long *Economic Manuscripts of 1861–63.* He seemed to believe that with the introduction of capitalist production the "development of productive power" is also possible in agriculture.

This emphasis on the positive side of capitalist agriculture looks quite different in *Capital,* written after he has read Liebig's *Agricultural Chemistry.* Marx in *Capital* deals with the diminishing productivity of the land precisely in relation to the capitalist form of intensive cultivation. Liebig's critique of the robbery system of agriculture makes it possible, in contrast to Ricardo, to investigate the causes of diminishing crop returns as a specific modern manifestation of material limits in the sphere of agriculture. As a result of the modern robbery system, the problem of soil exhaustion takes a more radical shape, and its analysis reveals the central contradiction of capitalist production.

First, Liebig points out that intensive cultivation through additional capital investments remains conditioned by the material properties of the soil and other natural elements in the production process. Neither mechanical or chemical operation realizes an infinite increase of productivity because it is limited by both organic and inorganic nutrients in the soil, by air, warmth, and light, and finally by the physiological functions of plants. These elements constitute the *transhistorical material aspect* of plant growth, by which any mode of production is essentially conditioned.

Liebig also argues that the natural conditions of agricultural production under capitalism appear in a specific form when the fertility of the land itself becomes the source for "ground rent." In other words, Liebig warns that intensive cultivation cannot always result in the increase of crops, but it can generate a decrease because of the violation of the natural "law of replenishment." According to Liebig, modern industrialization has created a new division of labor between town and countryside, so that foods are now produced as commodities and consumed by the working class in large cities. However, these products no longer return to and restore the original soils, but instead flow out into the rivers through flush toilets, without any further use. In addition, through the commodification of agricultural products and fertilizer, the aim of agriculture diverges from sustainability and becomes the mere maximization of profits, squeezing soil nutrients into crops in the shortest possible period. The maintenance of the circle of nutrients now becomes much more difficult due to the long distance between town and country. This historical development of the social division of labor, on the one hand, demands a rapid increase of agricultural production for sales in the cities. Through commodity exchange with the city, the countryside, on the other hand, receives machines and chemical fertilizer, which promote the intensification of agriculture and appear to increase its productivity. According to Liebig, there is no true development of productive forces, however, because this process only allows the farmer to squeeze the existing soil nutrients and let plants absorb them without replenishment. After all, more products are sold in large cities, which only reinforces the tendency of robbery agriculture. Liebig laments that it becomes ever more difficult and expensive to produce the same amount of corn; during production the cooperation of natural forces becomes weaker and a larger investment of chemical fertilizer becomes necessary.

It is not hard to see why Marx got so excited about Liebig's theory. In Liebig's work he found a scientific expression of the theme "antagonism between town and country," which had been an important topic for him since *The German Ideology*:

> The most important division of material and mental labor is the separation of town and country. . . . The contradiction between town and country can only exist within the framework of private property. It is the most crass expression of the subjection of the individual under the division of labor, under a definite activity forced upon him—a subjection which makes one man into a restricted town-animal, another into a restricted country-animal, and daily creates anew the conflict between their interests. Labor is here again the chief thing, power *over* individuals, and as long as this power exists, private property must exist.[67]

Referring to Liebig's theory of soil exhaustion in the famous chapter "Large-Scale Industry and Agriculture" in *Capital*, Marx thus criticized the irreparable disturbance of natural and social metabolism as a result of the separation of town and country:

Capitalist production collects the population together in great centers, and causes the urban population to achieve an ever-growing preponderance. This has two results. On the one hand it concentrates the historical motive power of society; on the other hand, it disturbs the metabolic interaction between man and the earth, i.e. it prevents the return to the soil of its constituent elements consumed by man in the form of food and clothing; hence it hinders the operation of the eternal natural condition for the lasting fertility of the soil. Thus it destroys at the same time the physical health of the urban worker, and the intellectual life of the rural worker.[68]

Based on Liebig's *Agricultural Chemistry*, Marx pointed to both the disturbance of natural metabolism in the sense of robbery of soil fertility and disturbance of social metabolism in the sense of destruction of life of the urban and rural worker. In this way, capitalism exhausts labor power as well as natural power.

Due to the disruption of the natural cycle of plant nutrients, the "relative increase in the price" of agricultural produce becomes more and more probable because production cannot occur by appropriating "a free natural power" but only by the exertion of "human labor."[69] It is precisely in this context that Marx reminds himself of the necessity to consult Liebig in elaborating "*the declining productivity of the soil when successive capital investments are made.*" According to Marx, this is certainly not the absolute tendency of capitalist agricultural intensification, but he comes consciously to integrate this aspect of negative development into his theory of ground rent, which is a self-critical process considering his earlier optimistic observation on the problem of intensification. In the new formulation, there lies a new critical insight that profit-oriented agriculture under capitalist relations is not capable of sustainable and long-term improvement of the soil and that production costs go up due to increasing capital investments as a countermeasure against soil exhaustion. Marx does not share any illusion that an infinite increase of agricultural productivity would be possible under the modern "agricultural revolution," but he recognizes the possibility that agricultural productivity remains much smaller in capitalism than it should be, and this is not because of the material and natural limitations of agriculture but because of the economic limitation of the capitalist mode of production.

The level and type of soil exhaustion in capitalist society takes a different shape than in the precapitalist mode of production. Modern large-scale farming exhausts the soil, but this is not because of a lack of technology and scientific knowledge but because squeezing out natural forces becomes the absolute goal:

> In both forms, instead of a conscious and rational treatment of the land as permanent communal property, as the inalienable condition for the existence and reproduction of the chain of human generations, we have the exploitation and squandering of the powers of the earth (not to mention the fact that exploitation is made dependent not on the level of social development reached but rather on the accidental and unequal conditions of the individual producers). In the case of small-scale ownership, this results from a lack of the resources and scientific knowledge needed to apply the social productive powers of labor. In the case of large-scale landed property, it results from the exploitation of these resources for the most rapid possible enrichment of the farmer and the proprietor. In both cases it results from dependence on the market price.[70]

Large-scale agriculture exhausts the soil more and more extremely not just because its level of squandering is much higher due to the strong dependence on machinery and fertilizer but also because production is oriented to the maximum utilization of the free forces of nature for profit-making. The progress presumably achieved through the conscious application of natural science and technology proves to be robbery of the foundation of all wealth. The relationship between humans and nature is emancipated from traditional and communal limitations, and even seemingly from any immediate natural limitation to the economic expropriation of the earth as a mere means for the production of profit and rent. Consequently, a pure commodity economy proves incapable of realizing the rational treatment of "the land as permanent communal property, as the inalienable condition for the existence and reproduction of the chain of human generations."

The problem here is not just the destruction of the natural fertility of the soil but the lack of freedom and alienation of human beings. Marx argues that the robbery of natural fertility is inevitably connected to the destructive processes of human life by the increasing productive forces of industry:

> Large-scale industry and industrially pursued agriculture go hand in hand. If they are originally distinguished by the fact that the former

lays waste and ruins labor-power and thus the natural power of man, whereas the latter does the same to the natural power of the soil, they link up in the later course of development, since the industrial system applied to agriculture also debilitates the workers there, while industry and trade for their part provide agriculture with the means of exhausting the soil.[71]

Life in the countryside as well as life in the city is fundamentally transformed and destroyed by the logic of capital. The development of productive forces and means of transportation under capitalism not only degrades the physical health of urban workers due to its utilization of the means of production as "means of enslaving, exploiting and impoverishing the worker" but also annihilates the "individual vitality, freedom and autonomy" of the rural worker.[72]

Against such a form of shortsighted agriculture, Marx continually insists on the necessity of sustainable cultivation of the soil for succeeding generations, arguing that neither individuals nor a society are the "owners" of the earth, but they are mere "occupiers" and thus responsible for the maintenance of the soil's fertility:

> From the standpoint of a higher socioeconomic formation, the private property of particular individuals in the earth will appear just as absurd as the private property of one man in another man. Even an entire society, a nation, or all simultaneously existing societies taken together, are not the *owners* of the earth. They are simply its *occupiers*, its *beneficiaries*, and they have to bequeath it in an improved state to the succeeding generations as *boni patres familias*.[73]

Capitalist relations of production create a pure economic "title" to the land, converting it in effect into a real estate monopoly. In the system of private property, the egoistic use of soil fertility for the sake of profit-making appears as a legitimate act because the use of one's own private property is seen as a right, a vital aspect of individual freedom. But private property plainly proves incompatible with the material presupposition for the realization of sustainable production. Who would give up a precious chance for a bigger profit under market competition simply for the benefit of future generations? Especially when such an altruistic act would not be compensated!

With the abolishment of the capitalist relation of production and of the system of private property, the human relationship to the earth needs to change in such a way that the use of natural resources is organized not for the sake of short-term profit-making but for future generations. That is, nature must be nurtured for "man as a species-being." But Marx does not demand a mere change in our moralistic perspective, toward the standpoint of a species-being, but there must be a radical change, with reified social relations replaced by conscious production realized through the association of free producers. Only this emancipation from the reified power of capital will allow humans to construct a different relationship to nature.

To people such as environmental sociologist Ted Benton, Marx's demand that humans behave as "*boni patres familias*" of the earth sounds like a Promethean hope for the domination of nature.[74] However, it is clear that what Marx criticizes is capitalism's alienated and reified domination over nature, which goes against humanity's potential to organize a universal and conscious interaction with nature. Accordingly, what is at stake is the future necessity for the *conscious* regulation of the metabolic exchange between humans and nature. This demand is fully understandable, not only because the influence of the universal production of humans on the whole ecosystem is much bigger than other animals, but also because it is *only* humans who are able to change their purposeful interaction with nature in the process of natural and social metabolism.

The new social intercourse with the earth from the standpoint of species-being is, in Marx's view, only possible by treating the material dimension as a central composition of the metabolism between humans and nature, which capital takes into account only in a seriously defective way. It is now clear why Marx's socialist project must be understood in its relation to his reception of Liebig. The more Marx becomes conscious, through his study of natural science, of the deterioration of the natural conditions of production as a fundamental contradiction of capitalism, the more strategic importance the transformation of our social intercourse with nature acquires for his project. Consequently, his political economy attains a clear ecological dimension. His demand is formulated particularly through his recognition of the limit of material modifications, which capital cannot recognize but only keep trying to overcome.

To sum up, thanks to Liebig's work, Marx in *Capital* has become capable of bestowing concrete content onto abstract natural limits, which the law of diminishing returns simply presupposed. He no longer sees diminishing returns as an abstract presupposition of the Ricardian school, but as a specific manifestation of capital's contradictions.[75] It is possible to observe the deepening of Marx's insight into how the relationship between humans and the earth is transformed by capital into an alien opposition. Whereas capital actively modifies nature for its valorization, natural forces also react to it in a "determinant" manner, as seen in soil exhaustion. The increase of production costs alone will not immediately pose a threat to the regime of capital accumulation because the soil has a material elasticity that can be intensively and extensively exploited through the introduction of machinery and chemical fertilizer. However, this does not transcend the capitalist contradiction of the relationship of humans and the earth. The material destabilization in various spheres of life cannot help but compel humans to recognize the need to establish a wholly different relationship to nature through transcending reification.

Ted Benton's claim with respect to Marx's supposed flight from the recognition of natural limits proves wrong on close inspection. Marx does not believe in the possibility of overcoming all natural limits through the development of productive forces. Rather, he analyzes the problem of natural limits intensively with regard to the contradiction of capital. Perelman's assertion about Marx's fear of Malthusianism misses the point as well, for Marx actually deals with the problem of the scarcity of natural resources as a critique of capitalism, whose systematic robbery aims to squander resources for more profit at the cost of environmental destruction. In this sense, Roscher's optimistic hope for market regulation of social and natural metabolism through value does not suffice for the realization of sustainable production. Clearly, Marx does not pretend that the transition to socialism would automatically solve all ecological problems. Rather, precisely because finite resources must be treated with great care for future generations, the realization of the conscious interaction with the material limits of nature demands the abolition of a social system of production based on value.

5

Fertilizer against Robbery Agriculture?

As examined in the last chapter, the problem of material limits of nature came to the foreground of Marx's political economy in the 1860s, to the extent that he deepened his critique of Ricardo's theory of ground rent through his intensive research on natural sciences during the preparation of *Capital*. Liebig played an essential role, although this was not the first time that Marx intensively studied agricultural chemistry. In the 1850s, he had already read various natural science books.

To trace the development of Marx's critique more precisely during the 1850s and 1860s, two natural scientists are of particular interest—Justus von Liebig and James F. W. Johnston. What makes them so important in the process of the emergence of Marx's ecological critique of political economy is that Marx carefully read their various works many times: in the beginning of the 1850s as noted in his *London Notebooks* (1850–1853) and in the mid-1860s during his preparation of the manuscripts for *Capital*.[1] When we examine Marx's excerpts, we realize that Marx's focus and interest clearly shifted over time. The new development of Liebig's theory of "metabolism" and "robbery cultivation" resonates with a significant critical turning point in Marx's socialist project, as the conscious rehabilitation of the unity of humanity and nature.

Without doubt, Marx owed to Liebig's *Agricultural Chemistry* the development of his concept of metabolism as a critique of modern capitalist agriculture.[2] On reading Liebig's work in 1865, Marx began to study in detail the negative consequences of modern agriculture, which was creating deep rifts in the transhistorical relationship between humans and nature. In this context, in 1851 Marx read the fourth edition of Liebig's *Agricultural Chemistry* and carefully copied excerpts from the book. In 1863, he read another book by Liebig, *On Theory and Practice in Agriculture* (*Ueber Theorie und Praxis in der Landwirtschaft*), published in 1856. Nonetheless, Marx's serious reception of Liebig's theory did not take place until he wrote a manuscript for the chapter on ground rent in volume 3 of *Capital* in 1865. In other words, Marx, following Leibig, developed his critique of modern agriculture as a robbery system relatively late. In contrast, his earlier excerpt notebooks on agricultural chemistry show that he was actually interested in such optimistic passages from Liebig's work, which explain how agricultural productivity can be enormously advanced through the introduction of chemical fertilizer.

Liebig eventually became more critical of capitalist agriculture, and thus his critique of the robbery system of agriculture in the seventh edition of *Agricultural Chemistry* (1862), especially in its Introduction, must have decisively contributed to Marx's critique of the metabolic rift.[3] This is not equivalent to saying that Marx failed to read anything critical about capitalist agriculture before 1865, however. To the contrary, he encountered critical books and articles in the early 1850s, but, astonishingly, paid hardly any attention at the time. Furthermore, though he repeatedly referred to his own notebooks in different economic manuscripts and in *Capital*, Marx did not use the excerpts from Liebig in the *London Notebooks* (see below). This leads to the hypothesis that Marx later came to regard his notebooks on agricultural chemistry as unsatisfactory for his critical investigation of capitalism because they only contained *positive* aspects of its modern development. In the *London Notebooks*, Marx's Prometheanism is still discernible, but as a result of integrating Liebig's critique he corrected his earlier optimistic vision about the potential agricultural revolution in the 1860s.

Despite the appearance in the last fifteen years or so of a number of pathbreaking studies of Marx's ecological thought, such studies were unable to throw sufficient light on the actual evolutionary process in which Marx's critique of modern agriculture emerged during his decades-long attempt to complete *Capital*. His notebooks on agriculture are thus indispensable in that they enable us to see precisely how he changed his attitude toward modern agriculture, in the process of developing his materialist conception of the metabolic interaction between humans and nature mediated by labor. It will be shown that Marx did not simply "copy" Liebig's theory. Instead, Marx's application of it to the

"Ireland question" opens up a new ecological paradigm that goes beyond Ricardo's politico-economic worldview.

PESSIMISM OR OPTIMISM?

After his exile to London in 1849, and despite severe financial hardships, Marx went to the British Museum every day and filled twenty-four notebooks that are today known as the *London Notebooks*. These contain a substantial number of excerpts on agricultural chemistry.[4] As shown in the last chapter, Marx's main aim in studying natural sciences was to reject a widespread assumption of the "law of diminishing returns." Marx gathered materials to prove the ungroundedness of Malthus's and Ricardo's presupposition, pointing to the potential of agricultural improvement through the introduction of drainage and chemical fertilizer. The natural fertility of the soil was treated as something fixed in the pessimistic prognoses of classical political economists. They ignored the existing possibilities of soil improvement.

Marx had already accepted this viewpoint in his 1845 *Manchester Notebooks*, in which he had written about the possibility of advancing the natural fertility of soils to a considerable degree, based on excerpts from James Anderson's *A Calm Investigation of the Circumstances That Have Led to the Present Scarcity of Grain in Britain* (1801). The Scottish agronomist and practical farmer passionately supported the idea of agricultural revolution. In the notebooks, Marx summarized Anderson's critique of Malthus, indicating that Anderson "explicitly poses the *population theory* as the most dangerous 'prejudice.'" Marx then quoted that "means of subsistence have rather augmented than diminished by that augmentation of its population: and the reverse. P. 55."[5] Furthermore, Marx documented Anderson's optimistic claim, summarizing: "The earth can be made *always better* through chemical influences and treatments. P. 38."[6] Anderson eventually argued that the soil is capable of further improvement by "human industry":

> Under a judicious system of management, that productiveness may be made to augment from year to year, for a succession of time to which no limit can be assigned, till at last it may be made to attain *a degree of productiveness, of which we cannot, perhaps at this time conceive an idea.*[7]

As this quote clearly documents, Anderson promulgated the vision of an enormous increase in agricultural productivity, which actually appeared plausible in the English agricultural revolution.

As a means for increasing productivity, Anderson recognized the utility of animal and human excrement for every farmer who aims at the rational treatment of the soil: "Of course, he must be sensible, that every circumstance which tends to deprive the soil of that manure ought to be accounted an uneconomical waste highly deserving of blame."[8] As Marx also wrote in his notebook, Anderson in this context problematized a "great waste of manure in England" due to the separation of town and countryside: "*The manure arising directly from the immense population of London is entirely lost to the purposes of agriculture. P. 73.*"[9] Anderson criticized this inefficient "waste of manure . . . without any beneficial effect" and demanded the realization of rational cultivation: "If the *running water*, which is wasted in Great Britain, were tidily employed, she could support four times as many as the current population in 100 years. P. 77."[10] In the last sentence, Anderson unmistakably criticized Malthus's population theory. He was firmly convinced of the future increase of agricultural productivity and strove for mass enlightenment about the merits of rational agriculture. He saw the causes of backwardness of agriculture as "moral" ones, which "are subjected to the influence of human wisdom."[11]

In this context, it is not surprising that in his later examination of Anderson's book in 1851 Marx again quoted a similar sentence that is critical of the law of diminishing returns. This time Marx read *An Inquiry into the Causes that Have Hitherto Retarded the Advancement of Agriculture in Europe*, published in 1779, where Anderson pointed out that the "infinite diversity of soils . . . may be so much altered from their original state by the modes of culture they have formerly been subjected to, by the manures etc. . . . . (5)"[12] Marx's intention is clear because later in the *Manuscripts of 1861–1863* he actually cited these passages from his own notebooks in the context of discarding the presupposition of Ricardo's differential rent theory.[13] In opposition to Ricardo's assumption, Marx continued to value Anderson's ideas about using drainage and manures to improve the productivity of soils to such a degree that the food supply would suffice to cover the increase of population, and the price of crops would remain the same or even fall.

Yet Marx expressed a certain reserve toward Anderson because as "a practical farmer" he did not treat the fundamental mechanism of agricultural production and the improvement of the soil fertility "*ex professo*" (as an expert) but only as an "immediate practical controversy."[14]

After his 1851 reading of Anderson, Marx felt it necessary to read more recent scientific works by agricultural chemists to gain a detailed knowledge about the ways of advancing agricultural productivity, especially the relationship between the use of synthetic fertilizers and the fertility of the soil. In the *London Notebooks*, there are two principal sources for this purpose: Justus von Liebig and James F. W. Johnston.

It appears that Marx encountered Johnston's *Notes on North America* (1851) through two articles in *The Economist*. The articles, dated May 3 and 24, 1851, sum up Johnston's book, with positive comments on his scientific contribution to the analysis of the actual state of American agriculture. It is likely that these reviews motivated Marx to study Johnston's more theoretical books on agricultural chemistry and geology. One of the articles mentions that despite the constantly growing commercial and cultural communication between England and North America, there was insufficient information about agricultural capacity in the New World. Consequently, a myth prevailed among English readers that a great improvement of virgin soils had been achieved, and the soil would be inexhaustible in North America. For the purpose of disproving this fallacy, the reviewer valued *Notes on North America* quite highly, as "the author's knowledge of science, and its practical relations with agriculture, enabled him to obtain very clear and accurate views." According to the article, "one of the most important of these conclusions" is "that the wheat-exporting power of North America has not only been much exaggerated, but is actually, and not slowly, diminishing" or even "worn out." Johnston furthermore showed that it is not in the farmer's interest to maintain the fertility of the land through good management because it is actually cheaper to sell it and settle upon new land, going farther west once the land becomes less agriculturally profitable. Thus the diminishment of crops is not at all surprising, once "we learn that in many districts the land has been cropped with wheat for fifty years with nothing more than *a ton of gypsum a year applied to the whole farm.*"[15] Succinctly summarizing Johnston's book to rebuff a widespread illusion about American agriculture, the conclusion is that it is still trapped "in a very primitive state," without proper investment or management, which quickly exhausts soils.[16]

Upon reading these articles, Marx quoted only one sentence in regard to the exhaustion of lands in North America: The "Atlantic States of the Union and the western part of New York, once so prolific in wheat, has now become almost exhausted, and Ohio is undergoing the same process."[17] This sentence explains neither a reason for the exhaustion nor its seriousness. In contrast, Marx was much more careful in recording the details about how the introduction of drainage was difficult in North America due to the low cost of abundant lands, and why a larger scale of farming was "not profitable" and "not popular":

> An objection to drainage is made in this country. The cost of this improvement, even at the cheapest rate, say 4*l.* or 20 dollars an acre, is [equal] to a large proportion *of the present price of the best land in this rich district of Western New York.*
>
> It is plain that there is too great an abundance of land, which, for little labor and with no skill, will produce, year after year, moderate crops.
>
> Husbandry by capitalists not yet available in North America . . . ; but on a larger scale, farming is not profitable. Beyond purchasing a farm for their own use, there is not much to be done with land, for renting land is not popular, and, in fact, the economic condition of North America is not yet such as to render such a mode of management necessary or desirable.[18]

Here, Marx seems more attentive to descriptions that there are no serious attempts to improve the soil through mechanical and chemical means due to the lack of a farmer's knowledge and capital. The excerpted passages give an impression that Marx was less interested in the exhausted state of soils in North America than in Johnston's reports about the primitive or precapitalist state of agriculture, which at the same time implies the future possibility of advancing the productivity of lands.

In order to examine Marx's interest at the time more carefully, it is necessary to consider other excerpts in the *London Notebooks*. In *London Notebook* VIII, Marx studied John Morton's *On the Nature and Property of Soils* (1838), one of the earliest studies on the relationship between geological composition and the productivity of land. Due to an inadequate knowledge of chemistry, Morton did not correctly grasp the role of inorganic materials, which he thought augment the productivity merely by changing the "texture" of the soil and thus by improving the effectiveness of plants to absorb moisture, air, heat, and organic materials:

> All mineral manures, such as lime, chalk, marl, sand, gravel, etc., act on the soil merely as an alternative, by changing the constituents of the soil and improving its texture, and by giving it an increased power of imbibing and decomposing water, air, and organic matter.[19]

As he missed the function of minerals and emphasizes the essential function of decomposed plants, Morton also optimistically insisted that "on a careful examination," one finds that "*the production of vegetables will never exhaust a land.*"[20] Morton argued that the "quality of the soil on each, is infinitely varied, and increases in value according to the degree of culture it receives," and that the soil is "susceptible to a continued improvement by every fresh application of capital judiciously employed. P. 221."[21] Like Anderson, Morton pointed to the possibility of the improvement of soil fertility precisely through constant cultivation. This is an important aspect of his book, and this is presumably why Marx made excerpts from it.

Despite the seemingly optimistic tone of Morton, who appears to neglect the problem of soil exhaustion, one should pay attention to the reason why he was naïvely convinced of the lasting fertility of the soil. According to him the "powers of nature to create vegetable productions appear never to diminish" only because "the decay of one crop becomes the nourishment of the next."[22] Even if Morton's insight is restrained by the theoretical and practical knowledge of his time, this limitation allowed him simply to presuppose the cycle of nourishment between old and new plants as a feasible condition for sustainable agriculture.

In this context, Marx's excerpts in *London Notebook* X from Henry C. Carey's book, *The Past, the Present, and the Future* (1848) are worth examining. Like Johnston in *Notes on North America*, Carey in his book explicitly challenged Morton's thesis by pointing out that the recycling of nourishment was in danger in North America because of an exhausting management of the soil. Carey's warning is based on the insight that rational treatment of soil requires replenishment of the soil's constituent elements in order to guarantee the nutrition cycle. If producers and consumers live next to each other and give up long-distance trade, the condition for the maintenance of soil fertility could be easily fulfilled, so that general fertility can increase through an effective return of refuse and excrement to the soil: "When the consumer and the producer come together, man is enabled to compel the rich soils to exert their powers in giving forth the vast supplies of food of which they are capable, and to pay them back by giving them the whole refuse."[23] Carey pointed to the actual state of U.S. agriculture under British economic domination and trade: "The tendency of the whole system of the United States is that of taking from the great machine all that it will yield, and giving nothing back."[24] This is because U.S. settlements, spread over an enormous land mass, impeded social interaction, and

the social division of industry and agriculture made it impossible to
return nutrients to the soil. The situation got even worse because the
U.S. economy was heavily dependent on its corn exports to England.
Carey reprimanded the nation that this squandering would proliferate
to the extent that corn trade, with its great distance between producer
and consumer, increased.

Carey provided some examples of the disturbance of the nutrition
cycle in North America due to the loss of manure:

> The farmer of New York raises wheat, which exhausts the land. That
> wheat he sells, and both grain and straw are lost. The average yield
> per acre, originally *twenty* bushels, falls *one-third*.
>
> The Kentuckian exhausts his land with hemp, and then wastes his
> manure on the road, in carrying it to market.
>
> Virginia is exhausted by tobacco, and men desert their homes to
> seek in the West new lands, to be again exhausted; and thus are labor
> and manure wasted, while the great machine deteriorates, because
> men *cannot come* to take from it the vast supplies of food with which
> it is charged. . . . South Carolina has millions of acres admirably
> adapted to the raising of rich grasses, the manure produced from
> which would enrich the exhausted cotton lands; but she exports rice
> and cotton, and loses all the manure.[25]

The social division of labor, which is based on "dispersion" in the
sense of the antagonism between town and country, requires long-distance transport of agricultural products and as a result wastes a large
amount of manure and labor. In order to prevent soil exhaustion due to
export and to utilize limited resources more efficiently, Carey fervently
argued for "concentration," that is, building an autarchic town-commu-
nity founded on a concentration of producers and consumers, which will
end the opposition between town and country.

Despite these explicit remarks by Carey, similar to those Marx found
in *The Economist* about the exhausted soils in the United States, Marx
does not seem to pay particular attention to them. He did not quote any
of these sentences, although he did copy various passages before and
after them. This is surprising because Liebig's critique of the modern
robbery practice directly refers to Carey's work.[26] The neglect implies
Marx's indifference to the problem of soil exhaustion.

Marx's excerpts have another focused, however. He focuses on Carey's
attempts to refute the existence of the natural limits of agricultural

development incurred by the scarcity of available fertile soils. Carey maintained, without much concrete historical analysis, that the development of society enables the cultivation of better soils: "We find invariably that the more dense the population and the greater the mass of wealth, the more the good soils are cultivated."[27] Carey formulated this historical tendency as a critique of the law of diminishing returns. Marx clearly recognized this point and wrote down a passage in which Carey argued against the classical political economist J. R. McCulloch, who, as a Ricardian, insisted upon the insurmountable natural "limits" of agricultural development due to the scarcity of best lands: "Man is always going from a poor soil to a better, and then returning on his footsteps to the original poor one, and turning up the marl or the lime; and so on, in continued succession . . . and at each step in this course, he is making a better machine. (129)."[28] Carey insisted upon the unilateral growth of agricultural productivity with the future development of society.

With a vertical line for emphasis, Marx also excerpted from Carey's book that, contrary to the law of diminishing returns, the increase in population and agricultural development would mutually reinforce each other, realizing the "harmonious" progress of civilization:

> Everywhere, with increased power of union, we see them exercising increased power over land. Everywhere, as the new soils are brought into activity, and as they are enabled to obtain larger returns, we find more rapid increase of population, producing increased tendency to combination of exertion, by which the powers of individual laborer are trebled etc. (48, 49).[29]

Carey rejects "Ricardo's system," founded on the assumption of the law of diminishing returns, as a system of "discords" and even says that Ricardo's book is "the true manual of the demagogue, who seeks power by means of agrarianism, war, and plunder. (74, 5)."[30] Marx bestowed a special notation (vertical lines) to mark the passage.

Carey's animosity toward everything connected to England could be interpreted as a critique of British imperialism from a colonized periphery. Marx does not accept such a polemic, because Carey dissolves class antagonism under the capitalist mode of production in North America into an illusory harmony of small-town communities. Despite this difference, Marx grasps Carey's historical comprehension of increasing agricultural productivity in an attempt to gather materials against Ricardo's and Malthus's law of diminishing returns.

Archibald Alison in his *Principles of Population* (1840), which Marx also read, argues against Malthus's assumption, pointing to increasing American population doubling every $33^1/_2$ years since 1640: "This long continued and astonishing multiplication for two centuries is the most luminous fact which the history of the globe has yet exhibited of the fixed superiority which the produce of human labor is able to maintain even over the most rapidly increasing multiplication of the species. (39, 40)."[31] At the time, there was still a popular opinion that U.S. agriculture would develop with the increasing population. Indeed, it partly reflected the reality. In this situation, it is actually not so surprising that Marx during his reading of Carey and Alison did not pay particular attention to the problem of land exhaustion in North America, a phenomenon that actually seemed to strengthen the validity of Ricardo's and Malthus's theory.

The *London Notebooks* contain research from various books on agronomic science, with an emphasis that only a conscious management of the soil—its potential was offered for the first time by the natural sciences, technologies with chemical fertilizer, drainage, and crop rotation—could realize a great advance in agricultural productivity. Marx's research on the agricultural revolution in the eighteenth and nineteenth centuries was in this sense definitely productive with regard to his critique against Ricardo and Malthus. Nonetheless, Marx did not yet commit to any serious critique of the actual situation of agriculture, which was characterized by a rapid decrease in soil fertility and was far from realizing the ideal rational cultivation based on a continual cycle of soil nutrients.

As a consequence, Marx seemed, too optimistically, to ascribe the problem of soil exhaustion to precapitalist and primitive societies. It was not analyzed as a specific problem of modern capitalist production. Accordingly, Marx emphasized the strategic importance of further agricultural progress for the coming revolution, as he stated in his letter to Engels dated August 14, 1851: "But the more I get into the stuff, the more I become convinced that agricultural reform, and hence the question of property based on it, is the alpha and omega of the coming revolution. Without that, Parson Malthus will prove right."[32] Malthus's theoretical fallacy, Marx argued, must be overcome through agricultural progress.

THE OPTIMISTIC CHEMISTS OF THE NINETEENTH CENTURY

Marx's optimistic tendency continues in the *London Notebooks* XII to XIV, in which he made careful excerpts from Justus von Liebig and James

F. W. Johnston in order to appropriate a systematic and scientific foundation for the improvement of agricultural productivity. In these excerpts, one clearly sees the widespread optimistic perspective of many European chemists about future agricultural development.

Liebig, one of the most famous German chemists in the nineteenth century, is often regarded as the "father of agricultural chemistry." In his epoch-making book *Organic Chemistry in Its Application to Agriculture and Physiology*, whose fourth edition Marx read while preparing *London Notebook* XII, Liebig applies his deep knowledge of chemistry and physiology to agriculture and argues that these sciences are quite useful to achieve the "general object of agriculture." They can be used to determine the components of soils and plants, how they function, and how they should be consumed and supplemented in an efficient manner. Marx notes the passage:

> The general object of agriculture is to produce in the most advantageous manner certain qualities, or a maximum size, in certain parts or organs of particular plants. Now, this object can be attained only by the application of those substances which we know to be indispensable to the development of these parts or organs, or by supplying the conditions necessary to the production of the qualities desired.[33]

Inadequate understanding of chemistry and plant physiology leads to the fallacy of the so-called humus theory, famously advocated by Johann Heinrich von Thünen, which wrongly assumes the direct contribution of the well-decomposed residue of plants as the source of plant food, absorbed through plant roots. Liebig persuasively demonstrates, based on his chemical experiments, that humus only indirectly contributes to plant growth by providing carbons and nitrogen in the process of its decay. He concludes from his observations that the importance of humus is therefore very limited or even nonexistent—in an earlier edition of *Agricultural Chemistry*, he had gone so far as to say humus "does not yield the smallest nourishment to plants"—because plants can later sufficiently absorb carbon from carbonic gas in the atmosphere through photosynthesis and receive nitrogen in the form of ammonium from the soil.

Liebig's "mineral theory," in contrast to the emphasis on organic materials in the humus theory, emphasizes the essential role of inorganic materials in soil for ample plant growth. However, according to Liebig, they can be exhausted by cultivation because neither atmosphere nor rainwater can sufficiently provide them as much as plants absorb them.

The loss of inorganic materials must be reduced as much as possible so that the soil can sustain its original fruitfulness over the long term. Such rational treatment of the soil occurs, according to Liebig, through various methods such as fallowing, crop rotation, and clover. Fallowing gives the soil a certain time during which new inorganic substances become available to plants through weathering. Crop rotation aims at a more sustainable production by growing different types of plants on the same land, so that different mineral substances can be absorbed each time. The cultivation of clover absorbs unused nutrients from deep layers of the soil und makes them available to other plants (and, as later discovered, fixes nitrogen in the atmosphere), and clover also becomes fodder to feed cattle and sheep whose excrement provides animal manure. Nevertheless, it is often necessary to add an amount of minerals directly to the soil either to avoid a state of exhaustion or to increase its productivity: "The fertility of a soil cannot remain unimpaired, unless we replace in it all those substances of which it has been thus deprived. Now this is effected by *manure*."[34] According to Liebig, fertility increases, for instance, by adding more animal and human excrement and bones to the soil.

Liebig thus recognizes the importance of supplementing mineral substances in manures to prevent soil exhaustion. Contrary to a vitalistic belief at that time, Liebig's analysis of the chemical reaction of manures in the soil comes to a provocative conclusion—that excrement and bones can be replaced by other materials with the same or similar chemical composition: "For animal excrement, other substances containing their essential constituents may be substituted."[35] Since chemical and physiological analyses of plants can show which mineral substances they need, Liebig hopes to replace animal excrement and bones through chemical fertilizers massively produced in factories in the future instead of painfully gathering and littering stall manure and bones over the field, as Marx documents in his notebook:

> Whether this restoration be effected by means of excrement, ashes, or bones, is in a great measure a matter of indifference. A time will come when fields will be manured with a solution of glass (silicate of potash), with the ashes of burnt straw, and with salts of phosphoric acid, *prepared in chemical manufactories*.[36]

As this passage plainly shows, Liebig is quite optimistic about the future development of natural science, which will lead to the production of a large amount of chemical manure in factories. This possibility, suggested by a famous chemist, must have appeared to Marx as a strong counterargument against the Ricardian law of diminishing returns.

Certainly, Liebig is aware that insofar as inorganic materials are finite, agriculture can exhaust soils if cultivation continues in succession. Some passages in the fourth edition of *Agricultural Chemistry* actually acknowledge the exhausted state of soils in Europe and the United States, but their tone of critique still remains weak. Liebig only mentions the fact of soil exhaustion to emphasize the essential role of minerals against humus theory.[37] After all, Liebig assumes that the exhausted state of soils can be cured through synthetic fertilizers. Marx studied Liebig carefully not because he was interested in the state of exhausted land due to agriculture but because he was striving to understand the function and mechanism of organic and inorganic materials for plant growth and a variety of methods for increasing crops, including chemical fertilizers.

Marx's intention in studying Liebig becomes clear in his excerpts from James F. W. Johnston's books in the *London Notebooks*. In his letter to Engels on October 13, 1851, Marx stated that he had "been delving mainly into technology, the history thereof, and agronomy" so that he could "form at least some sort of an opinion of the stuff" and affirmatively referred to Johnston's *Notes on North America* (1851), even characterizing him as "the English Liebig" (though a Scot).[38] Marx had already read Johnston's *Lectures on Agricultural Chemistry and Geology* (1847) and *Catechism of Agricultural Chemistry and Geology* (1849) and carefully studied these books in the *London Notebooks* XIII and XIV. Since Marx identified Johnston with Liebig, excerpted texts help us discern more clearly how Marx was reading Liebig and which aspects of agricultural chemistry he was trying to learn from these prominent agricultural chemists.

Johnston, a Scottish chemist and geologist, contributed to the development of agricultural praxis through the application of chemical and geological knowledge, acquired during his various travels through Europe and North America. Similar to Liebig, Johnston recognized that organic materials alone do not suffice for ample plant growth, but that inorganic materials must be constantly returned to the soil after plants absorb them.[39] It is certainly preferable to cultivate lands under better natural conditions, so Johnston investigated the mechanism of long-term "geological formation" that reveals the formation of the soil through weathering, and he proposed to conduct a geological survey and to prepare a geological "map" that highlights fruitful soils.[40]

Furthermore, Johnston's view of agriculture stood opposed to Ricardo and Malthus, though he did not directly refer to them. He also firmly believed, contrary to Ricardo, that "natural character and composition" is subjected to mechanical and chemical improvements. Marx was conscious of this, as he commented: "The differences of nature [are] quite big. But one can take control over the circumstances which they create, and these differences can be reduced."[41] Johnston promulgated the benefits of artificial modifications of soil fertility: The "farmer can change the *character of the land itself*. He can alter both its physical qualities and its chemical composition and thus can fit it for growing other races of plants than those which it naturally bears—or, if he chooses, the same races in greater abundance and with increased luxuriance."[42] It is thus clear that, according to Johnston, Ricardo's assumption is not immediately valid in reality as far as the modification of the soil's fertility makes the actual historical process of the formation of differential rent much more complicated. This is indeed the line of Marx's argument until the *Economic Manuscripts of 1861–63*.

For Johnston, the possibility of increasing the general fertility of the soil plays a central role, which gives an optimistic tone to his overall discussion. Though he is certainly conscious of the danger of soil exhaustion due to the irrational treatment of the soil, he is convinced of future agricultural improvement with the aid of chemistry and geology, as Marx documents from Johnston's *Catechism*:

> The special exhaustion [can be] prevented by returning to the soil the particular substances my crops had taken out. For example, the phosphoric acid is restored through bone dust or guano or phosphate of lime.... However, if the farmer puts in the soil proper substances, in the proper quantities, and at the proper times, he may keep up the fertility of the land, perhaps for ever. The farmer must put in to the land at least as much as he takes out. To make his land better, he must put in more than he takes out.[43]

Here it is possible to observe the same optimism as Liebig's, according to which soil exhaustion can be prevented by the supply of inorganic substances, and even the improvement of soil fertility is foreseen. In order to attain constant profits and maximize them without soil exhaustion, which is the objective of agriculture, Johnston advocates advancing productivity by changing the chemical composition of the land through mechanical and chemical means.[44] For this purpose, he also suggests importing from foreign countries "guano" and "bones" rich in mineral substances because they are suitable for transport over great distances, even though this is, as we will see later, exactly the view that Marx calls into question in the 1860s under Liebig's influence.[45]

Now we can better comprehend why Marx calls Johnston "the English Liebig." Both Liebig and Johnston appreciate the essential role of minerals for plant growth, but, more important, they share the same optimism about ameliorating agricultural productivity to a considerable degree through the application of natural science and technology. In the context of criticizing the Ricardian law of diminishing returns, claims made by Liebig and Johnston provide Marx with a scientific foundation about the possibilities of modern agricultural production based on the newest discoveries of natural sciences. Contrary to Ricardo, who assumes a strict natural limit to the improvement of the productivity of each soil, Marx comes to believe in a future great advancement of agriculture.

Of course, this would not immediately mean that the fertility of the soil could be multiplied infinitely, as if there were no natural limits at all for agricultural production. However, insofar as Marx presumes that the exhausted state of the soil can be cured by using synthetic fertilizers, guano, and bones, it is hard to find a concrete analysis on the relationship between the exhausting cultivation and the natural limits of the soil. This makes the general tone of Marx's notebooks from 1851 appear at times too optimistic, ascribing the problem of soil exhaustion to the technological and moral backwardness of "primitive" agricultural practice. Criticizing Ricardo's and Malthus's *ahistorical* understanding of the natural character of the soil, Marx too strongly emphasizes the *sociality* of agricultural productivity, as if the natural limit imposed upon agriculture does not really exist. By doing so, his theoretical framework tacitly assumes the static binary between naturalness and sociality without adequately considering the dynamic entanglement of the internal logic of the natural material world and its social and historical modifications under capitalism. However, thanks to his critique of political economy, Marx later deals with the problem of soil exhaustion in capitalism and sees it as a contradiction of modern society.

LIEBIG'S PROBLEMATIC POLEMICS

During the preparation of *Capital* in the 1860s, Marx again intensively studied natural sciences, reading Liebig at least twice. In June 1863, Marx made excerpts from *On Theory and Practice in Agriculture* (1856) and in 1865–66 from the seventh edition of *Agricultural Chemistry* (1862). Both excerpts are of great importance because they document the development of Marx's project, mediated by Liebig's critical turn.[46] As seen above, Liebig's theory in the fourth edition of *Agricultural Chemistry* was still optimistic, believing in the almost infinite effect of soil improvement through chemical fertilizer with inorganic substances produced in factories. After confronting a number of harsh critiques due to the exaggeration of his theory of inorganic minerals and the effect of his own patented commercial manure, he began to change his arguments. This change is also reflected in his *On Theory and Practice in Agriculture*. He now warned against the danger of soil exhaustion, but at the same time he emphasized the omnipotence of chemical fertilizer more strongly than ever. This ambivalence of Liebig is discernible in the debate between "mineral theory" and "nitrogen theory," which was initiated by his rejection of the necessity of introducing ammonia artificially.

Liebig changed his opinion in the fifth edition of *Agricultural Chemistry*, published in 1843, with regard to the source of nitrogen for plant growth. He now argued that ammonia (as a main source of nitrogen) as plant nutrients is provided to the soil through rainwater in a sufficient amount.[47] He explicitly repeated the same opinion in *On Theory on Practice in Agriculture* as well, and Marx recognized this new point as he noted: "Fertile soils contain as much as from five hundred to a thousand times more nitrogen than is required for the heaviest crop of wheat, or than is given to it in the most liberal supply of manure." Ammonia, so argued Liebig, is "always and eternally" transmitted from air to the soil and is thus "inexhaustible."[48]

One can see how drastic the change of Liebig's view on ammonia is by comparing this claim with another one in the fourth edition of *Agricultural Chemistry*, which Marx noted in triple vertical lines in his *London Notebooks*: "Cultivated plants receive the same quantity of nitrogen from the atmosphere as trees, shrubs, and other wild plants; but this is *not* sufficient for the purposes of agriculture."[49] Liebig still assumed the necessity of additional introduction of ammonia salt for attaining a larger amount of crops. One year later, in the fifth edition of *Agricultural Chemistry*, Liebig surprisingly reversed his opinion in this sentence: "Cultivated plants receive the same quantity of nitrogen from the atmosphere as trees, shrubs, and other wild plants; and *this is quite sufficient for the purposes of agriculture*."[50] In *On Theory and Practice in Agriculture*, Liebig repeated his new opinion, with "The supply of ammonia is unnecessary and superfluous for most of cultivated plants."[51]

This sudden change in opinion, after Liebig's research travel through England, inspired a number of severe critiques that reprimanded him for his undervaluation of the significance of nitrogen for the cultivation of crops. John Bennet Lawes, the first successful industrial producer of chemical fertilizer in England, harshly denounced Liebig's mineral theory. Through a series of experiments conducted with Joseph Henry Gilbert in Rothamsted, Lawes demonstrated that the supply of ammonia salt without doubt increased crops. Due to the total failure of Liebig's patented manure product, Lawes was even more convinced that mineral substances alone are not able to increase crops because the amount of nitrogen naturally existing in the soil is not sufficient for the ample growth of cultivated plants.[52] He concluded that the practical farmer should pay particular attention to the exhaustion of nitrogen in the soil: "But what we say is, that by the ordinary methods of practical agriculture, by which any soils are made to yield a fair produce of grain and meat only, for sale, their characteristic exhaustion, as grain-producers, will be that of NITROGEN; and that the mineral constituents, will, under this course, RELATIVELY TO NITROGEN, be in excess."[53] This critique caused a heated (in retrospect, overheated) debate between mineral theory and nitrogen theory.

Against the attempts by Lawes and Gilbert to demonstrate that nitrogen alone guarantees greater crops, Liebig defended his mineral theory in *On Theory and Practice in Agriculture*. Admitting that an additional supply of ammonia salt increases crops over a certain period of time, he argued that this temporary increase does not change the sum total of crops in the long run. Marx documented Liebig's response to Lawes and Gilbert:

> If, now, by the addition of ammonia and carbonic acid, or of ammonia alone, the produce of this soil, in one year, be doubled, then the soil thus treated will supply, in 50 years, as much produce as it would have done, without ammonia, in 100 years. The soil will have lost, in 50 years, as much of the mineral elements of nutrition as it would have lost, without ammonia, in 100 years. By this application of ammonia, the field will not have produced more wheat, on the whole, than it would have produced without ammonia, but only more *in the same time*.[54]

Since nature can slowly supplement mineral substances through weathering of the soil, it is absolutely necessary to add manure. The use of ammonia alone is not sufficient for maintaining soil fertility.

Additional ammonia salt exhausts soil more rapidly because plants take out other mineral substances in proportion to the increased amount of ammonia. Thus ammonia manure allows plants to absorb double, triple, or even quadruple amounts of nitrogen and the proportional amount of mineral materials, though the amount of the latter is more limited than that of nitrogen: "The amount of produce, in these cases, is unquestionably proportional to the quantity of mineral elements of nutrition present in the soils." It follows that "*exhaustion* of the soil by cultivation is directly proportional to that part of this quantity or sum which the soil has annually yielded to the crop raised on it."[55] Every necessary nutrient must be sufficient to increase the crop yield. When mineral substances are taken out of the soil together with nitrogen, it is necessary to return them to the soil. Therein lies the kernel of Liebig's "law of the minimum"—that the growth of plants is conditioned by the substance whose amount is smallest in the soil, that is, inorganic substances.

In the fourth edition of *Agricultural Chemistry*, Liebig talked about possible soil exhaustion due to a lack of mineral soil constituents. This had nothing to do with his critical turn against modern agriculture, because his remark was strategically aimed at highlighting the significance of mineral substances against nitrogen theory. It is "strategic" because he believed that the danger of soil exhaustion could be easily overcome with his own mineral theory. He insisted that chemistry should open up new possibilities to agriculture, demanding, for example, that animal excrement should be more efficiently replaced by chemical manures. He recognized the difficulties for the mass fabrication of ideal chemical fertilizers, given the knowledge of chemistry then, but his agricultural chemistry should soon "start a new era of agriculture."[56] Liebig was, after all, not just a chemist, but a capitalist producer of chemical fertilizer (his patented manure), and the increasing influence of his mineral theory is tightly connected with the increase of his wealth.

We should keep Liebig's self-interest in mind when considering his claim in *On Theory and Practice in Agriculture*:

> The object in view was a complete revolution in agriculture. Farmyard-manure was to be totally excluded, and all the mineral constituents removed in the crops were to be restored in the mineral manure. The usual rotations were to cease. . . . The manure was to give the means of raising, on one and the same field, uninterruptedly and yet without exhaustion, the same crop, whether clover, wheat, or any other, according to the wish or necessity of the farmer.[57]

Liebig foresees a similar future in *Principles of Agricultural Chemistry,* published in 1855:

> In our time, one problem worthy the attention of the scientific agri-
> culturist is this: to substitute for the rotation of crops a rotation of the
> proper manures, by which he shall be enabled to grow on each of his
> fields those crops, the sale of which, according to his locality and his
> special object, is the most profitable to him. How vastly would the
> labors of the farmer be simplified if he could succeed in growing, on
> the same piece of land, the same crop uninterruptedly, without injury
> to the soil![58]

Liebig's vision of agricultural revolution in the nineteenth century would require neither fallowing nor crop rotation, thanks to chemical fertilizer.[59] He even sharpens his claim against Lawes and Gilbert to emphasize the merits of his own mineral manure. One can hardly fail to see his overvaluation of mineral manure in this polemic. Some future chemical manure will allow for complete agricultural flexibility, so that the capitalist farmer can respond to the demands of the market without fallowing and crop rotation, independent of the natural properties of the soil. This naïve neglect of natural limits in agricultural production reflects nothing but the arrogance of modern science, which treats natural characteristics and properties as passive mediums that humans can arbitrarily modify. When new technology can transform this passive nature freely, in accordance with our needs, there is no room for a serious ecological investigation.

It is thus not surprising that, despite Liebig's warning about soil exhaustion, he did not develop a critique of the robbery practice of modern agriculture until the late 1850s. Accordingly, it would not be plausible that his work inspired Marx with regard to the negative consequences of modern agriculture, because the dominant tone of *On Theory and Practice in Agriculture* is still the transcendence of natural limits through mass production of chemical fertilizer. Even if Marx in the early 1860s had noted the problem of soil exhaustion, the *Economic Manuscripts of 1861–63* are sometimes characterized as an optimistic view of the progressive forces of capital. After reading Liebig's optimistic idea about the arbitrary manipulation of natural limits through natural sciences, there is still no detailed reflection upon the destructive effects of capitalist production in Marx's economic manuscripts. Thus it is safe to conclude that Marx's reading of Liebig before 1863 does not include a truly critical attitude toward modern agriculture. However, this changes in *Capital*. This indicates how decisive the seventh edition of *Agricultural Chemistry* was for Marx's development of his critique of the metabolic rift.

EMERGENCE OF A CRITIQUE OF MODERN AGRICULTURE

When Marx studied newer texts on agricultural chemistry in 1865–66, during his preparation for the chapter on ground rent in volume 3 of *Capital*, the development of his political economy allowed him to integrate Liebig's discoveries that were "fully confirming [his] theory."[60] Certainly, Marx believed that he had successfully criticized the law of diminishing returns in the *London Notebooks*. As seen above, Marx was aware of the concrete reality of exhaustion but not in regard to the specifics. Rather, he tended to hold on to an optimistic view of future agricultural development. He did not investigate the sociality of soil fertility, the entire panoply of social and technical relationships that determine it, that bestows the appearance of validity on Ricardo's law. When he wrote the chapter on ground rent, Marx focused more carefully on this issue. He primarily dealt with the capitalist form of agriculture; that is, how the alienated logic of capital modifies and even destroys the transhistorical universal metabolism between humans and nature, as the fundamental condition of all production. Humanity needs to work upon and transform nature to be able to reproduce its distinctly human-social species-being. However, the labor process, viewed from the standpoint of any given concrete reality, and not simply transhistorically, always takes on a certain determinate *historical economic* form (*Formbestimmung*), associated with a particular set of relations of production. This reflects the particular way in which humans carry out the metabolic interaction with their environment under capitalistically constituted social relations.

Marx's *Capital* reveals that the capitalist form of labor, that is, "wage labor," radically transforms and reorganizes the material dimensions of labor according to the logic of valorization. There emerges the domination of abstract labor as the sole source of value, which violently abstracts labor from other essential concrete aspects of reality and turns humans into a mere personification of the reified thing, through formal and real subsumption under capital. The process of accommodating human activity to the logic of capital causes various disharmonies in the lives of workers, such as overwork, mental and physical disorders, and child labor, as Marx described in the chapters on "Working Day" and "Machinery and the Large-Scale Industry." This domination by capital goes beyond the reorganization of labor in the factory, as the sphere of commodification enlarges to subsume agriculture. Consequently, it produces various discordances in the material world by disturbing the natural metabolic interaction between humans and nature. It is thus no coincidence that Marx's notebooks on agricultural chemistry also reflect a shift of his interest. He now studied it again to deal with such destructive transformations of the material world under capitalism.

Marx's excerpts of 1856–66 document why the seventh edition of *Agricultural Chemistry* must have been particularly insightful for his purposes, because Liebig also altered his arguments in the new Introduction and reinforced his critique of the robbery system of modern agriculture. He gave up the earlier and overemphasized optimism, and his warning about the decay of European civilization becomes dominant. As we have seen, Liebig's agricultural chemistry is characterized by the necessity of replenishing all nutrients taken out from the soil by plants. Since nature alone cannot provide enough inorganic material when such a large quantity of nutrients are removed annually, Liebig argued for the use of chemical mineral fertilizer. Though in the 1840s he was still optimistic about the future possibility of factory mass production of chemical manure, Liebig in the 1860s relativized this earlier thesis, putting forward a harsh criticism of the widespread neglect of the "law of replenishment."

Marx's excerpts carefully trace Liebig's explanations about the mechanism of soil exhaustion and reports on the concrete reality of the disruption of the metabolism between humans and nature due to the capitalist mode of production. Liebig argued that the shortsighted increase in production is nothing but robbery of the soil:

> One thus understands that the *increase of crops* that is aimed at through the improvement of the soil by such means as *drainage* and *dung* cannot have durability due to natural law. A larger amount of crop was achieved not because the nutrient matters in the soil became richer but because it was based on techniques that make them poorer more quickly.[61]

The more the farmer exploits the soil for the sake of maximizing profit and rent, the more difficult the maintenance of soil fertility becomes. Modern agriculture takes from the soil as many soil nutrients as possible, without replenishment. Instead of his earlier prediction, Liebig now harshly criticized the violation of the natural law of replenishment as a crime against humanity: "It is violation of one of the most rational laws of nature if today's generation believes it has a right to destroy them. What is circulating belongs to the present generation, and it is destined for it. However, what the soil holds in its womb is not the wealth of today's generation because it belongs to future generations."[62]

The modern social division of labor disrupts the plant nutrition cycle, as Liebig presages: "Each land" will inevitably become "more infertile not only by continuously exporting its crops, but also by uselessly wasting the products of metabolism [*Stoffwechsel*] that accumulate in large cities." He continues: "It is clear to everyone that labor as such gradually but constantly makes the soil poorer and exhausts it in the end."[63] Marx's critique of the disturbance of the metabolic interaction between humanity and nature in volume 1 of *Capital* is based on these passages. According to Liebig, the population growth in towns is the result of industrialization, which increases demand for agricultural products from the countryside; however, the mineral substances contained in food do not return to the original soil but flow into the river as sewage. Liebig points to "the terrifying fact that Great Britain is not producing food necessary for her 29 million population," and argues that "the introduction of water-closets into most parts of England results in the irrecoverable loss of the materials capable of producing food for three and a half million people every year."[64] Liebig thus argues that "the progress of cultivation and civilization" are dependent on the problem of urban toilets.[65]

Since the nutrition cycle is disrupted, short-term maintenance or increase of soil fertility through the addition of manure becomes necessary. Manure in the form of guano and bones is imported to Britain from foreign countries, as long as the large-scale producers are able to bear the higher production costs. The problem is that the long-distance transport of fertilizer deepens the rift in natural and social metabolism, as Britain's import of manure destroys the conditions for sustainable agriculture in the foreign countries:

> Great Britain robs all countries of the conditions of their fertility. She has already ransacked the battlefields of Leipzig, Waterloo and the Crimea for bones. She has ploughed up and used the skeletons of many generations accumulated in the catacombs of Sicily. And she still destroys yearly the food for a future generation of three and a half million people. We may say to the world that she hangs like a vampire

on the throat of Europe, and even the world, and sucks out its life-blood, without any real necessity or permanent gain to herself.[66]

Liebig problematizes this imperialist system of robbery cultivation in England as specific modern phenomena, for which the solution is decisive for all of humanity.

The change in tone from Liebig's earlier optimism is obvious. In the development of modern agriculture he now recognizes the destructive system of production. It is striking that his critique warns against the threat of diminishing returns, but he differentiates it from Ricardo's thesis because he does not analyze the phenomenon as a mere ahistorical law but as a specific modern one. The reason why Marx finds Liebig's theory attractive lies in this aspect. Marx's critique of Ricardo and Malthus is based no longer on the earlier optimistic prediction of the development of productive forces through the application of technology and natural science. In accordance with Marx's critique of political economy, he reveals the historically specific relations that bestow an appearance of general validity to Ricardo's "law." With natural science, Marx investigates in an exact manner how the profit-oriented development of technology in capitalism ends up causing unexpected and destructive consequences such as soil exhaustion and scarcity of natural resources.

Furthermore, Marx's 1865 excerpts from Johnston's *Notes on North America* reflect the same tone as his excerpts from Liebig. As we have seen, Marx did not pay any particular attention to the exhaustion of land in North America when he read the two articles in *The Economist* and Carey's books in 1851. Yet in 1865 Marx cited a sentence from Liebig's *Agricultural Chemistry* about this being "the natural course of the *robbery agriculture*, which has been pursued nowhere on a larger scale than in North America." Liebig, like Carey, writes about soil exhaustion in North America:

The history of agriculture in North America has made us acquainted with innumerable incontestable facts, which prove how proportionally short the period is in which crops of corn or commercial products can be obtained without interruption or manuring. After a few generations excess plant nutrients, which have been accumulating in the soil for thousands of years, is exhausted, and profitable crops cannot be obtained without manure. In the House of Representatives in Washington the delegate Morell from Vermont pointed out a number of statistical investigations, which included the States of *Connecticut,*

Massachusetts, Rhode Island, New Hampshire, Maine and *Vermont,* showing that in 10 years, *from 1840 to 1850,* wheat production had decreased in comparison with an earlier period by half and potatoes by one-third; in Tennessee, Kentucky, Georgia, and Alabama as well as in the State of New York corn crops had diminished by one-half.[67]

Liebig's argument prompted Marx to read again Johnston's *Notes on North America* in order to study the real agricultural state in North America, despite his general avoidance of travel reports. This time, Marx clearly concentrated on those passages that describe the diminution of the productivity of soils due to robbery culture, which Marx referred to as the "system of [soil] exhaustion in North America": "The common system, in fact, of North America of selling everything for which a market can be got [hay, corn, potatoes, etc.]; and taking no trouble to put anything into the soil in return."[68]

In the 1850s, Marx did not make excerpts from Carey's similar remarks in the *London Notebooks,* but instead follows Johnston's report carefully: "There was, however, no motivation for those American farmers who merely seek profits to conduct a more reasonable agriculture with a good management of their soils because careless and improvident farming habits . . . were thus introduced. . . . It was cheaper and more profitable to clear and crop new land than to renovate the old."[69] Consequently, farmers also have no interest in preserving or improving the fertility of their lands for their children: "The owner has already fixed a price in his mind at which he . . . hopes to sell, believing that, with the same money, he could do better for himself and his family by going still farther west."[70] In this situation, there is no serious attempt for the long-term improvement of the soil, and what is dominant among the farmers is idleness and ignorance:

> In Canada, as in every other part of North Eastern America, long under the cultivation of European settlers, the same change [is taking place]. "Everywhere idleness, ignorance, and *an avaricious spirit,* on the part of the cultivators, have led to the same results in diminishing the ability or disposition of the soil to produce good crops of wheat.... The spirit of fertility is every year retiring farther towards the West, shrinking from the abusive contact of European industry."[71]

Johnston concludes that the system in North America would sooner or later lead to "complete exhaustion."[72] Referring to Johnston's book,

Marx later writes in his manuscript about the tendency toward rapid soil exhaustion: "The possibility of this *superficial* cultivation is of course more or less rapidly exhausted in inverse proportion to the fertility of the new soil and in direct proportion to the export of its product."[73]

As long as agriculture, under the "monopoly of private property," is carried out on the basis of profit calculation, robbery practice prevails over society simply because the squandering exploitation of land is more profitable in the short term, in a manner similar to the intensive and extensive exploitation of labor power without caring about workers' mental and physical conditions. As capital does not compensate for the premature exhaustion of labor power, which shortens workers' lives, the natural fertility of the soil appears free to capital, and compensation for its destruction and pollution appears unnecessary. Thus there is an immanent tendency of capital to exploit both labor power and natural forces as quickly as possible, with no thought about its future consequences. Capital ignores the limits of the natural world, only to undermine the material conditions for sustainable production.

Nonetheless, Marx differs from Johnston on a decisive point. Facing this deep contradiction of the capitalist form of agriculture, "quite conservative agricultural chemists, such as Johnston (!) for example, admit that private property places insuperable barriers on all sides to a genuinely rational agriculture."[74] Though he values Johnston's work, Marx sees him as "conservative" because he feels the barriers to the realization of rational agriculture, but he does not see it as the manifestation of the immanent contradiction of the capitalist mode of production, but as the subjective inability, the lack of education, of individual farmers. Johnston repeatedly tries to justify the current situation as a necessary, but temporary, evil: "The emigration of this class of wilderness-clearing and new land-exhausting farmers, is a kind of necessity in the rural progress of a new country. It is a thing to rejoice in rather to regret, as I found some of my New Brunswick friends doing."[75] The solution to the robbery practice, short of the abolition of the capitalist mode of production, would be state administration of the entire land. Curiously, focusing on descriptions about the state of exhausting agriculture under this system, Marx stops his excerpts just *before* the passage cited above and also ignores other passages where the conservative agricultural chemist stresses, in vain, the possibility of introducing a more rational agricultural system through education and the development of technology under capitalism.

Obviously, Marx still recognizes the importance of "rational culture," an idea he obtained from Liebig and Johnston in the 1850s. Marx also makes it unambiguously clear that it is not the primitive agricultural state in North America but the *capitalist* relations of production that prevent such a rational form of agriculture by forcing American farmers to abandon lands, going farther west once they no longer produce enough profits. Capital actually constitutes a system of robbery economy with "techniques" of exploiting the productive force of nature for free; as Liebig writes, "crude robbery develops into techniques of robbery." The exhaustion of land in North America has its origin precisely in the development of capitalism. It is not simply due to the precapitalist backwardness of its agriculture, as the articles of *The Economist* indicated in accordance with Johnston. Marx plainly states in *Capital*: "All progress in increasing the fertility of the soil for a given time is a progress towards ruining the more long-lasting sources of that fertility." Thus the popular robbery practice is nothing but a *specific modern product*, and Marx characterizes the case of North America as the manifestation of the destructive dimension of capitalist production: "The more a country proceeds from large-scale industry as the background of its development, as in the case of the United States, the more rapid is this process of destruction. Capitalist production, therefore, only develops the techniques and the degree of combination of the social process of production by simultaneously undermining the original sources of all wealth—*the soil and the worker.*"[76] This destructive process extends to a global scale with the accumulation of capital.[77]

ECOLOGICAL IMPERIALISM AND GLOBAL CRISES

With regard to a possible countermeasure against the exhaustion of natural forces, Marx writes in *Capital*:

> Apart from the daily more threatening advance of the working-class movement, the limiting of factory labor was dictated by the same necessity that forced the manuring of English fields with guano. The same blind desire for profit that in the one case exhausted the soil had in the other case seized hold of the vital force of the nation at its roots. Periodic epidemics speak as clearly on this point as the diminishing military standard of height in France and Germany.[78]

Marx sees the legislation of a normal workday as an important gain for workers, extending their disposable time. Capitalists are forced to accept this regulation due to their class interest; otherwise, the reproduction of the working class and the accumulation of capital would be impossible. In a similar manner, the English farmer is driven to use guano as a means of sustaining soil fertility, even if it requires some additional costs. This manuring does not represent real progress, however, it only deepens the contradictions in capitalist agriculture. Here the limit of capitalist production clearly manifests itself, even if it always appears to overcome various difficulties imposed upon its aim of efficient and smooth capital accumulation. Liebig's critique of robbery agriculture contributed to Marx's theorization.

Guano is the excrement of sea birds native to South America. In 1802, Alexander Humboldt, during his short stay in Peru, noticed the local usage of guano in agriculture. He took some samples back to Europe from the Chincha Islands, hoping that guano would improve European soils. Investigation confirmed its effect. After this, guano was regarded as a superior guard against soil exhaustion, thanks to its rich content of phosphoric acid, nitrogen, and potash. In the nineteenth century, this excrement from the so-called guano islands was massively extracted and exported to Europe. This system worked fine, that is, until the guano reserve was completely plundered.

As Liebig came to comprehend modern agriculture in a more critical way in the seventh edition of *Agricultural Chemistry*, he toned down the effectiveness of this new natural manure. He now argued that dependence on guano does not contribute to maintaining soil fertility, but, on the contrary, disrupts the metabolic interaction between humans and nature on an enlarged scale. In the fourth edition of *Agricultural Chemistry*, he still treated the use of guano and bones as an effective way of supplying necessary plant nutrition. Just as Johnston recommended guano and bones as a favorable means of agricultural reform due to easy long-distance importation, Liebig wrote about the utility of guano as manure, as Marx documented in the *London Notebooks*:

> It is sufficient to add a small quantity of guano to *a soil, which consists only of sand and clay*, in order to procure the richest crop of maize. The soil itself (on the coast of Peru) does not contain the smallest particle of organic matter, and *the manure employed is formed only of urate, phosphate, oxalate*, and *carbonate of ammonia, together with a few earthy salts*.[79]

Liebig's high evaluation of guano is understandable, because the excellent effect of guano comes from its inorganic substances and thus proves the correctness of Liebig's mineral theory. Guano was eagerly collected from the coast of Peru and scattered over European lands as a savior. Guano export to England rapidly increased, and in 1859 amounted to 286,000 tons a year. However, this still did not suffice to replenish mineral substances in the soil lost by agriculture.

The scarcity of the guano reserve was keenly felt early in the 1850s, as Marx documented, based on the seventh edition of *Agricultural Chemistry*:

> Admiral Moresby, who was stationed on the coast of Peru, reported in 1853 to the English Government that according to his surveys and recordings, including the Chincha Islands, the reserves of guano at that time amounted to 8,600,000 tons or 172 million cwts [hundredweights]. Since then (according to Pusey) 3 million of cwts (150,000 tons) were annually imported by England alone and even more by the United States. . . . Thus, Moresby declares that by a moderate calculation of the exports these islands will be exhausted of the good quality guano saleable in the English market within eight or nine years.[80]

Liebig's new Introduction in the seventh edition was published exactly nine years after Moresby's report. So it is reasonable that Liebig added new passages in which he warned against excessive dependence on guano. Since the deep metabolic rift in the cycle of plant nutrients existed, due to the antagonism between town and countryside, use of imported manure could not provide a solution to the problem of soil exhaustion, but at best postponed it. English agriculture grew wheat by a successively greater sacrifice of its natural resources, so that, in the end, guano imports ultimately intensified the disruption of the metabolism between humans and nature.

The threat of soil exhaustion drove the English and Americans to a desperate search for new reservoirs of guano and saltpeter, first near the Chincha Islands and then in other islands in South America. The U.S. Congress voted for the "Guano Islands Act" in 1856, which approved annexing dozens of islands with guano reserves. This robbery of guano resulted in intensive economic exploitation of marginalized land, as well as the Chincha Islands War (the so-called Guano War) and the War of the Pacific. Furthermore, unregulated capitalist production in the periphery caused the gross exploitation of human labor in the extraction of guano, the violent oppression of original inhabitants and people from other colonies. Under colonial domination, not just aboriginal

people but also Chinese indentured laborers were enslaved and subjected to brutal conditions of work and life.[81] The original ecosystem was
also heavily modified. For example, Humboldt-penguins make nests in
guano hillsides, so that the rapid exploitation of guano reservoirs inevitably threatened them with extinction. As a whole, the system of guano
robbery lasted only for a relatively brief historical period. The number
of seabirds were diminished as their nests were destroyed during extraction, and thus guano was no longer reproduced.

The more urgent the scarcity of natural resources becomes, the more
violent imperialist politics becomes, as the example of guano clearly
illustrates. The process, however, is a vicious circle, as the extension of
imperialist domination accelerates the extent of exploitation of natural
resources, which causes more and more exhaustion of natural wealth.
Due to this ecological imperialism, the deep metabolic rift extends to all
of the earth.

The violent exploitation of natural resources and workers in periph-
eral countries, inherent in the capitalist competition exemplified by the
"guano imperialism" practiced by both England and the United States,
resulted in the squandering of Peru's guano. Yet it did not prevent the
decline in soil fertility in these two rich nations. The robbery system
simply caused the universal material condition of production to deteriorate by disrupting the nutrient cycle. When North America, after
importing enormous quantities of South American guano, ended up
exporting wheat to England, American lands were exhausted, as Carey
and Johnston reported. Inorganic substances exported to England and
absorbed by plants returned neither to American or English soils but
flowed into the Thames River as sewage, causing dramatic consequences
to the quality of life in London. Even if English capitalism imported more
guano, bones, wheat, and meat, made possible by rapidly developing
means of long-distance transportation, the existing system of squandering could hardly subsist in the long run.[82] With the development of
global capitalism, it only accelerated the desertification of the land.

In this context, it is important to emphasize that the problem of "ecological imperialism" is not at all limited to South America. Marx planned
to discuss the general danger of the international corn trade in capitalism, due to its destruction of soil fertility, as documented in this reference
to Leibig in his manuscript for volume 3 of *Capital*:

> Large-scale landownership, on the other hand, reduces the agricul-
> tural population to a constantly decreasing minimum and confronts

it with a constantly growing industrial population conglomerated together in large towns; in this way it produces conditions that provoke an irreparable rift in the interdependent process between social metabolism and natural metabolism prescribed by the natural laws of the soil. The result of this is a squandering of the vitality of the soil, and *trade carries this devastation far beyond the bounds of a single country* (Liebig).[83]

Since Marx only noted a relevant name without going into the detail, this passage requires further examination.

Marx pointed not just to the agglomeration of population in large cities but also to the desertification of soils due to international trade. Marx recognized the international exploitation of limited resources as the normal trajectory of capitalism. This insight confirms an important development in his ecology. In comparison to his initial reception of agricultural chemistry in the *London Notebooks*, his critique deepens in this passage as he problematizes not only Ricardo's abstract assumption of the law of diminishing returns but also its proponents' *politico-economic solution* to the issue.

According to the law of diminishing returns, Ricardo and Malthus argue that population increase requires the cultivation of less fertile lands. It requires more labor to produce the same quantity of crops and causes the general increase of the price of wheat, which also never fails to raise ground rent and the wages of labor. Corresponding to these increases, the profit rate falls. In order to eliminate this hindrance to capital accumulation, Ricardo supports the idea of abolishing the Corn Laws and insists upon importing cheaper crops from foreign countries and concentrating on industrial development within England, rather than cultivating less fertile lands, under pressure from the growing population to provide more food. Malthus, as an ideological apologist of the interest of landowners. not only speaks against the abolition of the Corn Laws but also applies the law of diminishing returns to legitimate the poverty of the working class, whose members cause absolute overpopulation, an inevitable result of the natural development of civilization. The assumptions made by both economists are problematic; they will only consider a retreat to less productive lands, excluding the uniquely capitalist dynamics of soil exhaustion from their analysis. Soil fertility is something simply given to them. As Ricardo formulates it, it is a question of the "*original and indestructible powers* of the soil."[84]

Ricardo recognizes a certain natural limit imposed upon agriculture in terms of differentials in natural productivity, but at the same time he believes that there are enough fruitful and unexhausted lands on the earth, at least sufficient for the development of capitalism in England. In this way, he neglects the problem of colonial domination and the global disturbance of social and natural metabolism. Marx clearly rejects Ricardo's ethnocentric assumption and argues that imports of North American, Irish, and Indian products only worsen the problem from the perspective of human species-being, as "trade carries this devastation far beyond the bounds of a single country." The natural power decreases all over the world to the extent that English capitalism flourishes.

It is therefore not a coincidence that ecological problems manifest more clearly in the periphery of capitalism, the sources of ever-growing exports of agricultural produce and raw materials to the capitalist center. Marx in *Capital* refers to an example of soil exhaustion due to English colonialism in Ireland: "If the product also diminishes relatively, per acre, it must not be forgotten that for a century and a half England has indirectly exported the soil of Ireland, without even allowing its cultivators the means for replacing the constituents of the exhausted soil."[85] Marx did not integrate Liebig's theory passively, but actively applied it to his own political analysis. In colonized Ireland, land was enclosed irrespective of the needs of the Irish people. Through England's "clearing of estates," Irish lands were transformed into "an English sheep-walk and cattle pasture" for the purpose of increasing ground rent and tenure, and despite consolidation of landed properties, rapid depopulation threw many lands out of cultivation.[86] The result of the nineteenth-century "agricultural revolution" for the population in Ireland was nothing but the enlargement of their unendurable suffering:

> The first act of the agricultural revolution was to sweep away the huts situated at the place of work. This was done on the largest scale, as if in obedience to a command from on high. Thus many laborers were compelled to seek shelter in villages and towns. There they were thrown like refuse into garrets, holes, cellars and corners, in the worst slum districts. . . . The men are now obliged to seek work from the neighboring farmers, and are only hired by the day, and therefore under the most precarious form of wage.[87]

Referring to various statistics, Marx showed that "progress" in agriculture under the agricultural revolution in Ireland did not bring improvement but rather the destruction of life. The population fell into poverty and famine: "The population of Ireland had, by 1841, grown to 8,222,664. In 1851 it had dwindled to 6,623,985; in 1861, to 5,850,309; and in 1866 5.5 million, approximately its level in 1801," which makes a clear contrast to the increasing number of cattle and sheep.[88] This process of transformation resulted not only in a massive emigration from Ireland, supplying new labor forces to the cities, but also drastic physical consequences for the Irish, such as deaf-muteness, blindness, and psychological problems. This "revolution" was quite successful from a capitalist perspective, for the rent of land and the profits of the farmers increased. The reason is simple: "With the throwing together of small-holdings and the change from arable to pasture land, a larger part of the total product was transformed into a surplus product."[89]

The increasing export of soils from Ireland together with its decreasing population undermined the material conditions for sustainable production.[90] The transformation from arable to pasture land disrupted the nutrition cycle, due to the consolidation of small landowners and to the emigration of lessees who had taken good care of the soil. Despite this situation, cultivation and stock farming were more intensively carried out.[91] Marx writes: "So result: Gradual expulsion of the natives. Gradual deterioration and exhaustion of the source of national life, the soil."[92] In the physical sickliness and soil exhaustion of Ireland, a periphery of the capitalist mode of production, the disharmony of "social metabolism," as well as the ecological crises of "natural metabolism" crystallized. The transformation of English agriculture found "its caricature in Ireland."[93] The "modernization" of Ireland occurred without the benefits of industrialization.

In this context, Marx's excerpts from Lavergne's *Rural Economy of England, Scotland and Ireland* (1855) are of interest. This French scholar illustrates the superiority of English farming in its comparison to his home country. Marx quoted the book in 1865 in the same notebook as his excerpts from Liebig, carefully documenting Lavergne's illustration of how sheep and cattle in England are artificially modified for the purpose of larger meat production and a shorter production period. The example of this "improvement," which Marx uses in a manuscript for volume 2 of *Capital* with regard to Lavergne, is on Bakewell sheep, named after the British breeder Robert Bakewell, known as one of the most important figures of agricultural developments in the eighteenth century. Marx notes that Lavergne is excited about the progress made by Bakewell sheep and discovers a proof of the superiority of English agriculture:

Bakewell. Earlier English sheep, as French now, not fit for the butcher, before 4 or 5 years. According to his system it may be fattened as early as one year old, and in every case has reached its full growth before the end of the 2nd year. By *System of Selection.* (19) (*Bakewell*—farmer of *Dishley Grange.*) (Reduced size of the sheep. Only so many bones as necessary for their existence) His sheep are called "new Leicesters." "The breeder can now send 3 to market in the same space of time that it formerly took him to prepare one; and broader, rounder, greater development in those parts which give most flesh. . . . Almost all their weight is pure meat."[94]

Lavergne is enthusiastic about the shortening of time necessary for the animals' maturity thanks to Bakewell's "system of selection," which also increased the amount of meat.

Since the beginning of the nineteenth century, many of Bakewell's "New Leicesters" were brought into Ireland and crossed with native sheep, creating new races, known as "Roscommon" and "Galway."[95] The original ecosystem in Ireland was transformed from the perspective of maximizing profits and ground rents, and this is exactly another example of ecological imperialism. Here the health and wealth of animals are not a primary concern, but what is important is their utility for capital. Notably, this type of progress did not impress Marx, and thus he wrote without hesitation in his private notebook: "Characterized by precocity, in entirety sickliness, want of bones, a lot of development of fat and flesh etc. All these are artificial products. Disgusting!"[96]

In the excerpts from Wilhelm Hamm's *Agricultural Tools and Machines in England* (*Die landwirthschaftlchen Geräthe und Maschinen Englands*), one finds a similar remark by Marx. As a reaction to Hamm's praise of intensive farming in England—Hamm translated Lavergne's work into German—Marx calls "feeding in the stable" the "system of cell prison" and asks himself:

In these prisons animals are born and remain there until they are killed off. The question is whether or not this system connected to the breeding system that grows animals in an abnormal way by aborting bones in order to transform them to mere meat and a bulk of fat—whereas earlier (before 1848) animals remained active by staying in free air as much as possible—will ultimately result in serious deterioration of life force?[97]

These remarks by Marx must be surprising to those who denounce him as a naïve anthropocentric apologist of technological development of any kinds. His notebooks document his honest reaction against the capitalist form of development that occurs at the cost of an animal's well-being.

Also, in India, the process of modernization penetrates, with the wanton destruction of traditional communities:

> There the broad basis of the mode of production is formed by the union between small-scale agriculture and domestic industry, on the top of which we have in the Indian case the form of self-sustaining communities. In India the English applied their direct political and economic power, as masters and landlords, to destroying these small economic communities. Insofar as English trade has had a revolutionary effect on the mode of production in India, this is simply to the extent that it has destroyed spinning and weaving, which form an age-old and integral part of this unity of industrial and agricultural production, through the cheapness (and the underselling) of English commodities.[98]

Through these "economic experiments," there emerged "a caricature of large-scale English landed property," analogous to colonialism in Ireland, where capital, despite its dissolution of the old system, does not bring about the positive effects of modernization.[99] Quite the opposite. These "economics experiments" first dissolve the traditional forms of communities, then transform the unity of agriculture and industry into their antagonistic separation, and finally destroy the entire national life. British colonialism in India did not recognize the importance of reserving water and drainage, once controlled by the state due to its importance for the people but then abolished by the colonialists. Thus a catastrophic famine occurred, not coincidentally, in 1866 in Orissa as the result of a severe drought.[100] In spite of various recommendations for delivering rice, for example, the British administration did not take any countermeasures against the famine. Marx shows the negative consequences of English colonialism when he writes, "It is sufficient to recall the famine of 1866, which cost the lives of more than a million Hindus in the district of Orissa, in the Bengal Presidency."[101]

In opposition to Ricardo's recommendation of corn imports and Malthus's simple acceptance of the poverty of the masses, Marx, referring to Liebig's theory of robbery cultivation, investigates not only the historical causes of the negative consequences of capitalist agriculture but also the imperialist brutality, which is tightly connected to capitalist "progress." He analyzes how the rifts in social and natural metabolism globalize when the demands for importing cheaper raw materials and agricultural produce increase. Marx comes to the conviction that, insofar as the infinite desire for capital accumulation organizes the relation of humans to nature, there is no effective method within capitalism to avoid production disasters. Though capital always tries to overcome this contradiction, it produces barriers to its own expansion: "The real barrier of capitalist production is capital itself."

In terms of an ecological perspective, Marx's analysis of marginalized colonial countries leaves no trace of a naïve faith in hyper-industrialism. Though Marx in articles in the *New York Daily Tribune* in the 1850s had argued about the progressive and civilizing power of English capital's colonial domination of India, his description in *Capital* without doubt differs from this earlier view. He now emphasizes colonialism's negative and destructive consequences.[102] There is no "great civilizing influence of capital" at work, but, on the contrary, there is the dissolution of traditional communities and communes, creating more poverty and suffering without hope for progress. Behind this change in his views there lies the development of his theory of metabolism.

The "caricatures" of the English modernization process present in colonized countries such as Ireland and India only serve to destroy traditional and sustainable agriculture. Marx's argument resonates with Liebig's critical remark on the dissolution of small-scale agriculture and with his warning about the decay of civilization, and he carefully notes:

> The fertility of the land is maintained without damage for thousands of years in only those places where the people engaged in agriculture gather to live within a relatively small area, and where the citizen or the craftsman of the small towns diffused over the same field cultivates a piece of his own land with his own companies. For example, when 3,000 to 4,000 people live within one square mile, they need the [entire] produce of the land just for themselves. The fertility of such land is maintained under the regular cycle of conditions [for sustaining fertility]. . . . One can think of the same land under the ownership of ten large landowners. Robbery replaces the position of replenishment. The small landowner almost completely replenishes to the soil what he takes out from it, but the large landowner exports corn and meat to large centers of consumption and loses the conditions for

reproduction. . . . This is the inevitable reason for the impoverishment of the lands by cultivation.[103]

Marx does not idealize the precapitalist form of production. However,
in Liebig's theory of metabolism Marx finds a scientific ground for the
"intimate relationship of humans to the earth." This is because Liebig
explains why modern agriculture must more rapidly exhaust the soil
compared to the traditional modes of production where agricultural
produce is consumed within the community. Since capital does not take
into account the traditional, more sustainable relationship of humans
and nature and radically destroys it for the sake of "free" capital accumulation, there emerge various material contradictions on a larger scale
than ever before.[104] Marx's critique of modernity deepened through his
natural science investigation in 1865. His attention to the topic of sustainability in precapitalist society, moreover, seems to correspond to his
further ethnological and agricultural study after 1868.

FROM SQUANDERING TO SUSTAINABLE PRODUCTION

In spite of the intensive usage of chemical fertilizer, capitalist agriculture
cannot help exhausting the soil in the long term. A communist project
therefore demands a radical transformation of humanity's relationship to
nature. In contrast to Ricardo and Malthus, Marx's project consistently
argues for the possibility of sustainable improvement of agricultural production under the operation of "rational agriculture." There is, in this
sense, no "pessimistic" turn in Marx's thought.

However, Marx is much more cautious about the limits of the material
world, the analysis of which, based on natural science, is indispensable
for any future vision of an alternative to capitalism. Precisely because
nature has limits, the social interactions with nature must be consciously
regulated by society. Marx's arguments come from his insight into the
inability of capitalism to fulfill this demand under reified social relations.
Marx's project of political economy repeatedly emphasizes the necessity
of a radical transformation of the relations of production and the conscious and rational management of natural and social metabolism by
"associated producers":

The moral of the tale, which can also be extracted from other discussions of agriculture, is that the bourgeois system runs counter to
a rational agriculture, or that a rational agriculture is incompatible

with the bourgeois system even if, technologically speaking, it promotes its development and needs either the touch of the small private cultivator or the control of the associated producers.[105]

Sustainable agriculture, due to its material characteristics and conditions, is incompatible with the capitalist mode of operation, which recognizes no such limits. Agricultural reform is thus a central task of the future revolution. However, Marx's project in *Capital,* in contrast to the *London Notebooks,* does not aim at an infinite increase in soil fertility. The smallholders maintained soil fertility by consciously following tradition, and given natural conditions, producing principally for satisfying their own concrete needs. The ownership of land constituted a basis for the "development of personal independence."[106] Capitalist agricultural production dissolves the old practice of peasant families and reorganizes the production process and its material and technological conditions solely from the perspective of capital's valorization. Nevertheless, it results in various disharmonies in the material world, and these require the transformation of the relations of production if they are to be resolved.

Against the one-sidedness of the capitalist production process, communist society must realize a conscious intercourse with nature. In a famous passage about the "realm of freedom," Marx emphasizes the significance of conscious regulation of metabolism with nature in the future society:

> In fact, the realm of freedom begins only when labor determined by necessity and external expediency comes to an end; it lies by its very nature beyond the sphere of material production proper. Just as the savage must wrestle with nature to satisfy his needs, to maintain and reproduce his life, so must civilized man, and he must do so in all forms of society and under all possible modes of production. This realm of natural necessity expands with his development, because his needs do too; but the productive forces to satisfy these expand at the same time. Freedom, in this sphere, can consist only in this, that socialized man, the associated producers, govern their metabolic interaction with nature rationally, bringing it under their collective control instead of being dominated by it as a blind power; accomplishing this metabolism with the smallest expenditure of energy and in conditions most worthy and appropriate for their human nature. But this always remains a realm of necessity. The true realm of freedom, the development of human powers as an end in itself, begins

beyond it, though it can only flourish with this realm of necessity as
its basis. The reduction of the working day is the basic prerequisite.[107]

Marx without doubt recognizes the positive side of modern technology and natural sciences, which prepares the material conditions for the
establishment of the "realm of freedom" by enabling humans to produce
various products in a shorter time. The producers in the future society
can modify their environment with larger freedom with the aid of technology. However, this is not an abolishment of natural laws. Nature still
maintains its own dynamics.

Also in the communist society, where the entire social production is
not organized by the commodity production of private producers but
by the social production of associated producers, the "realm of necessity" still remains. It continues to exist because material production is
definitely indispensable for any society. But in contrast to other societies,
the associated producers "govern their metabolic interaction with nature
rationally." This metabolic interaction cannot simply be abolished; its
conscious regulation persists as an eternal necessity. Otherwise humans
would be ignoring the power of nature. The regulation thus constitutes
the essential material conditions for the "realm of freedom" that will promote free human development. Marx is aware that the execution of labor
alone is not sufficient for free human development, but real free activity
only begins beyond the "realm of necessity." However, it is first necessary
to realize the rational interaction with nature and to shorten the workday. As Marx emphasizes here, the realm of freedom "can only flourish
with this realm of necessity as its basis," and in this sense there is no
utopian separation of these two realms. Human activity in the realm of
freedom is still a part of the transhistorical metabolism between humans
and nature and must not arbitrarily undermine its own material basis.
The conscious construction of the unity between humans and nature is
thus no one-sided domination and manipulation of the external sensuous world but aims at sustainable production without violating nature's
limits. The popular critique of Marx's so-called Prometheanism is false.
Marx does not overestimate the potential development of productive
forces in the future nor underestimate the negative consequences caused
by capitalism.[108]

What Marx repeats in *Capital* is the insurmountable limits of nature,
with which humans must be cautious, because all production is fundamentally dependent on nature. In addition to the objective possibility to
produce more, the subjective ability for the conscious interaction with the

environment, which needs to take place within nature's limits, is essential for the development of productive forces. In contrast, it is capitalism that clings to the myth of further technological innovations, because it cannot provide any solution to a series of serious ecological problems beyond more technological innovations.[109] Marx shows that the value-oriented system of production cannot realize a true development of productive forces. In this sense, there is no naïve praising of new productive forces, because in capitalism their material character is already fundamentally modified through the "productive forces of capital." If they contribute only to capital accumulation but not to sustainablility, such innovations do not count as "development" of productive forces, but mere "robbery." Even though this qualitative dimension of the category of "productive forces" is often neglected, and its characterization as a mere objective factor in material production is inadequate. Rather, the cultivation of the subjective capacity for conscious and sustainable control of production is essential for the concept of productive forces, viewed from a wider, more rational standpoint. The enlargement of disposable free time is indispensable for the cultivation of this wider sensibility.

Marx warns against an instrumental attitude toward nature for the purpose of capital's valorization, because "instead of a conscious and rational treatment of the land as permanent communal property, as the inalienable condition for the existence and reproduction of the chain of human generations, we have the exploitation and squandering of the powers of the earth."[110] However, insofar as the serious crises of the material conditions of life question the legitimacy of the capitalist system, he sees here the possibility that people with "enormous [new] consciousness," both subjectively and consciously, may resist the logic of capital and construct a new attitude toward nature.[111] Various ecological crises compel humans to conscious struggle with the problem of sustainability in order to overcome their alienation from nature and prevent the decay of civilization: "But by destroying the circumstances surrounding that metabolism, which originated in a merely natural and spontaneous fashion, it compels its systematic restoration as a regulative law of social production, and in a form adequate to the full development of the human race."[112] In the serious degradation of social and natural metabolism, there exists a fundamental ground for the emergence of a conscious regulation of the entire social production. The statement that the capitalist mode of production creates "the material conditions for a new and higher synthesis, a union of agriculture and industry"[113] is not a utopian prediction, with which Marx hoped for an "absurd elimination

of the problem of [ecological] disruption" but a practical demand for the
socialist movement.[114] On the contrary, Marx recognizes that the dominion of capital can endure as long as its valorization is possible, even if a
large part of the earth is made unsuitable for human life.[115] What Marx
sees here as necessary is the serious practical engagement with global
ecological crises, because capital cannot stop these crises but only accel-
erate them.[116]

By integrating Liebig's critique of robbery agriculture, Marx deepened his ecological critique of capitalism. It is true that he hardly wrote
on this theme after the publication of volume 1 of *Capital*. Yet one
cannot imagine that, after this intensive study on natural limits against
the formal logic of capitalist form determination, he suddenly abandoned his further research on ecological questions. With careful study
of his notebooks, one soon realizes the opposite is the case. After 1868,
Marx studied natural sciences seriously, but the actual theoretical significance of this in regard to completing his project of political economy
has remained unexamined until today. In his excerpt notebooks of 1868,
he continued his intensive research of agroscience and even modified his
judgment of Liebig's theory.

6

Marx's Ecology after 1868

In the last two chapters, we have seen in Marx's pre-1867 notebooks how Liebig's *Agricultural Chemistry* and Johnston's *Notes on North America* contributed to his project on political economy in an eco-logical sense. In opposition to his earlier writings, Marx came to clearly recognize natural limits as such, parting from a myth of an unlim-ited technologically driven increase in production. He also treated the exhaustion and deterioration of natural fertility and natural resources as a contradiction between nature and capital, which capital can never completely overcome, despite its endless endeavors to appropriate labor power and natural wealth. In addition to chapters on "The Working Day" and "Machinery and the Large-Scale Industry" in volume 1 of *Capital*, further hints in his unpublished manuscripts and notebooks indicate his intention to explicate various tensions between the formal logic of capital and the material properties of nature, such as in his analysis on the "turn-over of capital" in volume 2 and on "ground rent" in volume 3 of *Capital*. In this sense it is totally understandable that after 1868 he continued to study natural sciences for the sake of completing *Capital*, and did so more intensively than ever. Though Marx himself did not write much on this topic after the publication of volume 1 of *Capital*, it is worth recon-structing the new beginning of his research on natural science.

Unfortunately, we must wait until the full publication of the fourth section of the MEGA[2] in order to execute a complete study of Marx's excerpt notebooks after 1868.[1] Thus this chapter examines only his note-books of 1868 in order to show that his natural science investigation after 1868 is not a "flight from *Capital*" but a further development of his theory of metabolism.[2]

The notebooks Marx made in the winter of 1868 reveal how his theoretical horizon enlarged after confronting the heated debate on the validity of Liebig's theory of soil exhaustion, which prompted him to pursue research in the field of natural sciences such as chemistry, botany, geology, and mineralogy in the following years. A forgotten figure on the current topic is Carl Nikolaus Fraas, an agronomist in Munich in the mid-nineteenth century. Fraas is of importance because his books possess a unique position in Marx's notebooks. Though this German scientist was a harsh critic of Liebig's *Agricultural Chemistry*, which Marx affirmatively quoted in the first edition of *Capital*, Marx praised Fraas's contribution and even found in his work a "socialist tendency."

In the previous literature, Fraas was neglected, as well as his theoretical influence on Marx.[3] Here we will examine Fraas's books and Marx's excerpt notebooks to understand why Fraas's "agricultural physics," which, in opposition to Liebig's "agricultural chemistry," emphasized the "climatic influences" on vegetation and on human civilization, was important for Marx's project of political economy. Fraas's theory was so important to the development of Marx's theory of metabolism and agriculture that Marx even altered his evaluation of Liebig in the second edition of *Capital*. This change reflects the opening of his new field of research. One can observe another "emergence of a theory" in his notebooks of 1868.

DOUBT ABOUT LIEBIG?

Marx in volume 1 of *Capital* argues how capitalist agriculture, disregarding the needs of future generations, seriously disrupts the "metabolic interaction between humans and the earth" due to its shortsighted management of the soil. In this passage he refers to Liebig's *Agricultural Chemistry* and especially its Introduction, emphasizing its contribution to the ecology: "To have developed from the point of view of natural science the negative, i.e., destructive side of agriculture, is one of Liebig's immortal merits."[4] Marx continues to argue that Liebig's "historical overview of the history of agriculture, although not free from gross errors, contains more flashes of insight than all the works of modern political economists put together."[5] This astonishingly high valuation of Liebig's theory is not a careless formulation. Marx had already expressed the same opinion in a letter to Engels. Marx did not end his examination of the "negative" and "destructive" aspects of modern agriculture with Liebig's book, but that was only the beginning of his new research after

1868. This is not surprising, considering that after the publication of the seventh edition of Liebig's *Agricultural Chemistry* there emerged a number of debates on the validity of his theory of mineral fertilizer and soil exhaustion. The books that Marx read in 1868 clearly indicate that he was carefully following these debates.[6]

In reading the sentences on Liebig just quoted, a careful reader may immediately notice a difference between the first edition and later editions, although it was pointed out only recently by a German MEGA editor, Carl-Erich Vollgraf.[7] Marx modified this sentence in the second edition of *Capital* published in 1872–73. Consequently, we usually only read: "His historical overview of the history of agriculture, although not free from gross errors, *contains flashes of insight.*"[8] Marx deleted the statement that Liebig was more insightful "than all the works of modern political economists put together." Though he still continued to praise Liebig's contribution, the tone definitely became more sober. Why did Marx soften his endorsement of Liebig's contributions relative to classical political economy?

One might argue that this retraction of his previous claim, that Liebig was more important to the analysis of agriculture than all the economists, constitutes merely a trivial change, meant to clarify Liebig's original contributions in the field of agricultural chemistry and separate them from political economy, where the great chemist made some "gross errors." Also, Marx was very enthusiastic about one particular political economist's understanding of the soil problem, namely James Anderson, who, unlike other classical political economists, examined issues of the destruction of the soil. Hence, Marx might have thought that his own expression in the first edition of *Capital* was rather exaggerated.

Nonetheless, it should be noted that Liebig's *Agricultural Chemistry* was eagerly discussed by a number of political economists at the time, especially with regard to ground rent theory and population theory. Wilhelm Roscher integrated it into his *System of National Economy.* Liebig, himself, had a section on "National Economy and Agriculture" in the Introduction of *Agricultural Chemistry* and praised Adam Smith's recognition of the uniqueness of agriculture in contrast to industry. Thus it is reasonable to assume that Marx in the first edition of *Capital* was intentionally comparing Liebig to those political economists who postulated a transhistorical and linear development of agriculture, whether from more productive to less productive soils (Malthus, Ricardo, and John Stuart Mill), or from less productive to more productive (Carey and later Eugen Dühring). Liebig's critique of the "robbery system" of cultivation instead denounces the *modern form* of agriculture and its decreasing productivity as a result of the irrational and destructive use of the soil. In other words, Liebig's historicization of modern agriculture provided Marx with a useful scientific basis for rejecting abstract and linear treatments of agricultural development. Yet between 1867 and 1872–73, Marx's appraisal of his contribution to political economy changed somewhat. Could it be that Marx had doubts about Liebig's chemistry as well as his economic errors? In this context, close study of Marx's letters and notebooks helps us comprehend the larger aims and methods of his research after 1868.

Looking at the letters and notebooks from this period, it seems more probable that the change regarding Liebig's contribution in the second edition represents more than a mere correction. Marx was well aware of the heated debates surrounding Liebig's *Agricultural Chemistry*, so after the publication of the first volume of *Capital* he carefully followed up on the validity of Liebig's theory. In a letter to Engels dated January 3, 1868, Marx asked him to seek some advice from a longtime friend, the chemist Carl Schorlemmer:

> I would like to know from Schorlemmer what is the latest and best book (German) on agricultural chemistry. Furthermore, what is the present state of the argument between the mineral-fertilizer people and the nitrogen-fertilizer people? (Since I last looked into the subject, all sorts of new things have appeared in Germany.) Does he know anything about the most recent Germans who have written *against* Liebig's soil-exhaustion theory? Does he know about the alluvion theory of Munich agronomist Fraas (Professor at Munich University)? For the chapter on ground rent I shall have to be aware of the latest state of the question, at least to some extent.[9]

Marx's remarks in this letter clearly indicate his aim to study books on agriculture. He was not just looking for the recent literature on agriculture in general, but paid particular attention to debates and critiques of Liebig's *Agricultural Chemistry*. In the manuscript for volume 3 of *Capital*, Marx uncharacteristically pointed to the importance of Liebig's analysis while indicating that this needs to be filled in the future. That is, this was part of the argument he was continuing to research—and in such basic areas as "the declining productivity of the soil" related to discussions of the falling rate of profit.

As seen in the previous chapter, Liebig stated that the "law of replenishment" was violated as a result of the modern transformation of the way in which people lived and that the consequent soil exhaustion would threaten all of European civilization. Liebig's provocative thesis immediately caused great debate, as Julius Au, a contemporary of Liebig, conveys: "The questions raised by him became the topic of daily conversation for all cultivated men of practice: They came up to the agenda of almost all agricultural meetings and at the same time became a fertile source for literary and bibliopolic speculations."[10]

Liebig's thesis on soil exhaustion resonated positively with many political economists. Henry Charles Carey had already referred to wasteful agricultural production in the United States due to its corn export to England. He quoted from an American agronomist, George E. Waring: "Labor employed in robbing the earth of its capital stock of fertilizing matter, is worse than labor thrown away. . . . Man is but a tenant of the soil, and he is guilty of a crime when he reduces its value for other tenants who are to come after him."[11] Carey believed that when the producer and the consumer live next to each other it is possible to maintain the metabolic interaction between humans and nature without decreasing soil fertility. However, he noted a different reality, namely that scattered settlements over the enormous U.S. continent makes it almost impossible to return the soil nutrients taken out by plants.

Carey's theory of robbery agriculture is closely connected with his critique of British imperialism. In this vein he, like Marx, discussed the conditions in Ireland and India as British colonies in his book *Principles of Political Economy*:

The facilities of transportation throughout Ireland were greatly increased in the half-century that has just elapsed; but, with every stage of that improvement, famines and pestilences increased in number and in force. . . . With each such stage, the power of association declined—the soil was more rapidly impoverished—and now its laborers are everywhere flying from the homes of their youth. . . . Railroads are now being made *for*, but not *by*, the people of India, but their effects must, inevitably, be the same with those observed in Ireland. The object for the attainment of which they are being made, is the further promotion of the export of the raw produce of the soil, and the further extension of the centralizing power of trade; to be followed by increased exhaustion of the land, declining power of association among its occupants, and more rapid decay of commerce.[12]

Carey maintains that with the development of cheaper means of transport to England such as railways and ships, the export of raw materials from Ireland and India increases more than ever. This new economy results in a rapid exhaustion of the soil, so that populations and their forces of production decrease without the possibility of the development of their own manufacturing. With regard to the critique of imperialism, Carey's similarity with Marx is understandable because Liebig's theory plays a central role for both of them. Carey denounces once again the irrationality of colonial domination of the peripheries as "even worse than a crime."[13]

So for Carey as well, "dispersion" or "antagonism of town and country," which penetrates much of the world through international trade in favor (first) of English capitalism and worsens the national condition of the peripheries, is the fundamental cause of the disruption of the metabolism between humans and nature. In order to combat this, by increasing the power of "association" between the producer and the consumer, Carey proposes a "protective tariff" so that new manufactures in the peripheries can be effectively promoted, given that otherwise they have no chance for prosperity. He explains that agricultural productivity can also increase together with national manufactures because the latter offers new means for cultivating better soils. He envisions development built upon small autarchic communities within one nation through protectionist policies so that the refuse of industry can be effectively given back to the soils surrounding them.

Carey's protectionist policy was first received by Frédéric Bastiat in France, although Bastiat paid little attention to the problem of soil exhaustion. Marx had corresponded with Carey, who had sent him his book on slavery, which contained some of his arguments about soil exhaustion, and Marx studied Carey's economic works. But at the time Marx too did not pay much attention to the issue. Carey's role in the overall soil debate became more apparent when Marx encountered Eugen Dühring's work. Marx started studying Dühring's books in January 1868, after Louis Kugelmann sent him Dühring's review of *Capital* from the journal *Ergänzungsblätter zur Erkenntniß*—the first review of the book anywhere—published in December 1867.

It was Eugen Dühring, a lecturer at the University of Berlin and enthusiastic supporter of Carey's economic system, who clearly pointed to the commonality between Liebig and Carey. He integrated Liebig's theory into his own economic analysis as further validation of Carey's proposal to establish autarchic town-communities without wasting plant nutrients and thus without exhausting soils. In his book *Carey's Revolution of National Economy and Social Science* (*Carey's Umwälzung der Volkswirthschaftslehre und Socialwissenschaft*), Dühring emphasized the meaning of the theory of "soil exhaustion proved by Liebig" for Carey's economic system, maintaining that it "builds a pillar on [Carey's] system."[14] He argued:

> Also the problem of soil exhaustion, which has already become quite threatening in North America, for example, will . . . be halted in the long run only through a commercial policy built upon the protection and education of domestic labor. For the harmonious development of the various facilities of one nation will result in stable local economic activities. They promote the natural circulation of materials [*Kreislauf der Stoffe*] and make it possible for plant nutrients to be returned to the soil from which they have been taken.[15]

It is not accidental that Dühring's protectionism is explicitly directed against the neglect of the problem of soil exhaustion in political economy. This is because any serious concern about this problem "inevitably prompts to abandon the principle of *laissez faire*," a staple of classical political economy since Adam Smith. Dühring asks for "conscious regulation of material distribution" (*bewusste Regulirung der Stoffvertheilung*) as the "only countermeasure" against wasteful production in that it would overcome the division between town and country.[16]

In the manuscript for volume 3 of *Capital*, Marx envisioned a future society beyond the antagonism between town and country, one in which "the associated producers govern their metabolic interaction with nature rationally." He must have been surprised to learn that Dühring similarly demanded this, using Liebig's theory of soil exhaustion. In other words, Marx's claim, together with Dühring's, reflected a popular tendency of the "Liebig school." In subsequent years, Marx's view of Dühring grew more critical, as Dühring began to promote his own system as the true foundation of social democracy. This likely reinforced Marx's suspicion of Dühring's interpretation of soil exhaustion and its advocates, even if he continued to recognize the usefulness of Liebig's theory. In any case, at the beginning of 1868, the discursive constellation prompted Marx to intensively study books "*against* Liebig's soil-exhaustion theory," such as those by Karl Arnd, Franz Xavier Hlubek, Carl Fraas, and Friedrich Albert Lange.[17]

THE SPECTRE OF MALTHUS

Liebig's theory became popular in the 1860s among political economists not only because exhaustion of soil was a serious social problem in reality, but also because Malthus's theory of overpopulation was still influential. Liebig's warning rehabilitated, to borrow Dühring's expression, "Malthus's spectre," in that he gave a new natural science basis to the problem of diminishing agricultural productivity as a result of robbery agriculture. This Malthusian argument was successful in the sense that Liebig in the seventh edition of *Agricultural Chemistry* had actually aimed at regaining his influence by generating significant debates among farmers and scientific agronomists with his new polemics.[18]

The general tone of Liebig's argument shifted from one of optimism in the 1840s up through the mid-1850s to a quite pessimistic one in the late 1850s and 1860s. Sharply critical of British industrial agriculture, he predicted a dark future for European society, full of war and hunger, if the "law of replenishment" continued to be ignored:

> In a few years, the guano reserves will be depleted, and then no scientific nor, so to speak, theoretical disputes will be necessary to prove the law of nature which demands from man that he cares for the preservation of living conditions. . . . For their self-preservation, nations will be compelled to slaughter and annihilate each other in never-ending wars in order to restore an equilibrium, and, God forbid, if two years of famine such as 1816 and 1817 succeed each other again, those who survive will see hundreds of thousands perish in the streets.[19]

Liebig's pessimism appears distinct in this passage and gets close to Malthus's theory of absolute overpopulation. While his view of modern agriculture as a "robbery system" shows its superiority over the widespread ahistorical law of diminishing returns, his conclusion leaves his relation to Malthusian ideas ambiguous. In fact, many people criticized his "pessimistic view" by arguing that he ignored the statistical data and overemphasized the danger of a decay of civilization.[20]

However, at the same time his earlier optimism seems to still exist. At least it is possible to understand his warning of robbery agriculture in such a way that agricultural productivity would be able to increase one more time if the nutrition cycle was rehabilitated in the future.[21] Carey and Dühring were able to take advantage of this ambiguity because these supporters of Liebig were also sharp critics of Malthus, enthusiastically opposing an optimistic view of increasing agricultural productivity to the law of diminishing returns. According to Dühring, Carey's contribution consists in his discovery of the tendency of "concentration" in the process of the harmonious development of civilization, so that "Malthus's spectre is dissolved into nothingness."[22] Primitive agriculture first must contend with inferior soils—a view already at odds with Ricardo, who thinks cultivation begins with the best soil. But with the progress of civilization, more fruitful soils will be cultivated with better instruments and machines that industry provides, so that agricultural productivity will increase.[23] The situation in North America seemed unfavorable under British dominance, but Carey and Dühring believed that their protectionist policy could do away with the separation of producers and consumers, which would at the same time solve Liebig's pessimistic prediction.

Their demand for protectionist tariffs and close settlement of the producer and the consumer is not an arbitrary application of Liebig's theory of replacement. A small community is definitely more suitable for organizing the nutrition cycle without wasting refuse. Although Marx shared Liebig's theory as a theoretical basis with Carey and Dühring, he did not believe that protectionist tariffs alone would solve the problem of soil exhaustion and other metabolic rifts under the capitalist mode of production. He also did not agree with their assumption of a unilateral view—continuously proceeding from worse to better soils—of cultivation.[24]

While Carey and Dühring assume an optimistic solution to Liebig's view of modern agriculture, many works criticized both Liebig and Carey from an economic point of view, and Marx was prompted to read them after the publication of volume 1 of *Capital*.[25] In this context, his notebooks and the books in his personal library are of interest.

Friedrich Albert Lange, a German social democrat, elucidates his critique against the Liebig school in his 1866 book *J. St. Mill's Views on the Social Question and the Alleged Revolution of Social Science by Carey* (*J. St. Mill's Ansichten über die sociale Frage und die angebliche Umwälzung der Socialwissenschaft durch Carey*), the title of which ironically mocks Dühring's book. Marx made some excerpts from this book in the beginning of 1868 and possessed a copy in his library.[26] These excerpts are important because Marx focused on chapter 4 in which Lange criticizes Carey's and Dühring's view on agriculture. Marx documented a passage in which Lange rejects Carey's idea of the harmonious development, especially the latter's treatment of a "protective tariff" as "panacea," which should automatically lead to the establishment of an autarchic

community. Marx traced Lange's critique of Carey, first writing down
Lange's summary of Carey's ideal path to social progress:

> If, on the contrary, a well-chosen protective tariff is introduced, a fac-
> tory will be constructed next to the cultivated lands. Thanks to rich
> manure made from the refuse of industry and the growing popula-
> tion, the fertility of the soil will increase and become long-lasting:
> rational agriculture can develop, and agriculture attains the means
> for clearing forests, draining marshes—in a word, the means for the
> conquest of rich soils in fruitful low-lying areas, etc.[27]

Lange rejects the idea of the promotion of domestic industry by protective tariff alone. Carey's society, he says, would lead to a situation where
the development of domestic "industry," fully similar to "trade," ends up
creating a "centralizing tendency," which results in economic inequality.
Consequently, only a few enterprises would be rich, while masses are
"wrested from the land" and fall into poverty.[28] After all, argues Lange,
the only solution that Carey's harmonious system can offer is a protective
tariff, but in all other respects he holds firmly to the "principle of laissez-
faire," so that the social problem of the impoverishment of the working
class as a result of the market economy remains neglected. Lange concludes: "If new methods cannot be found to prevent *the centralization
of the industry in addition to the centralization of trade*, the protection
system only makes the situation even worse instead of improving it."[29]
Lange maintains that Liebig's theory was taken up by Carey only for
the sake of justifying the protectionist policy, and thus he contends that
Carey does not take natural limits seriously enough, as if agricultural
produce can be infinitely increased with the increasing power of association. In a manner similar to Roscher, Lange argues that "despite the
natural scientific correctness of Liebig's theory," robbery cultivation can
be justified from a "national economic" perspective.[30]

Julius Au, a German economist, opposes Liebig's view in an even more
detailed manner. Marx possessed a copy of Au's 1869 *Supplementary
Fertilizers and Their Importance for National and Private Economy*
(*Hilfsdüngermittel in ihrer volks-und privatwirthschaftlichen Bedeutung*),
in which he made various notes and comments.[31] Au agrees with Liebig
in that Agricultural Chemistry has correctly rejected the old humus
theory, but he refuses to acknowledge its "economic" conclusions. Liebig's
theory of soil exhaustion is, according to Au—in opposition to Lieibig's
pessimistic claim—not a "natural law," that is, it does not have a validity

that is "absolute," but is only "relative" to certain conditions.[32] So it is often meaningless from an economic standpoint to fulfill Liebig's mineral requirements in such countries as Russia, Poland, and Asia Minor, given that their extensive agriculture can produce crops over many years without soil exhaustion.

Au's critique goes so far as to undermine the irrationality of robbery cultivation as such: "The claim that the replenishment [of the soil nutrients] can be postponed until an actual decrease of fertility, that is, the soil exhaustion becomes discernible and as long as the economic relations allow to do so, . . . is not at all equal to '*après nous le déluge.*'"[33] According to Au, there is a certain point beyond which robbery would not be conducted in economic terms because the exploitation of soils beyond this point is no longer profitable. Like Roscher and Lange, Au also argues that profit-seeking farmers would be forced, by the logic of the market, to stop robbing the soil. There is thus "no threat to the public welfare, even if Liebig's law of replenishment is not respected."[34]

Marx's comment on Lange in a letter to Kugelmann of June 27, 1870, as well as his comment "donkey!" and many question marks in his personal copy of Au's book imply that he was not convinced by Lange's and Au's attempts to refute Liebig's theory.[35] They were, like Roscher, trapped in the national economic myth of realizing sustainable agriculture through fluctuations in market prices. Since Marx was also unwilling to support Carey's and Dühring's views, he set out to further study the problem of soil exhaustion in order to articulate a more sophisticated critique of the modern robbery system.

To sum up: Marx thought at first that Liebig's description of the destructive effects of modern agriculture could be used as a powerful argument against Ricardo's and Malthus's abstract law of diminishing returns, but began to question Liebig's theory after 1868, as the debates over soil exhaustion increasingly took on a Malthusian tone. Marx therefore backed off from his somewhat uncritical and exaggerated claim that Liebig's analyses "contain more flashes of insight than all the works of modern political economists put together," in preparation for the more extensive research into the problem that he clearly intended for volumes 2 and 3 of *Capital*.

Schorlemmer later replied to Marx in February 1868:

I was hardly able to follow up the progress of agricultural chemistry in the last years because I had no access to the literature. *The Annual Report on the Progress of Chemistry* of 1866 has not yet completely appeared, and I will only receive the volume which covers agricultural chemistry next month. I know about Fraas's theory of alluvion no more than you do…. [Take a look at] various articles by Lawes and Gilbert. Last year they received a prize from the Royal Society. For details, see *Proceedings of the Royal Society*, vol. 16, no. 96, where you can find a list of their writings.[36]

Schorlemmer knew the critique raised against Liebig by Lawes and Gilbert. However, Marx had followed the debate in 1863 when he read Liebig's *On Theory and Practice in Agriculture*. Furthermore, Schorlemmer was not able to say anything concrete about Fraas's "theory of alluvion." Thus it is likely that his reply was disappointing to Marx. Nevertheless, Marx continued to read other natural science books including Carl Fraas's work in the following months.

AN ENCOUNTER WITH "AGRICULTURAL PHYSICS"

If Liebig's Malthusian tendencies constituted a negative reason for Marx's alteration of the sentence on Liebig in the second edition of *Capital*, there was also a more positive one: Marx encountered several other authors who became as important as Liebig to his ecological critique of capitalism. Carl Fraas was one of them.

Fraas's name first appears in Marx's notebook between December 1867 and January 1868, when he notes the title of Fraas's 1866 book *Agrarian Crises and Their Remedies* (*Die Ackerbaukrisen und ihre Heilmittel*), a polemic against Liebig's theory of soil exhaustion.[37] When Marx wrote to Engels in January 1868 that "since I last looked into the subject, all sorts of new things have appeared in Germany," he was likely thinking of Fraas's book. Though Marx did not make excerpts from this book and his personal copy is lost, he read a series of books by Fraas, including *Climate and the Plant World Over Time, a Contribution to the History of Both* (*Klima und Pflanzenwelt in der Zeit, ein Beitrag zur Geschichte beider*) (Landshut, 1847), *The History of Agriculture* (*Die Geschichte der Landwirthschaft*) (Prague, 1852), and *The Nature of Agriculture* (*Die Natur der Landwirthschaft*) (Munich, 1857). Other books by Fraas are preserved in his personal library such as *Historical-Encyclopedic Outline of Agricultural Theory* (*Historisch-encyklopädischer Grundriß der Landwirthschaftslehre*) (Stuttgart, 1848) and *Root Life of Cultivated Plants and Increasing Returns* (*Das Wurzelleben der Kulturpflanzen und die Ertragssteigerung*) (Leipzig, 1872).[38]

A remark by Marx in his letter to Engels on March 25, 1868, confirms this:

> Very interesting is the book by Fraas (1847): *Climate and the Plant World Over Time: A Contribution to the History of Both*, namely as proving that climate and flora change in *historical* times. He is a Darwinist before Darwin, and admits even the *species* developing in historical times. But he is at the same time an agronomist. He claims that with cultivation—depending on its degree—the "moisture" so beloved by the peasants gets lost (hence also the plants migrate from south to north), and finally steppe formation occurs. The first effect of cultivation is useful, but finally devastating through deforestation, etc. This man is both a thoroughly learned philologist (he has written books in *Greek*) and a chemist, agronomist, etc. The conclusion is that cultivation—when it proceeds in natural growth and is not *consciously controlled* (as a bourgeois he naturally does not reach this point)—leaves deserts behind it, Persia, Mesopotamia, etc., Greece. So once again an unconscious socialist tendency! . . . His history of agriculture is also important. He calls Fourier this "pious and humorous socialist". . . . It is necessary to keep a close watch on the recent and very latest in agriculture. The *physical* school is pitted against the *chemical*.[39]

This passage is the only one where Marx discusses the content of Fraas's work. It is striking that Marx found even an "unconscious socialist tendency." His excerpts and notes are helpful in understanding why Marx was so strongly interested in Fraas's theory and why reading his works possibly prompted Marx to alter his evaluation of Liebig's theory in the second edition of *Capital*. Through a careful analysis of his reception of Fraas's theory, we can observe the emergence of a new horizon of his theory of metabolism after 1868.

In his letter to Engels, Marx makes it clear that he regards Fraas's "history of agriculture" as important. The expression alone does not say if Fraas's understanding of the history of agriculture is more important than Liebig's "historical overview of the history of agriculture," which is supposed to "contain more flashes of insight than all the works of modern political economists put together." However, Marx's statement is all the more interesting because the last sentence implies that he was clearly aware of Fraas's polemics against Liebig's mineral theory. Marx points to the debate between the "physical" and the "chemical" school.

Obviously, the "physical school" refers to Fraas's theories of alluvion and of climate, and the "chemical school" includes not only Liebig's mineral theory but also Lawes's and Gilbert's nitrogen theory.

In a letter to Engels on January 3, 1868, Marx expressed his interest in "the present state of the argument between the mineral-fertilizer people and the nitrogen-fertilizer people," that is, Liebig's polemic against Lawes and Gilbert. After two months of studying agronomy, and especially due to his reading of Fraas, Marx's interest shifted to the disagreement between the "physical" school and the "chemical school." Though he earlier thought it necessary to study the recent debates on Liebig's *Agricultural Chemistry* "to some extent," he came to think two months later that it is "necessary to keep a close watch on the recent and very latest in agriculture." He admitted the acute necessity for further research because the newest state of debate on soil exhaustion was not restricted to the debate between mineral theory and nitrogen theory.

Marx's reference to this debate indicates that he had already read Fraas's 1866 *Agrarian Crises and Their Remedies*. Fraas was not critical of Liebig's agricultural chemistry from the beginning but, on the contrary, he valued the latter as a talented chemist, inviting him in 1855 as an expert advisor to three Bayern experimental stations, where Fraas worked as the director. However, when Liebig lamented a lack of scientific knowledge among agricultural educators and practical farmers in Bayern in an article published in 1864, a heated controversy between the two agronomists emerged, which rapidly led to a strained relationship.[40] It is thus only after 1864 that Fraas began explicitly to criticize Liebig's theory, although he had, in the 1850s, pointed to a possible danger of overdependence on agricultural chemistry and had argued for the importance of "agricultural physics" for the development of agriculture.[41] By examining how Fraas changed his earlier position toward Liebig's agricultural chemistry after 1864, it will be possible to show what Marx learned from the debate between two German agronomists in 1868.

In his *Nature of Agriculture* (1857), Fraas begins his preface with a demand for the "cooperation of science" with the goal of further progress in agriculture. Fraas believes that "agricultural research of nature" should not simply "improve" the process or the means of cultivation, but "investigate" phenomena through a number of experiments, which would allow us to comprehend their functioning. In this passage, he affirmatively refers to "J. v. Liebig," whose work determines the path of Fraas's scientific investigation of agriculture.[42] In this vein, Fraas grounds his vision of the agricultural system as a continuation of Liebig's program. Liebig is repeatedly and affirmatively referred to in the main text with respect to the significance of mineral substances and of the chemical analysis of soils. This does not mean that Fraas is simply following Liebig's agricultural chemistry. On the contrary, in his *History of Agriculture* (1852) he pointed out that the *physical* aspects of soil and manure are often missing in Liebig's analysis.[43] Fraas's "agricultural physics" seek to complement what the famous chemist, as an enthusiastic supporter of chemical fertilizer, underestimates, that is, the meteorological and climatic effects on the formation of soils and the plant growth. It is this dimension to which Marx pays attention in his excerpts.

While James F. W. Johnston examined the "geological formation" and Liebig analyzed the organic composition of the soil in relation to plant growth, Fraas's originality lay in his detailed treatment of the relationship between climate and plant growth. According to Fraas, plants can absorb their nourishment from the soil through roots only when nutrients exist in a dissoluble form in the soil. The gradual weathering of rocks into friable components is the essential process in the formation of soil. In this process, what is both chemically and mechanically significant are, for example, "changes between the warm and the cold and between the wet and the dry," "oxygen in the atmosphere," "water containing ammonia and carbonic acid," and movements of "living organic bodies."[44] Marx writes down Fraas's claim that the investigation of chemical soil constituents alone is not practically useful because "the point is to comprehend what kind of and how many salts become available from a certain cultivated soil every year, when this happens, and what the level of their dissolution is. Only after answering these questions, can we decide the question with regard to the necessity of their [additional] supply."[45] Even if chemical soil analysis shows the existence of a large amount of mineral substances, the same soil could be infertile unless manure is added when weathering is slow. By contrast, under a favorable climatic condition of warmth and humidity the replenishment of mineral substances can take place without adding manure because weathering is fast enough. Marx notes: "The richer fertility of the soil in warm and hot countries without any manuring or only with very sporadic and meager manuring clearly owes to a faster speed of weathering of rocks, their mineral products, and the soil."[46]

Marx is clearly aware of Fraas's claim that the chemical analysis of soil elements alone cannot fully reveal the conditions for healthy plant growth: "Is there a more convincing proof *against* the great significance of chemical soil compounds for the existence of plants due to their dependence on them than a proof provided by plant geographers and farmers that the flora of lime soils in the *Carpathian Mountains* can be found on granite soil in Lapland, and the lime flora in Switzerland can be partly found on granite soil of the *Carpathian Mountains*?"[47] According to Fraas, climate influences can change material conditions for plant existence so strongly that a plant that usually requires a certain type of the soil (*bodenhold*) can often grow under favorable climatic conditions (*bodenvag*): "It is particularly remarkable that *all* cultivated plants became *bodenvag*, and only a few are *bodenhold*; however, this changes depending on climate, mostly on geographical climate."[48] So red clover, for example, which usually grows on loamy soil, can grow on chalky soil if summers are humid enough.

Fraas repeatedly argues that rational agriculture must seriously take climatic factors into account. Thus, even if inorganic constituent elements of the soil are "absolutely necessary," their artificial supply with chemical fertilizer is not a condition *sine qua non* for ample plant growth, but rather, functions as a "climatic adjustment":

> To the extent that favorable climatic conditions are missing to the cultivated plants and can*not* be replaced somehow, we must open up the sources of nutrition in the soil, that is, we must dung better. [It is] not because cereals consume more ash constituents (mineral constituents) than meadow plants, but because they are alien to our climate and do not have enough warmth to assimilate salts of the soil as well as gases of the air into our desired amount of organic substance within an artificially and naturally measured time of vegetation.[49]

Nonetheless, Fraas does not fully reject Liebig's theory. He attributes a particular role to phosphoric acid, as Liebig does, and praises the discovery of its importance for plant growth as the main contribution of agricultural chemistry.[50] Yet at the same time, he maintains that agricultural chemistry must not be overemphasized. The assimilation and diffusion of elements of the soil "take place in relation to climatic conditions."[51] Climatic influence upon vegetation constitutes an essential object of the scientific investigation of agronomy, for it also significantly affects the growth of agricultural produce.

For Fraas, the problem of soil exhaustion must be modified accordingly, because it exists also in relation to climatic factors. In fact, soils without manure can provide successful crops over a long time period under certain conditions of climate, as Marx documents in his notebook:

> In southern Europe cereals (barley) can be quite successfully cul-
> tivated on the same land every year for many years even without
> rotation and without manure, maybe not corn and cotton, but at least
> melons. . . . Cereals are thus *soil-exhausting plants in the cold tem-
> perature zone* as they strongly require favorable climate, particularly
> corn, durra, wheat, barley, rye and oat, legumes and buckwheat less
> so, and clovers, *our* pasture, asparagus etc. not at all. In the *warm and
> moderate* temperature zone cereals and legumes are no longer soil-
> exhausting plants with exception of corn, rice and durra, but hardly
> tobacco that is already cultivated often without manure.[52]

Under favorable climatic conditions, cultivation, Fraass suggests, can take place without exhaustion even if the soil nutrients that plants absorbed are not returned to the soil by humans. This is why traditional agriculture under tropical or subtropical conditions of climate is often sustainable. While Liebig enthusiastically explicates the sustainability of traditional agriculture in Japan and China, which successfully organized the cycle of soil nutrients by effectively gathering human excrement, Fraas offers another image of traditional sustainable agriculture in Europe where the power of nature itself takes care of the replenishment of the soil nutrients. While Liebig thinks of the supply of mineral substances by human hands as essential, Fraas's vision of sustainable agriculture emphasizes the power of nature and the metabolic cycle based on it.

Only in the very last two pages of volume 2 of *The Nature of Agriculture* does Fraas, directly referring to Liebig's *Chemical Letters*, develop his critique of the theory of soil exhaustion, which Marx notates. First of all, Fraas argues that there were "ancient civilized societies such as *Greece* and *Asia Minor*" where people conducted sustainable agriculture "*without* any manure." Civilized life did not necessarily result in a robbery system of agriculture. Secondly, even if farmers sell their products in the market, they also receive various materials useful for the replenishment of soil nutrients from "brewery, distillery and limekiln." Thirdly, robbery praxis does not exist in forestry. Fourthly, Fraas emphasizes that fallow is a state of weathering and thus allows more plant nutrients to be available in the soil, but Liebig underestimates its importance. Finally, referring to Chinese agriculture, Fraas points out that even Liebig admits the possibility of increasing agricultural productivity together with an increase of population. In other words, Malthusian pessimism is not an inevitable conclusion of Liebig's mineral theory.[53] Carefully excerpting from this passage, Marx learns from Fraas's critique of the exaggeration of Liebig's

theory of soil exhaustion. Fraas disagrees with Liebig by emphasizing
the possibilities of intensive agriculture without soil exhaustion because
replenishment of inorganic substances takes place naturally and artificially in various places. He warns against a hasty generalization of the
risk of soil exhaustion as natural law.

Even though the seventh edition of *Agricultural Chemistry* had not
yet been published, the tension between Fraas and Liebig is discernible. Nonetheless, Fraas in the *Nature of Agriculture* does not conduct
a ruthless critique against Liebig, which would be the case later in the
1860s. On the contrary, Fraas argues that his project is a "supplement" of
Liebig's mineral theory and in this way defines the future task of "agricultural physics":

> Agricultural chemistry recently enlightened agriculture a lot through
> the determination of unknown amounts that designate the *wealth* of
> the land, but the [research] area that it wanted to designate as *activity*
> of the soil is still hardly studied. It will probably be agricultural phys-
> ics, though it does not encompass the area of study completely, that
> will build the future of agricultural scientific efforts.[54]

Fraas does not want to replace agricultural chemistry completely with
agricultural physics. Rather, they should support each other:

> Not only the theory of supply of plant nutrition but also the prepara-
> tion for a widely abundant and adequate usage [of plant nutrition]
> with an aid of agricultural chemistry, agricultural physics, and physi-
> ology is the task of the future for agricultural science.[55]

In Fraas's opinion, agricultural chemistry is a subdiscipline of agronomy. It is essential for the development of agriculture, but the analysis of
chemical soil constituents alone must not be absolutized. Though Marx
does not write down these passages, Fraas's intention was quite clear
throughout the text.

Eventually, the relationship between Liebig and Fraas ended in conflict,
but this situation after 1864 is exactly what Marx at the beginning of 1868
called "the recent and very latest in agriculture." It is important to examine
in more detail what exactly this debate between the two agronomists was
about. Fraas primarily attempted a scientific intervention into a problem
of agriculture in Germany, but what is most interesting in the current context is his attempted refutation of Liebig's theory of soil exhaustion.

FRAAS'S POWER CULTIVATION AND ALLUVIAL THEORY

In contrast to his earlier books, Fraas's 1866 *Agrarian Crises and Their Remedies* is characterized by a polemic against Liebig. He ironically calls Liebig's theory of soil exhaustion a variation of "quietism," which regards the lowering of the corn prices in Germany as a temporary phenomenon without asking for a countermeasure. According to the assumption of Liebig's "quietism," Fraas summarizes: "This overproduction, even if it is the true ultimate cause of [the current] lower crop price, must end soon, as the theory of 'robbery agricultur' shows this, . . . due to the misrecognition of the theory of exhaustion and replenishment."[56] Fraas rejects this conclusion, arguing that Liebig's warning is based on illusions and promotes a false prediction without actually paying attention to a more urgent problem of West European agriculture.

Even if Liebig were to prove correct in predicting that "one day" soils all over the world would be exhausted due to the robbery system of agriculture and would be unable to provide enough food for growing populations, Fraas believes that the realization of Liebig's prediction will still take a long time, namely until the fertile soils of the Danubian Lowland or the extensive plains in Poland and Galicia become fully exhausted.[57] Furthermore, if the soil exhaustion of enormous lands in North America and South Russia are factored into the calculation, German and other West European farmers surely cannot survive international competition in the corn market, which would lower prices until worldwide soil exhaustion occurs. In the past the long physical distances functioned as a "protective wall" for European producers, which balanced out the cheaper production costs of crops under more favorable climatic conditions, with the more expensive transportation costs of foreign producers seeking access to European markets. However, the development of the means of transportation, especially railways, enabled a cheaper and faster transport of agricultural produce to Western Europe, so that the "protective wall" was de facto abolished.

The modern crisis of agriculture is thus not characterized by the underproduction that Liebig is worried about but by *overproduction*: "The crisis of this disease [of agriculture] comes into existence with import of a large amount of crops from the countries that have more fertile lands and produce more cheaply."[58] Since the import of cheaper crops corresponds to the growing needs of industry in Western countries, cheap prices of corn will be "chronic" in capitalist societies: "The periods of cheap crops must increase, and this occurs with a seriously deteriorating effect for the producers."[59] Fraas is primarily thinking about the economic situation of the farmers in Germany, and to protect them from ruin, he insists upon the urgent need for agricultural reform. After the fall of the natural protective wall, there is only one way left for the German farmers if they are to survive international competition: "Produce more cheaply!"[60] Fraas laments that the hope for increased prices for crops in the future, the one that Liebig's "quietism" propagates, circumvents the need for essential reforms.

Here note that in criticizing Liebig, Fraas neither negates the possibility of soil exhaustion nor the utility of mineral fertilizer. What he problematizes is Liebig's *"exaggeration of a proposition that is correct in itself* by arguing that if the population should increase and the land should maintain its power, it is necessary to return all mineral substances that are taken out by crops because they existed in the soil only in an exhaustible way."[61] It is true that Liebig's law of replenishment is correct, insofar as mineral substances in the soil are indispensable for plant growth and they can be quickly exhausted under incautious treatment of the soil. Nonetheless, Fraas doubts Liebig's implicit assumption that this return of *all* mineral substances must be arranged by human hands alone, especially through chemical fertilizer. Given that the seventh edition of Liebig's *Agricultural Chemistry*, in contrast to the optimism of his earlier works, downplays the omnipotence of chemical manure, he all of a sudden falls into a Malthusian-like pessimism, particularly because he is not able to find an alternative way to replenish mineral substances effectively. This conclusion is, according to Fraas, too hasty and false.

What is missing in Liebig's exaggerated argumentation is an investigation into the eternal force of replenishment that exists *in nature itself*, the utilization of which can realize the full replenishment of soil nutrients:

> However, as said, nature offers the full replenishment through weathering, alluvion, irrigation, meteorous materials in rain and meteoritic dust, and usage of refuse in manure and excrements.[62]

However, "once the presupposition, that is, soil exhaustion, is accepted, the rest of the argument follows automatically, and no one dares to object to the presupposition against the zealots."[63] Indeed, as seen in the last chapter, Liebig first introduced the theory of soil exhaustion in order to emphasize the necessity of mineral chemical fertilizer. Neither the power of nature, which brings rich mineral substances, nor farmers' actual careful treatment of their lands receive enough attention in Liebig's theory. Fraas proposes that the famous chemist strategically overemphasizes the risk of soil exhaustion for the sake of popularizing his theory of mineral fertilizer.[64]

In other words, Fraas recognizes the importance of Liebig's warning against robbery, but he argues that there are other possibilities for the improvement of soil fertility. Since Liebig's law of replenishment is now widely accepted, it is necessary to take a step forward instead of falling into Malthusian pessimism: "The most importatnt consequence of the new theory of plant nutrition is not the old and now generally accepted conviction about the necessity to replenish soil constituents taken out by cultivated plants as crops but the discovery of numerous sources that increase them."[65] Fraas's research on climatic influences on vegetation opens up a fully new way to generate and maintain sustainable production. He calls the agriculture of increase "power agriculture" (*Kraftkultur*), which he envisions being introduced on the basis of traditional agriculture. As Marx noted in his letter to Engels, Fraas's "alluvial theory" is the most effective method for power agriculture, which makes a clear contrast to Liebig's recommendation to use chemical fertilizer. As a result, Marx finds another way to consciously regulate the metabolic interaction between humans and nature.

The renowned geologist Charles Lyell defines alluvion in the following way: "Earth, sand, gravel, stones, and other transported matter which has been washed away and thrown down by the rivers, floods, or other causes, upon land not permanently submerged beneath the waters of lakes or seas."[66] Alluvion is a geological formation consisting of silt that contains a rich amount of mineral substances. Alluvion that is overserved in the alluvial plain of the Danube, and in the deltas of the Mississippi, Nile, and Po rivers, created by tidal bore, provides a large amount of crops over many years without manure because the river water carries a sufficient amount of mineral substances and replaces the plant nutrients taken from the soil as crops. For example, an alluvial plain with rich minerals builds a fertile surface soil with "height of 7 to 10 feet" in the Chiana Valley and around rivers in Toscana.[67] Inspired by these examples, Fraas, in *Nature of Agriculture,* suggests, in a passage that Marx wrote down, constructing artificial alluvion as "the most radical means to cultivation."[68] By constructing canals and water gates, silt contained in the river water is regulated to cover the fields, so that it provides the fields with necessary plant nutrition.

Fraas's belief in further possibilities for increasing agricultural productivity is based on the power of nature itself: "Nature itself showed…

this way."[69] What Fraas recognizes is the limitation of human intervention. The maintenance of soil fertility is not possible without the cooperation and support of nature. This explains why Fraas ascribes only a secondary role to the use of chemical fertilizer in his vision of a more sustainable agriculture. He argues many times that chemical fertilizer is often too costly for farmers, and with international competition it is not the best choice. And, in the end, it is not sustainable.

Fraas explicitly claims that "the remedy for soil exhaustion is not to be found in chemical fertilizers," because their effect lasts only for a short period of time despite its high costs:[70]

> Chemical fetilizers are an excellent means for increasing crops, if they are used in the correct composition and form adequate to the need and *if they match the cost calculation*. But overall they can never protect the land from exhaustion because their constituents are much more expensive than the same constituents we can receive a) through soil weathering, b) through irrigation and alluvion, and c) through natural manure of farm animals, dung, and sewage.[71]

According to Fraas, chemical fertilizer is not a panacea but only a "climatic adjustment." Clearly his tone differs here from that of Liebig's earlier optimism.

In contrast, Fraas urgently demands agrarian reform, using such methods as artificial alluvion, which continues to work "eternally" and without further costs after installation because the power of nature is lasting and free: "The future of European agriculture depends on irrigation, and particularly on artificial alluvion because it will produce *the same amount with less costs*. It is exactly what the progress needs, not the price increase."[72] Chemical fertilizer alone is, on the contrary, not able to achieve this goal. Realization of truly sustainable agricultural production is not possible without aid from an already existing natural metabolism. In fact, Fraas argues, the usage of natural power is much more cost-efficient and effective than strong dependence on chemical fertilizer.

Reading Fraas's books, Marx realized another vision of sustainable agriculture, which tempers Liebig's theory of mineral fertilizer and soil exhaustion. He points to the possibility that the power of nature can be used to more efficiently and sustainably satisfy human needs without exhausting the soil, and also provides an explanation of why chemical fertilizer alone cannot solve the problem. Clearly, this is why Marx's focus shifted after two months of intensive research on agriculture in the beginning of 1868 from the debate between "mineral fertilizer people" and "nitrogen fertilizer people" to the polemics between the "physical" school and the "chemical" school. He recognized that the problem of sustainability is not just about deciding which fertilizer is better, mineral or nitrogen. Marx's new interest is actually a reflection of what Fraas argued against in the debate. According to Fraas, both "mineral fertilizer people" and "nitrogen fertilizer people" are basically the same in that they presuppose soil exhaustion as a given fact. In the theory of soil exhaustion, Fraas says, "lies the reconciliation between nitrogen and mineral theory. Both theories were from the beginning stretched to the extreme by the 'inventors,' saying that the amount of nitrogen is the sole measure of manure estimation, while phosphoric acid is also used for the same purpose [by the supporters of mineral theory]."[73] Beyond this debate, Fraas opened up a third way to the rational arrangement of metabolism between humans and nature. His critique of Liebig provides a probable reason why Marx in 1868 saw the acute necessity for more study of natural sciences in envisioning the sustainable metabolism in the future society. Its concretization was important for Marx in order to dispel "Malthus's spectre."

CLIMATE CHANGE AS DANGER TO CIVILIZATION

Marx's interest in Fraas's theory is not limited to his critique of Liebig's theory of soil exhaustion. His comments about an "unconscious socialist tendency" in his letter relates to another Fraas book, *Climate and the Plant World Over Time*. The reason Marx found the book important provides a helpful hint in terms of why he so intensively studied natural science in the 1870s. In this context Marx's excerpts prove useful again.[74]

Fraas based his 1847 book on his experience and research during his stay in Greece as a director of the Royal Garden in Athens and professor of botany at the University of Athens (1835–1842). The work consists of various historical reports about the influence of climate changes on humans and plants over a long historical period. These reports grounded his thesis on the significance of climate as an essential material condition for plant growth. Fraas's provocative thesis is that cultivation conducted by humans brings a climate change, which in the end counts as the most important factor for the decay of civilization. This is because naturally developed forms of agriculture must leave a desert behind due to the disruption of nature's universal metabolism. There is also an important departure from Liebig's view on the history of agriculture. Marx did not make excerpts from Liebig's overview of the collapse of ancient civilizations, not only because he was primarily interested in Liebig's critique of modern agriculture, but perhaps also because Roscher already doubted the validity of Liebig's historical explanation.[75] Since Marx this time focuses on Fraas's history of agriculture, the comparison between Fraas and Liebig is useful.

In *Agricultural Chemistry*, Liebig illustrates the history of precapitalist societies from the perspective of the natural law of robbery cultivation: "It is one and the same natural law that controls the emergence and the downfall of nations. Robbing countries of the conditions of [soil] fertility causes their ruin."[76] He points to modern deserts in those places where old civilizations had flourished: "In those areas where powerful kingdom used to flourish and a dense population obtained food and wealth from the soil, today the same field no longer brings enough fruits to pay off the cultivation." The "only cause" for the disappearance of old civilizations is "soil exhaustion due to robbery cultivation," and not wars, famines, and epidemics. Liebig argues that "the collapse of a nation" is possible "only when the property of the soil has changed."[77] The problem of soil exhaustion determines the limit of civilization's progress because, with a decrease of agricultural produce, society begins to suffer from a lack of food and overpopulation.

In Greece, Liebig says, depopulation and emigration existed as early as 700 BCE. As a result, according to Aristotle, Sparta was unable to recruit a thousand men suited for warfare, though the city had been able to provide 8,000 soldiers in the Battle of Plataea, a century before in 479 BCE. Soil exhaustion became much worse after a hundred years, so much so that Strabo lamented that out of a hundred cities of Laconia only thirty villages remained.[78]

Furthermore, Liebig argues that the same destiny fell upon the Roman cities. Cato (234–149 BCE) did not talk about a decrease of crops but about the great fertility of Roman lands. A census carried out under Julius Caesar (46 BCE) confirmed a decrease of population, and under Augustus (63–14 BCE), the shortage of men suitable for militaryservice was so grave that "due to the annihilation of a small battalion under the leadership of Varus in the Teutoburg Forest the capital and its ruler were put into fear and terror."[79] Import of crops to Rome kept increasing and its population suffered from inflation and hunger.

Liebig concludes:

> While outwardly the Roman state [at the time of Augustus] presented every sign of prosperity and the most luxuriant affluence and power, the evil worm was already busy destroying its march of life, and it began the same work two hundred years ago in the European states. … What could the might of the mightiest, which, in its presumption, arrogantly had its own altar built and made people worship it as a god; what could the wisdom of philosophers, or the deepest acquaintance with jurisprudence, or the valor of the most competent commanders, the most formidable and well-organized armies, effect against the operation of a Law of Nature! All the greatness and strength shrank to smallness and weakness, and in the end it even lost a glimmer of its ancient splendor![80]

For Liebig, the fertility of the soil is what ultimately determines the course of civilization's progress. If the law of replenishment is violated, the foundation of a nation is necessarily destabilized, which leads to a shortage of soldiers and means of subsistence, and this undermines the material conditions for the prosperity of a nation. Referring to historical witnesses, Liebig warns that the same crisis was approaching modern European countries because the popular practice of robbery agriculture is disrupting the universal metabolism of nature more than ever.

Fraas chooses another approach in his *Climate and the Plant World Over Time*. He poses the same question as Liebig in addressing desertification in those areas that used to have very fruitful lands, such as Persia, Mesopotamia, and Egypt. Yet he explains the emergence and collapse of old civilizations from changes of "natural climate" (*physikalisches Klima*). For him, climatic influence proves to be a stronger factor for vegetation than the chemical composition of the soil. The supply of disposable plant nutrition is dependent on the weathering of the soil, which is essentially determined by humidity, temperature, and rain.[81] Using various botanical examples, Fraas illustrates that the accumulative process of changes in climate and the plant world is slow but much bigger in the long run than was usually assumed.[82] He tries to demonstrate that these changes of local climate have a significant impact on human civilization because the modified conditions, characterized by increasing temperature and dryness of the air, are unfavorable for local plants. In other words, when the material conditions for cultivation deteriorate, it leads the civilization to its collapse. Thus, according to Fraas, the effect of climate on plants is the most decisive factor for the development of society.

In contrast to the widespread undervaluation of human influence upon climate, Fraas describes the historical dynamics in which human practices in building civilizations are transformed by climate over a long period. According to Fraas, it is not robbery of a certain mineral substance in the soil but changes in climate that cause such a great disturbance in the metabolic interaction between humans and nature. Even if these changes proceed so slowly that they are often unnoticed or undervalued, they can be reconstructed by finding their traces documented in nature. Plants give Fraas hints that the climatic conditions have gradually but continuously changed, so that vegetation actually can look quite different over historical time.[83]

The impact of climate change is not to be underestimated. As Fraas writes:

> Great damage of natural vegetation in a region results in a deep transformation of its entire character, and this modified new state of nature is never so favorable to the region and its population as before; certainly, people change with it. Such great transformations of the natural state of the region can hardly remain without effects, or, if they occur extensively and together with many regions, never remain without effects, and, of course, the old state of affairs cannot be rehabilitated.[84]

Since flora are largely dependent on the key variables of the local climate, the migration of native plants from south to north or from the plains to the mountains is an indicator of change toward desertification. Some kinds of plants become extinct in this process because they cannot adapt to the new environment; other plants transform their organs by, for example, sharpening their leaves and extending their roots, in order to be able to use less water and soil nutrients. When native plants migrate, other foreign plants come in, but they usually do not completely replace the original vegetation, and flora changes. Gradually the desert climate becomes more and more apparent in those places where many plants used to flourish. The formation of steppes begins in an irreversible manner, bringing negative consequences to the original cultivation in the area.

As Marx summarizes in his letter to Engels, Fraas argues that "deforestation" is the most significant cause of desertification, in that it generates rising temperatures and lower humidity. For example, Marx documents the following passage in his notebook:

> *Deforestation of a region,* particularly when it possesses a very arid and sandy or furthermore even calcareous soil, is counted as the most powerful cause for creating heat. . . . The composition of the soil [conditions] the rainfall, from which the climatic influences described above follow. The forested areas covered by vegetation retain moisture more firmly and are less heated up by sunlight than infertile areas. [As a result,] they also attract more rainfall, and thus these areas are not just cool but also distribute refreshing cool airstream to hot surrounding areas. The distribution of moisture in the air greatly changes temperature and various capacities of heat conduction of matter on the surface of the earth.[85]

Marx then notes Humboldt's remark: "The scarcity or absence of forests without exception increases temperature and dryness of the air."[86] With eradication of forests climate change of the entire region proceeds, and one day various negative effects become apparent even in the plain area, such as increase of steppe formation, disappearance of streams, narrowing river valley.

Fraas analyzed flora to illustrate how the loss of humidity and increase of temperature changed the plant world and impeded the further development of civilizations. Marx was interested in Fraas's concrete description of historical transformations and of today's totally different situation. It is useful to look at exactly what Marx paid attention to.

Mesopotamia, where in the past there were a number of canals and ditches with fertile alluvial soils between the Euphrates and Tigris rivers, was now, according to Fraas, "totally desolate and deserted without villages and settlement, a withering dilapidation! Now woody saltwort, vines of capparaceae, and bushes of mimosas cover the most fertile alluvial soil cut through by numerous lines of dried-up canal channels and ditches, but this is where 'the garden of the world' used to flourish."[87] It is not hard to identify the cause of this desertification with climate change:

> The great transformation of climate and change of vegetation are most convincingly proved by an escalating *steppe formation* and the transition to a complete desert in the places the ancient people knew as the most fruitful regions of the world. The unique, loose, saliferous soil in very fertile Mesene used to be covered by

grus sand and mud in every flooding. But if this soil is not constantly irrigated, covered by mud and then drained, it is exposed
to a unique transformation, one similar to the decomposition of
mud of the Nile river in Egypt as [Joseph] Rußegger illustrated or
the coasts in Greece as we observed. [Namely,] salt and grus sand
become dominant, and steppe flora comes in.[88]

Fraas, moreover, points to a "record in the past of a ten-month-long
winter and only a two-month-long summer."[89] This comparison between
the soil fertility of the past and today, said Fraas, eliminates any doubts
about a huge climate change.

After documenting some passages on Palestine, Marx makes notes on
Egypt. In Egypt, which in modern times is categorized as having an arid
or desert climate, the same transformation of climate and the plant world
took place over historical time. Fraas derives from the "migration of so
many cultivation plants from south to north" that "today's climate in
the Lower Egypt (totally different from the Upper Egypt) was stretched
farther south in ancient times."[90] Climate change was so extreme that
the increasing dryness of the air and the rapid change of temperature
during the day and night limited arable fields to the coast area. The situation was dramatically different in the past, as Fraas points out that the
upper reaches of the Nile River was "where the oldest people's cultivation [Völkerkultur] took place" and where existed "Thebes with 100 gates
8,000 years ago."[91]

In Meroe, an island city surrounded by the Nile and Atbar, the land
was not only successfully cultivated, but also served as the center of
the caravan trade. Fraas gives the account of ancient Greeks about the
wealthy state of the peoples living around Meroe:

> Meroe was surrounded by various peoples and partly inhabited.
> According to the ancient reports (Agatharchides, Strabo) they
> remained far from engaging in agriculture. They are glorified by us as
> Troglodyten [hole dwellers] in the coastal mountain of the Red Sea, as
> Ichthyophagen [fish eaters], the same ones as those Nearchus encoun
> tered in the south Persian Gulf, though this time in the Arabic Gulf,
> and as meat-feeding Makrobier [people who live a long time], who
> treated wheat bread as garbage; in short, these inhabitants in ancient
> Ethiopia were "beloved by God."

Such a fruitful gift of nature can no longer be found in today's desert climate in the region. According to Fraas, this area also suffered from climate change:

> With constant pushing back of the plant world from south to north due to cultivation, plants look for an adequate temperature sphere. The process continues until the area of dissemination is more and more limited due to the increasing influence of climatic factors, so that plant [species] often become almost extinct.[92]

For example, Theophrastus von Eresos (371–287 BCE) records that many acacia were flourishing in Egypt, but due to the increasing dryness of the air they grew sparsely in Fraas's time, and carob trees grew instead, which were not found in Theophrastus's time.

The great transformation of Egyptian vegetation is also proved by the fact that agriculture in Egypt came to be so dependent upon the cultivation of cotton that "the most part of export from Egypt is related to cotton." Cotton can grow "only on non-overflooded lands": "What a difference between the ancient *swamp dweller who grew lotus* and today's fellah who grows cotton!"[93] Could the cotton example give some comfort that even under new climatic conditions different types of useful plants could flourish, which support the farmers economically? Fraas answers this question by stating that the cultivation of cotton is not guaranteed in the future if climate change continues: "As a result of the constant decrease of the amount of water and the increasing height of [river] banks, it is likely that one day the fertility of Egypt will be finally limited to very tiny parts where artificial irrigation is possible."[94]

Greece is the most important region for Fraas's study not only because there were documents of scientific investigations by ancient Greeks available but also because the case of Greece is geographically insightful for other modern European countries. Its history experienced the same historical transformation of climate and the plant world. Though Fraas provides detailed proofs for climate change in Greece, what comes to the foreground in his treatment is the problem of deforestation, a theme also reflected in Marx's notes in his own copy of the book.[95] Civilization consumes an enormous amount of wood as raw material for constructing houses and ships, as fuel for iron and sugar production. Goatherds need open fields; farmers burn brushwood into ash for manuring their lands; tanners need root cortex. Planting timber forests or maintaining existing forests, Fraas argues, is simply "unfeasible" in this situation.[96]

As a result of deforestation, the forests of which the ancient Greeks often spoke were no longer to be found in modern Greece. According to Strabo, "Eratosthenes said that Cypriots could not eradicate the forests *on the plains* by mining operations and ship construction, so that they finally decided to cede a piece of land to anyone that cleared it and brought it under cultivation." The situation in modern Greece was, said Fraas, much different, because "today modern Greece does not have any forests in easily accessible regions."[97] There existed forests in the areas higher than 3,000 meters where forestry was still too costly due to the height and distance from the cities: "There are ample trees only in higher mountains, that is, in areas where forestry continued to be impossible until today and any use of forest remained extremely difficult."[98] Even those forests would soon disappear with technological development, warns Fraas.

The more arid the local climate becomes, the more the original indigenous plants will be pushed back into the mountains—only if they can accommodate to a mountainous climate:

> Most oak trees from ancient times are maimed remnants that survived various attacks from cultivation and destruction, now withdrawing into shady gullies of high mountains where there is still ample spring water and the air is more humid.[99]

Fraas observed that cornus mas, oak, hophornbeam, holly, ash tree, maple, which used to grow in the plains, according to Theophrastus, were all pushed away to higher mountains. Instead of them flourishing in the plains, "bushes with thick and hard leaves, covered by felt, and with a lot of spine thorn" became common, which are similar to those plants in the savanna in South America or steppe in northern Asia: this is how the steppe formation proceeded in Greece.

Fraas observed that in the past a large number of cattle herds were pastured on rich fields of lowland near the coast, where "winter grain as well as summer grain of spelt, einkorn, wheat, and barley" were able to produce rich amounts of crops, but now in these regions "two-thirds of the land is dedicated to poorly managed winter grain without any manure, and in summer the field is inevitably left in fallow."[100] Climate change, he surmised, must have negatively affected the people in Greece because, though altering the natural conditions, it did not change the soil conditions to such an extent that other agricultural products could normally be cultivated with success.

Fraas's historical investigation shows in detail that cultivation with commerce and industry results in new material conditions that are no longer favorable to crops and humans. The difference between Fraas and Liebig is explicit. Both agree that a decrease of soil productivity due to irrational human interaction with their environment undermines the fundamental material conditions of civilization. However, the ultimate cause of a decrease is, according to Fraas, not the exhaustion of mineral substances in the soil, but excessive deforestation. Marx's excitement with Fraas's work expressed in a letter to Engels documents the enlargement of his interest in the capitalist disruption of metabolism between humans and nature in 1868. He subsequently attempted to integrate the new knowledge into his own political economy.

CLIMATE CHANGE AS A LIMIT OF THE MATERIAL WORLD

Historical investigation of the influence of human civilizations on the climate prompts Fraas to an almost Darwinian thesis of change or even creation of new species over historical time. He maintains that due to climate change "plants emigrate from their homeland," to the extent that we "can hardly recognize their homelands again."[101] Though the migrating plants can no longer attain the same homeland, accommodation under new climates is necessary for the sake of the plants' reproduction. In *Climate and the Plant World Over Time*, Fraas argues that "even the essential characteristics of plants can change through the long-lasting effect of climatic relations."[102] Newly emerged characteristics can be handed down to the next generation. Required by the metabolic interactions with the environment, such transformations often occur without human intervention, though humans can also modify physical shape and properties of plants directly and indirectly.[103] This is why Marx calls Fraas a "Darwinist before Darwin."

Human labor transforms the natural process of metabolism in two ways. First, it relates to nature *purposefully* and *consciously* in industry and agriculture. Nature provides human labor with materials for production, which can be modified in accordance with human needs and desires. This elasticity of nature strengthens humans' instrumentalist attitude toward nature. Second, humans change nature *unintentionally*, as industry and agriculture modify the universal metabolism between humans and nature as a whole. The cumulative result is, as Fraas illustrates in detail, exhaustion of the soil, the formation of steppes and desertification, which finally leads to the decay of civilization. In other words, humans are not in a position to change and manipulate their environment at will. Rather, human labor is confronted by the limits of the material world, when humans find themselves incapable of regulating metabolic rifts due to their instrumentalist treatment of nature. Their purposeful actions cause various negative effects over long historical periods. Fraas sums up his obervation:

> Man in various ways changes his environment, on which he is quite dependent, and he changes nature more than one usually imagines. In fact, he is able to change nature to such an extent that later it completely malfunctions as the indispensable means for the realization of a higher level of mental and physical development, forcing him to confront extreme physical obstacles. . . . There is no hope of overcoming this reality.[104]

Social production is not possible without the cooperation of the external sensuous world, and in this sense production is essentially dependent on it. However, the changes in climate and the plant world show that the expansion of civilization ends by leaving a desert behind it.

In relation to Marx's project of political economy as an analysis of dynamic entanglement between "form" and "material," Fraas's historical investigation opens up an even more expanded vision of ecology than the earlier reception of Liebig's theory of soil exhaustion. Climate change is a new and important element for Marx's investigation into the historical disturbances in natural metabolism caused by humans. Although Fraas focuses on ancient civilizations, *Climate and the Plant World Over Time* makes Marx aware that this development of modern capitalist production accelerates the disturbance of metabolism between humans and nature due to a more massive deforestation than previously in human history. Marx documents a passage in his notebook in which Fraas laments the rapid forest decrease in Europe: "France now has no more than 1/12 of its earlier forest area; in England out of 69 woodlands there remain only 4 big forests; in Italy and the southeastern peninsula of Europe the stands of trees in the mountains are less than what was common even in the plains in the past."[105] The future of European civilization appears dark because the modern development of productive forces not only requires more woods but also enables the cutting of trees in the higher mountain areas that were not hitherto accessible. The robbery practice worsens in the long run and undermines the universal physical conditions of the entire social production. According to Fraas, the only solution is to regulate the speed of deforestation as much as possible:

Civilized states with dense population inevitably need to add artificial constructions to meadow and forest that damage nature, replace
forests with fields for farming, dry out swamps and marshes, and
burn peat and forests that sustain humidity. In short, without such
supports civilized societies cannot be what they are. However, without actual necessity such changes of the state of nature should never
be carried out. . . . That is, *trees in mountain areas should never be cut
down without the highest necessity because they are most influential.*[106]

Once the mountain becomes bald, it causes increasingly harmful
effects on weather and vegetation, and material interests of European
nations can be threatened, as were those of earlier civilizations. Fraas
admits that this warning will not be appreciated by the public because
deforestation has built the economic foundation for the masses of people.
Thus he concludes pessimistically that the "biggest enemy" of nature is
"cultivation accompanied by commerce and industry."[107]

In opposition to Fraas, Marx thinks it possible and necessary that
the harmony between civilization and nature should be realized by the
conscious collective governance of the metabolism by the associated producers. But "as a bourgeois [Fraas] naturally does not reach this point."
Marx differs from Fraas with his insight that the great ecological crises
threaten the material foundation of social production, but humans will
be compelled to construct a more conscious and sustainable relationship
to nature. In this sense, Fraas's theory still remains within the realm of an
"*unconscious* socialist tendency."

Marx argues in the same letter of March 25, 1868, that one is often
trapped into "a certain judicial blindness," so that "even the best minds
fail to see, on principle, what lies in front of their noses." A "socialist
tendency" emerges only later as a "reaction" to the earlier situation,
only to find everywhere the traces of what has been overlooked. What
Fraas found "in what is oldest," Marx writes, is at the same time "what
is newest," which is also significant for modern society. In this vein,
Georg Ludwig von Maurer, a historian in the time of Marx and Fraas,
though he did not identify himself as a socialist, found in precapitalist
communities an "unconscious" socialist tendency that was "even egalitarian to a degree which would have made Proudhon shudder."[108] Fraas's
investigation of ancient societies also shows the same socialist tendency
toward the necessity of conscious regulation of metabolism between
humans and nature. Marx thus recognizes that the problem of deforestation treated by Fraas's work is not a problem of the past but of "what is

newest." In other words, the realization of sustainable production with regard to climate and the plant world is, like egalitarianism, one of the most important practical tasks of post-capitalist society. Herein lies Marx's *conscious* socialist tendency.

Given the wide range of Marx's research on ecological destruction from the perspective of the whole of human history, it is also important to clarify the point that ecological contradictions in the material world with which modern society is confronted are *not* purely economic. An understanding of this helps us to avoid falling into economic determinism.[109] Fraas shows that despite the appearance of long-term sustainable production in precapitalist societies there was always a certain tension between nature and humans. Capitalism alone does not create the problem of desertification *ex nihilo*, which would be nothing but economic determinism. Rather, it transforms and deepens the transhistorical contradiction by radically reorganizing the universal metabolism of nature from the perspective of capital's valorization.[110]

Marx separates himself from a popular reductionistic understanding that a non-contradictory unity between humanity and nature existed before the emergence of capitalism and must be reconstructed on a higher level in socialism. The rifts in natural metabolism have existed throughout history, for the entire human relationship to nature was never consciously arranged. This does not mean, of course, that the problem of an unconscious interaction between humans and nature remains the same throughout the course of history, but Marx's research on the transhistorical contradiction primarily aims at highlighting the specificity of the capitalist disruption of metabolism. In other words, he seeks to show how the transhistorical contradiction of the capitalist intercourse with nature gets strengthened, so that enormous disharmonies come to exist in the material world.

Fraas's theory contributes to understanding the deepening of metabolism rifts, as his analysis of historical transformations of climate and the plant world warns against shortsighted deforestation. Liebig's critique of the robbery system does not entirely cover the destructive tendency of modern production, and Marx, reading Fraas's work, rightly thinks it necessary to study much more thoroughly the negative aspect of the development of productive forces and technology and their disruption of natural metabolism with regard to other factors of production. Marx aims at strengthening Liebig's critique of the squandering of limited natural resources over the entire ecosystem, going beyond Liebig's analysis.

Although no direct reference to Fraas is found in Marx's later economic manuscripts, his interest in deforestation can be confirmed in his notebooks of 1868. In the beginning of 1868, he also read John D. Tuckett's *History of the Past and Present State of the Labouring Population*, noting the numbers of important pages. On one of those pages, Tuckett argues:

> The indolence of our forefathers appears a subject of regret, in neglecting the raising of trees as well as in many instances causing the destruction of the forests without sufficiently replacing them with young plants. This general waste appears to have been greatest just before the use of sea coal [for smelting iron] was discovered, when the consumption for the use of forging iron was so great that it appeared as if it would sweep down all the timber and woods in the country. . . . However, at the present day the plantations of trees not only add to the usefulness, but also tend to the embellishment of the country, and produce screens to break the rapid currants of the winds. . . . The great advantage in planting a large body of wood in a naked country is not at first perceived. Because there is nothing to resist the cold winds, cattle fed thereon are stunted in growth and the vegetation has often the appearance of being scorched with fire, or beaten with a stick. Moreover, by giving warmth and comfort to cattle, half the fodder will satisfy them.[111]

The thematic similarity with Fraas's work is explicit. Tuckett points to the fact that deforestation has significant economic consequences in agriculture and stock farming.

The influence of the ideas of Fraas and Tuckett is visible in the second manuscript for volume 2 of *Capital*, written between 1868 and 1870. Marx had noted in the manuscript for volume 3 that forestry would not be sustainable under the system of private property, even if it could be more or less sustainable when conducted under state property.[112] After 1868, Marx paid great attention to the problem of the modern robbery system, which he now expanded from crop production to include deforestation. In this vein, Marx made detailed excerpts from Friedrich Krichhof's *Manual of Agricultural Business Operations* (*Handbuch der landwirthschaftlichen Betriebslehre*; 1852) in support of the incompatibility between the logic of capital and the material characteristics of forestation. He pointed out that the long time required for forestation imposes a natural limit, compelling capital to try to shorten the cycle of deforestation and regrowth as much as possible. In the manuscript to volume 2 of *Capital*, Marx commented on a passage from Kirchhof's book: "The development of culture and of industry in general has evinced itself in such energetic destruction of forest that everything done by it conversely for their preservation and restoration appears infinitesimal."[113] Marx was certainly conscious of the danger that this deforestation will cause not only a wood shortage but also a changing climate, which is tied to a more existential crisis of human civilization. Indeed, Kirchhof also pointed to the climatic influence of deforestation:

> On the contrary, where forests disappeared, air becomes unfavorably dry and its flows are wilder and more violent. Springs of mountain valleys dry up, and many streams dry out. Many regions lost their fertility by cutting down trees, causing the balance of power to be disturbed.[114]

The thematic similarity between Fraas and Kirchhof is clear. It is probable that in his analysis of the turnover of capital in volume 2 of *Capital* Marx was not thinking about economic implications but a possible crisis in civilization due to deforestation.

Marx in the same manuscript also refers to Léonce de Lavergne in analyzing the same problem of material limits in the shortening of capital's turnover in stock farming. This time, he supplements his thesis by quoting a passage from William Walter Good's *Political, Agricultural and Commercial Fallacies* (1866):

> For this reason, remembering that farming is governed by the principles of political economy, *the calves* which used to come south from the dairying counties for rearing, *are now largely sacrificed at a week and ten days old*, in the shambles of Birmingham, Manchester, Liverpool, and other large neighboring towns. . . . What these little men now say, in reply to rear recommendations, is, "We know very well it would pay to rear on milk, but it would first require us to put our hands in our purse, which we cannot do, and then we should have to *wait a long time for a return, instead of getting it at once* by dairying."[115]

Capital is confronted by a natural limit, which impedes the shortening of necessary production time, due to "physiological necessity" as it sells the product "before it reaches the economic normal ages, which causes a great damage to agriculture."[116] Here Marx's ecological vision describing the contradiction between "capital" and "nature" is quite clear, and other excerpts in the 1870s can be interpreted from the same perspective.

A comparison with the writing of the young Marx illustrates this dramatic development of his ecological thought. In the *Communist Manifesto*, Marx and Engels write of the historic changes brought by the power of capital:

> The bourgeoisie, by the rapid improvement of all instruments of production, by the immensely facilitated means of communication, draws all, even the most barbarian nations into civilization. The cheap prices of its commodities are the heavy artillery with which it batters down all Chinese walls, with which it forces the barbarians' intensely obstinate hatred of foreigners to capitulate. It compels all nations, on pain of extinction, to adopt the bourgeois mode of production; it compels them to introduce what it calls civilization into their midst, i.e., to become bourgeois themselves. In one word, it creates a world after its own image.[117]

Marx and Engels here emphasize the progressive character of capital in opposition to the "barbarian" state of precapitalist society. Though they famously criticize in a subsequent discussion the negative aspects of capitalism in Europe, the problems of colonial domination remain outside the scope of their critique. It is as if the marginalized countries could be subsumed by capital and modernized through colonialism and the world market.[118]

Marx and Engels are also optimistic about capital's subjugation of nature based on increasing productive forces as a basis of emancipating humans from the alien forces of nature:

> The bourgeoisie, during its rule of scarce one hundred years, has created more massive and more colossal productive forces than have all preceding generations together. Subjection of Nature's forces to man, machinery, application of chemistry to industry and agriculture, steam-navigation, railways, electric telegraphs, clearing of whole continents for cultivation, canalization of rivers, whole populations conjured out of the ground—what earlier century had even a presentiment that such productive forces slumbered in the lap of social labour?[119]

Michael Löwy has criticized this passage as a manifestation of Marx's naïve attitude toward modernization and ignorance of ecological destruction under capitalist development: "Paying homage to the bourgeoisie for its unprecedented ability to develop the productive forces," he writes, "Marx and Engels unreservedly celebrated the 'Subjection of Nature's forces to man' and the 'clearing of whole continents for cultivation' by modern bourgeois production." Löwy's reading of Marx's alleged "Prometheanism" might seem hard to refute here.[120]

Löwy's criticism, even if his interpretation accurately reflects Marx's thinking at the time, can hardly be generalized across Marx's entire career, since his critique of capitalism became steadily more ecological with each passing year. As seen above, the evolution of his thought subsequent to volume 1 of *Capital* shows that in his later years, Marx became seriously concerned about the problem of deforestation, and it is highly doubtful that the late Marx, after reading Fraas and Kirchhof, would praise mass deforestation in the name of progress without regard for the conscious and sustainable regulation of the metabolic interaction between humanity and nature. On the contrary, it is much more likely that ecological issues attained increasingly more strategic significance for Marx in the 1860s as a manifestation of the contradictions of capitalism, to which socialism must provide a practical answer. Fraas's "unconscious socialist tendency" is discernible in his attempt to demonstrate the practical necessity to consciously reorganize the metabolism between humans and nature, based on which Marx much more consciously demanded human emancipation by radically abolishing the private character of production and wage labor and thus by constructing a fully different metabolic interaction with nature in a more sustainable way.

One sees more clearly why Marx was interested in Fraas's works. The polemics between Liebig and Fraas showed him that ecological problems in modern society must not be limited to that of soil exhaustion and that many other problems such as massive deforestation and climate change exist. Fraas's alluvial theory provides another vision of agriculture that becomes more sustainable thanks to the power of nature itself. Alluvial theory alone, of course, does not provide a final solution to the capitalist metabolic rifts. Deforestation alone does not explain climate change, either. Marx was witnessing a rapid development of natural sciences and technologies at that time, and he rightly thought it essential to study various natural science disciplines much more carefully in order to figure out how far capitalism can postpone the ecological crisis caused by itself and what kind of problems are actually emerging out of capital's infinite desire for self-valorization. As he subsequently changed his evaluation of Liebig slightly in the second edition of *Capital*, a new ecological field of research lay behind it.

Conclusion

In the 1970s, Hans Jonas, in his principal work *The Imperative of Responsibility*, insisted on the necessity of a critique of utopia precisely because "Marxist utopia, involving the fullest use of super-technology, served as an 'eschatologically' radicalized version of what the worldwide technological impetus of our civilization is moving toward anyway."[1] Today, nobody really believes in such a Marxist utopia, after its power of enchantment disappeared without trace along with the collapse of "really existing socialism." This "crisis" of Marxism, however, provided a new opportunity for Marxists, because Marx's theoretical legacy can be soberly analyzed again independently of party dogma. One can now investigate whether Marx really did envision such a technocratic emancipation. In the discussion in this book, it has become clear that a popular critique of Marx's utopian and anti-ecological thought is nothing but a retrospective projection of the Promethean idea of the nineteenth and twentieth centuries imposed on Marx's materialist thought.

The new historical edition of *Marx-Engels-Gesamtausgabe* enables us to reconstruct how, in the course of deepening his theory of political economy, Marx developed his ecological thought as a critique of capitalism. A more complete investigation of new materials published by the MEGA showed that a stereotypical (and false) critique of his indifference to the scarcity of natural resources and the burdening of our ecospheres, and another critique of his Promethean superstition on limitless economic and technological development, are not tenable. Furthermore, a more *systematic* investigation of excerpts and notes enables us to comprehend the central role of ecology in his critique of capitalism. We can derive ecological theory consistently from his theory of value, as an integral part of his system of political economy. And, accordingly, his vision of socialism clearly includes a project to rehabilitate the social and natural metabolism that has been seriously distorted in capitalism.

Modern discussions of ecology owe a great debt to Marx's deep insight into the fundamental nature of a society of generalized commodity production. He shows that value as the mediator of the transhistorical metabolism between humans and nature cannot generate the material conditions for sustainable production. Rather, it causes rifts in the process of material reproduction. When value becomes the dominant subject of social production as capital, it only strengthens the disturbances and disruptions of that metabolism, so that both humanity and nature suffer from various disharmonies. This includes overwork as well as physical and mental illness and deformations with regards to human beings; and desertification, devastation of natural resources, and extinction of species with regards to nature. According to Marx, this disruption of the metabolism of human beings and nature ultimately poses material limits to the measureless drive to capital accumulation and demands that humans have a more conscious interaction with their environment. It is possible to "crack capitalism" here.[2]

Of course, Marx was not thinking "ecologically" when he first attempted to develop his critique of capitalism. Nevertheless, it is important to recognize that in the notebooks of 1844 he had already demanded the abolition of modern alienation as a radical transformation of the human relation to nature, though this project of the young Marx has long been overlooked due to the dominant "philosophical" interpretation of his theory of alienation. Considering the history of debates on ecology, it is important to emphasize that Marx consistently bestowed a central role in his critique of modern society to the problem of the "separation" of humans from the earth.

Recently, some ecosocialists, in contrast to Marx, have come to stress the "monistic synthesis" of society and nature: "Not the separation *from*, but the terms of humanity's place *within* nature, is crucial to understanding the conditions of capitalist renewal (if any) and crisis."[3] However, this understanding overlooks Marx's original insight that the constitutive condition of the capitalist regime is the *separation* of humans from nature. The unity of humanity and nature exists transhistorically from an abstract general perspective, in that human labor not only always modifies nature, but is also a part of nature and conditioned by it. What Marx's analysis shows is the *historical* deformation of the relationship between humans and nature in modern capitalist society, which is based on the alienation of nature. Marx investigates, as the primary task of his political economy, how this material condition of social production is transformed and deformed under capitalistically constituted social relations.

In spite of this theoretical continuity, underlying all of his thought, Marx gradually corrected his optimistic vision of the human mastery of nature, following his break with philosophy in 1845. In comparison to the *Communist Manifesto*, in *Capital* Marx clearly rejects the illusion that the development of productive forces in technological terms allows for the arbitrary manipulation of nature by completely transforming the external sensuous world into a second nature. In *Capital*, Marx argues differently: the neglect of material characteristics causes deterioration of the material conditions of production and prevents free human development. In contrast to a widespread critique that Marx is a blind supporter of absolute domination over nature, his vision of the future society demands a careful and sustainable interaction with nature, based on a distinct recognition of its limits.

Against the popular opinion that sustainable production is possible on the basis of market mechanisms, Marx's theory of value also demonstrates in a convincing manner that capital contradicts the fundamental limitedness of natural forces and resources because of its drive toward infinite self-valorization. This is the central contradiction of the capitalist mode of production, and Marx's analysis aims at discerning the limits to this measureless drive for capital accumulation within a material world. The discrepancy between nature and capital appears in an increasing number of spheres, such that the domination of capital subsumes various branches of production and organizes the entirety of social and private life.

In this situation, Marx does not call for going back to "nature as such," existing independently of human beings, because, as he argues in *The German Ideology* in his critique of Feuerbach, that nature as such exists only in the philosopher's head. Instead, Marx says, "nature" exists only in relation to social production, and he calls this fundamental material relationship the "metabolism" between humans and nature. Both nature and society must be comprehended in their dynamic interrelation to each other, and his scientific analysis explains the specificity of the capitalist mode of production as the historical organization of that transhistorical metabolism and the resultant destabilization of our ecosystems.

Marx's theory of reification plays a central role in this context. It reveals how economic form determinations are tightly ossified as a *property of a thing* in the course of capitalist development, and how human needs, along with the external sensuous world, are radically transformed according to the logic of capitalism. Material properties are modifiable, and the whole reorganization of the world by capital is based on this material "elasticity," though capital cannot, after all, completely and arbitrarily overcome natural limits. In order to elucidate the fundamental tension between capital and nature, Marx developed his value theory in a close systematic relation to the problem of metabolic rifts. After parting from philosophy, Marx stopped collapsing this problem into a general ontological understanding of the human-nature relationship. He aimed instead at comprehending material limits under respective concrete conditions of natural sciences and technology. Where exactly this contradiction manifests itself is not given a priori; it requires a concrete analysis of each situation. Natural sciences provide the basic knowledge for such an analysis. Otherwise, a critique would only be able to say that capitalism must destroy the environment. Marx was never satisfied with such an abstract thesis.

Instead, he was aware that the contradiction between capital and nature does not immediately lead to the collapse of the regime of capital. Thanks to material elasticity, capital can, for example, overcome its limitations by intensively and extensively exploiting workers, inventing new technologies, discovering new raw materials, and opening up global markets and colonies. However, the limits of material, such as labor power, natural resources, social needs, exist objectively, even if they can be displaced by technological and scientific development to a considerable degree, as seen in the history of capitalism. The concrete manifestation of material limits is thus quite diverse, because the outcomes of the formal logic of capital develop in various ways, depending on capital's relation to respective natural conditions. To thematize these limits of capital more precisely, Marx studied the natural sciences more intensively after 1868 in order to complete *Capital*. Even though Marx's *Capital* remained incomplete, it not only provides a solid methodological foundation for the analysis of capital's historical process of antagonism between humanity and nature, but also enables us to envision a counterstrategy against the reified domination of capital and the alienation of nature, from the standpoint of the material world itself. In this sense, Marx's ecological critique is far from "apocalyptic."

Speaking of socialist strategy, the gradual formation of Marx's theory of metabolism parallels another important shift of his vision of social change. Though earlier, in the *Communist Manifesto*, Marx optimistically tended to believe that a serious economic crisis would suffice for a socialist revolution, he gradually gave up this optimism after the failure of the Revolution of 1848 and subsequent political repression and restoration. The capitalist system proved itself much more pertinacious and capable of survival in the economic crisis of 1857–58. As a consequence, Marx began to agitate for constraints on reification through workers' unionism and the construction of a more sustainable form of social metabolism. As illustrated in the chapters on "The Working Day" and "Machinery and Large-Scale Industry," Marx's point is that struggle is not immediately about policies but about a transformation of social practice itself, a practice that, under capitalism, bestows to a thing a social power independent of humans. Such reforms can extend the social and political realm and thus give rise to further progressive changes against the reified power of capital.

Marx emphasized the same point with regard to nature. Not only in his discussion about modern agriculture, but also in his reference to Fraas's "socialist tendency," he attempted to comprehend the destruction of ecosystems in relation to the reified power of capital from the perspective of the material world. The rehabilitation of the universal metabolism of nature disrupted by capitalism is only possible when the autonomous power of capital is fully abolished. Even if capitalism does not automatically collapse, despite the scarcity of natural resources, the disharmonies in the material world impede the free and sustainable development of humanity and compel people to struggle for a new social system beyond capitalism. Counter to the logic of capital, a more rational form of social production must be realized, and it must be based on the abolition of "private labor" and "wage labor." For Marx, it is moreover necessary to examine the concrete processes of transformation of the material world, as he read a number of Parliamentary reports and reports by factory inspectors while writing the chapter on "The Working Day." Only by doing so can a concrete socialist strategy against reified exploitation of nature become possible.

The investigation of Marx's ecology through his notebooks also showed that the common identification of the nineteenth century as a century of naïve Prometheanism proves one-sided, since a number of theorists such as Liebig, Johnston, and Fraas were seriously engaged with the problems of scarcity and exhaustion of natural resources. Also William Stanley Jevons's prediction about decreasing coal reserves in England in his famous book *The Coal Question* (1865) repeatedly refers to Liebig and caused heated discussions in the English Parliament. Marx knew this work, as in 1868 he noted the title in his notebook and checked next to it with an intent to buy a copy.[4] Matthias Jakob Schleiden, whose *Physiology of Plants and Animals* (*Physiologie der Pflanzen und Tiere*, 1850) Marx read in 1876, wrote of the "desertification of forests" in his later work *For Wood and Forest* (*Für Baum und Wald*), in which Schleiden refers to George P. Marsh's important book *Man and Nature* (1864).[5]

Diverse serious discussions on the destruction of the environment and the deterioration of conditions for humanity's survival were underway as early as the 1860s. It is not a coincidence that Marx, constantly studying new books and articles in various disciplines, was prompted to integrate the emergence of ecological thought in the nineteenth century into his own critique of political economy, as this dimension had been largely neglected. If we examine Marx's notebooks and trace Marx's working process, it is difficult to continue claiming that he shared a naïve and optimistic idea of human progress, one that believed in the infinite development of productive forces. Carl Fraas is of importance in this context because he offers another vision of sustainable production, which differs from Liebig's dependence on synthetic manures. His theory of alluvion attempts to show the possibility of sustainable production, using the power of nature itself purposefully, but without exhausting it. His historical investigation also showed Marx how serious the consequences of excessive deforestation were to local climates and the plant world.

Among Marx's writings, it is possible to find various clear arguments that indicate his strong interest in ecological problems. If the statement that Marx's ecology is only of secondary importance for his critique of political economy was accepted as convincing for a long time, the reason can be partially found in the tradition of Western Marxism, which primarily dealt with social forms (sometimes with an extreme fetishism of Hegel's *Science of Logic*), while the problem of "material" or "content" was largely neglected. If the "material" becomes integrated into his system, Marx's texts open the way to ecology without much difficulty.

In this sense, the present volume is more systematic and complete than earlier works on the issue of Marx's mature ecology, yet its scope is still limited. Manuscripts and excerpt notebooks that I have dealt with in this book are only part of what Marx wrote during his life. Especially in the 1870s, his theory of metabolism was further developed. There are some examples indicating this tendency in his personal library: Bernard Cotta, *German Soil, Its Geological Composition and the Latter's Influence on Human's Life* (*Deutschlands Boden, sein geologischer Bau und dessen Einwirkung auf das Leben der Menschen*; Leipzig, 1858); Jean Charles Houzeau, *Climate and Soil* (*Klima und Boden*; Leipzig,

1861); Adalbert Adolf Mühry, *Climatographical Overview of the Earth* (*Klimatographische Uebersicht der Erde*; Leipzig, 1862); and Robert Russell, *North America: Its Agriculture and Climate* (Edinburgh, 1857). Marx also followed the debates on Liebig's theory of soil exhaustion: Adolf Mayer, *Fertilizer Capital and Robbery Cultivation* (*Das Düngerkapital und Raubbau*; Heidelberg, 1869); Clement Mandelblüh, *Tables for the Calculation of Soil Exhaustion and Replenishment of Soil Power* (*Tabellen zur Berechnung der Bodenerschöpfung und des Bodenkraft-Ersatzes*; Leipzig, 1870); and Johannes Conrad, *Liebig's View on Soil Exhaustion and Its Historical, Statistical, and National Economic Reasoning* (*Liebig's Ansicht von der Bodenerschöpfung und ihre geschichtliche, statistische und nationalökonomische Begründung*; Göttingen, 1866). This is only a sample of the books relevant to the topics dealt with here, and Marx's own interests in this respect are still more encompassing than even these suggest.[6] As a result of these investigations, Marx came to see in his later years that metabolic rifts were the most serious problem of capitalism.

In this context, it is important to emphasize that his later research was not limited to natural sciences. Marx also read various books on pre-capitalist and non-Western societies and communities, with a particular focus on agriculture and landed property, as can be seen in the famous *Ethnological Notebooks*.[7] In terms of this theme, Marx's expression "an unconscious socialist tendency" is again insightful. In the same March 25, 1868, letter to Engels in which Marx discussed Fraas's *Climate and the Plant World Over Time*, he also judged quite positively Georg Ludwig Maurer: "*Ad vocem Maurer*: his books are extremely significant. Not only the primitive age but also the entire later development of the free imperial cities, of the estate owners possessing immunity, of public authority, and of the struggle between the free peasantry and serfdom, get an entirely new character."[8] Marx admitted in the letter that he paid too little attention to the continuation of precapitalist (Germanic) elements until his time. In the following years, Marx seriously studied precapitalist societies, engaging in a self-critical move to overcome this blind spot, even learning Russian, so that he could read books on Russian village communities and agriculture in the original.[9]

How do natural sciences and ethnology relate to each other for the late Marx? We find a key in a textual connection between Fraas and Maurer: Fraas himself positively evaluates Maurer's historical investigation about Germanic communities because this German historian shows that "the first Germanic village formation always followed the law of necessity to increase the soil's power."[10] Moreover, Fraas continues to argue about the sustainable way of life of Germanic communities, with a reference to Maurer's text:

> If the Mark village did not allow sales except among village members of wood, straw, dung, and even livestock (pigs!) and also ordered that all the crops harvested within the village, and even wine, should be consumed within the village (out of this practice various socage rights [Bannrechte] were to emerge), the means must have been retained for the maintenance of land power, and furthermore, the use of additional nutrients from forests and pastures, and even the use of meadows manured by rivers served to increase the [soil's] power everywhere (Maurer, op. cit., 313 sq.).[11]

Germanic communal production based on the Mark association is, according to Fraas, not only egalitarian but also sustainable because everything is produced and consumed within the community. It is very likely that this reference prompted Marx to read Maurer's book in the beginning of 1868 and to make excerpts from it.[12]

At this time, it is not possible to investigate the enormous entirety of Marx's manuscripts and excerpts after 1868 because not all are published yet. However, it is reasonable to assume, based on his high evaluation of Maurer and Fraas and his characterization of them as "unconscious" socialists in the same letter, that he wanted to study the various concrete ways of organizing the metabolism between humans and nature through precapitalist and non-Western communities and societies, especially with regard to agriculture and landed property. Kevin Anderson argues with regard to volume IV/27 of the MEGA[2] that Marx's research in the 1870s focuses on precapitalist and non-Western agriculture "in transition."[13] In other words, Marx analyzed how far earlier ways of organization of natural and social metabolism must be modified through formal and real subsumption under capital, or whether they can resist capital. In this sense, the relationship between humans and nature remained central in the late Marx as well.[14]

Some remarks by Marx in the last years of his life confirm the thematic connection. It is known that he recognized the possibility of an alternative way to the socialist revolution in Russia in his letter to Vera Ivanovna Zasulich, a Russian revolutionary. Referring to Maurer directly, Marx pointed to the great "natural vitality" of archaic communes and argued that the later village communes, especially those that the Germans introduced, "became the only focus of liberty and popular life throughout the Middle Ages."[15] According to Marx, this vitality was founded on a different organization of the metabolism between humans and nature—the communal form of production. Thus the Russian village communes could function as the place of resistance against capital and establish socialism without going through capitalism. "Historically very favorable to the preservation of the 'agricultural commune' through its further development is the fact not only that it is contemporaneous with Western capitalist production and therefore able to acquire its fruits without bowing to its *modus operandi*, but also that it has survived the epoch when the capitalist system stood intact."[16]

At the same time, Marx, in the next sentence, points to the "crisis" of capitalism in Western Europe: "Today it finds that system, both in Western Europe and the United States, in conflict with the working masses, with science, and with the very productive forces which it generates—in short, in a crisis that will end through its own elimination, through the return of modern societies to a higher form of an 'archaic' type of collective ownership and production."[17] The "crisis" emerges not only out of the experience of alienation, whose transcendence is loudly demanded by workers, but also out of capital's conflict with "science." It is not enough for science simply to enable the invention of new technologies that increase productive forces and prepare material conditions for the future society. As is clearly visible in Liebig and Fraas, science also highlights the crisis of capitalism by demonstrating the irrationality of robbery under the capitalist mode of production and its consequent metabolic rifts, which accordingly demand the realization of a more sustainable form of production. Taking into account the deepening of Marx's theory of metabolism, it is plausible that Marx in 1881 recognized not only non-Eurocentric, multilinear ways to socialism but also developed a more ecological vision of socialism. However, this expansion of Marx's interest made it extremely hard to complete his project of *Capital*.

Even if late Marx's ecosocialism will become more apparent through future publications of MEGA[2] volumes, the project of *Capital* remains unfinished. Marx did not answer all the questions and did not predict today's world, but it does not follow that his ecology is of no use today. It is undeniable that his critique of capitalism provides an extremely helpful theoretical foundation for further critical investigation of the current ecological crisis, and that with regard to ecology Marx's notebooks can prove their great importance. Careful examination of Marx's excerpt notebooks is not minor"philological" work, and that analysis will lead us to unknown dimensions of Marx's critique.[18] It is too early to "forget

Marx," as Immler provocatively declared. At the end of this book, the opposite imperative sounds more convincing: "Marx lives!"

Notes

INTRODUCTION

1. John Passmore, *Man's Responsibility for Nature: Ecological Problems and Western Traditions* (New York: Scribner, 1974), 185.

2. Anthony Giddens, *A Contemporary Critique of Historical Materialism,* vol. 1: *Power, Property and the State* (Berkeley: University of California Press, 1981), 60. Although totally neglected by Giddens and others, it is noteworthy that there is actually a rich classical Marxist tradition that integrated ecological thinking into its critique of capitalism in the 1960s and '70s. Scholars in this tradition include Shigeto Tsuru, Paul Sweezy, Herbert Marcuse, Raymond Williams, and István Mészáros. For more detail, see John Bellamy Foster and Paul Burkett, *Marx and the Earth: An Anti-Critique* (Leiden: Brill, 2016), 2.

3. A stereotypical view can be found, for example, in Alexander Gillespie's summary: "Traditional Marxism involved a realization of 'productivism,' and how it can be applied to serve the needs of all, and not just the ruling classes. This trend has continued through to modern doctrines of socialism. Therefore, it is still argued that full mobilization of modern productive forces is necessary before socialism can be established. This perception suggests that 'there is too little growth' and any limits that do eventuate represent political and social issues, *not* ecological ones." Alexander Gillespie, *The Illusion of Progress: Unsustainable Development in International Law and Policy* (New York: Earthscan Publications, 2001), 16, emphasis in original.

4. Thomas Petersen and Malte Faber, *Karl Marx und die Philosophie der Wirtschaft* (Freiburg: Karl Alber, 2014), 139.

5. Rolf P. Sieferle, *Karl Marx zur Einführung* (Hamburg: Junius, 2011), 215.

6. Hans Immler and Wolfdietrich Schmied-Kowarzik, *Marx und die Naturfrage: Ein Wissenschaftsstreit* (Kassel: Kassel University Press, 2011), 36.

7. Ibid., 12.

8. Paul Burkett, *Marx and Nature: A Red and Green Perspective* (New York: Palgrave, 1999); John Bellamy Foster, *Marx's Ecology: Materialism and Nature* (New York: Monthly Review Press, 2000).

9. Paul Burkett, "Marx's Vision of Sustainable Human Development," *Monthly Review* 57/5 (October 2005): 34–62, 34.

10. John Bellamy Foster, "Paul Burkett's *Marx and Nature* Fifteen Years After," *Monthly Review* 66/7 (December 2014): 56–62, at 56. See also John Bellamy Foster, *The Ecological Revolution: Making Peace with the Planet* (New York: Monthly Review

Press, 2009); John Bellamy Foster, Brett Clark, and Richard York, *The Ecological Rift: Capitalism's War on the Earth* (New York: Monthly Review Press, 2010).

11.   Ariel Salleh, *Ecofeminism as Politics: Nature, Marx and the Postmodern* (London: Zed, 1997); Del Weston, *The Political Economy of Global Warming: The Terminal Crisis* (London: Routledge, 2014); Stefano B. Longo, Rebecca Clausen, and Brett Clark, *The Tragedy of the Commodity: Oceans, Fisheries, and Aquaculture* (New Brunswick, NJ: Rutgers University Press, 2015); Brett Clark and Ricard York, "Carbon Metabolism: Global Capitalism, Climate Change, and Biospheric Rift," *Theory and Society* 34/4 (July 2005): 391–428; Rebecca Clausen and Brett Clark, "The Metabolic Rift and Marin Ecology," *Organization & Environment* 18/4 (December 2005): 422–44; Stefano Longo, "Mediterranean Rift," *Critical Sociology* 38/3 (May 2012): 417–36; John Bellamy Foster and Brett Clark, "Ecological Imperialism: The Curse of Capitalism," in Leo Panitch and Colin Leys, editors, *Socialist Register 2004: The New Imperial Challenge* (New York: Monthly Review Press, 2004), 186–201. .

12.   Naomi Klein, *This Changes Everything: Capitalism vs. the Climate* (New York: Simon and Schuster, 2014), 177.

13.   Major works by the "first-stage ecosocialists" that contributed to establish a stereotype of Marx's productivism are Ted Benton, "Marxism and Natural Limits," *New Left Review* 178 (November–December 1989): 51–86; André Gorz, *Capitalism, Socialism, Ecology* (London: Verso, 1994); Michael Löwy, "For a Critical Marxism," *Against the Current* 12/5 (November–December 1998): 33–34; James O'Connor, *Natural Causes: Essays in Ecological Marxism* (New York: Guilford, 1998); Alain Lipietz, "Political Ecology and the Future of Marxism," *Capitalism Nature Socialism* 11/1 (March 2000): 69–85. For a general critique see also Foster, "Paul Burkett's *Marx and Nature* Fifteen Years After," 57–58.

14.   Joel Kovel, *The Enemy of Nature: The End of Capitalism or the End of the World?* (London: Zed Books, 2002), 232; Salvatore Engel-Di Mauro, *Ecology, Soils, and the Left: An Eco-Social Approach* (New York: Palgrave, 2014), 136–42.

15.   Daniel Tanuro, *Green Capitalism: Why It Can't Work* (London: Fernwood Publishing, 2013), 138–39. Foster and Burkett recently provided a convincing "anticritique." See Foster and Burkett, *Marx and the Earth*, 15–25.

16.   Jason W. Moore, *Capitalism in the Web of Life. Ecology and the Accumulation of Capital* (London: Verso, 2015), 80; "Toward a Singular Metabolism. Epistemic Rifts and Environment-Making in the Capitalist World-Ecology," *New Geographies* 6 (2014): 10–19, 13.

17.   Hubert Laitko, "Marx' theoretisches Erbe und die Idee der nachhaltigen Entwicklung," in *Beiträge zur Marx-Engels-Forschung Neue Folge 2006: Karl Marx und die Naturwissenschaften im 19 Jahrhundert* (Hamburg: Argument Verlag, 2006), 63–81, 65.

18.   Lipietz, "Political Ecology and the Future of Marxism," 74.

19.   Gorz, *Capitalism, Socialism, Ecology*, vii.

20.   Helmut Reichelt, *Zur logischen Struktur des Kapitalbegriffs bei Karl Marx* (Freiburg: Europäische Verragsanstalt, 1970); Hans-Georg Backhaus, *Dialektik der Wertform: Untersuchungen zur marxschen Ökonomie* (Freiburg: Ca ira, 1997); Michael Heinrich, *Wissenschaft vom Wert: Die Marxsche Kritik der politischen Ökonomie* (Münster: Verlag Westfälisches Dampfboot, 1999); Ingo Elbe, *Marx im Westen:. Die neue Marx-Lektüre in der Bundesrepublik seit 1965* (Berlin: Akademie Verlag, 2010); Werner Bonefeld, *Critical Theory and the Critique of Political Economy: On Subversion and Negative Reason* (New York: Bloomsbury, 2014).

21.   Helmut Brentel, *Soziale Form und ökonomisches Objekt: Studien zum Gegenstands-*

und Methodenverständnis der Kritik der politischen Ökonomie (Opladen: Westdeutscher Verlag, 1989), 13; Ingo Elbe "Soziale Form und Geschichte. Der Gegenstand des *Kapital* aus der Perspektive neuerer Marx-Lektüren," *Deutsche Zeitschrift für Philosophie* 58/2 (April 2010): 221–40, 228.

22. Though not available in English, Teinosuke Otani in his four-volume *Marx's Theory of Interest-Bearing Capital* (Tokyo: Sakurai Shoten, 2016) conducted an astonishingly careful comparison between Section 5 of Marx's original manuscript and Part 5 of the Engels edition on "interest-bearing capital." I translate here some examples of his discoveries from his recent address upon receiving a Distinguished Achievement Award of World Political Economy of the 21st Century from the World Association for Political Economy: "By the way, in Chapters 25 and 27 in the Engels edition, certain sentences have been repeatedly quoted as a hint to understanding the task and the theoretical structure of Section 5 of Marx's original manuscript. However, Engels changed some of them significantly, even changing their original meanings. Two examples would be sufficient for now. First, in the beginning of Section 5, 'Credit. Fictitious Capital,' Marx writes: 'It lies outside the scope of our plan to give an analysis of the credit system and the instruments this creates, as credit money etc.' Engels changed the term 'analysis' into 'detailed analysis.' With 'our plan' Marx is referring to the whole plan of *Capital* as a 'general analysis of capital,' so he means that an 'analysis of the credit system' lies outside the scope of *Capital*. But Engels, adding an adjective 'detailed,' changed the meaning in such a way that an 'analysis of the credit system' is actually included in *Capital*, though not a detailed one. Indeed, many repeatedly referred to this sentence to argue that Marx does treat the problem of the credit system in Part 5. Secondly, toward the end of Chapter 27 Marx writes about what he is going to analyze: 'Now we pass into consideration of interest-bearing capital as such.' And he continues to write within brackets: 'Effect on this by credit system and the form this takes.' Engels changed the part 'Now we pass into consideration of interest-being capital as such' to 'In the following chapter we discuss credit in relation to interest-bearing capital as such.' What is the object of analysis here? According to Marx, it is 'interest-bearing as such,' but according to Engels, it is 'credit.' Moreover, Marx bracketed 'Effect on this by credit system and the form this takes,' but Engels changed it to 'Both effect of credit on interest-bearing capital and the form that the credit assume in this connection.' That is to say, Marx intended to analyze 'interest-bearing capital,' but Engels changed the object of an analysis to 'credit.' Due to Engels' modification, Marx's statement was fully reversed from the analysis on 'interest-bearing capital as such' in its relation to credit system to the analysis of 'credit,' i.e., credit system in its relation to interest-bearing capital. This sentence too was often quoted as a place where Marx explicitly states that the following passages deal with the credit system. Why did Engels make such changes that modify the meanings? The only possible reason is that he was falsely convinced that Chapter 25 and the following chapters deal with credit or credit system, and he modified the sentences according to this idea."

23. Richard Sperl, "Der Beitrag von Anneliese Griese zur historisch-kritischen Edition der naturwissenschaftlichen Manuskripte von Marx und Engels," in *Beiträge zur Marx-Engels-Forschung: Neue Folge 2006* (Hamburg: Argument Verlag, 2006), 10–25, 15. It is true that deteriorating health prevented Marx from writing *Capital*, and thus spent more time reading books. However, this fact alone does not explain why he read so many books on natural sciences.

24. Burkett and Foster refer to Marx's notebooks in order to emphasize his serious

commitment to ecology. Nonetheless, they do not directly deal with them. As a result, their chronology and internal connection are not discernible. See Paul Burkett and John Bellamy Foster, "The Podolinsky Myth: An Obituary Introduction to 'Human Labour and Unity of Force' by Sergei Podolinsky," *Historical Materialism* 16/1 (2008): 115–61.

25. Cited in Richrd Sperl, *Edition auf dem hohen Niveau: Zu den Grundsätzen der Marx-Engels-Gesamtausgabe* (Hamburg: Argument Verlag, 2000), 68–69.

26. David Riazanov, "Neueste Mitteilungen über den literarischen Nachlaß von Karl Marx und Friedrich Engels," *Archiv für die Geschichte des Sozialismus und der Arbeiterbewegung*, 11 (1925): 385–400, 392, 399.

27. Benedikt Kautsky, "Die Marx-Engels-Gesamtausgabe," *Die Gesellschaft* 7/2 (1930): 260–70, 261–62.

28. Karl Marx and Frederik Engels, *Gesamtausgabe*, section IV, vol. 32 (Berlin: De Gruyter, 1976–), 21, emphasis in original. When I quote from the *Marx-Engels-Gesamtausgabe*, I will use an abbreviated expression "MEGA²" followed by the section and volume numbers and then by the page number (ex. MEGA² IV/32, 21 in this case).

29. Martin Hundt, "Der Fortgang der MEGA und einige aktuelle Debatten um Marx' Werk," *Z. Zeitschrift Marxistische Erneuerung* 85 (March 2011): 105–21, at 116.

30. Only Annelise Griese's introduction to MEGA² volumes IV/26 and IV/31 and Carl-Erich Vollgraf's introduction to MEGA² volume II/4.3 examine Marx's natural science notebooks in detail. With regard to other literature on Marx's notebooks in general, there are a handful: Fred E. Schrader, *Revolution und Restauration: Die Vorbereiten zum "Capital" von Karl Marx in seinen Studienheften 1850–1858* (Hildesheim: Gerstenberg, 1980); Kevin Anderson, *Marx at the Margins: Nationalism, Ethnicity, and Non-Western Societies*, 2nd rev. ed. (Chicago: University of Chicago Press, 2016); Kolja Lindner, "Marx's Eurocentrism. Postcolonialism Studies and Marx Scholarship," *Radical Philosophy* 161 (May–June 2010): 27–41.

31. Foster and Burkett do not see any significant difference between Marx and Engels in terms of the ecology. Nonetheless, I will focus only on Marx's ecology without going into that of Engels.

32. See also Hans Jörg Sandkühler, "Wissenschaftliches Weltbild als naturalisierte Philosophie. Der Theorietypus Marx und die epistemologische Bedeutung der Naturwissenschaften im Marxschen Werk Teil 1," in *AG Marx-Engels-Forschung, Naturwissenschaften und Produktivkräfte bei Marx und Engels. MarxEngels-Forschung heute 3* (Frankfurt am Main: IMSF, 1991), 11–23, at 22; Manfred Kliem, *Karl Marx: Dokumente seines Lebens 1818 bis 1883* (Leipzig: Reclam, 1970), 482.

33. Carl-Erich Vollgraf, "Marx auf Flucht vor dem *Kapital*?," in *Beiträge zur Marx-Engels-Forschung, Neue Folge 1994: Quellen und Grenzen von Marx' Wissenschaftsverständnis* (Hamburg: Argument, 1994), 89–93, 92.

34. Paul Burkett, *Marxism and Ecological Economics: Toward a Red and Green Political Economy* (Chicago: Haymarket Books, 2009), 136.

1. Alienation of Nature as the Emergence of the Modern

1. The *Paris Notebooks* are now available in the MEGA² IV/2 with the exception of the so-called *Economic and Philosophic Manuscripts*, which is also published in volume I/2. This separate publication reflects the German editors' preference to treat the bundle of texts as an independent work. The decision to make a separate publication made it harder to trace Marx's working process and contradicts the

editorial principle of the MEGA² to present the texts as original (*Originaltreue*). Jürgen Rojahn argues that the artificial separation between volumes I/2 and IV/2 by the editors, treating some of the notebooks as "manuscripts" and the rest as "excerpts," made it impossible for readers to attain the full vision of the *Paris Notebooks*. See Jürgen Rojahn, "Die Marxschen Manuskripte aus dem Jahre 1844 in der neuen Marx-Engels-Gesamtausgabe (MEGA)," *Archiv für Sozialgeschichte* 25 (1985), 647–63, at 658–59.

2. Iring Fetscher, *Marx and Marxism* (New York: Herder and Herder, 1971), 314.

3. Eric Fromm, *Marx's Concept of Man* (New York: Frederick Ungar Publishing, 1961).

4. Louis Althusser, *For Marx* (London: The Penguin Press, 1969), 33.

5. Mandel gives a good summary of the debate. See Ernest Mandel, *The Formation of the Economic Thought of Karl Marx* (New York: Monthly Review Press, 1971), 163–75.

6. Jürgen Rojahn, "The Emergence of a Theory: The Importance of Marx's Notebooks exemplified by Those from 1844," *Rethinking Marxism* 14/4 (2002): 29–46, 45. The false impression of Marx's intention to write a work for publication was created by the editors of the *Manuscripts* when they took the Preface from the third manuscript and brought it to the beginning, as if it were a preface to the entire work. Musto also offers some explanation in English based upon Rojahn's research. See Marcello Musto, "Marx in Paris. Manuscripts and Notebooks of 1844," *Science & Society* 73/3 (July 2009), 386–402.

7. Humanists criticize Althusser for his overemphasis on the importance of Marx's "epistemological break" in 1845. However, their "absolutization" of the young Marx also requires another breakthrough. For example, Merleau-Ponty justifies his complete dismissal of *Capital* by pointing to Marx's breakthrough ca. 1850 when he abandoned the theory of alienation in favor of constructing a dehumanized scientific system of political economy. Maurice Merleau-Ponty, *Adventures of the Dialectic* (Evanston, IL: Northwestern University Press, 1973), 62–65. Daniel Bell also argues in a similar way, in *The End of Ideology: On the Exhaustion of Political Ideas in the Fifties* (Cambridge, MA: Harvard University Press, 2001), 366–67. Others refer to Mészáros's careful analysis of the *Grundrisse* as a proof that Marx used the term "alienation" or "alien"; see Ivan Mészáros, *Marx's Theory of Alienation* (London: Merlin, 1970), 221–26.

8. Axel Honneth and Daniel Brudney, who emphasize the necessity of a normative critique of capitalism, miss Marx's main object. Marx's project after 1845 is not concerned with judging capitalism as a good or bad system. It was clear to him that capitalism is not sustainable due to its destruction of the labor force and nature. Proving the wrongness of capitalism was not the task of theory. Rather, Marx aims at comprehending the social and material relations of capitalism that structurally produce the misery of workers and exhaustion of natural resources. See Axel Honneth, *Reification: A New Look at an Old Idea* (Oxford: Oxford University Press, 2012); Daniel Brudney, *Marx's Attempt to Leave Philosophy* (Cambridge, MA: Harvard University Press, 1998).

9. Marx and Engels, *Collected Works*, vol. 3 (Moscow: Progress Publishers, 1975), 272.

10. Ibid.

11. Ibid., 274, emphasis in original. Here Marx explicitly refers to the similarity in religious alienation: "Just as in religion the spontaneous activity of the human imagination, of the human brain and the human heart, operates on the individual

independently of him—that is, operates as an alien, divine, or diabolical activity—so the worker's activity is not his spontaneous activity."

12. Ibid., 276, emphasis in original.

13. See Ludwig Feuerbach, *Gesammelte Werke*, vol. 5 (Berlin: Akademie Verlag, 1973), 29.

14. There is a debate whether this concept of "inorganic body" is anthropocentric and anti-ecological. As an ecological defense of the concept, see John Bellmay Foster and Paul Burkett, *Marx and the Earth: An Anti-Critique* (Leiden: Brill, 2016), chap. 1.

15. Marx and Engels, *Collected Works*, vol. 3, 277.

16. Ibid., 276, emphasis in original.

17. Ibid., 277, emphasis in original.

18. Ibid., 328, emphasis in original.

19. Feuerbach, *Gesammelte Werke*, vol. 5, 99.

20. Marx and Engels, *Collected Works*, vol. 3, 175, emphasis in original.

21. Herbert Marcuse, *Studies in Critical Philosophy* (Boston: Beacon Press, 1972), 7.

22. Before his stay in Manchester in 1845 Marx read books on political economy in French translation and translated them into German in his notebooks. He also directly cited from Wilhelm Schulz, Constantin Pecqueur, and Eugène Buret.

23. Marcuse refers to the first half of the first manuscript only once.

24. Erich Fromm, *Marx's Concept of Man: Including "Economic and Philosophical Manuscripts"* (London: Bloomsbury, 2013).

25. Marx and Engels, *Collected Works*, vol. 3, 279–80, emphasis in original.

26. Ibid., 281, emphasis in original.

27. Lars Tummers, *Policy Alienation and the Power of Professionals* (Cheltenham: Edward Elgar, 2013), 26; Ignace Feuerlicht, *Alienation: From the Past to the Future* (Westport, CT: Greenwood Press, 1978), 130. In Germany, recently, Ingo Elbe negatively judged the failure of Marx's explanation in "Entfremdete und abstrakte Arbeit: Marx' Ökonomisch-philosophische Manuskripte im Vergleich zu seiner späteren *Kritik der politischen Ökonomie*," *Oldenburger Jahrbuch für Philosophie 2012* (Oldenburg: BIS Verlag, 2014), 7–69, 45.

28. Michael Quante, "Kommentar," in Karl Marx, *Ökonomisch-philosophische Manuskripte* (Frankfurt am Main: Suhrkamp, 2009), 231, 258.

29. Marx, *Collected Works*, vol. 3, 268.

30. Ibid., 266. Last emphasis in quote added by K.S. Although Marx does not name the source here, he builds up his own critique with Engels's *Outline of a Critique of Political Economy*. Prior to Marx, Engels had written about this theme in the following manner: "To make land an object of huckstering—the land which is our one and all, the first condition of our existence—was the last step towards making oneself an object of huckstering" (ibid., 429). Marx takes up Engels's idea in his own analysis in order to comprehend alienation, the huckstering of oneself, as a result of huckstering the land.

31. See MEGA² II/2, 20.

32. It is precisely this specific form of capitalist alienation that the "philosophic" interpretation cannot adequately explain. As a result, it shares a one-sidedness with the Romantics. Any critical analysis requires an investigation into how alienated labor in capitalism differentiates itself from its feudal form. Margaret A. Fay is one of the few who take Marx's comparison of alienation between capitalist and feudal society into account, but she ends up negating any "rupture" in the process of the emergence of modern society. Rather, she emphasizes the "continuity" and "similarity"

between the two. Fay argues that because of "private property" under feudalism the serf was exploited by the owner of the means of production as day-laborers were. Consequently, the whole problematic of alienation is reduced to the problem of private property of the means of production. However, Marx questions not just the fact of alienation and exploitation but the specific historical ways of appropriation. See Margaret A. Fay, *Der Einfluß von Adam Smith auf Karl Marx' Theorie der Entfremdung: Eine Rekonstruktion der Ökonomisch-philosophische Manuskripte aus dem Jahr 1844* [Marx's Theory of Alienation: A Reconstruction of the *Economic and Philosophic Manuscripts of 1844*] (Frankfurt am Main: Campus 1986), 166–72.

33. Marx, *Collected Works*, vol. 3, 266, emphasis in original.
34. Ibid.
35. Ibid, emphasis in original.
36. Masami Fukutomi, *Keizaigaku to Shizen Tetsugaku* [Political Economy and Philosophy of Nature] (Tokyo: Sekaishoin, 1989), 23.
37. Marx, *Collected Works*, vol. 3, 267.
38. Ibid.
39. Ibid.
40. Marx did not idealize the feudal life, even when he emphasized its positive aspects in contrast to modern alienated life. He was clearly aware of the relations of domination in the past and thus argued that the full development of the free individual can only take place through the experience of modern alienation and its conscious transcendence in the future society.
41. Notably, Marx owed this view to Engels, who wrote in *Outline of a Critique of Political Economy*: "The immediate consequence of private property was the split of production into two opposing sides—the natural and the human sides, the soil which without fertilization by man is dead and sterile, and human activity, the first condition of which is that very soil" (ibid., 432). When he read Engels's *Outline*, Marx indeed paid attention to this modern "split" as it is documented in his *Paris Notebooks*: "Split between land and humans. Human labor separated into labor and capital." MEGA² IV/2, 486.
42. Marx and Engels, *Collected Works*, vol. 3, 286, emphasis in original.
43. Ibid., 267.
44. Ibid., 284.
45. Ibid., 267.
46. Ibid., 283.
47. It is also clear that Marx at this time differentiates himself from Feuerbach. Feuerbach's critique of religious alienation is based on an ontological argument that finite individuals feel powerless in the face of God. Religious alienation as such is not a specific product of modern society, even if its conscious transcendence requires modern subjectivity. Feuerbach, in contrast to Hegel, does not reveal the dynamic movement of history through the negation of the negation. Ibid., 329.
48. Ibid., 268, emphasis added.
49. Ibid., 296, emphasis in original.
50. Ibid., 298, emphasis in original.
51. Ibid., vol. 6, 201.
52. Ibid., vol. 29, 430, emphasis added.
53. Ibid., 431.
54. Ibid., vol. 30, 364.
55. Karl Marx, *Marx's Economic Manuscript of 1864–1865* (Leiden: Brill 2015), 715–17.
56. Karl Marx, *Grundrisse* (London: Penguin Books, 1973), 488.

57. Ibid., 471.

58. Ibid., 452–53, emphasis in original.

59. Ibid., 604.

60. Ibid., 489, emphasis in original.

61. Ibid., 488.

62. Masami Fukutomi, *Keizaigaku to Shizen Tetsugaku*, 72–74.

63. Marx, *Grundrisse*, 510.

64. Marx, *Capital*, vol. 1 (London: Penguin Books, 1976), 927.

65. Marx and Engels, *Collected Works*, vol. 33, 340. Marx did not idealize family-based small-scale agriculture, pointing out that it did not possess the necessary means for conducting sustainable agriculture, such as fertilizer and machines, due to a lack of capital and scientific knowledge.

66. Marx, *Capital*, vol. 1, 896.

67. Marx, *Grundrisse*, 295–96.

68. Marx and Engels, *Collected Works*, vol. 3, 343.

69. Ibid., vol. 33, 340.

70. Ibid., vol. 34, 109.

71. Ryuji Sasaki comprehends Marx's critical turnaround against Feuerbach as the moment he established his own "materialist method" and his final parting from philosophy. Marx writes in *Capital* about his own "scientific" and "materialist" way of conducting his analysis: "It is, in reality, much easier to discover by analysis the earthly kernel of the misty creations of religion than to do the opposite, i.e., to develop from the actual, given relations of life the forms in which these have been apotheosized. The latter method is the only materialist, and therefore the only scientific one" (*Capital*, vol.1, 494). Its kernel lies in another type of question in comparison to *The Economic and Philosophic Manuscripts*. Earlier Marx tried to figure out what the human essence hidden under alienation and private property is; accordingly, he opposed the species-being as the "essence" to estranged reality. In *The German Ideology* Marx asks "how" and "why" alienation is objective and inevitable under certain concrete social relations. As Sasaki points out, instead of imposing a certain philosophical truth upon the alien reality, Marx now recognizes the necessity to analyze concrete material conditions to reveal the possibility of a radical social transformation. Ryuji Sasaki, *Marx no Busshouka Ron* (Tokyo: Shakai Hyoronsha, 2011), 39.

72. In this application Marx follows Moses Hess's work *On the Monetary System* (Über das Geldwesen). See Auguste Cornu, *Karl Marx und Friedrich Engels: Leben und Werk*, vol. 1 (Berlin: Aufbau Verlag, 1954), 516.

73. Marx and Engels, *Collected Works*, vol. 5, 3.

74. Ibid., 39.

75. Ibid., vol. 3, 142, 144, emphasis in original.

76. Ibid., 79.

77. Ibid., 168.

78. Ibid., 183, 186.

79. Ibid., 181.

80. Ibid., 302, emphasis in original.

81. Ibid.

82. Marx and Engels, *Collected Works*, vol. 5, 30.

83. Max Stirner's *Ego and Its Own* published in 1845 argues from a nominalist standpoint that the universal categories such as Feuerbach's "species-being" and Hegel's

"spirit" are mere illusions in philosophers' heads. As indicated in the volume of Marx's critique of Stirner in *The German Ideology*, the work was of great importance for Marx's theoretical development at the time because he was also supportive of the concept of "species-being." Nonetheless, Marx also rejects the idea of Stirner's "ego" in *The German Ideology* because Stirner only offers another illusionary existence as a basis for a self-claimed racial philosophy, as if the subject could exist fully outside the social relations. In other words, Stirner also presupposes the "true" subject *within* the paradigm of the Young Hegelians.

84. Ibid., 236.
85. Žižek emphasizes the same point: "The illusion is not on the side of knowledge, it is already on the side of reality itself, of what the people are doing. What they do not know is that their social reality itself, their activity, is guided by an illusion, by a fetishistic inversion. What they overlook, what they misrecognize, is not the reality but the illusion which is structuring their reality, their real social activity." For example, it is meaningless to point out that money is actually a mere piece of paper under a situation where it possess a real social power to exchange with any other commodities. In this sense, the critique of "false consciousness" misses Marx's point because the scientific task lies in an explanation of *why* a mere piece of paper functions as money in certain social relations. It is thus necessary to investigate the social relations and practice that constitute the objective structure of ideology. This is the only way to open up a possibility to reveal the objective conditions for a radical praxis. Slavoj Žižek, *The Sublime Object of Ideology* (London: Verso, 1989), 32.
86. Marx and Engels, *Collected Works*, vol. 5, 4.
87. Andreas Arndt, *Unmittelbarkeit* [Immediacy] (Berlin: Eule der Minerva Verlag, 2013), 84.
88. In other words, it is not effective to propagate the importance of environmental protection with the aid of "deep ecology." Education about the fundamental significance of nature for human beings alone cannot ground a new ecological movement. Marx thus asks why under capitalist social relations environmental destruction is an inevitable result, even though many people are now without doubt aware of the importance of environmental protection for the coming generations. Only after conceiving the immanent relationship between the capitalist mode of production and the current environmental destruction, does it become possible to investigate the concrete conditions for establishing more sustainable production. Marx is not advocating the absolute primacy of theory, as if theory should first comprehend all the necessary conditions and then simply apply theory to practice. His point is that everyone engaged in social movements is constantly required to pose this type of question investigating the concrete social relations, because otherwise he or she would fall into a utopian practice.
89. Marx and Engels, *Collected Works*, vol. 5, 57, emphasis in original.
90. Ibid., 41, emphasis in original.
91. Ibid., 3.
92. Ibid., 40.
93. Ibid., vol. 3, 345, emphasis in original.
94. Ibid., vol. 5, 58–59.
95. Ludwig Feuerbach, *Principles of the Philosophy of the Future* (Indianapolis: Hackett Publishing, 1966), § 27, emphasis in original.
96. Marx and Engels, *Collected Works*, vol. 5, 58.
97. Ibid., 31.

2. Metabolism of Political Economy

1. Interestingly, Haeckel was critical of the one-sided analysis of physiology that only deals with functions and relations of each parts of the organism, and thus he proposed the importance of analyzing the "economy of nature's totaltiy" including the organism's interaction with the external world. See Ernst Haeckel, *Generelle Morphologie der Organismen* [General Morphology of the Organisms], vol. 2, (Berlin: G. Reimer, 1866), 287. Marx knew Haeckel's work, but he chose to use the physiological concept of "metabolism" in such a way that the incessant process of interaction between humans and their environment, that is, "economy of nature as a whole," can be thematized. This is not odd because the scientific discipline of ecology came out of physiology, and the term "ecology" came to be fixed only in the twentieth century, whereas in the nineteenth century there were a number of other terms such as "bionomics" (E. Ray Lankester) and "ethology" (St. Hilaire) that were used to determine the sphere of new scientific investigation. See Robert P. McIntosh, *The Background of Ecology: Concept and Theory* (Cambridge: Cambridge University Press, 1985), 29.

2. Immler and Schmied-Kowarzik, *Marx und die Naturfrage*, 10. As Immler's claim "Forget Marx, discover Schelling!" indicates, he is primarily concerned with Marx's philosophical analysis of nature. To refute his claim, it is necessary to investigate Marx's systematic treatment of ecology in his political economy. In chapter 3, I will come back to Marx's critical project of political economy from an ecological perspective, based on his theory of reification.

3. Burkett, *Marx and Nature*, 26.

4. Marx and Engels, *Collected Works*, vol. 3, 276, 273, emphasis in original.

5. Ibid., 276, emphasis in original.

6. Marx, *Grundrisse*, 489, emphasis in original.

7. Quante, "Kommentar," 312.

8. Ibid., 315; Michael Quante, "Karl Marx," in Otfried Höffe, ed., *Klassiker der Philosophie: Von Immanuel Kant bis John Rawls* [Classics of Philosophy: From Immanuel Kant to John Rawls] (Munich: C. H. Beck, 2008), 129–42, at 137.

9. Fielding H. Garisson, *An Introduction to the History of Medicine, with Medical Chronology, Bibliographic Data and Test Questions* (Philadelphia: W. B. Saunders, 1914), 414–15.

10. William H. Brock, *Justus von Liebig: The Chemical Gatekeeper* (Cambridge: Cambridge University Press, 1997), vii, 80–82.

11. Justus von Liebig, *Animal Chemistry, or Organic Chemistry in Its Application to Physiology and Pathology* (Cambridge: John Owen, 1843), 48.

12. Franklin C. Bing in his historical analysis of the concept of metabolism refers to G. C. Sigwarts's article of 1815 as the oldest usage. See Franklin C. Bing, "The History of the Word 'Metabolism,'" *Journal of the History of Medicine and Allied Sciences* 26/2 (1971): 158–80, 168. Today it is easier to find an older example thanks to the digitalization of books, and it is possible to point to an earlier usage, for example, Friedrich L. Augustins, *Lehrbuch der Physiologie des Menschen*, vol. 1 (Berlin: Christian Gottfried Schöne, 1809), 279. But it is not important to find the earliest appearance of the concept. In any case, Bing's claim that the concept of metabolism became popular in the 1840s remains valid. Other authors used the concept almost at the same time as Liebig. As Reinhard Mocek points out, Rudolf Wagner dedicated an entire section to metabolism in *Lehrbuch der speciellen Physiologie*, the manuscript of which he finished writing by 1838. See Reinhard Mocek, "Roland Daniels' physiologischer Materialismus," in Roland Daniels, *Mikrokosmos*

(Frankfurt am Main: Peter Lang, 1988), 261–74. A one-sided focus on Liebig as the founder of the concept of metabolism may be misleading, as it hides the complexity of the discourse around the concept at the time. Yet it is beyond the scope of this study to do an extensive historical analysis, because the focus here is the concept in relation to Marx's political economy.

13. David C. Goodman, "Chemistry and the Two Organic Kingdoms of Nature in the Nineteenth Century," *Medical History* 16/2 (1972): 113–30, 117–18. The vitalist dualism of Dumas and Boussignault manifests in their claim that animals consume and destroy what plants provide to them without being able to produce sugar and starch within their body. Liebig showed in his laboratory that animals can actually produce these substances. Nonetheless, it is also true that he did not fully abandon vitalism and maintained the view that there is a unique non-physical element of animals that cannot be found in inanimate things.

14. Justus von Liebig, *Die Organische Chenmie in ihrer Anwendung auf Agriculture und Physiologie* (Braunschweig: Friedrich Vieweg und Sohn, 1840), 332.

15. It is important to note that Liebig was not able to overcome his "vitalism" immediately in the sphere of physiology and recognized the unique "vital force" of living organisms, which cannot be fully reduced to a chemical process. See Timothy O. Lipman, "Vitalism and Reductionism in Liebig's Physiological Thought," *Isis* 58 (1967): 167–85, 175–77. Robert Julius Mayer in his *Organic Movement in Connection with the Metabolism* (*Organische Bewegung im Zusammenhang mit Stoffwechsel*, 1845) criticized Liebig's presupposition of vital force as not necessary because mechanical and chemical forces are convertible to each other. In the face of Mayer's critique Liebig later partly corrected his earlier view in his *Chemical Letters* (4th ed., 1859), though in other places in that book he still defended the existence of vital force. See Brock, *Justus von Liebig*: 312–13.

16. Robert Ayres, "Industrial Metabolism: Theory and Policy," in *Industrial Metabolism: Restructuring for Sustainable Development*, ed. Robert Ayres et al. (Tokyo: United Nations University Press, 1994), 3–20; Maria Fisher-Kowalski and Walter Hütter, "Society's Metabolism: The Intellectual History of Materials Flow Analysis, Part I," *Industrial Ecology* 2/1 (1998): 61–78; Fisher-Kowalski et al., "A Sociometabolic Reading of the Anthropocene: Modes of Subsistence, Population Size and Human Impact on Earth," *The Anthropocene Review* 1/1 (April 2014): 8–33.

17. Alfred Schmidt, *The Concept of Nature in Marx* (London: NLB, 1971); Foster, *Marx's Ecology*; Amy E. Wendling, *Karl Marx on Technology and Alienation* (New York: Palgrave, 2009).

18. Foster, *Marx's Ecology*, 155–63.

19. MEGA² IV/8, 227–34.

20. Ibid., 233–34, emphasis added.

21. Ibid., 233.

22. Gerd Pawelzig, "Zur Stellung des Stoffwechsels im Denken von Karl Marx," in Annelise Griese and Hans Jörg Sandkühlerm, eds., *Karl Marx: Zwischen Philosophie und Naturwissenschaften* (Frankfurt am Main: Peter Lang, 1997), 129–50, 133.

23. MEGA² I/11, 480

24. MEGA² III/4, 308.

25. Ibid., 336.

26. Ibid., 308.

27. Ibid., 78. Unfortunately, Marx's letters to Daniels have not been preserved. It is only possible to speculate about Marx's critiques from Daniels's reactions.

28. Pawelzig, "Zur Stellung des Stoffwechsels," 133. As the first usage of the concept

Pawelzig referred to Marx's letter to his wife, Jenny, dated June 21, 1856, where his remark on "Moleschottian metabolism" can be found: "But love, not for Feuerbachian Man, not for Moleschottian metabolism, not for the proletariat, but love for a sweetheart and notably for yourself, turns a man back into a man again" (*Collected Works*, vol. 40, 56). From this statement Pawelzig immediately inferred Moleschott's influence on Marx. However, this is not the first usage of the concept, and also Marx's theory is incompatible with Moleschott's. Indeed, it is clear in this sentence that Marx referred to Moleschott's "metabolism" in a negative way in juxtaposition with Feuerbach's concept of "love."

29.　Roland Daniels, *Mikrokosmos: Entwurf einer physiologischen Anthropologie* (Frankfurt am Main: Peter Lang, 1988), 29, emphasis in original.

30.　Ibid., 20. In terms of "mental metabolism" Liebig remained within the vitalist framework. It seems thus consistent to infer that Rudolf Wagner's *Handwörterbuch der Physiologie* is a source of Daniels's theory of metabolism. This confirms that the earlier debate on metabolism must be expanded beyond Liebig and Moleschott. See also Daniels, *Mikrokosmos*, 158. Marx later talked about "mental metabolism" in the *Grundrisse*. See Marx, *Grundrisse*, 161.

31.　Daniels, *Mikrokosmos*, 135.

32.　See Reinhard Mocek, "Roland Daniels' physiologischer Materialism: Der naturwissenschaftliche Materialismus am Scheideweg," in Daniels, *Mikrokosmos*, 261–74, 269.

33.　Marx and Engels, *Collected Works*, vol. 38, 326.

34.　Daniels, *Mikrokosmos*, 119.

35.　Marx and Engels, *Collected Works*, vol. 39, 548–49.

36.　Marx, *Grundrisse*, 320.

37.　Ibid., 339.

38.　Ibid., 637.

39.　Marx, *Capital*, vol. 1, 198–99.

40.　MEGA IV/32, 1135.

41.　Wilhelm Roscher, *Principles of Political Economy*, vol. 1 (Chicago: Callaghan and Company, 1878), 111. Roscher writes about his own method: "We refuse entirely to lend ourselves in theory to the construction of such an ideal system. Our aim is simply to describe man's economic nature and economic wants, to investigate the laws and the character of the institutions which are adapted to the satisfaction of these wants, and the greater or less amount of success by which they have been attended. Our task is, therefore, so to speak, the anatomy and physiology of social and national economy!"

42.　Ibid., 154.

43.　Jean-Baptiste Say, *A Treatise on Political Economy or the Production, Distribution and Consumption of Wealth* (Philadelphia: Clement C. Biddle, 1880), 107.

44.　Justus von Liebig, *Familiar Letters on Chemistry, in Its Relation to Physiology, Dietetics, Agriculture, Commerce, and Political Economy* (London: Walton and Maberly, 1859), 480.

45.　Carl Fraas, "Die Natur in der Wirthschaft: Erschöpfung und Ersatz," *Westermann's Jahrbuch der illustrirten Deutschen Monatshefte*, vol. 3 (1858): 561–65, 562.

46.　Marx also saw a similarity between the task of political economy and physiology, as both aimed at penetrating "the inner physiology of the bourgeois society" and comprehending "its internal organic coherence and life process." *Collected Works*, vol. 31, 391.

47.　Marx, *Grundrisse*, 271.

48. Marx, *Capital*, vol. 1, 289.

49. Marx, *Grundrisse*, 360.

50. We will not deal with *Herr Vogt*, because the text was written in a specific political controversy and has little to do with Vogt's natural scientific materialism as such.

51. Alfred Schmidt, *The Concept of Nature in Marx* (London: NLB, 1971), 87.

52. It is surprising that many authors simply accepted Schmidt's claim without examining Marx's text; see Gernot Böhme and Joachim Grebe, "Soziale Naturwissenschaft: Über die wissenschaftliche Bearbeitung der Stoffwechselbeziehung Mensch-Natur," in *Soziale Naturwissenschaft. Weg zur Erweiterung der Ökologie*, ed. Gernot Böhme and Engelbert Schramm (Frankfurt am Main: fischer alternativ, 1985), 19–41, 30; Maria Fischer-Kowalski, "Society's Metabolism: The Intellectual History of Materials Flow Analysis, Part I, 1860–1970," *Industrial Ecology*2/1 (1998): 61–78, 64; Joan Martinez-Alier, "Marxism, Social Metabolism, and International Trade," in *Rethinking Environmental History: World-System History and Global Environmental Change*, ed. Alf Hornborg et al. (Lanham: AltaMira Press, 2007), 221–38, 223. Foster has rejected such views; see Foster, *Marx's Ecology*, 161.

53. Schmidt, *The Concept of Nature in Marx*, 218n129.

54. Ibid., 76.

55. Ibid., 87.

56. Jakob Moleschott, *Kreislauf des Lebens: Physiologische Antworten auf Liebig's Chemische Briefe* (Mainz: Verlag von Victor von Zabern, 1852), 83.

57. Karl Vogt, "Physiologische Briefe für Gebildete aller Stände: Zwelfter Brief. Nervenkraft und Seelenthätigkeit," in *Der Materialismusstreit*, ed. Walter Jaeschke et al. (Hamburg: Meiner, 2012), 1–14, 6.

58. Moleschott, *Kreislauf des Lebens*, 401.

59. Ibid., 369.

60. Jakob Moleschott, *Physiologie der Nahrungsmittel. Ein Handbuch der Diätetik* (Giessen: Ferber'sche Universitätsbuchhandlung, 1850), 101.

61. Moleschott, *Kreislauf des Lebens*, 3rd rev. ed., 1857, 80. "*Dammsäure*" does not exist according to today's scientific knowledge. As Liebig and others demonstrated at the time, humus decomposes into various organic and inorganic matter before absorption by plants. One can say that "Dammsäureammoniak" was an illusionary discovery envisioned with a hope of refuting the validity of Liebig's mineral theory.

62. Ibid., 81.

63. Ibid., 83.

64. Justus von Liebig, *Chemische Briefe*, 4th ed., vol. 1 (Leipzig: C. F. Winter'sche Verlagshandlung, 1859), 362.

65. A similar claim to Moleschott's statement about roast beef and vegetables can be found in Daniels's explanation about "the meat-eating American Indian and the plant-eating Indian etc.—what a great difference with regard to the way of their thinking!" But Moleschott's mechanistic determinism is less attractive for Marx because he does not treat knowledge in a genetic and historical manner, while Daniels at least puts forward his demand for a historical explanation in terms of human production. See Daniels, *Mikrokosmos*, 112.

66. MEGA² III/4, 336.

67. Jakob Moleschott, *Für meine Freunde: Lebenserinnerungen von Jacob Moleschott* (Giessen: Verlag von Emil Roth, 1894), 251.

68. Moleschott, *Kreislauf des Lebens*, 3rd rev. ed., 393–94, emphasis in original.

69. Feuerbach, *Gesammelte Werke*, vol. 10, 356.

70. Ibid., 358.

71. This does not mean, however, that Feuerbach fully accepted Moleschott's theory. He distanced himself from Moleschott's radical reduction to matter as he expressed his concern in a letter to F. W. Heidenreich of June 24, 1852. Feuerbach, *Gesammelte Werke*, vol. 19, 393–94. For Feuerbach it was vital to remain within a philosophical and anthropological perspective of the *human* essence, and in this sense natural scientific materialists went too far in their monistic explanation of all phenomena with the movements of eternal matters. See Walter Jaeschke, "Ludwig Feuerbach über Spiritualismus und Materialismus," in *Materialismus und Spiritualismus: Philosophie und Wissenschaften nach 1848*, ed. Andreas Arndt and Walter Jaeschke (Hamburg: Meiner, 2000), 23–34, 32.

72. Feuerbach, *Gesammelte Werke*, vol. 10, 358.

73. Schmidt, *The Concept of Nature in Marx*, 79.

74. Ibid., 92.

75. Ibid., 88.

76. Theodor W. Adorno, *Negative Dialectic* (London: Routledge, 1973), 355.

77. Alfred Schmidt, *Emanzipatorische Sinnlichkeit: Ludwig Feuerbachs anthropologischer Materialismus* (Frankfurt am Main: Ullstein, 1977).

78. Alfred Schmidt, "Vorwort zur Neuauflage 1993: Für einen ökologischen Materialismus," *Der Begriff der Natur in der Lehre von Marx*, 4th ed. (Hamburg: Europäische Verlagsanstalt, 1993), xi.

79. Schmidt, *Emanzipatorische Sinnlichkei*, 34. Schmidt also points out the "Romantic nature-speculation in Marx" without giving any textual evidence. See Schmidt, *The Concept of Nature in Marx*, 220n18.

80. Schmidt, "Vorwort zur Neuauflage," xii.

81. Marx, *Grundrisse*, 661.

82. Ludwig Büchner, *Force and Matter or Principles of the Natural Order of the Universe: With a System of Morality Based on Thereon* (New York: P. Eckler, 1920), 16, emphasis added. See also Army W. Wendling, *Karl Marx on Technology and Alienation* (New York: Palgrave, 2009), 64.

83. Ibid., 64.

84. Ludwig Büchner, *Stoff und Kraft: Empirisch-naturwissenschaftliche Studien* (Frankfurt am Main: Verlag von Meidinger Sohn, 1858), 11, emphasis added. An older English translation translated the passage correctly: see Ludwig Büchner, *Force and Matter: Empirico-Philosophical Studies, Intelligibly Rendered* (London: Trüner & Co., 1864), 11.

85. Ibid.

86. The "thermodynamic" model must not be completely rejected. For example, Kozo Mayumi provides a more productive interpretation of this model in relation to Marx's and Liebig's theory of metabolism. See Kozo Mayumi, "Temporary Emancipation from the Land: From the Industrial Revolution to the Present Time," *Ecological Economics* 4 (1991): 35–56.

87. Wendling, *Karl Marx on Technology and Alienation*, 97.

88. See Lipman, "Vitalism and Reductionism," 170.

89. MEGA III/4, 391; Daniels, *Mikrokosmos*, 88–89.

90. Carl Gustav Carus, *System der Physiologie umfassend das Allgemeine der Physiologie, die physiologische Geschichte der Menschheit, die des Menschen und die der einzelnen organischen Systeme im Menschen, für Naturforscher und Aerzte*, vol. 2 (Dresden: Gerhard Fleischer, 1839), 32–33.

91. Carl Fraas, *Natur der Landwirthschaft. Beitrag zu einer Theorie derselben*, vol. 2 (Munich: Literarisch-artistische Anstalt, 1857), 106.

92. Justus von Liebig, *Animal Chemistry, or Organic Chemistry in Its Application to Physiology and Pathology* (London: Taylor and Walton, 1842), 227, emphasis in original.
93. Marx and Engels, *Collected Works*, vol. 40, 282.
94. Marx, *Grundrisse*, 268.
95. Ibid., 670.
96. Ibid., 722.
97. Ibid., 694.
98. Ibid., 692. Marx at that time still confused the concepts of "circulating capital" and "circulation capital," though he clearly distinguishes the two in terms of the content.
99. Ibid.
100. Ibid., 646.
101. Marx and Engels, *Collected Works*, vol. 32, 145–46, emphasis in original.
102. Schematically, economic crisis is the disturbance of social metabolism. Ecological crisis is the manifestation of the disturbance of natural metabolism through the capitalist form of social metabolism.
103. Luxemburg believed that Marx's diagram of simple reproduction should be realized in a socialist planned economic order. See Rosa Luxemburg, *The Accumulation of Capital* (London: Routledge and Kegan Paul Ltd, 1951), 75.
104. Marx, *Capital*, vol. 1, 758.
105. Marx, *Grundrisse*, 409.
106. Ibid.
107. Ibid., 410.
108. Ibid., 421.
109. Burkett, *Marx and Nature*, 196.
110. James O'Connor, *Natural Causes: Essays in Ecological Marxism* (New York: Guilford Press, 1998).
111. John Bellamy Foster, "The Great Capitalist Climacteric, Marxism and 'System Change Not Climate Change.'" *Monthly Review* 67/6 (November 2015): 1–18, 9.
112. Marx and Engels, *Collected Works*, vol. 30, 64.

3. Capital as a Theory of Metabolism

1. Salvatore Engel-Di Mauro, *Ecology, Soil, and the Left: An Eco-Social Approach* (New York: Palgrave 2014), 137; Michael Löwy, *Ecosocialism. A Radical Alternative to Capitalist Catastrophe* (Chicago: Haymarket Books, 2015), 3.
2. Moore, "Toward a Singular Metabolism," 10.
3. Larry Lohmann, "Fetishisms of Apocalypse," *Occupied Times*, October 30, 2014.
4. Helmut Reichelt, *Zur logischen Struktur des Kapitalbegriffs bei Karl Marx* (Freiburg im Breisgau: ça-ira-Verlag, 2001); Hans-Georg Backhaus, *Dialektik der Wertform: Untersuchungen zur marxschen Ökonomiekritik* (Freiburg im Breisgau: ça-ira-Verlag, 2011); Michael Heinrich, *Wissenschaft vom Wert: Die Marxsche Kritik der politischen Ökonomie zwischen wissenschaftlicher Revolution und klassischer Tradition* (Münster: Westfälisches Dampfboot, 2011); Ingo Elbe, *Marx im Westen: Die neue Marx-Lektüre in der Bundesrepublik seit 1965* (Berlin: Akademie Verlag, 2010); Christopher Arthur, *The New Dialectic and Marx's Capital* (Leiden: Brill, 2002); Tony Smith, *The Logic of Marx's Capital: Replies to Hegelian Criticisms* (Albany: State University of New York Press, 1990).
5. Marx, *Capital*, vol. 1, 283.
6. Ibid., 133–34.
7. Ibid., 290, emphasis added.

8.   Ibid.

9.   Marx, *Grundrisse*, 86, 88.

10. Marx, *Capital,* vol. 1, 137, emphasis added.

11. Ibid., 164.

12. Isaak Rubin, *Essays on Marx's Theory of Value* (Detroit: Black and Red, 1972); Riccardo Bellofiore, "A Ghost Turning into a Vampire: The Concept of Capital and Living Labour," in *Re-Reading Marx: New Perspectives after the Critical Edition*, ed. Riccardo Bellofiore and Roberto Fineschi (New York: Palgrave, 2009), 183; Werner Bonefeld, "Abstract Labor: Against Its Nature and Its Time," *Capital & Class* 34/2 (June 2010): 257–76, 266.

13. Heinrich, *Wissenschaft vom Wert*, 210; Werner Bonefeld, *Critical Theory and the Critique of Political Economy: On Subversion and Negative Reason* (New York: Bloomsbury, 2014), 10.

14. In an article published in German, Ryuji Sasaki and I argued against Rubin's and Heinrich's interpretation in detail, explaining why Marx regards abstract labor as material not because of his ambivalences but intentionally. See Ryuji Sasaki and Kohei Saito, "Abstrakte Arbeit und Stoffwechsel zwischen Mensch und Natur," *Beiträge zur Marx-Engels-Forschung 2013* (Hamburg: Argument, 2015), 150–68. A similar interpretation on the transhistorical character of abstract labor can be found in Alex Kicillof and Guido Starosta, "On Materiality and Social Form: A Political Critique of Rubin's Value-Form Theory," *Historical Materialism* 15/1 (2007): 9–43. Despite these attempts, there is no agreement. Just focusing on this issue would make the debate futile, so in this chapter I will take another approach, by showing how a transhistorical understanding of abstract labor can provide a more productive reading of Marx's project that can include "ecology."

15. I hope this situation will change when the new edition of Kuruma's book translated by Michael E. Schauerte appears from the Historical Materialism series published through Brill.

16. There is no real historical stage of simple commodity production in history, but society based on simple commodity production is a product of scientific abstraction of the capitalist mode of production. Marx is decisively different from Engels in this regard.

17. Kuruma Samezo and Yoshiro Tamanoi, *Keizaigakushi* (History of Political Economy) (Tokyo: Iwanami Shoten, 1954), 83–90.

18. Marx, *Capital*, vol. 1, 165.

19. Marx does not use the terms "allocation" and "distribution." Here I follow Teinosuke Otani's categorization. Paul Sweezy clearly recognized this problem and consistently developed Marx's value theory. See Sweezy, *The Theory of Capitalist Development: Principles of Marxian Political Economy* (London: Dobson Books, 1946), 25.

20. Kuruma and Tamanoi, *Keizaigakushi*, 85.

21. Marx, *Capital*, vol. 1, 166.

22. Ibid., 128. In order to express this invisible phantom-like property a commodity has to go through a "detour" expressing it in another use value, i.e., it enters into a "value form."

23. Ibid., 164.

24. Ibid., vol. 1, 166–67.

25. Ibid., 165–66.

26. Teinosuke Otani, "Shohin oyobi Shohinseisan" (Commodity and Commodity Production), *Keizai Shirin* 61/2 (1993): 49–148, 96.

27. Marx, *Capital*, vol. 1, 167–68. This does not exclude the epistemic inversion. Marx famously discusses how a social characteristic of a thing appears in a naturalized form, as if it is a natural material property of a thing. He calls this epistemic fallacy "fetishism," as observed, for example, in a belief that gold is by nature valuable. The fact that money functions as a universal equivalent is, in contrast, not an epistemic misunderstanding because under commodity production it receives a social power exchangeable with other commodities.

28. Marx and Engels, *Collected Works*, vol. 34, 398. Marx's critique of religion in the economic manuscript *Results of the Direct Production Process* documents an important difference from the *Paris Manuscript* and a continuity with *The German Ideology*. In 1844 Marx referred to an analogy between capitalism and religion in the context of Feuerbach's theory of alienation: "It is the same in religion. The more man puts into God, the less he retains in himself. The worker puts his life into the object; now his life no longer belongs to him but to the object. Hence, the greater this activity, the more the worker lacks objects" (Ibid., vol. 3, 272). He simply pointed out that the essence of God is human nature as a species-being, and the essence of objective material wealth is the human activity of labor. After parting from Feuerbach's philosophy Marx did not deal with the inversion of religion as a "false consciousness" but as an inevitable "appearance" (*Schein*), which necessarily emerges out of the alienated and inverted reality. Marx in *Capital* also explained how and why under the capitalist relations of production such an inversion of the subject and the object actually occurs, and he did not aim at revealing the hidden essence.

29. Otani, "Shohin oyobi Shohinseisan," 101; Marx, *Capital*, vol. 1, 209.

30. Ibid., 280. See also Teinosuke Otani, *A Guide to Marxian Political Economy: What Kind of Social System Is Capitalism?* (Berlin: Springer, forthcoming).

31. Marx, *Grundrisse*, 687. Roman Rosdolsky also discusses this paragraph in order to investigate the economic role of use values. See Rosdolsky, "Der Gebrauchwert bei Karl Marx: Eine Kritik der bisherigen Marx-Interpretation," *Kyklos* 12 (1959): 27–56. Kuruma's *Marx-Lexikon* is more pertinent to this discussion because its volume 3, titled "Method II," deals with this problem in detail.

32. Marx, *Grundrisse*, 258.

33. Ibid., 881.

34. Ibid.

35. Ibid.

36. Ibid., 646.

37. Marx, *Economic Manuscript of 1864–1865*, 897.

38. Marx and Engels, *Collected Works*, vol. 24, 546.

39. Marx and Engels, *Collected Works*, vol. 34, 397–98.

40. A mere opposition between "use value" and "value" or "concrete labor" and "abstract labor," defending the material side against the capitalist economic determinations, still remains in the Feuerbachian standpoint. A plea for going back to "use value" and "concrete labor" alone is too idealistic for Marx because the material sides are actually always modified through reification and personification. In this sense the denunciation of "false needs" opposing "genuine needs" only sounds elitist to the audience. Marx does not aim at "demystification" of an illusion in order to discover "genuine" human life but at a genetic explanation of the dynamics of the inverted world of capitalism.

41. An important exception is Paul Burkett. He consistently asks for analyzing the "mutual constitution of the social forms and material content of human-nature interaction." See Burkett, *Marx and Nature*, 18.

42. Alfred Sohn-Rethel, *Geistige und körperliche Arbeit: Zur Epistemologie der abend-ländischen Geschichte*, rev, ed. (Weinheim: VCH, 1989), 22. Sohn-Rethel's "real abstraction" is still influential today among adherents of a new reading of Marx. Michael Heinrich argues that abstract labor "cannot be 'expended' at all" because it is "a *relation of social validation* that is constituted in exchange." See Michael Heinrich, *An Introduction to the Three Volumes of Karl Marx's Capital* (New York: Monthly Review Press, 2004), 50. Accordingly, Heinrich does not see the relationship between the metabolism between humans and nature and the category of "value." Notably, he also argues in his commentary on *Capital* regarding the category of "the sum total of labor" that the concept "is not used by Marx in a transhistorical sense" but rather describes a specific society under commodity production. See Michael Heinrich, *Wie das Marxsche Kapital lessen? Leseanleitung und Kommentar zum Anfang des Kapital*, Teil 2 (Stuttgart: Schmetterling Verlag, 2009), 172. One should say that this category is by nature *transhistorical* and *material* because the necessity of the allocation of the sum total of social labor exists in every society insofar as its quantity is always some finite sum.

43. Sohn-Rethel, *Geistige und körperliche Arbeit*, 58, emphasis added.

44. Obviously, precapitalist forms of production were not necessarily sustainable. Marx's reading of books by Carl Fraas in 1868 indicates some aspects of environmental destruction that threatened the existence of civilization due to their unconscious treatment of nature, as I discuss in detail in chapter 6. A truly sustainable production is, according to Marx, only possible in the future society where the human-nature interactions are fully consciously organized.

45. Marx, *Capital*, vol. 1, 147, 230.

46. Ibid., 255.

47. Ibid.

48. Ibid., 252.

49. Ibid., 375.

50. Tony Smith says that Marx's project is "nothing more than the Hegelian goal of reconstructing the world in thought through working out a systematic theory of categories." See Smith, *The Logic of Marx's Capital*, 35. Marx's interest is, however, not a reconstruction of the capitalist totality in thought. As seen in chapter 1, the philosophical transcendence of Hegel's dialectic was not so important for Marx after 1845.See also Andreas Arndt, "'. . . unbeding das letzte Wort aller Philosophie': Marx und die hegelsche Dialektik," in *Karl Marx: Pespektiven der Gesellschaftskritik*, ed. Rahel Jaeggi and Daniel Loick (Berlin: Akademie Verlag, 2013), 27–37.

51. Marx, *Capital*, vol. 1, 341.

52. Ibid., 345. The social meaning of exploitation of labor has become something totally different from the precapitalist societies. Slaves were treated as mere means of production and forced to produce surplus labor through violence, but the precapitalist production of surplus products remained more or less limited within a realm of certain concrete desires for use values. Desire after surplus labor becomes *boundless* only after the establishment of endless quantitative movement of capital's valorization, and in this sense the boundless extension of the workday and the ruthless intensification of labor are a specific modern product.

53. This natural elasticity functions as a material property of capital itself. The elasticity of labor power can, for example, be used during an economic crisis in such a way that fewer workers are compelled to work longer hours with the same loan to boost up the profit rate.

54. Marx, *Capital*, vol. 1, 376–77.

55. Ibid., 611.
56. Ibid., 381.
57. Ibid., 739.
58. Ibid., 344.
59. Ibid., 610.
60. Ibid., 415, emphasis added.
61. Harry Braverman, *Labor and Monopoly Capital: The Degradation of Work in the Twentieth Century,* 25th anniversary ed. (1974; repr. New York: Monthly Review Press, 1998), 78–79.
62. Marx, *Capital,* vol. 1, 618.
63. Ibid., 618–19; Sasaki, *Marx No Busshouka Ron,* 390–91.
64. Marx, *Capital,* vol. 1, 619.
65. Marx and Engels, *Collected Works,* vol. 30, 98.
66. Marx talks explicitly about his plan in his *Manuscript of 1864–1865.* After pointing out that "the development of labor productivity is far from uniform in the various branches of industry, and, besides being uneven in degree, often takes place in opposite directions since the productivity of labor is to such a degree bound up with natural conditions that it may fall while the *social* productivity of labor is increasing," Marx adds in parentheses that "the whole investigation of the extent to which *natural conditions* influence the productivity of labor independently of the development of *social* forces of production, and often in opposition to them, belongs to our consideration of *ground-rent.*" See Marx, *Economic Manuscript of 1864–1865,* 368, emphasis in original.
67. Marx, *Capital,* vol. 1, 376.
68. Marx repeated the same parallel of labor-power and the land in the *Economic Manuscripts of 1861–1863*: "*Anticipation* of the future—real anticipation—occurs in the production of wealth only in relation to the worker and to the land. The future can indeed be anticipated and ruined in both cases by premature overexertion and exhaustion, and by the disturbance of the balance between expenditure and income. In capitalist production this happens to both the worker and the land." (Marx and Engels, *Collected Works,* vol. 32, 442). Marx recognized the penetration of the same capitalist tendency in the exhaustion of workers and land due to the "disturbance of the balance between expenditure and income." As the capitalist mode of production compels workers to maximally expend labor power without necessary rest, it also devastates the land. Marx in *Capital* discussed this theme with Liebig's critique of the "robbery" system of agriculture, as we will see in chapter 4. Here it is sufficient to say that Marx recognized a certain material limitation regarding soil fertility that capital cannot arbitrarily modify because the soil without adequate treatment in accordance with its natural characteristics must quickly lose its fertility.
69. Marx and Engels, *Collected Works,* vol. 33, 146.
70. Marx, *Capital,* vol. 1, 508.
71. Marx, *Economic Manuscript of 1864–1865,* 883.
72. Marx and Engels, *Collected Works,* vol. 33, 146, emphasis in original.
73. The object of labor and the means of labor are even more carefully treated than forces of labor if they are more expensive than the means of labor. Or labor becomes intensified and extended in order to avoid physical and moral loss of fixed capital. This is another case where human labor is subjugated to the logic of value.
74. Marx, *Economic Manuscript of 1864–1865,* 185, emphasis in original.
75. Stefan Baumgärtner, *Ambivalent Joint Production and the Natural Environment* (Heidelberg: Physica-Verlag, 2000), 107.

76. Jess Shantz, *Green Syndicalism: An Alternative Red/Green Vision* (Syracuse: Syracuse University Press, 2012), xlvi.
77. Marx illustrates this problem between the capitalist as buyer of labor power and the worker as its seller. Marx, *Capital*, vol. 1, 344.
78. MEGA² II/4.3, 80. MEGA volume II/4.3 includes new materials that consist of various economic manuscripts for volumes 2 and 3 of *Capital*, written after 1868. They are still sketches but they are of importance because they document Marx's new interests after the publication of volume 1 of *Capital*.
79. Marx, *Economic Manuscript of 1864–1865*, 329.
80. Marx, *Capital*, vol. 1, 667.
81. Despite a popular critique that Marx's optimism undervalued the problem of wastes, his theory of metabolism confirms the opposite. See Baumgärtner, *Ambivalent Joint Production*, 107. Metabolism between humans and nature is an interactive and circular process in which humans not only take from nature but also give back to it. Marx's critique aims at showing that "value" as the mediation of the metabolism cannot sufficiently take this aspect of returning into account.

4. Liebig and *Capital*

1. *Marx and Engels, Collected Works*, vol. 3, 436.
2. Here Engels refers to Alison's similar argument. See Archibald Alison, *Principles of Population, and Their Connection with Human Happiness*, vol. 1 (London: Thomas Cadell, 1840), chaps 1 and 2.
3. Benton, "Marxism and Natural Limits," 77, emphasis in original.
4. Volumes 2 and 3 of *Capital*, edited by Engels after Marx's death, do not thus represent the final shape of Marx's theory, which led to debates in terms of the adequacy of the editing by Marx's lifelong friend and supporter. The publication of the original economic manuscripts in MEGA² reveals various differences between Marx as an "author" and Engels as an "editor" of *Capital*. See Regina Roth, "The Author Marx and His Editor Engels: Different Views on Volume 3 of *Capital*," *Rethinking Marxism* 14/4 (2002): 59–72.
5. Foster, *Marx's Ecology*, 155; Burkett, *Marx and Nature*, 126.
6. Engels also did not remain true to the arguments in the *Outline of a Critique of Political Economy*. Burkett and Foster thus see no decisive difference between Marx and Engels in terms of the theme "ecology."
7. "The exchangeable value of all commodities, whether they be manufactured, or the produce of the mines, or the produce of land, is always regulated, not by the less quantity of labor that will suffice for their production under circumstances highly favorable, and exclusively enjoyed by those who have peculiar facilities of production; but by the greater quantity of labor necessarily bestowed on their production by those who have no such facilities; . . . meaning by the most unfavorable circumstances, the most unfavorable under which the quantity of produce required, renders it necessary to carry on the production." David Ricardo, *Principles of Political Economy, and Taxation* (Cambridge: Cambridge University Press, 1951), 73.
8. Ibid., 71.
9. Edward West, *Essay on the Application of Capital to the Land, with Observations Shewing the Impolicy of Any Great Restriction of the Importation of Corn and that the Bounty of 1688 Did Not Lower the Price of It* (London: Underwood, 1815), 2–3.
10. According to Ricardo, the increase of agricultural productivity with fertilizer and better instruments is possible to some extent, but he adds that through such an

improvement the tendency of the profit rate to fall can only be "checked at repeated intervals." See Ricardo, *Principles of Political Economy*, 120.

11. David Harvey, *The Enigma of Capital: And the Crises of Capitalism* (Oxford: Oxford University Press, 2010), 72.

12. Marx and Engels, *Collected Works*, vol. 6, 200.

13 Ibid., 206.

14. Ibid., vol. 38, 261–62.

15. Ibid., 262. Marx seems to correct his earlier view that ground rent would decrease with increasing agricultural productivity.

16. Ibid.

17. Ibid., vol. 31, 490, emphasis in original.

18. This limited disposability of the land, which immunizes it from the free competition of capital, is natural. Here the material dimension again becomes an object of investigation in political economy.

19. Ibid., vol. 33, 346.

20. Marx, *Economic Manuscript of 1864–1865*, 864, emphasis in original.

21. Marx and Engels, *Collected Works*, vol. 31, 476–77.

22. Ibid., 327, emphasis in original.

23. Ibid., 341, emphasis in original.

24. This difference is based on the lower organic composition of capital in agriculture, which is of a historical nature. Absolute rent can disappear when this difference no longer exists. This is why Marx wrote to Engels, August 9, 1862: "All I have to prove *theoretically* is the *possibility* of absolute rent, without infringing the law of value." Ibid., vol. 41, 403.

25. Marx referred to the "exhaustion of forests, coal seams, mines and the like," but he argued that the growth of productivity in these fields is "*yet* far from keeping pace with the development of the productive powers in the manufacturing industry." Ibid., vol. 33, 135, emphasis added.

26. Michael Perelman, *Marx's Crises Theory: Scarcity, Labor and Finance* (New York: Praeger, 1987), 52.

27. Marx and Engels, *Collected Works*, vol. 42, 227, emphasis in original.

28. Marx, *Economic Manuscript of 1864–1865*, 882, emphasis in original.

29. Marx, *Capital,* vol. 1, 638–39.

30. Marx-Engels Archive (MEA), International Institute of Social History, Amsterdam, Sign. B 106, 32.

31. Joseph Esslen, *Das Gesetz des abnehmenden Bodenertrages seit Justus von Liebig: Eine dogmengeschichtliche Untersuchung* (Munich: J. Schweitzer,1905), 58. In Japan, Shigeaki Shiina argued in the same way, in *Nougaku no Shiso: Marx to Liebig* [Agricultural Theory. Marx and Liebig] (Tokyo: Tokyo University Press, 1976).

32. Liebig, *Einleitung in die Naturgesetze des Feldbaues* (Braunschweig: Vieweg & Sohn, 1862), 111.

33. James Anderson, *An Inquiry into the Causes that Have Hitherto Retarded the Advancement of Agriculture in Europa: With Hints for Removing the Circumstances that Have Chiefly Obstructed Its Progress*, vol. 4 (Edinburgh: T. Caddell and C. Elliot, 1799), 375–76, emphasis added.

34. Justus von Liebig, *Chemistry in Its Applications to Agriculture and Physiology* (New York: John Wiley, 1849), 201–2.

35. John Bennet Lawes, "On Agricultural Chemistry," *Journal of the Royal Agricultural Society of England* 8 (1847): 226–60, 245, emphasis added.

36. MEA, Sign. B 106, 32–33, emphasis in original; Liebig, *Einleitung*, 143.

37. According to Liebig, not only is the absolute quantity of nutrients in the soil lim-
     ited, but also in its availability to plants. If the mineral substances should function
     as nutrients, they must first turn into a dissoluble form so that plants can absorb
     them. But this transformation is fundamentally conditioned by the weathering
     process through warmth, air, and water.
38. MEA, Sign. B 106, 106; Liebig, *Einleitung*, 117.
39. MEA, Sign. B 106, 120.
40. Esslen, *Das Gesetz des abnehmenden Bodenertrages*, 10.
41. Marx, *Capital*, vol.1, 639.
42. Liebig's confusion might be explained by his personal friendship with John Stuart
     Mill. Mill highly valued Liebig's contributions to chemistry, and Liebig arranged a
     German translation of Mill's *System of Logic*. See Pat Munday, "Politics by Other
     Means: Justus von Liebig and the German Translation of John Stuart Mill's *Logic*,"
     British Journal for the History of Science 31 (1998): 403–18.
43. Marx, *Economic Manuscript of 1864–1865*, 768, emphasis added.
44. It is noteworthy that James Anderson also recognized the social aspect in terms of
     increase and decrease of soil fertility, especially when he warned against the wasteful
     usage of stall manure, a cause of soil exhaustion. See Foster, *Marx's Ecology*, 145–47.
45. Leszek Kołakowski, *Main Currents of Marxism: Its Rise, Growth and Dissolution*,
     vol. 1: *The Founders* (Oxford: Oxford Unviersity Press, 1978), 413–14.
46. Carl-Erich Vollgraf, "Einführung," in MEGA² II/4.3 (Berlin: Akademie Verlag,
     2012), 421–74, 454.
47. Marx and Engels, *Collected Works*, vol. 31, 352.
48. Wilhelm Roscher, *Nationalökonomik des Ackerbaues und der verwandten Urpro-
     ductionen*, 4th ed. (Stuttgart: Cotta, 1865), vi.
49. Ibid., 66.
50. MEGA² II/5, 410.
51. Marx's personal library contained other later editions of the book. See MEGA²
     IV/32, no. 1136. In the later edition, Marx marked pages in the last part of the
     book, which Roscher had newly added. This implies that Marx had already read
     the earlier pages in a previous edition.
52. Marx, *Economic Manuscript of 1864–1865*, 831, emphasis added.
53. Roscher, *Nationalökonomik des Ackerbaues*, v.
54. Ibid., 98.
55. Wilhelm Abel, *Agrarkrisen und Agrarkonjunktur: Eine Geschichte der Land- und
     Ernährungswirtschaft Mitteleuropas seit dem hohen Mittelalter* (Hamburg: Paul-Pa-
     rey, 1966), 240.
56. Roscher, *National Ökonomie des Ackerbaues.*, 64, emphasis in original.
57. Ibid., 65.
58. Ibid., 66.
59. Ibid, 64–65.
60. Ibid., 65. Johannes Conrad formulates the point more clearly: "Why isn't the farmer
     allowed to take out and circulate the hoarding of his soil as mineral constituents
     of corn just as the owner of a mine does so with iron? Later generations may face
     a dire need for iron due to our squandering of it, but no one has come up with an
     idea to limit mining. Just as the people in England leave it to their descendants to
     find out substitutes for stone coal, they can also leave it to them with the same right
     to build expensive facilities in order to obtain London's manure for the fields when
     guano import stops or to provide the land with phosphoric calcium contained in
     [bones of] herrings, now wasted to the River Thames." Johannes Conrad, *Liebig's*

Ansicht von der Bodenerschöpfung und ihre geschichtliche, statistische und national-ökonomische Begründung (Jena: Friedrich Mauke, 1864), 150.

61. Marx, *Economic Manuscript of 1864–1865*, 716, emphasis in original.

62. Léonce de Lavergne, *The Rural Economy of England, Scotland, and Ireland* (Edinburgh: William Blackwood and Sons, 1855), 50–51; MEA, Sign. B 106, 214, emphasis in original.

63. Marx, *Economic Manuscript of 1864–1865*, 729.

64. There are some debates on this point between John Bellamy Foster and Paul Burkett, on the one hand, and Daniel Tanuro, on the other. See Foster and Burkett, *Marx and the Earth*, 27–30.

65. Marx and Engels, *Collected Works*, vol. 19, 39.

66. Ibid., vol. 32, 433.

67. Ibid., vol. 5, 64, emphasis in original.

68. Marx, *Capital*, vol.1, 637.

69. Marx, *Economic Manuscript of 1864–1865*, 882–83.

70. Ibid., 797.

71. Ibid., 798.

72. Marx, *Capital*, vol. 1, 638.

73. Marx, *Economic Manuscript of 1864–1865*, 763, emphasis in original.

74. Ted Benton, "Greening the Left?: From Marx to World-System Theory," in Ted Benton et al., *The SAGE Handbook of Environment and Society*, ed. Ted Benton (London: Sage Publications, 2007), 91–107, 98.

75. In contrast, Heinz D. Kurz characterizes such remarks in *Capital* as "Marx's retreat to Ricardo's position" and says that Marx's "case is more serious with respect to the long-run trend of the rate of profits than Ricardo's case of extensive and intensive diminishing returns, because in Marx the use of ever more types of land goes hand in hand with their successive deterioration." His understanding is dulled by the fact that Marx intentionally distanced himself from Ricardo's law. Marx's originality lies in his investigation into the cause of the *specific modern* form of successive deterioration of the soil. See Heinz D. Kurz, "Technical Progress, Capital Accumulation and Income Distribution in Classical Economics: Adam Smith, David Ricardo and Karl Marx," *European Journal of the History of Economic Thought* 17/5 (2010): 1183–222, 1217.

5. FERTILIZER AGAINST ROBBERY AGRICULTURE?

1. Furthermore, in the 1870s Marx read Johnston's *Elements of Agricultural Chemistry and Geology* (Edinburgh: William Blackwood, 1856). This excerpt is available in MEGA IV/26, but I will not go into it because Marx's interest in natural sciences expanded even more after 1868 in relation to his analysis of precapitalist and non-Western societies. In order to reveal Marx's project after 1868, it is first necessary to trace Marx's theoretical development until 1867 with his excerpt notebooks, which is the aim of the current chapter.

2. Foster, *Marx's Ecology*, 155.

3. Brock, *Justus von Liebig*, 177–78.

4. Marx told Joseph Weydemeyer in a letter of June 27, 1851: "I am usually at the British Museum from 9 in the morning until 7 in the evening. The material I am working on is so damnably involved that, no matter how I exert myself, I shall not finish for another 6–8 weeks." Marx and Engels, *Collected Works*, vol. 38, 377.

5. MEGA^2 IV/4, 64. Marx included page numbers as references to the work being quoted.

6.   Ibid., 63.
7.   Ibid., 62, emphasis added.
8.   James Anderson, *A Calm Investigation of the Circumstances that Have Led to the Present Scarcity of Grain in Great Britain* (London: John Cummins, 1801), 73.
9.   MEGA² IV/4, 64–65.
10.   Ibid., 65.
11.   Ibid., 64. Anderson also stated: "Whenever population increases, the produce of the country must be augmented along with it, *unless some moral influence is permitted to derange the economy of nature.*" Anderson, *A Calm Investigation of the Circumstances*, 41.
12.   MEGA² IV/9, 119.
13.   Marx and Engels, *Collected Works*, vol. 31, 372, 374.
14.   Ibid., 344.
15.   "North American Agriculture," *The Economist* 401, May 3, 1851, 475.
16.   "Husbandry in North America," *The Economist* 404, May 24, 1851, 559–60, 559.
17.   MEGA² IV/8, 87.
18.   Ibid., 88–89, emphasis in original.
19.   Ibid, 306–7. Morton erred when he wrote about the role of soil in plant growth: "The most important elements of vegetation being water, air, light and heat; man, without these, may spend his strength for nought.... The soil, being therefore merely the reservoir of water, air, and heat, and of decomposing organic matter, may be rendered either fertile or sterile by giving it the power of storing and retaining these elements for use in a much greater quantity than before, or by abstracting from it, or depriving it of the power of receiving, retaining, and transmitting these to plants." John Morton, *On the Nature and Property of Soils*, 2nd ed. (London: James Ridgway Piccadilly, 1840), 123.
20.   MEGA² IV/8, 306, emphasis added.
21.   Ibid., 309, 311.
22.   Ibid., 305.
23.   Henry Charles Carey, *The Past, the Present, and the Future* (Philadelphia: Carey & Hart, 1848), 299.
24.   Ibid., 304–5.
25.   Ibid., 305–7, emphasis in original.
26.   Justus von Liebig, *Naturwissenschaftliche Briefe über die moderne Landwirthschaft* (Leipzig: C. F. Winter'sche Verlagshandlung, 1859), 202–3; Foster, *Marx's Ecology*, 153.
27.   MEGA² IV/8, 743.
28.   Ibid., 746. Carey's thesis on future growth is primarily about the progressive order of cultivation in more fertile soils, and not much about the improvement of infertile soils through manure and drainage, though he does not exclude the possibility. Carey's model thus presupposes a certain fixed fertility of soil to illustrate the unilateral process of cultivation as a law opposed to Ricardo's.
29.   Ibid., 744.
30.   Ibid., 745.
31.   MEGA² IV/9, 257.
32.   Marx and Engels, *Collected Works*, vol. 38, 425.
33.   MEGA² IV/9, 200.
34.   Ibid., 207.
35.   Ibid., 209.
36.   Ibid., 210, emphasis in original.

37. Ibid., 202. Marx notes a passage in which Liebig describes the exhausted state of lands in New England, which have produced plenty of wheat and tobacco without manure but become unproductive. Nonetheless, Liebig mentions this only to substantiate his demand for realizing the system of "rational culture" of fallowing, crop rotation, and synthetic fertilizer. In fact, Liebig makes no critical comments on the agricultural praxis that has caused such soil exhaustion in New England.

38. Marx and Engels, *Collected Works*, vol. 38, 476.

39. James F. W. Johnston, *Lectures on Agricultural Chemistry and Geology*, 2nd ed. (Edinburgh and London: W. Black and Sons, 1847), 855–56.

40. James F. W. Johnston, *Catechism of Agricultural Chemistry and Geology*, 23rd ed. (Edinburgh and London: W. Black and Sons, 1849), 44.

41. MEGA² IV/9, 277.

42. Ibid., 299.

43. Ibid., 380.

44. Johnston writes about the objective of agriculture: "To raise the largest crops at the smallest cost and with the least injury to land." (Ibid., 372.)

45. Ibid., 381.

46. These excerpts will be published in MEGA² IV/17 and IV/18 respectively.

47. Justus von Liebig, *Die Chemie in ihrer Anwendung auf Agricultur und Physiologie* (Braunschweig: Friedrich Vieweg und Sohn, 1843), 368.

48. MEA, Sign. B 93, 37–38.

49. MEGA² IV/9, 189, emphasis added.

50. Liebig, *Die Chemie in ihrer Anwendung auf Agricultur und Physiologie* (1843), 68, emphasis added.

51. Liebig, *Ueber Theorie und Praxis in der Landwirthschaft* (Braunschweig: Friedrich Vieweg und Sohn, 1856), 45.

52. John Bennet Lawes, "On Agricultural Chemistry," *Journal of the Royal Agricultural Society of England* 8 (1847): 226–60, 243–44. Critiques against Liebig intensified due to the failure of his mineral fertilizer. His patented manure did not work due to a lack of nitrogen, and he later admitted the failure. See Brock, *Justus von Liebig*, 123.

53. John Bennet Lawes and Josepf Henry Gilbert, "On Agricultural Chemistry—Especially in Relation to the Mineral Theory of Baron Liebig," *Journal of the Royal Agricultural Society of England* 12 (1851): 1–40, 23.

54. MEA, Sign. B 93, 39.

55. Ibid., 38, emphasis in original.

56. Justus von Liebig, "On Some Points in Agricultural Chemistry," *Journal of the Royal Agricultural Society of England* 17 (1856): 284–326, 314.

57. Liebig, *Ueber Theorie und Praxis in der Landwirthschaft*, 59–60.

58. Justus von Liebig, *Principles of Agricultural Chemistry, with Special Reference to the Late Researches Made in England* (London: Walton & Maberly, 1855), 47–48.

59. In the *Principles of Agricultural Chemistry* Liebig pointed to the squandering of mineral soil constituents in England: "An enormous quantity of these substances, indispensable to the nourishment of plants, is annually withdrawn from the soil, and carried into large towns in the shape of flour, cattle, &c. It is certain that this incessant removal of phosphates exhausts the land and diminishes its capability of producing grain. The fields of Great Britain are in a state of progressive exhaustion because of this, as is proved by the rapid extension of the cultivation of turnips and mangel-wurzel—plants that contain the least amount of the phosphates, and thus require the smallest quantity for their development" (130). In this sense, Liebig

already recognized facts that support his critique of the robbery system of agriculture in 1862, but he did not develop it because he still believed in the omnipotence
of chemical fertilizer.

60. Marx knew that Liebig became more concerned with the difficulty of recycling
     minerals to achieve lasting fertility of lands by 1860, as he wrote in *Herr Vogt*:
     "Liebig rightly criticizes the senseless wastefulness which robs the Thames of its
     purity and the English soil of its manure" (Marx and Engels, *Collected Works*, vol.
     17, 243). Marx possibly got this information from Liebig's article in *The Times*
     (London), December 23, 1859. As Brock points out (*Justus von Liebig, the Chemi-
     cal Gatekeeper*, 259), this article in which Liebig talked about "the question of the
     sewage of towns" was widely read at that time. However, Marx did not immediately
     integrate Liebig's insight into his economic manuscripts.

61. MEA, Sign. B 106, 36, emphasis in original; Liebig, *Einleitung*, 146.

62. MEA, Sign. B 106, 37; Liebig, *Einleitung*, 147–48.

63. MEA, Sign. B 106, 30–31.

64. Ibid., 56.

65. Ibid., 39. Liebig wrote letters to the mayor of London, stressing the urgency of tak-
     ing action against this problem. See Justus von Liebig, *Two Letters on the Subject of
     the Utilization of the Metropolitan Sewage: Addressed to the Lord Mayor of London*
     (London: W. H. Collingridge,1865).

66. MEA, Sign. B 106, 58.

67. Ibid., 46–47; Liebig, *Einleitung*, 107–8.

68. MEGA² II/4.3, 239; MEA, Sign. B 106, 345.

69. Ibid., 346.

70. Ibid., 348.

71. Ibid., 355–56, emphasis in original.

72. Ibid., 356.

73. Marx, *Economic Manuscript of 1864–1865*, 829.

74. Ibid., 716.

75. Johnston, *Notes on North America*, vol. 1, 54–55.

76. Marx, *Capital*, vol. 1, 638. It is also possible in his excerpts from Johnston's book
     to observe a change in Marx's view of Carey on another matter. In the beginning
     of the 1860s Marx seems to believe the possible correctness of Carey's historical
     sequencing of cultivation: "It is therefore clear . . . that this is also historically incor-
     rect for the settlement in the United States which, in common with Adam Smith,
     he has in mind; therefore Carey's objections were justified on this point" (Marx and
     Engels, *Collected Works*, vol. 31, 525–26). In contrast, after reading Johnston, Marx
     explicitly argues against Carey's explanation, as he writes to Engels on November
     26, 1869: "As far as the development of cultivation in the United States is con-
     cerned, Mr. Carey ignores even the most familiar facts. For instance, Johnston, the
     English agricultural chemist, shows in his *Notes* on the United States [that] the set-
     tlers in Virginia exploited so abominably the land, so suitable both in *location* and
     fertility for tobacco, their main product, that they had to move on to Ohio, where
     the land was worse for their product (if not also for wheat, etc.)" (Marx and Engels,
     Collected Works, vol. 43, 384).

77. An important aspect of soil fertility was not yet recognized by scientists, and there-
     fore also not recognized by Marx. Plants generally do not directly use nutrients
     that are part of organic matter. They are first converted into inorganic elements
     that plants use during the process of decomposition by soil organisms. It is now
     understood that soil organic matter is a critical part of building and maintaining

healthy and productive soils. It positively influences almost all soil properties—chemical, biological, and physical. Though it is true that organic matter (or humus) is not taken up directly by plants, its depletion from soils is one of the main causes of decreased productivity. Adding only inorganic chemical nutrients to replenish those removed by crops can leave soils in poor biological and physical condition leading to numerous problems, including accelerated erosion, droughty soils (that do not store much water), low nutrient holding capacity, more disease and insect problems, and so on. In modern industrial agriculture these are corrected to an extent with greater capital input in the form of pesticides, fertilizers, more powerful equipment, and more frequent irrigation. See Fred Magdoff and Harold van Es, *Building Soils for Better Crops* (College Park, MD: Sustainable Agriculture Research and Education Program, 2010).

78. Marx, *Capital*, vol. 1, 348.
79. MEGA² IV/9, 187, emphasis in original.
80. MEA, Sign. B 106, 53; Liebig, *Einleitung*, 122.
81. Brett Clark and John Bellamy Foster, "Ecological Imperialism and the Global Metabolic Rift: Unequal Exchange and the Guano/Nitrates Trade," *International Journal of Comparative Sociology* 50/3–4 (2009): 311–34, 318.
82. The squandering of guano was compensated for by the industrial production of ammonia manure, thanks to the Harber Bosch method. It goes without saying that the same type of squandering still can be found in extractive industries such as oil and fracking.
83. MEGA² II/4.2, 752–53, emphasis added. The new translation, *Economic Manuscript of 1864–1865*, unfortunately overlooks the fact that Engels modified the sentence and obscured the meaning: "In this way it produces conditions that provoke an irreparable rift in the interdependent process of social metabolism, a metabolism prescribed by the natural laws of life itself" (798).
84. David Ricardo, *On the Principles of Political Economy, and Taxation*, 67. Earlier Marx pointed out the fallacy of this "original and *indestructible powers of the soil*," though he did not explain why Ricardo's assumption is false. MEGA² II/3, 888.
85. Marx, *Capital*, vol. 1, 860.
86. Ibid., 869.
87. Ibid., 865. Marx added in the French edition new passages about the condition of Ireland. Engels did not integrate all the changes into his German edition of *Capital*, which he published after Marx's death, though the paragraph quoted here was. The French edition possesses its own unique value for Marx study. See Kevin Anderson, "The 'Unknown' Marx's *Capital*, vol. 1: The French Edition of 1872–1875, 100 Years Later," *Review of Radical Political Economics* 15/4 (1983); 71–80.
88. Marx, *Capital*, vol. 1, 854.
89. Ibid., 860.
90. Eamonn Slater and Terrence McDonough, "Marx on Nineteenth-Century Colonial Ireland: Analyzing Colonialism as a Dynamic Social Process," *Irish Historical Studies* 36 (November 2008): 153–72, 169–70.
91. Marx writes: "Since the exodus, the land has been underfed and overworked, partly from the injudicious consolidation of farms, and partly because, under the corn acre system, the farmer in a great measure trusted to his laborers to manure the land for him." MEGA² I/21, 19.
92. Ibid. Marx repeats the same point in another text for the lecture on December 16, 1867. MEGA² I/21, 30.
93. MEGA² I/21, 28.

94. MEA, Sign. B 106, 206, emphasis in original; MEGA² II/11, 189.

95. Janet Vorwald Dohner, *The Encyclopedia of Historic and Endangered Livestock and Poultry Breeds* (New Haven: Yale University Press, 2001), 121.

96. MEA, Sign. 106, 209. Vollgraf points out that Marx later read Hermann Settegast's book about sheep rearing and marked in red critical passages regarding the fact that modern attempts to maximize wool yields caused a deterioration in the health of the sheep as well as in the quality of wool. Hermann Settegast, *Welche Richtung ist der Schafzucht Norddeutschlands der Concurenz des Auslandes gegenüber zu geben?* (Breslau: Wilh. Gottl. Korn, 1869), 33; MEGA² IV/32, No. 1231.

97. MEA, Sign. B 106, 336.

98. Marx, *Economic Manuscript of 1864–1865*, 439–40.

99. Ibid., 440.

100. Marx read various Parliamentary reports on this event. The amount of rain that fell in 1865 was not significantly less than in previous years, but it came before the regular rain season and not after. Thus the reservoir of water for later use was of great importance, which the British officers were not able to recognize.

101. Marx, *Capital*, vol. 1, 650.

102. Sunti Kumar Ghosh, "Marx on India," *Monthly Review* 35/8 (January 1984): 39–53.

103. MEA, Sig. B 106, 94.

104. In the seventh edition of *Agricultural Chemistry*, Liebig added a new appendix based on Hermann Maron's research trip to Japan. Maron found a counterexample to European agriculture in Japan, praising the effective use of human excrement in the large cities and with no dependence on guano and stock farming.

105. Marx, *Economic Manuscript of 1864–1865*, 229.

106. "The free ownership of the peasant who farms his land himself is evidently the most normal form of landed property for small-scale cultivation. . . . Ownership of land is just as necessary for the complete development of this activitiy as is ownership of the instrument of labour for the free development of handicraftsman's trade. It forms here the basis for the development of personal independence. It is a necessary transitional point in the development of agriculture itself." Ibid., 792.

107. Ibid., 885–86.

108. There used to be debates among Marxists whether technology in communism would be transformed into a fully ecological technology when emancipated from capitalist use. Grundmann points to negative characteristics of technology that cannot be overcome with the mere abolition of its capitalist form. He criticizes Marxists for dealing with the form of technology without fully going into its content. Nonetheless, he hardly pays attention to how the capitalist form itself is reified (*versachlicht*) and materialized (*verdinglicht*) into a thing. Not only the form but the content of technology is surely a problem, but it is necessary to examine how the capitalist form actively modifies the material contents of technology, which appear as productive forces of capital. Reiner Grundmann, *Marxism and Ecology* (Oxford: Clarendon Press, 1991), 83–84.

109. One can think about new projects such as DESERTEC or solar radiation management (SRM).

110. Marx, *Economic Manuscript of 1864–1865*, 797.

111. Marx and Engels, *Collected Works*, vol. 34, 246.

112. Marx, *Capital*, vol. 1, 637–38.

113. Ibid., 637.

114. Kurt Jakobs, "Bruchstücke Sozialismus und Ökologie," *Das Argument* 197 (1993): 31–46, 45.

115. Burkett, *Marxism and Ecological Economics*, 136.

116. The contradiction of capitalism is not a purely formal one. Rather, it exists between the formal logic of capital and the material logic of nature. Since the latter is modifiable, one cannot deduce from the formal contradiction alone the necessity of the collapse of capitalism.

6. Marx's Ecology after 1868

1. Marx's excerpts on chemistry, geology, mineralogy, and agricultural chemistry from the 1870s and 1880s are available in MEGA² IV/26 and IV/31. For a fuller analysis it will eventually be necessary to examine those natural science excerpts that affect Marx's theoretical horizon after 1868, a project that lies outside the scope of this book.

2. Carl-Erich Vollgraf, "Marx auf Flucht vor dem *Kapital?*," *Beiträge zur Marx-Engels-Forschung: Neue Folge 1994* (Hamburg: Argument, 1994), 89–93, 89.

3. References to Fraas appear in Iring Fetscher, *Überlebensbedingungen der Menschheit: Ist der Fortschritt noch zu retten?* (Munich: Piper, 1985), 124–25; Grundmann, *Marxism and Ecology*, 79.

4. MEGA² II/5, 409.

5. Ibid., 410.

6. Marx's notebooks of 1868 will be published, together with his excerpts from Liebig's *Agricultural Chemistry*, in MEGA² IV/18.

7. Vollgraf, "Einführung," in MEGA² II/4.3, 461.

8. MEGA² II/6, 477, emphasis added. This is one of the clearest examples of how Marx actually changed his sentences in different editions of *Capital*. The problem of any editions based on *Marx-Engels-Werke*, including *Marx Engels Collected Works*, is that they only publish the Engels version.

9. Marx and Engels, *Collected Works*, vol. 42, 507–8.

10. Julius Au, *Die Hilfsdüngermittel in ihrer volks- und privatwirthschaftlichen Bedeutung* (Heidelberg: Bassermann, 1869), 85.

11. Henry Charles Carey, *Letters to the President on the Foreign and Domestic Policy of the Union and Its Effects as Exhibited in the Condition of the People and the State* (Philadelphia: J. B. Lippincott & Co., 1858), 55; George E. Waring, "The Agricultural Features of the Census of the United States for 1850," *Organization & Environment* 12/3 (1999): 298–307, quote at 306. See also Foster, *Marx's Ecology*, 152–53. Liebig and Carey knew each other personally after Eugen Dühring invited Carey to Europe in 1859.

12. Henry Charles Carey, *Principles of Social Science*, vol. 1 (Philadelphia: J. B. Lippincott & Co., 1858), 367–68, emphasis in original.

13. Ibid., 371. Even though Carey did not use Liebig's mineral theory in his critique of soil exhaustion, he quoted long passages from Peshine Smith's *Manual of Political Economy* (ibid., 67). Referring to Liebig and Johnston, Smith investigated in the same chapter the cause of "special exhaustion" due to a lack of necessary inorganic substances. E. Peshine Smith, *Manual of Political Economy* (New York: George P. Putnam & Co., 1853), 36. Carey was also aware of Liebig's explanation of soil exhaustion. See Arnold W. Green, *Henry Charles Carey: Nineteenth-Century Sociologist* (Philadelphia: University of Pennsylvania Press, 1951), 77–78.

14. Eugen Dühring, *Carey's Umwälzung der Volkswirthschaftslehre und Socialwissenschaft* (Munich: E. A. Fleischmann, 1865), xv.

15. Ibid., xiii.

16. Eugen Dühring, *Kritische Grundlegung der Volkswirthschaftslehre* (Berlin: Alb. Eichhoff, 1866), 230.

17. Hlubek is regarded as the last defender of humus theory. Marx was already familiar with various critiques against it, as both Liebig and Lawes were highly critical of it. Marx's reading of Hlubek's *Theory of Agriculture* (*Landwirthschaftslehre*) published in 1853 indicates how encompassing his study of agriculture was in the beginning of 1868. He wrote to Kugelmann on March 6, 1868, and reflected that in the past two months despite his health condition he had "gobbled up enormous masses of 'material,' statistical and otherwise; this alone would have made sick those whose stomachs are not accustomed to this type of fodder and the rapid digestion of the same." Marx and Engels, *Collected Works*, vol. 38, 544.

18. The expression "Malthus's spectre" is employed by Dühring, though he does not relate this term to Liebig. Dühring, *Carey's Umwälzung*, 67. Karl Arnd, in contrast, clearly direct in his critique, calls Liebig's theory a "spectre of soil exhaustion." Karl Arnd, *Justus Liebig's Agrikulturchemie und sein Gespenst der Bodenerschöpfung* (Frankfurt am Main: H. L. Brönner, 1864).

19. Liebig, *Einleitung*, 125–26.

20. Arnd, *Justus Liebig's Agrikulturchemie*, 56. Liebig proposed state intervention into building latrines and sewers in cities as a solution to rehabilitating the nutrition cycle: "To render the execution of a plan of this kind possible, government and the police authorities should take measures to insure the proper construction of latrines and sewers in towns, to guard against the waste of the night-soil, &c." However, it is not quite clear whether he was satisfied with this idea as the most effective countermeasure. Justus von Liebig, *Letters on Modern Agriculture* (London: Walton and Maberly, 1859), 269.

21. Au, *Hilfsdüngermittel*, 151.

22. Dühring, *Carey's Umwälzung*, 67.

23. Carey, *The Past, the Present, and the Future*, 34.

24. Marx and Engels, *Collected Works*, vol. 43, 384.

25. Notably, even Hermann Maron, whose report on Japanese agriculture Liebig used as an appendix to his *Agricultural Chemistry*, changed his opinion after 1862 and began to criticize Liebig's theory of soil exhaustion in his article "Spectre of Soil Exhaustion." See Hermann Maron, "Das Gespenst der Bodenerschöpfung," *Vierteljahrschrift für Volkswirthschaft und Culturgeschichte* 2 (1863): 146–61, 161.

26. MEGA² IV/32, no. 722.

27. MEA, Sign. B 107, 31–32.

28. Ibid., 32.

29. Ibid., emphasis in original.

30. Albert F. Lange, *J. St. Mill's Ansichten über die sociale Frage und die angebliche Umwälzung der Socialwissenschaft durch Carey* (Duisburg: Falk and Lange, 1866), 203.

31. MEGA² IV/32, no. 42.

32. Au, *Hilfsdüngermittel*, 179.

33. Ibid., 209–10.

34. Ibid., 212.

35. Marx and Engels, *Collected Works*, vol. 43, 527; MEGA IV/32, no. 42.

36. MEA, Sign. D 3986.

37. MEA, Sign. B 107, 13.

38. MEGA² IV/32, no. 435–37. Fraas's *Agrarian Crises and Their Remedies* is included in the list of lost books from the personal library of Marx and Engels. See Inge Werchan and Ingrid Skambraks, "Verzeichnis von verschollenen Büchern aus den Bibliotheken von Marx und Engels. Part 2," *Beiträge zur Marx-Engels-Forschung* 12 (1982): 3–106.

39. Marx and Engels, *Collected Works*, vol. 42, 558–59, emphasis in original. Fraas's reference to Fourier comes from *Die Geschichte der Landwirthschaft oder geschichtliche Übersicht der Fortschritte landwirthschaftlicher Erkenntnisse in den letzten 100 Jahren* (Prag: Calve, 1852), 12. Marx's text in *Marx-Engels-Werke* is not correctly deciphered and I have corrected the translation here.
40. Fritz Andreas Zehetmair, *Carl Nikolaus Fraas (1810–1875): Ein bayerischer Agrarwissenschaftler und Reformer der intensiven Landwirtschaft* (Munich: Herbert Utz Verlag, 1995), 178.
41. For example, Fraas in his *Historical-Encyclopedic Outline of Agricultural Theory* pointed to a potentially antagonistic relationship between the "physical school" and the "chemical school." His tone was not so critical of Liebig. See Carl Fraas, *Historisch-encyklopädischer Grundriß der Landwirthschaftslehre* (Stuttgart: Franckh, 1848), 64.
42. Carl Fraas, *Natur der Landwirthscahft. Beitrag zu einer Theorie derselben*, vol. 1 (Munich: Literarisch-artistische Anstalt, 1857), iii.
43. Fraas, *Die Geschichte der Landwirthschaft*, 221.
44. Fraas, *Natur der Landwirthscahft*, vol. 1, 3.
45. MEA, Sign. B 107, 89.
46. Ibid.
47. Ibid., 123, emphasis in original.
48. Ibid., 124, emphasis in original.
49. Ibid., Sign. B 111, 2.
50. Fraas, *Natur der Landwirthschaft*, vol. 1, 132.
51. MEA, Sign B. 111, 24.
52. Ibid., 17, emphasis in original.
53. Ibid., 102.
54. Fraas, *Nature der Landwirthschaft*, vol. 1, 357.
55. Ibid., 368.
56. Carl Fraas, *Die Ackerbaukrisen und ihre Heilmittel. Ein Beitrag zur Wirthschaftspolitik des Ackerbauschutzes* (Leipzig: Brockhaus, 1866), 53.
57. According to Liebig, the necessity of a ruthless war is scientifically grounded and guaranteed: "For their self-preservation, nations will be compelled to slaughter and destroy each other in cruel wars. These are not vague and dark prophecies nor the dreams of a sick mind, for science does not prophesy, it calculates. It is not if, but when, that is uncertain." Cited in Brock, *Justus von Liebig*, 178.
58. Fraas, *Ackerbaukrisen*, 81.
59. Ibid., 87.
60. Ibid., vi.
61. Ibid., 141, emphasis added.
62. Ibid., 142–43.
63. Ibid., 141.
64. The wide acceptance of Liebig's exaggeration, argues Fraas, owes to the material interests of landowning nobility looking for an ideological figure to replace Malthus because Liebig's solution to the problem of soil exhaustion required state intervention. The feudal lord enthusiastically talked about the risk of soil exhaustion, hoping to retain some political privilege or territorial power under new social policies. In other words, the maintenance of soil fertility was connected to the maintenance of power of landlords, and the popularity of the discourse was not purely scientific but, rather, political. Ibid., 143.
65. Ibid., 156.

66. Charles Lyell, *Principles of Geology, Being an Attempt to Explain the Former Changes of the Earth's Surface, by Reference to Causes Now in Operation*, vol. 3 (London: William Clawes, 1833), appendix, 61. Fraas also refers to Lyell in his discussion of alluvion in *Natur der Landwirthschaft*, vol. 1, 15.

67. Fraas, *Natur der Landwirthschaft*, vol. 1, 19.

68. MEA, Sign. B 107, 94.

69. Ibid., 19.

70. Fraas, *Die Ackerbaukrisen und ihre Heilmittel*, 155.

71. Ibid., 141–42, emphasis in original.

72. Ibid., 164.

73. Ibid., 141.

74. Marx also acquired a copy of the book while he was making excerpts, and made a number of marginal notes. I will pay equal attention to these notations to figure out Marx's interest.

75. Roscher, *Nationalökonomik des Ackerbaues*, 66.

76. Liebig, *Einleitung*, 110.

77. Ibid., 109–10.

78. Ibid., 96.

79. Ibid., 98.

80. Ibid., 99.

81. Fraas, *Die Natur der Landwirthschaft*, vol. 1, 11.

82. Fraas argued that Alexander Humboldt did not consider this dimension sufficiently. See Alexander von Humboldt, *Fragments de géologie et de climatologie asiatiques* (Paris: Gide, 1831).

83. Today's scholars do not necessarily agree with Fraas's claim, and Joachim Radkau's opinion about Liebig is more positive. See Joachim Radkau, *Nature and Power: A Global History of the Environment* (Cambridge: Cambridge University Press, 2012), 132. In this chapter I primarily investigate the work in relation to an enlargement of Marx's theory of metabolism that led him more intensively to study natural sciences in the 1870s.

84. Carl Fraas, *Klima und Pflanzenwelt in der Zeit, ein Beitrag zur Geschichte beider* (Landshut: J. G. Wölfe, 1847), xii.

85. MEA, Sign. B 112, 45–46, emphasis in original.

86. Ibid., 46.

87. Ibid., 49.

88. Ibid.

89. Fraas, *Klima und Pflanzenwelt*, 24.

90. MEA, Sign. B 112, 51.

91. Ibid., 52.

92. Ibid.

93. Ibid., 53, emphasis in original.

94. Ibid.

95. When Marx read James F. W. Johnston's *Notes on North America*, he did not write down passages in which Johnston lamented a rapid decrease of forests in North America, which he termed a "lavish cutting of timber." See Johnston, *Notes on North America*, vol. 1, 36.

96. Fraas, *Klima und Pflanzenwelt*, 67.

97. Ibid., 63, Marx's marginal note in his personal copy.

98. Ibid., 65, Marx's marginal note in his personal copy.

99. Ibid., 63–64, Marx's marginal note in his personal copy.

100. Ibid., 96, Marx's marginal note in his personal copy.
101. Ibid., 31.
102. Ibid., 57–58.
103. Ibid., 32.
104. Ibid., 59.
105. MEA, Sign. B 112, 45.
106. Fraas, *Klima und Pflanzenwelt*, 136, emphasis in original.
107. Ibid., 68. Fraas was perhaps too pessimistic. George Perkins Marsh in his *Man and Nature*, originally published in 1864, valued Fraas's work as a pioneer of his own project. Marsh's book had been a strong influence on forest protection movements in the United States. See George Perkins Marsh, *Man and Nature: Or, Physical Geography as Modified by Human Action* (Seattle: University of Washington Press, 2003), 14.
108. Marx and Engels, *Collected Works*, vol. 42, 557.
109. Raya Dunayevskaya emphasized the same point with regard to Marx's treatment of gender issues in his late notebooks on precapitalist societies. See Dunayevskaya, *Rosa Luxemburg, Women's Liberation and Marx's Philosophy of Revolution*, 2nd ed. (Chicago: University of Illinois Press, 1991), 180–81.
110. Grundmann's investigation of Marx's ecology, on the contrary, focuses on the transhistorical dimension, which exists in "every social form," so that he cannot comprehend the specific capitalist form of ecological problems. See Grundmann, *Marxism and Ecology*, 83.
111. MEA, Sign B 111, 1. John Devell Tuckett, *History of the Past and Present State of the Labouring Population* (London: Longman, 1846), 402.
112. Marx, *Economic Manuscript of 1864–1865*, 716.
113. MEGA² II/11, 203.
114. Friedrich Kirchhof, *Handbuch der landwirthschaftlichen Betriebslehre: Ein Leitfaden für praktische Landwirthe zur zweckmäßigen Einrichtung und Verwaltung der Landgüter* (Dessau: Katz, 1852), 57.
115. MEGA² II/11, 188.
116. Ibid., 187.
117. Marx and Engels, *Collected Works*, vol. 6, 488.
118. Anderson, *Marx at the Margins*, 10.
119. Marx and Engels, *Collected Works*, vol. 6, 489.
120. Michael Löwy, "Globalization and Internationalism: How Up-to-Date Is the Communist Manifesto?" *Monthly Review* 50/6 (November 1998): 16–29, 20; Foster provides another view. See John Bellamy Foster, *The Ecological Revolution* (New York: Monthly Review Press, 2009), 213–32. Marx's remark is not surprising if contemporaries such as Carey also optimistically argued that steel and iron would replace the need for wood in Europe in the future: "Population increases, and the great forests and swamps disappear, giving place to rich farms, through which broad roads are made, with immense bridges, which enable the merchant to transport his wool and his cotton to exchange with his now rich neighbours for their surplus corn or clothing." Carey believed that "the almost boundless powers of the earth are developed in the progress of population and wealth." Carey, *The Past, the Present, and the Future*, 82. Here Carey's critique of soil exhaustion suddenly disappears.

Conclusion

1. Hans Jonas, *The Imperative of Responsibility: In Search of an Ethics for the Technological Age* (Chicago: University of Chicago Press, 1984), 201.

2.   John Holloway, *Crack Capitalism* (London: Pluto Press, 2010). Holloway's project to "crack capitalism" simply and optimistically assumes a space *outside* the power of reification. There is, however, no such space. The contradiction, on which Marx focuses, emerges out of the immanent antagonism between the logic of capital and the logic of the material world. It is thus necessary to first study the logic of capital carefully and then to analyze various contradictions in relation to it.

3.   Moore, "Toward a Singular Metabolism,"12, emphasis in original.

4.   MEA, Sign. B 112, 2.

5.   Carl-Erich Vollgraf, "Marx über die sukzessive Untergrabung des Stoffwechsels der Gesellschaft bei entfalteter kapitalistischer Massenproduktion," *Beiträge zur Marx-Engels-Forschung Neue Folge 2014/15* (Hamburg: Argument, 2016), 106–32.

6.   Ibid., 113.

7.   Hans-Peter Harstick published a large portion of the excerpts. The complete version will be published in MEGA² IV/27.

8.   Marx and Engels, *Collected Works*, vol. 42, 557.

9.   See Tomonaga Tairako, "A Turning Point in Marx's Theory on Pre-Capitalist Societies," *Hitotsubashi Journal of Social Studies* 47 (2016): 1–10.

10. Fraas, *Ackerbaukrisen*, 209.

11. Ibid., 210. Here Fraas refers to Maurer's *Einleitung zur Geschichte der Mark-, Hof-, Dorf-, und Stadt-Verfassung und der öffentlichen Gewalt* (Munich: Christian Kaiser, 1854).

12. Marx read Maurer's work again in the 1870s. Surprisingly, he read Maurer's *Einleitung* again and made extensive excerpts, which he usually did not do. They will be published in MEGA² IV/24.

13. Anderson, *Marx at the Margins*, viii.

14. Marx's ecological interest continued to expand in the 1870s. For example, in 1878 Marx notated in his notebook: "The *extinction of species* is still going on (Man himself [is] the most active exterminator)." MEGA² IV/26, 233, emphasis in original.

15. Teodor Shanin, ed., *Late Marx and the Russian Road: Marx and "The Peripheries of Capitalism"* (New York: Monthly Review Press, 1985), 108.

16. Ibid., 111.

17. Ibid.

18. Recently, Lucia Pradella commented rather ironically on the "new mode" in MEGA-study. She said that the fourth section of the MEGA² "provides some elements for assessing continuity and changes in Marx's elaboration more accurately, *without succumbing to a now influential trend in MEGA studies in pursuit of a 'new Marx.'*" However, as shown throughout this book, a fully unknown and in this sense "new" Marx exists in his late notebooks. See Lucia Pradella, *Globalization and the Critique of Political Economy* (London: Routledge, 2014), 173, emphasis added.

Index

Büchner, Ludwig, 65, 78, 80, 91; materialism of, 89; in Moleschotts, 90; organic analogy used by, 87–88; "thermodynamic" theory of value in, 86
Burkett, Paul, 11, 96, 99

Canada, 200
Capital: contradiction between nature and, 129–37, 260; elasticity of, 95–96; fixed and floating, 86, 87, 92–94; money as, 121; Ricardo's definition of, 114; value as, 121–23
Capital (Marx): on agriculture, 169; anti-philosophical trait in, 67; on capitalist production, 123–27; on deforestation, 252; on downfall of feudalism, 48–49; Fraas and Tuckett's influence on, 251; on landed property, 45–46; Liebig cited in, 205–6; on manipulation of nature, 259; on metabolic interaction between humans and nature, 101; on metabolism, 15, 19, 68, 78; theory of ground rent in, 148–49; theory of reification in, 109–13; uncompleted volume 3 of, 142; on variation in labor processes, 128; volumes two and three of, 16–17
Capitalism: agriculture under, 166, 169, 172–74, 201–2, 210–11; alienation in, 29; destruction of nature under, 16; domination in, 40; ecological crises under, 64, 99; environmental unsustainability of, 142; Marx on crisis in, 265; metabolic interaction in, 71–72; metabolic rifts as serious problem of, 263; monopoly of landed property as precondition for, 45–46; relationship between capital and nature under, 19; second contradiction of, 97; transformation of metabolism under, 119–29

Carey, Henry Charles, 160, 183–86, 221–26
Carus, Carl Gustav, 88–90
Cato, 240
Chemistry, 68–70; agricultural, 152–62, 178–81, 197; agricultural physics and, 228–34; optimism in, 186–91
Child labor, 125, 126
China, 233
Chincha Islands War (Guano War), 204
Climate, 229, 231–33
Climate change: as danger to civilization, 239–47; deforestation and, 252; as natural limit, 247–55
Coal, 261
Colonialism, 210–12, 221–22, 253
Commodities, 114–17
Commodity exchange, 107–10; nature and, 133; reification in, 111
Commodity production, 104–6; reification in, 110–11; value in, 120–21
Communism: Marx on, 31, 43–44; sustainable agriculture in, 213–14
Communist Manifesto (Marx and Engels), 253, 259–61
Concrete useful labor, 103
Consciousness, 52–53
Content and form, 113–19
Contribution to the Critique of Hegel's Philosophy of Right (Marx), 53
Contribution to the Critique of Political Economy (Marx), 44–45
Cotton, 245

Dammsäure, 80–81
Daniels, Amalie, 74
Daniels, Roland, 72–74, 78, 82
Deforestation, 242–43, 246–52, 254; *see also* Trees
Democracy, 53
Desertification, 205, 241–43, 250
Differential rent, 149